ACCLAIM FOR

BIBLE
BABEL

"*Bible Babel* is wide-ranging, objectively factual, and written for the common reader. . . . Swenson's book possesses a singularly breezy tone, a kind of *Jesus Christ Superstar* approach to the sacred. . . . This is not your father Abraham's guide to the Good Book. . . . A solid, readable work that doesn't shy away from the tough issues."

—Michael Dirda, *Washington Post*

"Hats off to Kristin Swenson: She has done what I really thought was impossible. . . . Ms. Swenson combines meticulous scholarship with an original eye and a sense of fun. She has succeeded in presenting the Bible anew in a highly accessible way. . . . A most welcome achievement."

—Martin Sieff, *Washington Times*

"Swenson successfully shows why, in spite of all its difficulties, the Bible remains a thought-provoking and infinite source of inspiration and debate for all kinds of people."

—*Publishers Weekly*

"Finally, a book on the Bible for the rest of us! In a world where almost all of our conversation about religion seems to spill out of ideologues on the far reaches of the secular left or the religious right, this broadside against our collective biblical illiteracy hits the sweet spot between blind belief and angry atheism. Who said a book on the Good Book can't be brave, smart, and fun?"

—Stephen Prothero, author of *Religious Literacy: . . . American Needs to Know—and Doesn't*

"*Bible Babel* is a breath of fresh air in the musty library of introductions to the Bible. Kristin Swenson's writing is brisk and lively. She has an informed sense of everything relevant to the Bible, from source criticism to the archaeological record, as well as an apt perception of what goes on in the biblical texts themselves. Keenly aware of how the Bible gets into popular culture and is also often distorted by it, she is an engaging corrector of misconceptions and a helpful guide to the common reader." —Robert Alter, author of *The Book of Psalms: A Translation with Commentary*

"Kristin Swenson offers a confident, well-paced, well-informed, and accessible guide to Bible basics and biblical literacy. The reader may expect some surprises, some confirmation of hunches, and some challenges—exactly what ought to arise from serious, sustained treatment." —Walter Brueggemann, author of *An Unsettling God: The Heart of the Hebrew Bible*

BIBLE
BABEL

BIBLE BABEL

Making Sense of the Most Talked About Book of All Time

Kristin Swenson

HARPER ⬤ PERENNIAL

NEW YORK • LONDON • TORONTO • SYDNEY • NEW DELHI • AUCKLAND

HARPER ● PERENNIAL

FIRST HARPER PERENNIAL EDITION PUBLISHED 2011.

The Library of Congress has catalogued the hardcover edition as follows:

Swenson, Kristin M.
      Bible babel : making sense of the most talked about book of all time / Kristin Swenson.—1st ed.
        xix, 343 p. : ill., 1 map ; 24 cm.
      Includes bibliographical references (p. [286]-323).
      ISBN 978-0-06-172829-7
      1. Bible—Introductions. 2. Bible—Use. I. Title.
   BS475.3 .S846 2010
   220.61 22

                                                      2010278280

ISBN 978-0-06-172826-6 (pbk.)

HB 12.05.2019

For my parents, L. Cecile and Richard E. Swenson,
with admiration, gratitude, and love

ACKNOWLEDGMENTS

Help comes in lots of ways. Sometimes it's flat-out aid; sometimes it's a push in the right direction. Often it comes in the form of support, which demands of its giver flexibility and endurance. In the course of my writing of *Bible Babel*, many people have graciously offered all kinds of help, and I've taken it—every bit. My gratitude is small change.

My parents, Cec and Dick Swenson, are truly amazing people. What can I say?—I lucked out. Besides unflagging support and genuine delight in my work, they model a love for learning, ageless curiosity, and authentic engagement with the Bible. Brad Graff has provided all sorts of encouragement. He's been a sympathetic ear, my champion, and quick to celebrate each milestone. Told that we met as six-year-olds in Sunday school, I can't remember Brad's ever not being there. I also appreciate the enduring love and support of my sisters and their families.

The subject of this project elicits immediate and strong reactions. Some people assume that a book about the Bible must be an effort to convert them, others that it's going to try to debunk their faith. So, I've found myself all but grabbing lapels to say, "Wait, wait! It's not what you think!" My agent, Chris Park, "got" *Bible Babel* from the start. I am incredibly grateful for her confidence in the project and strong advocacy on my behalf. She's tough, she's kind, and she makes me laugh. My editor, Rob Crawford, has been absolutely wonderful. Calm, conscientious, and delightfully upbeat, he carefully considered every feature and helped calibrate the tone to get it as close as is humanly possible to just right. I deeply appreciate having his keen eyes and ears on this book, and I also appreciate him for being such a joy to work with. I never would have thought that it could be so much fun.

A number of friends deserve hearty thanks. A couple of summers ago, in conversation with Donna Freitas at an outdoor bistro in Brooklyn, I mused about writing a book such as this. Donna gave me the nudge (actually an enthusiastic push), and I was on my way. Since graduate school, Kirsi Stjerna has cheered me on, and for this project she offered important insight into Martin Luther and the Reformation. Brooks Schramm read an early version of the whole manuscript and provided valuable comments along the way. Making a strong case for our collective need to improve biblical literacy, Stephen Prothero's book *Religious Literacy* paved the way for *Bible Babel*. Turns out, he's also a gem of a human being—thoughtful and generous, whip-smart, and funny, too.

Kathleen Gacek is as good a friend as anyone could ask for; and it's a boon to have come to know, through her, Joab Jackson, who shares a name with one of the most intriguing men in the Bible. Friday evening on the porch with Denise Honeycutt and Pat Watkins is a snapshot of many moments graced by easy conversation and the simple comfort of old friends. I never doubt their support—a real gift. I am grateful, too, for supportive neighbors—the Adams-Rileys—and for great, diversion-ready friends such as Jim Burke and Emilie Raymond. Susann Cokal's support might be measured by the huge quantities of her chocolate cake that I've eaten while working on this book, but it's been even more than that. John and Gigi of Trigo provided a great place to work and flaky croissants in Panama City, while Gretchen Kainz helped me talk it out and walk it off. I appreciate Kelly Justice's steadfast interest in this project. Thanks, too, to Gene LeCouteur.

The folks at James River Writers are a wonderful bunch, and I treasure their support. I am grateful to my colleagues, teaching assistants, and students at Virginia Commonwealth University. In ways both large and small, our family of Religious Studies faculty members inspire and support me. I also wish to thank VCU's School of World Studies and

College of Humanities and Sciences for giving me time, in the form of a course release, to write. Eric Jarrard ably assisted me with the final form of the manuscript.

Despite all the help that I've had with this book, any errors or infelicities are mine.

CONTENTS

Appendixes

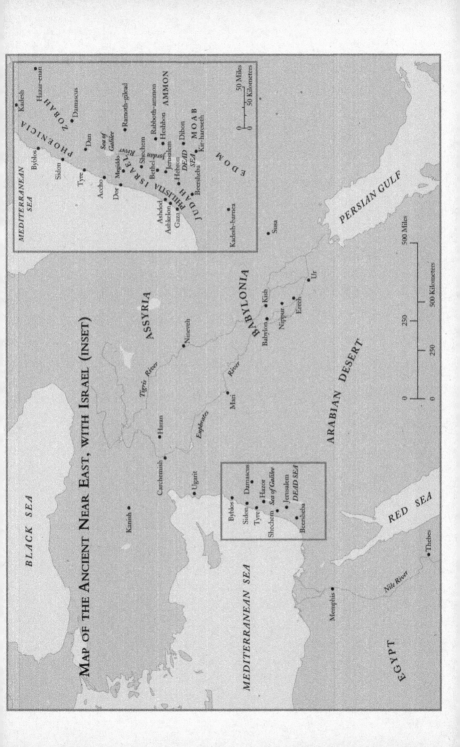

Map of the Ancient Near East, with Israel (inset)

INTRODUCTION

> The Bible is a book that has been read more and
> examined less than any book that ever existed.
>
> —THOMAS PAINE

> Bible reading is an education in itself.
>
> —ALFRED, LORD TENNYSON

In an effort to help reunite lost pets with their owners, Bay County
Animal Control in Florida's Panhandle offered to put a tiny microchip
in cats and dogs free of charge. This seemingly harmless public service encountered surprising resistance. "Some residents . . . feel there
might be a snake behind microchipping in general."[1] The opposition
had nothing to do with reptiles, stray animals, or the veterinary procedure: it stemmed from the Bible. "They feel like it's the mark of the
devil. . . . I've had people tell me that," said Bridgett Miller, a techni-
cian who performs the procedure. Biblical references abound in our
culture, often with far-reaching effects—from shaping personal belief
to informing public policy. Unfortunately, few people know enough
about the Bible to tell how or explain why.

For secular and religious people alike, there aren't many opportunities to learn about the Bible. As a result, many think that the Adam
and Eve story in Genesis equates its talking snake with Satan, that the
fateful fruit was specifically an apple, and that to this day men have
one less rib than women. None of these are true—not as that particular

biblical narrative spells it out, anyway. Others are shocked to discover
that the Jewish bible constitutes the bulk of the Christian bible, and
predates the New Testament by centuries; that Paul wrote much of the
New Testament (and Jesus didn't write any); and that the shepherds and
three kings do not appear together in any biblical story of Jesus' birth.[2]
The fear expressed by the Floridians is based on an interpretation of
the New Testament book of Revelation. Yet, citing the relevant text, one
commentator noted, "Where there is an important translation dispute
like this I go for the Jewish translator as being more familiar and pains-
taking with the language."[3] But the New Testament is not part of the
Jewish bible, and its language is Greek (not the Hebrew of the Jewish
bible). The errors abound.

Most people know that the Bible has been enormously influential
in the western world for millennia and continues to be so today, but
there are surprisingly few opportunities to learn about it, believe it or
not. Many churches and synagogues don't have the time or resources
to devote to instructing about the Bible's historical context or the finer
points of its literary characteristics, and public schools are understandably nervous about teaching the Bible. However, the Bible is the religious foundation for the vast majority of Americans, who read it for
inspiration and instruction. And it continues to crop up in politics and
popular culture. People argue whether or not the Ten Commandments
should be posted in courthouses. Democratic presidential candidates
were asked to name their favorite Bible verse in a 2007 debate. The
Bible shows up frequently in *The Simpsons*, and in popular television
dramas such as *Law and Order* and *Lost*. Biblical references permeate
The Matrix film trilogy. What the Bible does and doesn't say is crucial
to the plot and popularity of *The Da Vinci Code*; and the Bible is so
much a part of country music that it's easy to confuse Country with
Christian rock. Devout individuals contemplate the sense and meaning
of scripture for their lives, basing their thoughts and actions on it above
all else. Others want to understand how such religious readers do this,
and to have fruitful discussions about issues of mutual concern. Some
people grew up with the Bible but feel they know little *about* it. Others

simply want to understand how something like the Sistine Chapel's *Creation of Adam* interprets the biblical creation story.

A lot of people are curious and eager to learn about the Bible, but they don't want to be preached to on the one hand, or have their religious beliefs disrespected or belittled on the other. This book doesn't take a religious position or attempt to convert readers to a particular faith perspective. Neither does it scoff at belief or scorn those for whom the Bible is, well, the Bible. Rather, it gives big-picture information about the Bible—what it is, what's in it, and how to understand "Bible speak." This book aims to provide the kind of information that people want, no matter what their (non)beliefs, in order to make sense of and talk sensibly about the Bible; to help readers understand and evaluate for themselves biblical references; and to appreciate how people can get so riled up about it.

The Bible is a deceptively difficult book. It appears to be straightforward, but it's really very complicated and seems downright contradictory at times. People today can be excused for approaching it like any other book (that's how it appears) and then promptly stumbling over its bewildering commands both to kill and not to kill, its strident monotheism and matter-of-fact references to other gods, its pages of genealogies, patriarchal declarations to silence women in church, strange agrarian metaphors, and plethora of Jesus portraits, not to mention the diversity of translations. Given all this, it helps to have a guide or at least some foundational information about the Bible's development, contents, and history. But there are so many candidates clamoring for that role and championing interpretation under the guise of "information" that it's tough to know what to do.

This book begins with some background information about the Bible as a whole before it gets into specifics such as who's who, what's what, and where's where, or modern debates for which the Bible is used on both sides. Although this book assumes no preliminary knowledge about the Bible, some chapters build on others, so it's best to read this book straight through from the beginning. After all, it's easier to understand how one person can argue that the Bible condemns homosexuality and another that it doesn't (and both have sound arguments), why David is such a big deal, why women get short shrift, why Jerusalem is also Zion, and why Catholics venerate the Virgin Mary, if you've learned about the different bibles, if you know some history in and behind the Bible, and if you are familiar with the drama of translation.[4]

The opening chapter describes what the Bible is in the first place, a little about the different ways that people read it, and how to find one's way around in it, including Bible lingo and organization. The second chapter briefly describes the different bibles that exist, notes a seldom-considered version that influenced them all, and gives a whirlwind overview of the Bible's contents, book by book. (A chart at the back compares the versions, in a side-by-side layout.) The third, fourth, and fifth chapters tell about history—in, behind, and of the Bible, respectively. (In other words, the third chapter relates the Bible's telling of history; the fourth chapter illustrates the historical contexts out of which particular biblical texts came; and the fifth chapter discusses how the Bible as a whole came to be the sacred scripture that it is today. Timelines at the back of the book help to visualize the order of these events.) The sixth and final chapter on foundational information deals with translation in history and today. There is no original Bible that we can consult, and few people other than academic specialists and some seminary graduates know biblical Hebrew, Aramaic, or koine Greek, so Chapter 6 takes some time to discuss issues of translation—how translators determine what text they'll translate from, some of the most influential translations of all time, and the variety that exist today.

The seventh and eighth chapters, "We've Got Issues" and "Quotes and Misquotes," focus on some of the ways people use particular biblical texts today. What are those texts? How do they show up in contemporary culture? And how do they underscore or undermine an ideological point or position? In the process of describing such texts, including their historical and literary contexts, these chapters aim to help readers understand for themselves the texts' modern uses. Although the matter of women's roles and expectations would fit well in Chapter 7, that topic is instead addressed in the chapter on women characters (Chapter 10).

The remaining chapters—Chapters 9 through 13, on people, places, and things—need little introduction. Jesus gets double play, in both the chapter on men (Chapter 9) and the chapter on God (Chapter 13, "God Names, Beings, and Doings"). Satan, on the other hand, gets the most complete treatment only in the chapter on things (Chapter 11, "Flora, Fauna, Etcetera"). I didn't intend to make a theological statement with this organization; but in hindsight, it certainly reflects orthodox Christian theology—Jesus as simultaneously human and divine, and the personification of evil as utterly unworthy of worship. Items associated with Satan such as significant numbers and creatures identified with evil are discussed in Chapter 11, as are angels and demons. Because there are so many ways in which God is identified throughout the Bible, I devote an entire chapter (the last one, Chapter 13) to "God Names, Beings, and Doings."

The relatively small size of this book, and the fact that it is only a single volume, should signal to readers that it is in no way exhaustive. People have been using, studying, and commenting on the Bible from before its ink, so to speak, had even dried. From before the time that biblical literature was ever even assembled as such, people were asking some of the same kinds of questions about it that we ask today and using the biblical texts in any number of ways. This book, then, is necessarily just a tidbit of the feast that is biblical study. Maybe it will stimulate the reader's appetite to learn more. (A brief section at the back describes some helpful resources.) There certainly is more to learn about the Bible (and with every day yet more) than a person could master in a single lifetime. That said, this book should suffice to provide a respectable level of biblical literacy and to enable its readers to make sense of references to and uses of the Bible—that most popular, controversial, and talked about book of all time.

BIBLE
BABEL

BIBLE
BABEL

ONE

What Is the Bible, Anyway?

The familiar is not the thing it reminds of.

—JANE HIRSHFIELD

Year after year, the Bible tops best-seller lists. Polls show that it is the runaway favorite book for Americans of all kinds, and it is considered holy by a full 84 percent of the U.S. population.[1] It comes in every imaginable form. Leather-bound and embossed, in raggedy paperback, pink poofy cover, audio, multimedia, or clutched in the perfectly manicured fingers of Paris Hilton en route to jail. People swear on it in courtrooms. Families record births, marriages, divorces, and deaths in its pages. Soldiers take it into battle, and peaceniks wave it in demonstrations of opposition. The Bible is a singular document of inestimable influence; but all evidence to the contrary, it can be really hard to understand. For one thing, it isn't just one thing.

The Bible didn't fall out of the sky in King James English. Neither was it etched into stone tablets during a thunderstorm and handed to a tunic-clad Charlton Heston. The Bible grew up over a long period of time, and like anything that takes its own sweet time to mature, it has depth and richness and a few wrinkles, too. Actually, the word "Bible" means something like "little library." In this case, not only is the whole Bible a collection of books, but most of those books are themselves collections—the product of long development and many hands. In other words, the Bible and its individual books are more like a Wikipedia entry growing out of the contributions of various people of faith than a Hemingway short story composed in one mojito-fueled evening.

Plus, those biblical books don't all work in the same way. Just as we read the lyrics of a Neil Young song differently than we do directions for setting up a stereo or the arguments of Galileo's opponents, so the devotional poetry of Psalms should be read differently from Leviticus's logistical instructions for consecrating a sacrifice and differently from the early Christian missionaries' letters of encouragement to new congregations.

The Bible's present form—pages bound between two covers just like other books—masks its spectacular complexity and its radical difference from anything else you might find on Amazon.com. Although some of what became biblical was composed by a single author and designed for general consumption, much of what's in the Bible developed before books even existed—before most people could read, for that matter. For the most part, those prebiblical texts were disparate documents (many reflecting ancient oral traditions), coproduced, redacted, and exchanged among the elite few who could read and write. Yet one can pick up a Bible today and read it just like any modern book, from cover to cover. Doing so is problematic at best, though, because a careful reader will quickly discover that the Bible's "voice" is really a (sometimes dissonant) chorus.

Think about how many times you've heard someone say, "Well, the Bible says . . ." Then another person retorts, "But the Bible also says . . . ," and proceeds to give the opposite argument. For example, the Bible both condemns and commands killing, divorce, religious ritual, and putting family first. Unless you understand the social situation out of which those texts come and something about the peculiarities of ancient Near Eastern literature, the Bible could seem to say everything and nothing. Without knowing something about the

Bible's development, a reader would be understandably flummoxed trying to figure out exactly how many animals were supposed to be on Noah's ark, based on God's command first to take a pair and then to take seven pairs of clean and one pair of unclean animals—let alone how big such a boat would have to be, *Evan Almighty* notwithstanding. The Bible is all around us, yet as alien as E.T.

SCRIPTURE IS AS SCRIPTURE DOES

New Yorker A. J. Jacobs lived "biblically" for a year and wrote a clever, amusing, and best-selling account of the effort. Not that it isn't an entertaining read, but the project had some real problems. For one thing, some of the biblical "laws" he followed may, like other ancient Near Eastern "laws," never have been intended for such literal application. They may have been meant and functioned as more generally instructive than absolutely applicable. Isn't it a timeless and universal fact that adolescents curse their parents at some point during the tribulation that is "growing up"? Yet if young people who rebelled against their parents were to be killed as "commanded" in the Bible,[2] the human race would have trouble surviving past a single generation.

Without some background information, people of course read the Bible in the way that they're accustomed to reading: assuming a single origin (at least for individual biblical books), for example, or that the Bible tells things from start to finish in direct, chronological order. In other words, they read somewhat "literally"; but the Bible doesn't easily lend itself to such reading. Matters of translation aside, the Bible's bio alone—it developed over a long period of time and reflects input from a number of times, places, and perspectives—virtually guarantees that it says many (sometimes varied and even contradictory) things. And it doesn't attempt to reconcile these voices, but rather proceeds as though its meaning is transparent. We are left to puzzle over ambiguity and the relationship of seemingly contradictory texts.

Also, most people read the Bible in translation, and the act of translating necessarily requires interpretation. For example, the Bible's

very first words allow for at least three equally good translations: "In
the beginning, God created the heavens and the earth"; "When God
began to create"; or "In the beginning when God created." To translate sensibly, though, we must choose one. Also, there is no punctuation or capitalization in the Hebrew, so we have to add both ourselves
in order to make sense of the text in English. And as *Eats, Shoots &
Leaves: Why, Commas Really Do Make a Difference!* demonstrates, punctuation alone can make a world of difference.

As the next chapter (Chapter 2) explains in detail, "the Bible"
means different things to different people, including those who believe
in it. Consider Handel's lofty and moving *Messiah*, sung in countless
churches and community centers around the country at Christmastime. The chorus triumphantly sings, "For unto us a Child is born,
unto us a Son is given, and the government shall be upon His shoul-
der; and His name shall be called Wonderful, Counselor, the Mighty
God, the Everlasting Father, the Prince of Peace." Those lyrics indeed
come from the Bible, but depending on whose Bible you're using, the
poetry may or may not refer to Jesus. (Also, depending on whose Bible
you read, "a virgin shall conceive" may not show up at all, the story
of Esther may or may not include God, and there may or may not be
four horsemen of the apocalypse.)

This part of Handel's *Messiah* comes from a section that Jews and
Christians share, in the Old Testament book of Isaiah. Because Christian bibles also include a New Testament, which reflects ideas about
Jesus that Jews do not share, Christians and Jews sometimes read passages from the Old Testament differently. Hundreds of years before
Jesus was born, Isaiah's poetry gave hope to a nation in exile, hope
that in God's grace, God would provide a leader to establish justice
and peace in the world. Later, Christians interpreted that leader to be
their Christ, Jesus, and applied the poetry to him. This and other Old
Testament messiah passages are foundational for Christianity because
the first followers of Jesus (who were themselves Jews) interpreted the
identity and significance of Jesus in light of their Hebrew scriptures.

In other words, that passage did not refer to Jesus in its original literary form. Yet because such Old Testament texts are also read

through a Christian lens of faith, informed in part by New Testament texts, Christians are on solid theological ground when they claim that it did indeed refer to Jesus originally. After all, although the passage predates a historical Jesus by nearly half a millennia, Christians believe (based in part on the New Testament gospel of John's declaration) that Jesus was present with God at the beginning of creation. According to such Bible-based thinking, Jesus came to fulfill those scriptures.

However, if a person doesn't believe that Jesus was divine, then he or she can appeal to the text's literary and historical context to state with confidence that the passage has nothing to do with Jesus. A Jewish translation of that same text reads, "He has been named, 'The Mighty God is planning grace; The Eternal Father, a peaceable ruler.'"[3] Translations reflect different perspectives, and in this case, the original Hebrew supports both the Jewish translation and the Christian one that Handel used. Each is valid and accurate; just different, from different perspectives.

People appeal to the Bible differently and for a variety of reasons, both secular and religious. We've already seen one example of how a person's faith perspective informs his or her reading and interpretation. Because the Bible is both a peerless collection of ancient literature and believed by many to be the word of God, learning *about* it—its development, for example—inevitably raises questions of faith. How can the Bible come from historically based, real people, who lived and died a long time ago, reflecting their particular ideas, concerns, and even biases, and yet come from God? How can it be God's Word, yet subject to the vicissitudes of history and human failings?

Many believers who have learned about the Bible's origins and development locate God's "authorship" of the Bible in the process of its development, inspiring the human hands that made it what it is today.[4] Some identify God's word itself as a dynamic matter defined in part (and with God's intent) by the ever-changing relationship readers and communities have to the text. Many people for whom the Bible is sacred apply modern tools of investigation and academic study to it and find that what they learn along the way actually enriches their faith. Believers who accept the models and findings of modern biblical scholarship do not always read the Bible "literally," but for them that does not make the Bible any less true, claiming that, on the contrary, they discover deeper truths and more spiritually rewarding implications than reading at face value allows.

Understanding that the Bible was composed over a long period of time by many different people, and all of it a long time ago, we can appreciate more easily how different people today derive different meanings from it. Much of what's in the Bible wasn't written with the goal of becoming biblical. Most of its contents were deemed authoritative and sacred scripture only long after those texts were first developed and used. These facts make interpretation today, both secular and religious, a richly layered business.

BIBLE ORGANIZATION AND LINGO

Before there ever was a Bible that would be recognizable to us today, there were bits and pieces of literature preserved orally, written on plant-based papyrus or on animal hide, or etched in stone. Images of Moses holding the Ten Commandments usually depict him with a heavy stone tablet in each arm. That the commandments were "written in stone" reflects an ancient method of writing described in the story of God's giving the commandments to the Israelites through Moses.[5] The individual bits of ancient tradition and literature came to be collected in the form of scrolls—rolled-up sheets of writing. Over time, the texts were recorded on discrete sheets, stacked and bound between two covers like books today, in what's called a codex.

When you pick up a Bible today, you'll quickly notice that it is divided into big sections. These are called "books." Genesis is a book, Isaiah is a book, Psalms is a book, John is a book, 1 Corinthians is a book. Each book is subdivided into chapters, which are numbered; and each chapter is subdivided into verses, which are also numbered. Within each book as they appear today, the texts, no matter what they are—narratives, regulations, poems, letters—are organized numerically by chapters and verses. The big numbers indicate chapters. Within the chapters, little numbers designate verses. There is no minimum or maximum number of chapters that a book can have or verses that a chapter can have. The Old Testament book of Obadiah and the New Testament book of Philemon each have only one chapter. Psalm 117 is the shortest chapter in the Bible (each psalm in the book of Psalms is its own chapter). And there is no maximum or minimum number of words that a verse can have. John 11:35, "Jesus wept," is the shortest verse in Christian bibles.

When the debate moderator Tim Russert asked the 2008 Democratic presidential candidates to name their favorite Bible verse, Dodd, Obama, and Richardson cited passages consisting of numerous verses—the parable of the Good Samaritan and the Sermon on the Mount. Biden made an odd, threatening reference to Pharisees. Gravel said, "The most important thing in life is love," likely meaning (in a very loose paraphrase) to refer to the verse that concludes, "The greatest of these is love." Kucinich went with the nonbiblical "Lord, make me an instrument of your peace" prayer of Saint Francis. Only Clinton and Edwards actually named a verse. Clinton named "Do unto others as you would have them do unto you"; Edwards said, "What you do unto the least of these you do unto me."[6]

To cite a particular text, one notes the book, followed by the chapter number, followed by a colon (or a comma—this book uses a colon), followed by the verse or verses. Names of books are often abbreviated. In a table at the end, I've included a list of conventional abbreviations, which this book uses. In the movie *Evan Almighty*, in which Steve Carell plays a reluctant modern-day Noah, the numbers 6:14 show up frequently. For example, when Evan Baxter's alarm clock rings, the camera shows the time as 6:14. A light auspiciously burned out in the clock's display masks the "-eral Electric" to read "Gen 6:14."

Throughout the beginning of the movie *Magnolia*, the numbers 8 and 2 appear in all sorts of places. They refer to the book of Exodus, chapter 8, verse 2 (Exod 8:2), which reads, "If you refuse to let [them] go, I will smite your whole territory with frogs."[7] The context is Moses' confrontation with the Egyptian pharaoh, in which God—through Moses—threatens the pharaoh unless the Hebrew slaves are liberated. At a turning point toward the end of *Magnolia*, when the alienated and wounded characters begin to connect and heal, the sky rains down huge frogs. A popular book by the Christian author Max Lucado has the title *3:16: The Numbers of Hope*. Its title refers to one of the most popular texts in the New Testament—John 3:16: "For God so loved the world that he gave his only son so that everyone who believes in him may not perish but have eternal life."

You may have heard the expression "chapter and verse" used with a word such as "quote" or "recite" as a way to indicate that a person knows something in great detail. For example, "Chapter and Verse on Vegetarianism" is the title of an article in the *Boston Globe* (January 3, 2007) about a man who amassed an impressive collection of books on vegetarianism. The article has nothing to do with the Bible. The expression comes from the practice of demonstrating one's mastery of biblical texts by an ability to cite a text's chapter and verse. In Mark Twain's *Tom Sawyer*, young Tom is instructed to "get his verses" in Bible study at Aunt Polly's house. Today, citing chapter and verse is usually done to prove a particular idea's basis in or to show a person's facility with the Bible.

Yet some people who can cite chapter and verse may not know that this organizational system is not original to the texts. Although the Bible's books do indeed have precursors in stand-alone volumes (scrolls, actually), their chapter-verse organization came along much later. It was only when librarians at the University of Paris standardized a Latin bible in the thirteenth century that Stephen Langton (1150–1228) came up with the chapters that appear as big numbers in our bibles today. Centuries after that, in the 1500s, Robert Estienne subdivided the chapters into verses, designated by the little numbers that appear every sentence or so throughout the Bible. The whole purpose of the numerical chapter-verse system was to help people find their way to a particular biblical text.

This numerical chapter-verse system, developed long after the biblical texts that it organized, is a product of interpretation. That is, as editorial additions, these divisions and subdivisions suggest a certain way to read biblical texts that may allow other ways of reading. For example, Genesis, the first book in all bibles, begins with a story about the creation of the universe in seven days, but most scholars agree, based on its literary style, that the conclusion of the narrative doesn't appear until midway through the fourth verse of chapter 2. Nevertheless, the editors who provided the chapter-verse system seemed to think that "and there was evening and there was morning, the sixth day" (1:31) made a better ending than "these are the generations of the heavens and the earth when they were created" (2:4a), following the description of the seventh day.[8]

Many bibles also include headings and subheadings throughout the text. For example, in the New International Version, "Abram Rescues Lot" introduces Gen 14:1–24, and "The Sun Stands Still" introduces Josh 10:1–15. These titles may appear to readers to be as biblical as the rest, but they're not. Such aids to reading are the product of modern editors who mean to direct readers by summing up stories or otherwise explaining what's coming next in the text. The titles and phrases can indeed be helpful but shouldn't be taken as part of the Bible (except as the modern editorial additions that they are).

Some bibles are identified as "study" bibles, or as "annotated." These bibles have yet more modern editorial help in the form of cross-references and marginal notes. Many of them also include essays providing background information about historical context and literary characteristics, and notes about milestones in biblical studies. I recommend that everyone have at least one study bible on hand. If the scholarship behind them is sound, they can be a valuable help. For example, the *Oxford Annotated Bible with the Apocrypha* explains how God's speech after the great Flood revised his earlier command of vegetarianism.[9] The marginal notes may simply tell readers where a text is unclear in the earliest version we have by noting something like "Meaning of Heb uncertain" or "The Greek is plural." Or they may have detailed background information about a particular word or idea.

Cross-references are citations of biblical texts that have some relationship to the text in question. For example, a Bible with such editorial help directs readers of Matt 24:31 to look at Isa 27:13, so that they can see how Matthew's prediction that the Son of Man will send out his angels with the blare of trumpets and gather his elect (Matt 24:31) reinterprets Isaiah's prophecy of a day when, with a trumpet blast, God would gather the people of Israel from their exile (Isa 27:13).

TWO

Different Bibles and a Hidden Bible, Too

"I've got a book right here that's jam packed with answers!"

—FLANDERS (presenting the Bible to Homer, who has just asked a question about God), from *The Simpsons*

The Bible is a collection of books that millions of people take to be religiously authoritative, yet when people talk about the Bible, they're not always talking about the same thing. When the pregnant Abby Quinn (played by Demi Moore) and the Jewish teenager Avi (Manny Jacobs) are desperately trying to figure out how to avert the end of the world in the movie *The Seventh Sign*, Abby turns to Avi for help in identifying the fifth, sixth, and seventh signs. Earlier, Avi proved his biblical know-how by translating a cryptic Hebrew text from the Old Testament prophet Joel. However, the later signs are enumerated in Revelation, a New Testament book. "You should know this!" Abby exclaims. But Avi counters, "That's not my book; that's the New Testament."

The biggest difference is between Jewish and Christian bibles, but not all Christian bibles are the same, either. Even though Joel Osteen and the pope both believe in Jesus, they do not have identical bibles. Nevertheless, all these sacred scriptures have more in common than not. Christian bibles include all the same texts as Jewish bibles (the entire Jewish bible is part of the Christian bible); and Roman Catholic Christian bibles, though longer, include all the same texts as Protestant Christian bibles. This chapter tells how the Jewish bible and two varieties of Christian bibles differ, and it uncovers the hidden bible that influenced all of them.

WHOSE BIBLE IS IT?

The earliest bible is the Jewish bible, and it is the one on which Christian bibles depend. But the Jewish bible was not finalized as such until after the Christians came along. That said, most of what would constitute this bible already had a long history of use as authoritative scripture by Jewish communities. The pre-Bible scriptures that both traditional Jews and Jews who were followers of Jesus used at that time were translations from ancient Hebrew manuscripts into a common language, Greek. This Greek version is a kind of hidden bible because its existence, assumptions, language, and structure lie behind many differences in bibles today.

There is a fantastic legend that grew out of an account attributed to a certain Aristeas telling how this translation took shape: Ptolemy II (a.k.a. Philadelphus, "of brotherly love"), who ruled from Egypt (285–246 BCE) a territory that included Judah, commissioned a copy of the first five biblical books for his library.[1] He brought seventy-two Jewish translators to Alexandria and wined and dined them. Then they holed up to work. After exactly seventy-two days, as the story goes, the scholars had each individually finished identical translations, and that version has remained unchanged ever since. (Aristeas's story has some internal errors, and evidence from ancient manuscripts reveals that the project of translating from Hebrew into Greek dragged on for centuries.[2]) The result is called the Septuagint and abbreviated LXX (seventy) as a nod to the seventy-two scholars and days of legend. That title also came to apply to Greek translations of the rest of the Hebrew Bible.[3]

Because the Bible as a whole had not yet been finalized, the Septuagint developed to include more than simply strict translations of Hebrew scriptures. It appears to have incorporated variations on existing books as well as whole new books. Traditional Jews excluded the newfangled books and defined their canon—their "bible"—in the first century CE as a specifically *Hebrew* Bible composed of Torah, Prophets, and Writings.

The Jewish bible, composed as it is of these three sections, is sometimes called by the acronym *Tanakh*, in which T, N, and Kh represent the names of the sections. The T stands for *Torah*—the first five books. The N stands for the Hebrew word *Nevi'im*, meaning "Prophets"—a section comprising books of history and books whose titles are the names of individual prophets. The Kh stands for *Kethuvim*, meaning "Writings"[4]—a collection of a variety of books, including Psalms, Proverbs, Job, and Ecclesiastes. The collection ends (and with it the whole Jewish bible) with a historic call for Jews to return to Jerusalem. Both Passover and Yom Kippur, the most important annual Jewish festivals, end with "Next year in Jerusalem!"—reflecting the ring of hope that concludes the Jewish canon. The Jewish bible, *Tanakh*, and the Hebrew Bible are three terms for exactly the same thing. Sometimes, Jews also refer to the whole Hebrew Bible as Torah.

The Christian Old Testament includes all the same material, but it's organized differently, to end with an eye to a coming savior. In an effort to avoid suggesting that these books are obsolete or otherwise out of date, some people choose to call the Old Testament the Hebrew Bible. However, the Old Testament is not strictly identical to the *Tanakh*/Hebrew Bible.[5] For one thing, the Roman Catholic and Eastern Orthodox Old Testaments include books and sections from the Greek version that are not in the Hebrew Bible. For another thing, even the Protestant Old Testament, based as it is on the Hebrew Bible, nevertheless orders its books differently from the Jewish bible.

Because the Jesus-following, proto-Christian Jews also used the

Septuagint, they had not only variations due to translation and the additions mentioned above, but also a different ordering of the contents. The first Christians did not set about to develop an alternative bible (they believed that the world was going to end within their lifetimes), but as time went on, they amassed a collection of authoritative and beloved texts in addition to the Greek version of their bible. When they did develop their own canon of sacred texts, it reflected the Greek version of Hebrew scriptures with its variations, additions, and different order (Old Testament), plus new texts that reflected their beliefs about Jesus as a divine Messiah (New Testament). Generally speaking, this is the Bible of Roman Catholic and Eastern Orthodox Christians.[6]

Jerome, the man who translated the Christian bible into Latin (between the years 385 and 405), called the Septuagint's extra books—those not included in the Hebrew Bible—"apocrypha." He didn't coin the term. It means something like "hidden things," and those books were thought to include hidden or secret ideas and teachings. Jerome wanted to distinguish them from the original books of the Bible, so he chose to separate out the books that didn't have Hebrew originals and put them at the end of the Old Testament. They nevertheless crept in and came to be formally acknowledged by the Roman Catholic Church as part of the Bible: a secondary part ("deuterocanonical") but a part nonetheless.

CHRISTIAN BIBLE: TAKE 2

Centuries later, when Protestant Christians distinguished themselves from Roman Catholic Christians, they appealed to the Hebrew Bible to define their Old Testament. In the process, they excluded the Septuagint's additions but retained its arrangement of order. Rather than following the arrangement of the Hebrew Bible—Torah, Prophets, Writings—the Protestant Old Testament reflects the Septuagint's arrangement in the sections: Torah, historical books, poetry and wisdom, and prophets.

Consequently, just like the Hebrew Bible, the Protestant Christian story of Esther makes no mention of God. Roman Catholic and

Orthodox Christian bibles, on the other hand, include the Greek additions with plenty of references to God, which make the story more religious. (And the 2006 movie *One Night with the King* makes additions unknown in anybody's Bible.)[7]

I've specified "Protestant Christian" to distinguish this from other forms of Christianity. Just as Christianity grew out of Judaism as a kind of reform movement, Protestant Christianity grew out of Roman Catholic Christianity as a reform movement. Unlike the Jewish-Christian relationship, though, Protestants do not belong to a different religion from Catholics. One thing that the father of the German reformation, Martin Luther, sought to do was to reinstate the reading and use of the Bible by ordinary people. Actually, he wanted to be sure that the primary basis for people's religious orientation was the Bible, not the church or its traditions. *Sola scriptura*—"by Scripture alone"—was his principle.

Somewhat like our noting how "the Bible" means different things to different believers, Luther distinguished between the Church's bible and the original bible. The Bible of the Roman Catholic church was Jerome's Latin translation (with some modifications), called the Vulgate. Martin Luther was troubled by the fact that not only was Latin a dead language by his time (ironically, Latin was no longer *vulgare*, the common tongue), but also that the Vulgate was itself a translation, at least one step removed from the original. So Luther went back to the Hebrew for the Old Testament and Greek for the New Testament and translated directly into the common people's language, finishing a complete German bible in 1534.[8]

Countering Luther, the Church reintroduced into its bible texts from the Septuagint that do not appear in the Hebrew Bible. Consequently, the Roman Catholic and Orthodox Christian Old Testaments include everything the others have, plus additions and several other books, too. These extra books are called Apocrypha by Protestant Christians, who don't consider them part of the biblical canon. Roman Catholic and Orthodox Christians accept these books as "deuterocanonical," meaning "second canon"—not quite of the same authority as the rest, but inspired nonetheless.

These extra books are full of colorful stories and thought-provoking ideas. Without them, we'd have no Maccabees (now the name of a popular Israeli beer), and no archangel Raphael (who consequently shows up in some traditions of Judaism, Christianity, and Islam, and is identified with the tarot's Suit of Swords). We'd have none of the hundreds of lavish paintings about Susanna, a gorgeous woman who maintains her virtue and innocence despite the evil machinations of lecherous voyeurs determined to have sex with her, or of "Judith beheading Holofernes," favorite themes of Italian artists during the Renaissance (the more suggestively erotic and gory a scene, the better). Judith, also a strong and virtuous woman, took the opportunity to behead an enemy of the Jewish people by taking him to bed.[9] These subjects were especially popular during the period when artists were conscripted by the church to counter the reformation begun by Luther by painting "biblical" scenes from the books that Protestants rejected.

A BRIEF REVIEW OF BIBLICAL BOOKS: HEBREW BIBLE–OLD TESTAMENT

The first five books, called Torah, are also called the Pentateuch or Five Books of Moses because tradition attributes them to Moses. They are Genesis, Exodus, Leviticus, Numbers, and Deuteronomy. They follow the rough chronology of a story line beginning with the creation of the universe to include the creation of a people bound to their God by a promise of loyalty and ending with a liminal moment, when the people stand poised to take the land they understood to have been promised to them by God. The books include, then, stories about the successive generations from Adam and Eve to Moses and details about the terms of agreement between this God and this people.

The next part, the *Nevi'im* (N) or "Prophets," includes the books of Joshua, Judges, Samuel (divided into two parts, 1 and 2), and Kings (also divided into two parts). It also includes the books whose titles are the names of prophets: Isaiah, Jeremiah, and Ezekiel (the Big Three, sometimes called the "major prophets"), plus the "twelve minor prophets" ("minor" because their books are little in size, not because they're less important) Hosea, Joel, Amos, Obadiah, Jonah, Micah, Nahum, Habakkuk, Zephaniah, Haggai, Zechariah, and Malachi. Collectively, these are sometimes called "the book of the twelve" because they all fit onto a single scroll.

Joshua through Kings is largely a historical narrative telling the story of the people's becoming "Israel." It begins with their entry into the land of Canaan, the development of a nation called Israel, the division of that nation into two, and the destruction of one and then the other. It ends with reference to the defeated people's life in Babylonian exile. The books whose titles are the names of prophets are predominantly poetry relating God's message to Israel as mediated by individual prophets during the period of the two kingdoms and through the dissolution of both.

The third and final part, the *Kethuvim* (Kh) or "Writings," includes all the rest—the poetry, stories, advice, and historical narratives of the disparate remaining books. Those books are Psalms, Proverbs, Job, the Song of Songs, Ruth, Lamentations, Ecclesiastes, Esther, Daniel, Ezra, Nehemiah, and Chronicles (1 and 2). As a whole, they do not follow a historical, chronological story line, though Esther through Chronicles reflects the historical circumstances of the Persian period. The end of Chronicles, which ends the whole Hebrew Bible, is a declaration for Jews to return to Jerusalem.

As noted above, the Christian Old Testament follows a different order from the Jewish Hebrew Bible, though it includes all the same books. It begins in the same way, with the same order of the Torah or Pentateuch, but it puts Ruth between Judges and Samuel because of the setting of Ruth's story. It situates Chronicles, Ezra, Nehemiah, and Esther after Kings because they share a historical focus and make rough chronological sense. The rest of the books of *Tanakh*'s Writings section appear next in the Christian Old Testament, but in a slightly different order. At the end are the books whose titles are the names of prophets because several of them can be interpreted as telling about the coming of Jesus and so look forward to the New Testament. Daniel is among the Christian grouping of prophets for two reasons: the book was set (though not composed) in a prophetic period, during the Babylonian exile; and Daniel is portrayed as discerning the future.

Roman Catholic and Orthodox Christians include the apocryphal books throughout the Old Testament. One of several ways that these deuterocanonical books are arranged is evident in *The Catholic Study Bible*.[10] Following the historical books of Chronicles, Ezra, and Nehemiah are the deuterocanonical books of Tobit, Judith, additions to Esther, and 1 and 2 Maccabees. The books of Wisdom and Sirach are tucked in among other so-called wisdom books (following Ecclesiastes and Song of Songs), and the deuterocanonical Baruch is situated after Jeremiah and Lamentations, since Baruch is the name of Jeremiah's secretary. Like Esther, the Orthodox version of the book of Daniel has additions not found in the original Hebrew or Protestant Christian bibles. The three additions to Daniel are named Susanna, The Prayer of Azariah and the Song of the Three Jews, and Bel and the Dragon. To complicate matters yet further, Greek Orthodox bibles include a few more deuterocanonical books than Roman Catholic bibles: 1 and 2 Esdras, the Prayer of Manasseh, Psalm 151, and 3 Maccabees.

There is no right or wrong order for the books of the Old Testament/Hebrew Bible. They are simply arranged according to different, all quite sensible, criteria. The most striking difference between Jewish and (all) Christian bibles, though, is the New Testament. Put simply: the New Testament is not part of the Bible for Jews, and it's the most determinative part for most Christians. Whereas Jewish bibles begin and end with the Hebrew Bible (though there are other texts of great religious import for Jews—the Talmud, for example), Christian bibles include several books more. They date to a period after the books of the Hebrew Bible were written, and are arranged following them. These additional books compose the New Testament, which lays out the information and ingredients for the theology that makes a Christian a Christian.

A BRIEF REVIEW: NEW TESTAMENT

The New Testament is standard for all Christians. It tells about Jesus and the significance of Jesus by and for people who believe(d) him to be unique as the incarnation of God and the Messiah who brings eternal salvation. Based on evidence of the books' ordering in the early church it seems that they were generally arranged in four groups: the gospels; Acts and General (or Catholic) Letters; the Pauline Letters; and the Apocalypse.[11] Within each group, there was considerable variation. The groups remained, but their order changed a bit by the time the books were fixed in their present form.

The gospels begin the New Testament, and they profess to be "good news," from the Greek *evangelion*. In other words, they were written by people who believed in Jesus. Each gospel narrates its own version of Jesus' biography, professing not to be primarily a dispassionate reporting of actual events but rather proclaiming what they believed to be good news about Jesus and attempting to convince others of it.

There are four such books, and their authors are called the four evangelists. The books' titles are the names of those evangelists: Matthew, Mark, Luke, and John. Some include Jesus' birth; all include his death; and all include some reference to his resurrection. The bulk of each is devoted to what Jesus did and said during the last three years or so of his adult life. Matthew, Mark, and Luke share many similarities and so are sometimes called "synoptic" (literally, "see together"). That we have four gospels shows that the early Christian community responsible for the New Testament as we have it did not think there was only one way to remember or think about Jesus. That they appear together in the document of ultimate authority to Christians would seem to suggest that no one of them has the final and absolute truth. Rather, somehow, taken together, competing and even contradictory claims get closer to that truth.

Although the gospels begin the New Testament, they are not the earliest literature in it. Paul's letters are. Paul (originally named Saul), a Jewish man who never met Jesus, claimed to have had a conversion experience on the road to Damascus in which, with a blinding light, the resurrected Jesus spoke to Paul (then called Saul) and asked why Paul was persecuting him.[12] Paul became an ardent missionary and developed Christian churches throughout the eastern Mediterranean. He kept in touch with them through letters, some of which were collected, circulated, and came to be held as authoritative texts by early Christians. Although we have only a part of what Paul wrote, those letters make up the majority of the New Testament. They were probably read aloud and circulated as diatribes, explanations, and encouragement immediately relevant to the particular communities that he addressed and more generally representative of the ideas that would become the foundation of Christianity. Most scholars agree that the earliest New Testament book we have is one of Paul's letters to the Thessalonians (1 Thessalonians), composed around 50 CE. The earliest gospel, Mark, was composed twenty years later, around 70 CE, a full generation (forty years) after Jesus' death.

Most of the letters that appear as books in the New Testament are associated with Paul, yet among these, some might and others definitely do come from other people. Ancient traditions of authorship were very unlike ours today. Back then, people didn't so much claim authorship as claim authority for their texts. It was better to write in the name of someone famous and get an audience than claim authorship for yourself and let your work die on the vine.[13]

The letters that most scholars agree Paul wrote are, in probable order of composition: 1 Thessalonians, Galatians, Philippians, Philemon, 1 and 2 Corinthians, and Romans. Colossians and 2 Thessalonians are tricky to determine—some scholars think they're Pauline (from Paul himself), while others are certain they come from Paul's disciples who wrote in the spirit of Paul, so to speak. Ephesians continues to be debated by some, though the great majority of biblical scholars think it's "deutero-Pauline" (not by Paul, but like Paul). The books of Timothy (1 and 2) and Titus, which concern times well after Paul's death, probably do not come from Paul, and the same can be said for the seven letters called the catholic epistles ("catholic" here meaning "universal")—James; 1 and 2 Peter; 1, 2, and 3 John; and Jude.

Hebrews is not a letter, by Paul or anyone else. Hebrews uses an allegorical interpretation of the Hebrew Bible together with Greek philosophy to argue for an image of Jesus as High Priest and royal Messiah. It is a sophisticated work of an anonymous Christian that concludes its dualistic discourse with an eloquent sermon on faith.

The New Testament concludes with a book that has gotten loads of attention over the years as people try to predict the end of the world. And recently, it's garnered even more attention owing to the popularity of the *Left Behind* series and a number of other movies, including *The Seventh Sign* and *The Omen*. It's called Revelation (*not* Revelations), the Revelation to John, or the Apocalypse of John. (The Greek title of the oldest available manuscript is *apokalypsis ioannou*.) Amazing and bizarre, it conforms to a type of literature called apocalyptic. The Old Testament has some apocalyptic literature, too—in a couple of the prophets' books and fully in the book of Daniel. Filled with symbolism and alarming statements about end-times, apocalyptic literature lends itself well to interpretation and reinterpretation throughout time and place. Besides, it's fun to read—fantastic and exciting.

THREE

As It Is Written:
History in the Bible

Tell all the Truth but tell it slant.

—EMILY DICKINSON

Unless we know something about the worlds out of which the Bible comes and about its thoroughly unmodern and counterintuitive process of development, the Bible may seem to be full of nonsense and contradictions. By way of seeming nonsense: there's an odd story in Genesis about gods mating with human women.[1] Yet rather than describing a particular point in semihuman or human history, it's probably based on an ancient story, included in part to tell that God disallowed humans from becoming divine.

By way of seeming contradiction, the Bible both condemns and commands divorce. Much of the Bible reflects a patriarchal culture in which a woman's welfare was completely dependent on her relationship to a man. To divorce one's wife, then, was to make her destitute. Prophets including Malachi were especially concerned with social justice, interpreting it as a crucial part of doing God's will. Forbidding divorce in the case of Mal 2:10–16, then, was an act of social justice in favor of women. By contrast, Ezra 10:1–44 commands that the people divorce. In Ezra's situation, a tenuous postexilic period, there was a real question about whether or not the people of Israel would survive. They were at risk of losing their identity as people of God because they had married women from other places and cultures. In an act of piety (and great sadness), then, they divorced their foreign wives.

Three kinds of history are relevant for understanding the Bible: the history *in* the text (the Bible's telling of events—the focus of this chapter), the history *behind* the Bible (circumstances out of which the biblical texts were written and so reflect—the focus of Chapter 4), and the history *of* the Bible (how the Bible as we know it came to be— the focus of Chapter 5). These histories overlap (and so each chapter will include some information that's relevant to the others too), but they are not the same. The Bible does not aim to be a disinterested reporting of events such as we expect from journalists or other modern chroniclers of history. It is a book of faith written, copied, and edited by people of faith who interpreted all of their experiences through faith. Sometimes the Bible narrates things that may very well have happened exactly as told; sometimes it does not. Always, it reflects traditions of faith.

THE FURNACE OF BABYLON

Five hundred eighty-seven years before 1 CE, Israel experienced a cataclysmic event that reverberates today. From the northeast, a great army descended, and in a violent assault, destroyed the nation, razed its temple, and took its people captive. Although such violent destruction and seizure are hardly unique in human history, what happened next would change the world forever. Like dust that seeds a heavy cloud to let loose the rain, the Babylonian destruction of Judah and the temple in Jerusalem and the subsequent exile of the population provoked a flurry of scribal activity profoundly affecting the content and shape of what would ultimately become the Bible. In the decades that followed Judah's defeat, its exiled intellectuals codified, edited, and added to the stories, songs, laws, and lists that defined this particular people's identity and defended its God.

For a people who understood themselves to be singled out for a special relationship with God, who interpreted the king as God's vice-regent on earth, and who believed that God had chosen the temple in Jerusalem as God's earthly home, the Babylonian destruction called everything into question. Is God real or just a joke? And if real, is our god too weak to withstand the Babylonian god? Where did God go when the temple was destroyed? Is God just and fair?

The invading Babylonians took from among the defeated the best and the brightest people and brought them back to Babylon to fertilize the already prosperous and sophisticated center of the empire. In the decades that followed, some of those intelligent and industrious Israelites and their children simply became Babylonian. Perhaps they answered the theological questions in favor of Marduk, the god of the Babylonians. Perhaps they dismissed the idea of God altogether. Others, though, refused to assimilate into the culture of Babylon. They saw themselves not as Babylonians, but as exiles. They defined themselves over against their captors and held on to their traditions and their God. Much of the Hebrew Bible developed to answer those questions in favor of God, even if it meant accusing and admonishing themselves.

There's a famous story in the biblical book of Daniel in which Daniel and his three Jewish friends were dramatically and divinely rescued from the Babylonian furnace into which they had been cast because they refused to bow down to the king's golden statue.[2] Although we may quibble about the historicity of Daniel's escapades, it's safe to say that Babylon itself was a kind of furnace in which the founding texts and religion of Judaism were forged.[3] Still, most scholars agree that scribes who experienced the devastating events of Babylonian destruction and exile didn't compose the whole Bible (though they did write some of it). Rather, they collected, edited, and added to what would become the earliest collection—the first five books, a.k.a. the Pentateuch or Torah. They also saved and edited some of the texts that are preserved among the Prophets and Writings sections of the Old Testament or Hebrew Bible.

When the crucible of Babylon eased and relented in the face of a new power, Persia, the momentum of textual development increased.

It appears that Persian officials encouraged, even required, conquered groups to codify their norms and traditions because these rulers preferred to sanction native, grassroots legislation rather than to superimpose their own. As far as the conquering Persians were concerned, the law of the land was good enough for them (and diplomatically easier to maintain).[4]

THE BIBLE'S STORY OF EVENTS

What follows in this section is a summary of what the Bible says happened. As noted above, the Bible's report is sacred history in which God is a character in the people's drama. It's not to be confused with the kind of secular history that we try to teach our kids in public school civics classes about just exactly what happened just exactly when and where. In the Bible's "history," God's relationship to people is in, under, over, and behind it all, making it unapologetically unverifiable. That is, bringing God into the equation necessarily takes the stories out of the realm of disinterested, historical reporting, making them instead faith-based interpretations of events.

What's more, the Bible does not tell its version of history in some linear way. The following summary, then, risks implying that the Bible goes from creation to destruction and new creation in a grand, single narrative. The fact is that its telling twists and turns, circles back, bounds ahead, and sometimes hunkers down for pages and pages to expand on a particular moment or idea. Nevertheless, it's useful to have some sense of the arc of the biblical narrative (e.g., to understand why "a new king in Egypt who didn't know Joseph" could make your stomach sink, or the point of the prophet Hosea's marrying a prostitute, or why Amos claims that sacrifice is useless and Haggai finds it indispensable, or Daniel's visions of the rise and fall of empires, or why Jesus must be situated in David's family line). So here in a nutshell is the Bible's telling of history, from the beginning of the Hebrew Bible through the New Testament.

Not all books are relevant for this whirlwind tour of the Bible's narrative of events. Within the Hebrew Bible, scholars observe three different historical narratives. One is the Pentateuch, whose final form is probably the work of priestly scribal editors. The second is composed of the books immediately following the Pentateuch (Joshua, Judges, Samuel, and Kings), called the "Deuteronomistic history" because its central ideology reflects the book of Deuteronomy. The third historiography, "the Chronicler's," is in the books of Chronicles, Ezra, and Nehemiah. This one is primarily a retelling of history from Adam to Cyrus II's edict of return from a perspective that makes David and his monarchy the central, shining moment.

The New Testament's telling of history picks up a few centuries later than the latest events told in the Old Testament, with the people back in Israel during a new period with its own problems (the Romans). This history focuses on one particular Jew named Jesus—specifically, how he came to be understood by his followers and the effect he subsequently had on the development of a new people. This longer bible ends with the cosmic destruction of the world and its re-creation in God. Its historical trajectory is narrated in the gospels, Acts, and Revelation.

A brief caveat: Not all the biblical books that tell history do so equally. For example, Genesis covers a great deal of the history in the Pentateuch. Also, the New Testament, in contrast to the Old, tells very little history, reflecting the fact that it was composed over a much shorter period of time (about 100 years by comparison to the Old Testament's possibly 1,500 years of development). Consequently, the section below on the New Testament's telling of history is much shorter than that concerning the Old Testament.

THE OLD TESTAMENT'S STORY OF EVENTS

Genesis begins with the creation of the universe and then focuses on a particular place, Eden, and the first human couple, Adam and Eve. After their disobedience, this couple lived east of Eden, where one son, Cain, murdered his brother and fathered a son. As humans increased, so too did their violence and arrogance until, brokenhearted, God regretted creating people at all. God consequently determined to wipe out the world with a great Flood. But he commissioned the one righteous person, Noah, and his family to build a boat, an ark, on which Noah and token pairs of creatures would survive the coming catastrophe. They did—built the ark, loaded the animals, and survived—and God promised never to destroy the earth by flood again.

The stories up to this point in the narrative are universal in scope and do not distinguish any one people from another. That changes in chapter 12, where we meet Abraham and his wife Sarah. God made a binding agreement with Abraham, and the rest of Genesis focuses on this particular family, specially chosen by God, following them through three generations (Abraham's, Isaac's, and Jacob's). The book concludes with a multi-chapter story (chapters 37–50) focused on one of Jacob's sons, Joseph. At the end of Genesis, the family is safely established in Egypt, where Joseph had risen to such power that he was second only to the king.

The book of Exodus begins with a description of how Abraham's family has grown—a sign of God's blessing. Then the narrator tells that "a new king [pharaoh] arose over Egypt who did not know Joseph." Because Joseph was the people's ticket to a good life in Egypt, the ignorance of this pharaoh bodes ill for them. Sure enough, threatened by the great number of Hebrews, the pharaoh enslaved them. Enter Moses.

What happens next, when Moses was commissioned by God to liberate God's chosen people by appealing to the pharaoh to "let my people go," makes for all sorts of exciting renderings, not only Cecil B. DeMille's iconic film, *The Ten Commandments*. It's the story of an imperfect, star-crossed person filled with self-doubt and standing between two cultures, of a cruelly oppressed people dramatically freed by greater than human powers yet fickle and unappreciative. It's got magicians; strange happenings in a fantastic environment; human conflict and resolution; the bad guy getting what he deserves; death; and new life. This story has resonated through the ages not just among Jews, but with many people subject to injustice and oppression. It is the cornerstone of liberation theology, a perspective that declares God's solidarity (even violent solidarity) with the oppressed. It isn't hard to see why slaves in the American South would identify with this story and call one of their most amazing liberators—a woman named Harriet Tubman—Moses. Finally, after a succession of ten brutal plagues, the last of which (the death of the firstborn) is commemorated in the annual Jewish festival of Passover, the pharaoh told the Hebrews to leave. Under Moses' leadership, they set out, only to be pursued (again) by the capricious pharaoh. God enabled them to cross a sea that swamped the pharaoh's army, and they are free at last.

Free to be servants of God. The next stop was the mountain of Sinai (also called Horeb), where God gave detailed instructions to the people through Moses. These instructions include the Ten Commandments plus hundreds of others concerning how to be in relation to God, each other, and the world. The forging at Sinai of this agreement between God and the Hebrew-speaking proto-Israelites takes up the second part of the book of Exodus and all of Leviticus.

Finally, in Numbers, the people set out again, to wander for a total (since leaving Egypt) of forty years in the wilderness. Dueteronomy takes place at the far edge of the wilderness, where the people stand poised to enter the land that they understood to have been promised to them by God beginning with Abraham—the Promised Land. The whole book of Deuteronomy is Moses' final sermons to the people reiterating the agreement to be faithful to their one God, with special emphasis on the idea that if they instead worshipped other gods and goddesses, things would go badly and God would wrest the land away from them.

Having agreed again to these terms, the people passed into the land, where, under Joshua's leadership, they were enabled by God to defeat the resident Canaanites, take the territory, and settle the tribes in what we can at this point in the story call Israel. They lived for a time as semi-independent tribal groups, united occasionally by "judges," who served as military and religious leaders.[5]

By the beginning of the book of Samuel, and faced with a greater threat than ever before (the Philistines), the people clamored for a fully unifying king. Saul became their first; but it's with King David that the people (composed of twelve tribes descended from the twelve sons of Jacob, Abraham's grandson) became truly united, a bona fide nation Israel with its capital in Jerusalem. In the movie *King David*, Richard Gere marked the moment of bringing the religiously (and politically) significant covenant container, the Ark, into the capital by dancing around in a miniskirt of sorts. This loose display ticked off David's wife Michal, whom he had acquired from her father Saul for 100 Philistine foreskins. Gere could be excused for showing a little leg, since they're such nice legs, and in any case that moment of bringing the Ark into Jerusalem is also a significant moment in the biblical narrative. There, David's son (by a different wife, this one gained through adultery and murder—more on that later) and successor, Solomon, built the great temple as the central site wherein God promises to be specially present to and with the people.

After Solomon's death, the situation went downhill. For one thing, the ten northern tribes seceded from the union to form a separate nation confusingly called Israel. (Yes, "Israel" is a name for both the entire nation of twelve tribes and the northern kingdom of ten tribes. It's also another name for the patriarch Jacob whom we meet in Genesis, and it's used of the people in general, nation or not.) The southern kingdom, which retains the capital of Jerusalem with its temple and a monarchy descended from David, is called Judah.

According to the story, the people of the northern kingdom angered God by setting up worship sites rivaling Jerusalem's temple and occasionally worshipping other gods and goddesses. Finally fed up, God allowed the northern kingdom to be destroyed by the Assyrians. The southern kingdom of Judah continued for some time with a couple of very good kings ("good" because they set the people on a righteous track, recognizing the singular worship of God) until its offenses under especially bad kings overwhelmed the beneficent grace of God, and God allowed the Babylonians to destroy them and to take captives back to Babylon.

When Cyrus, king of Persia, conquered Babylon, he allowed the exiled people to return to Jerusalem. The books of Ezra and Nehemiah relate stories about the return of exiles and their efforts to rebuild community, temple, and Jerusalem's city walls. Ezra is portrayed as bringing the Torah back to the people and instructing them as if they'd forgotten its tenets. Rebuilding Jerusalem's temple and city walls is portrayed as fraught with the difficulties of poverty among the returnees and conflict with people who, never taken into exile, lived there or in the vicinity.

THE NEW TESTAMENT'S STORY OF EVENTS

The New Testament tells history as it's relevant for understanding the implications of Jesus' birth, life, death, and resurrection for believers. Its scope is consequently much smaller both geographically and temporally. That so much of the New Testament is about Jesus' life, together with the fact that I discuss the details of Jesus' character and significance in later chapters, means that this particular section is very brief by comparison with the Old Testament's story of events.

The four books of gospels that begin the New Testament tell about the person, Jesus. They variously narrate his birth, skip nearly all of his childhood and adolescence, and concentrate on the three years of his preaching, teaching, and healing in the Galilee region. They describe his execution in Jerusalem, at the time of the Jewish Passover, by Roman crucifixion, and they tell that he came alive again.

The narrative continues after Jesus' death by detailing in the book of Acts the missionary work of his followers, concentrating especially on Paul. That book of history (Acts) and what history is incidentally related in the New Testament's books of letters and epistles tells about the church's development related both to its Jewish, biblical roots and to the greater Roman empire. The last book, Revelation, is the exception. Its scope is universal, cosmic even. Although its language transcends history, it tells of events leading up to and including the violent second coming of Jesus and the end of the world as we know it.

FOUR

Contexts and Culture: History behind the Bible

> It might be a good idea if the various countries of
> the world would occasionally swap history books,
> just to see what other people are doing with the
> same set of facts.
>
> —BILL VAUGHAN

Because the Bible grew up over a long period of time, any timeline of related historical events is bound to be as long as Midsummer Day in northern Norway. Also, especially in the case of the earliest contexts, it's often difficult to assign dates to particular events. Nevertheless, through archaeology, other writings contemporary with the biblical literature (even if they focus on different things), and notations within the Bible itself, we can be confident about identifying a number of significant historical moments that are reflected in the biblical texts. Knowing about the history behind the Bible helps us to appreciate how and why the Bible says what it does and also to understand how people use those texts today.

The trouble is that although the Bible speaks as if the whole world were equally spellbound by the events it tells, we sometimes have precious little nonbiblical evidence, literary or otherwise, to corroborate those events. What's more, rather than simply reporting, the Bible interprets events in light of particular traditions and faith. Told by believers, the biblical narratives emphasize God's part in human history and the implications for God's relationship with people. The Bible is, then, not a pure recording of observable facts. It is seldom concerned with such concrete details as a scientific explanation of origins or the logistics of moving 600,000 men plus their families and livestock across the Sinai peninsula. Sometimes the evidence actually contradicts the biblical telling.

For example, Joshua is remembered in the biblical book by the same name for leading the ancient Israelites in a decisive victory over the city of Jericho.[1] Following God's instruction for seven priests to blow seven trumpets while walking with the warriors around the city for six days, all the people were to shout on the seventh day, and the walls would come a-tumblin' down. And so they did—the priests, the warriors, the people, and the walls—according to the Bible. But the archaeological record indicates that at the time of Joshua, Jericho was a small, unfortified village. There were no walls.[2] Even regarding the latest biblical periods, for which we have quite a lot of extrabiblical information, there isn't much attention in the extrabiblical sources to the things that the Bible focuses on. Jesus himself, the central figure of the New Testament, gets scant mention (arguably, none at all) in Roman records of the day.[3]

Although I encourage interested readers to learn in detail about what there isn't room to discuss here, a word of warning: There are loads of modern books that claim to describe the historical background of biblical texts but simply repackage the Bible's telling of events.[4] Unfortunately, a lot of believers have worked under the assumption that to question the Bible's telling of history is to question God's integrity, and so they have gone to great lengths (straining credibility and occasionally the principles of physics) to force the Bible to fit modern expectations for historical reporting. But finally, with a wink and a whistle, the Bible merrily blows such a house of cards down.

BEGINNINGS

The first eleven chapters of Genesis are sometimes called the "primeval history," because they tell about times before there were any people at all and then about times when people were said to have lived for hundreds and hundreds of years (the longest-lived being Methusaleh, at 969 years). These stories include semi-humans and talking animals and concern the whole world. Things change after the Flood, when the narrative begins to focus on one particular family (Abraham's) in a particular, geographically specific locale.

For a long time, scholars have situated Abraham at around 1850 BCE, even though we have no record outside the Bible for him or his family.[5] Yet on the basis of archaeological evidence about the life and times of people in ancient Canaan and literary records from places such as Mari in Mesopotamia, Ugarit in modern Syria, and Egypt, most scholars agree that if Abraham and Sarah lived at all, they probably lived during a period when cities made a comeback in Palestine, Israel's mother culture in Canaan took shape, Egypt experienced a similar revitalization, and the alphabet on which ours is based was born.

Although the Bible is usually the starting point for trying to determine a historical context for the Exodus from Egypt, the narrative doesn't mention a single pharaoh by name, and doesn't include much at all in the way of concrete references to Egypt. Like the ancestral narratives, the biblical story of the Israelites' liberation and departure from Egypt probably has some historical background, but the form that we have today represents a long tradition of development combining disparate sources and told primarily for theological purposes.

That said, if an exodus from Egypt like that described in the Bible occurred, it may have been around 1250 BCE. This date is partly based on the huge building projects of Ramses II, who ruled Egypt at the time and relied on a great number of laborers. Ramses is also the name of a place in the biblical narrative. Also, during the period around 1400–1200 BCE there is evidence of mass migrations in the areas of Egypt and Canaan; and letters from the Canaanite city of Amarna reveal frustration on the part of Egyptian officials over their inability to govern the feisty *apiru* peoples in Canaan. *Apiru* sounds a lot like "Hebrew," but it is difficult to determine their relationship to the proto-Israelites of the biblical texts.[6] Nevertheless, there is considerable evidence that people from the area of Canaan made their way into (and out of) Egypt over the centuries, after fleeing hard times back home, being taken as slaves, or simply looking for a better life.

Dating the Exodus to 1250 BCE is due in no small part to the fact that this is about forty years (a formulaic period of the biblical wandering in the wilderness, equal to a generation) before 1200 BCE. Also, around 1200 BCE we have the earliest known reference outside the Bible to "Israel." The reference, "Israel is laid waste, his seed is no more," is part of the Egyptian pharaoh Merneptah's lengthy victory declaration, inscribed on a freestanding pillar called a stele.[7] It spells "Israel" with a sign designating this as a people, not a nation, and we cannot say exactly what or who composed Israel in Merneptah's mind. Nevertheless, the stele's date and its mention of the people Israel are definitive and constitute a valuable piece of evidence in reconstructing the history behind the Bible.

Following the biblical narrative, and based on some general sociological, anthropological, and archaeological evidence, it seems that from about 1200 BCE to about 1000 BCE, the Hebrews in the territory of Palestine-Canaan-Israel operated in tribal groups that may have been related to one another. Perhaps these groups joined forces occasionally to combat a common enemy; but for the most part they operated independently. A poem in the biblical book of Judges (chapter 5) may well have this historical background. The archaeological record shows that settlements in the heart of ancient Israel began to flourish at this time.

KINGDOMS

Due to a combination of pressure from their enemies and economic interests, and under the umbrella of shared religious beliefs (which used familial language such as "people" or "kindred" of God), the tribes formed a confederacy that became a modest nation with centralized leadership. Archaeological evidence of settlements, fortresses, and pottery indicating a common culture fits the general biblical picture of a nation that reached its peak under the kings David and Solomon. Most people situate David and the establishment of a unified monarchy around the year 1000 BCE. David gets far more press in the Bible than anyone else except God or Jesus; yet until a few decades ago, we had no reference to him or his kingdom outside the biblical texts themselves. (We still have no nonbiblical reference to Solomon.) Then, in 1993–1994, archaeologists discovered an inscription at a site called Tel Dan that dates from around 800 BCE, and seems to mention the "house of David" (an idiom referring to the people or nation that David founded).

The inscription from Tel Dan tells about affairs between two nations: Israel and Judah. Scholars date the split of a united Israel into these two in part on the basis of nonbiblical references, such as the Tel Dan stele, which assume that Israel and Judah were two separate kingdoms. We also have a reference from Egypt, the earliest definitive extrabiblical source that agrees with a biblical telling of an event concerning Pharaoh Shishak (Shoshenq I). Together with the biblical narrative, the Egyptian account lends confidence to dating the division of kingdoms to around 922 BCE.[8]

After that schism, the northern kingdom (Israel) had its own national and economic system independent of the southern kingdom (Judah). Israel's capital city became Samaria, while Judah's continued as Jerusalem. Some of what we read in the Bible is specific to one or the other kingdom. For example, when the Old Testament prophet Amos railed against Israel, it was against the fat and happy northern kingdom. Since Amos was actually from Judah, he got a less than friendly reception and was not so kindly asked to take his acerbic tongue back home. Hosea was a native of the northern kingdom who also prophesied the coming judgment of God on Israel. He reasoned that Israel's determination to worship other gods and goddesses, thereby breaking its covenant of fidelity to God, justified national destruction. Hosea made his point by marrying a prostitute to exemplify the "marriage" of God to a nation that promiscuously hooked up with other deities.

We don't know about these individual prophets as real, historical figures outside the Bible. We do know, however, that the northern kingdom (Israel) enjoyed the prosperity of a fertile area under a succession of kings. During this period, Israel and Judah are mentioned in several texts from other nations—a dubious honor because such attention invariably led to meddling and an eventual takeover. Indeed, the prophets' words of impending destruction rang true, and the northern kingdom was defeated by the Assyrians, a nation based in the northern part of Mesopotamia, to the east of Israel. Shalmaneser V brought them down (722 BCE), but his successor Sargon II delivered the fatal blow (721 BCE). The Assyrians' empire-building policy included shuffling population groups around, probably because it's harder to unite and rise up if your neighbors speak different languages and if most aren't *from* where they happen to be living. As a result, the northern kingdom's tribes were scattered throughout the wide-ranging Assyrian empire. They came to be called the "ten lost tribes."

There's a tradition of the "ten lost tribes" that continues to generate all sorts of speculation. After 9/11, Americans were introduced to the Pashtun people of Afghanistan and Pakistan. They are one of many groups that claim to be descended from ancient Israel. So, too, people in China, Japan, Great Britain, Russia, and Zimbabwe, among others.[9] The Book of Mormon associates Native Americans with the ten lost tribes, and many Ethiopian Jews have recently made their way (back) to Israel in part by association with the ancient Israelite tribe of Dan. Wherever it was that the Assyrians deported and scattered people from Israel, the Assyrians also imported and settled others in Israel.

Meanwhile, King Hezekiah of Judah kept his head down, paid dues to Assyria, concentrated on religious reform and local literary patronage,[10] and tried to stay out of trouble. The southern kingdom escaped an Assyrian takeover but wasn't spared assault. In a remarkable Bible-versus-Assyrian telling of events, both the Bible and the (Assyrian) Annals of Sennacherib, plus an inscription on Assyrian palace walls, provide a detailed account of an Assyrian siege on Jerusalem in 701 BCE.[11] The biblical and Assyrian versions vary somewhat, in predictable ways. In the Bible, an angel of God gets credit for killing the enemy army the morning before they had planned to attack, and Sennacherib retreated back home. The nineteenth-century, club-footed British poet and ladies' man, Lord Byron, memorialized the biblical side of the story in dactylic tetrameter (the rhythm of a galloping horse) that begins, "The Assyrian came down like the wolf on the fold." In the Assyrian account, there is no mention of casualties due to an avenging angel, but there is much description of the Assyrians' destruction of surrounding towns. Rather than slinking back home, the Assyrian annals tell how Sennacherib secured a lot of money and goods from Judah's king, Hezekiah. The accounts apparently agree that Jerusalem was not destroyed.

As far as we can tell, Judah continued to function as a semiautonomous nation under a succession of kings, occasionally paying tribute to the power brokers of the day—Egypt, Assyria, and Babylonia—to keep one or another of them at bay. (Assyria succumbed to Babylonia in the late seventh century BCE. Its capital, Nineveh, fell in 612 BCE.) Judah enjoyed a brief rejuvenation and flowering under good king Josiah (reigned 640–609 BCE), who is associated in the Bible with the discovery (621 BCE) of and reforms based on "the book of the law," which modern scholars identify as some form of Deuteronomy.[12] But rather than enjoying the long life of a righteous man, Josiah was killed in a shocking defeat by the Egyptians.

After that, Judah resumed its vassal status, first to Egypt and then to Babylon. Then, tired of funneling resources to appease the big dogs and sensing that Babylonia might be weakening, the hotheaded Judean king Jehoiakim rebelled—with devastating results. Babylonia came down hard. Overwhelmed by Babylonian might, Jerusalem surrendered to Nebuchadnezzar II. We can date that event with confidence—March 15 and 16, 597 BCE—because besides the biblical witness, the Babylonians made clear note of it in enduring records.[13] The victors removed prominent Judahites, including the king and also the priest-prophet Ezekiel, to Babylon (in modern Iraq).

EXILE

With the Babylonians' approval, Judah continued to operate with some measure of independence until, in 587 BCE, emboldened by Egypt, it revolted again. Bad choice. The Babylonian response under Nebuchadnezzar II was swift and decisive, and Egyptian support was lukewarm. The Babylonians razed the Jerusalem temple; destroyed much of the surrounding area; killed a lot of people, including King Zedekiah's sons, before blinding the king; and took another group of elite Judahites into exile in Babylon.

This is arguably the most crucial event in the history of the Bible, not because the report takes up so much space—it doesn't[14]—but because it profoundly affected the pace and shape of the Bible's development. This catastrophe informs much of the Bible's ideas about God, community identity, and human accountability. And it spurred efforts among this particular people to record in a definitive and lasting way, so as to pass along to their children and their children's children, who, how, and why "we" are. Without a nation, a king, or a central place of worship, the Israelites became a people of the book (specifically the Pentateuch, which probably took its shape during the Babylonian exile). It seems that during this time of exile, the religion of Judaism began to take shape.

FREEDOM AND RESTORATION

It was in the subsequent, Persian period, however, that Judaism flowered and the first biblical books were compiled and accorded the authority of scripture. That period began for the biblical witnesses in 539 BCE. After the span of about a generation since Babylon defeated Judah, Babylon capitulated to a new world leader—Cyrus II, aptly called "The Great." This ruler—a brilliant strategist, religiously tolerant, and culturally literate—based his empire (which became the largest of any up to that time) in Persia, the area of Mesopotamia that is modern-day Iran. On a clay cylinder, about the size of a small thermos, he wrote (or commissioned a scribe to write) what has come to be called the "first declaration of human rights."[15] It announced his renunciation of terror, his efforts at peace, his release of slaves, and the right of people to worship however they saw fit. A replica sits today in the United Nations building in New York City. Cyrus allowed exiles, including the Jews, to return to their places of origin and to rebuild their places of worship.

Using details based on the biblical narrative, most scholars agree that with the prompting of the postexilic prophets, Haggai and Zechariah, the (second) temple was completed around 515 BCE. Again based primarily on the biblical witness, most think that Ezra and Nehemiah returned to Jerusalem from Babylon in the middle of the fifth century BCE. The Torah (Pentateuch) was probably completed toward the end of that century. Conditions for restoration were hardly as easy as the returnees may have hoped or even expected, however. Despite Cyrus's encouragement to rebuild the temple in Jerusalem, Haggai and Zechariah (in quite different ways) implore, chasten, and encourage their Judean audience to persist in the task despite adversity and economic hardships. Ezra and Nehemiah also faced opposition from the "people of the land,"[16] possibly composed in part of people who had never been taken into exile, and from neighboring people, threatened by Jerusalem's restoration.[17]

Although we have little nonbiblical material corroborating these details,[18] and the texts themselves make no effort to hide their ideological bias or point of view, conditions of the greater historical context are clear to us: Cyrus was succeeded by a series of variously capable Persian leaders until Alexander of Macedon took the world by storm before his death in 323 BCE. The enduring influence of Alexander's Greek empire on the Bible is indisputable. During this period, hellenization (the introduction of Greek language and culture into existing cultures) became the norm. Take the Septuagint, for example. Because it was this translation of the Hebrew scriptures that the New Testament writers used, the New Testament reads the Old through Greek eyes. Among Jews, the question of just how much they should

assimilate was a source of contention, and some of the strongest biblical voices argued against it,[19] preferring to maintain a distinct identity
no matter how intense the pressure to conform.

Sometimes that pressure was painfully great, intolerable even. The
book of Daniel, set in the Babylonian exile, was actually composed
around 165 BCE, after one of Alexander's successors (Antiochus IV)
forced the Jews to behave and worship in a Greek manner. Antiochus
IV even took over the Jerusalem temple, desecrating Judaism's most
holy site. The historical result was a full-scale revolt instigated by one
Judean family, the Hasmonaeans, nicknamed the Maccabees—after
their military genius leader Judas "The Hammer" (Maccabaeus).
They were remarkably successful. In 164 BCE, they regained control of
the Jerusalem temple and ritually purified it; the Jews commemorate
this event each year in the menorah-lighting, dreidel-spinning winter holiday of Hanukkah. Call it ironic, but the books that recall this
moment of national *Jewish* glory, 1 and 2 Maccabees, are apocryphal:
they have become part of some Christian bibles but not of the Jewish
bible. At any rate, the Maccabees brought national independence to
the Jews in Palestine and went on to rule Judah through a succession
of Hasmonaean kings from 142–63 BCE.

Not every Jew was thrilled about all this; and people differed over
a number of critical points, including what a king should look like,
who constitutes a proper priest, and just how Greek Jews should be.
During this time the varieties of Jews about whom the historian Josephus wrote—Pharisees, Sadducees, Essenes, and Zealots—really came
into their own.[20] Fractures in the community concerning religion and
politics led some to appeal to the new world power for assistance.
Happy to resolve this civil conflict, Rome, under the military leadership of Pompey, simply ended Jewish independence in 63 BCE.

UNDER ROMAN RULE

Things were pretty messy in Judea after that, with considerable up-
heaval in religious and political leadership until 37 BCE, when Herod I,
the Great, was installed by the Romans as king in Jerusalem. Herod

the Great ruled the province of Judea as a king answerable to Rome for thirty-three years. During that time, he kept close and friendly relations with Rome, renovated the Jerusalem temple into a structure nearly as grand as the memories of Solomon's temple, and went a bit crazy. Herod's insecurity (an understatement) led him to execute his own family and earned him quite a reputation. This reputation got him a character role in the Bible as the paranoid king who, threatened by a Jewish baby's birth, consequently ordered that all babies in and around Bethlehem under two years of age be killed.[21] (A similar reputation earned his successor son, Herod Antipas, a flamboyant wardrobe and a manic showgirl dance in the movie *Jesus Christ Superstar.*)

The challenge of walking a line between maintaining some measure of control over a notoriously problematic population while keeping a fine-tuned imperial system happy could have made anyone insane. Unlike most other peoples of the Roman empire, the Jews stubbornly held to their exclusivist traditions, some of which created a logistic nightmare for the Roman security forces. Passover, for instance, was a Jewish holiday that required anyone capable of travel to go to Jerusalem. The surge in population coupled with the excitement of religious celebration in this heart of Judea must have made the Romans nervous. Indeed, during this volatile time, the charismatic Jewish healer and teacher Jesus, from the Galilean town of Nazareth, came under suspicion as an agitator of sorts and was executed.

Jesus' followers continued to hope for his immediate return. Violence and social unrest fed apocalyptic expectations, most colorfully expressed by the imprisoned author of Revelation.[22] The emperor Nero accused Christians of starting the conflagration of Rome in 64 CE and persecuted them accordingly. In 70 CE, in response to a Jewish revolt against Rome, Titus and his Tenth Legion burned to the ground the Jerusalem temple (its renovations and rebuilding had only recently been completed). Despite the strident declarations of many people, the earth was not destroyed in a great cosmic battle between divine forces of good and evil, with or without Jesus. Instead, both Jews and Christians had to find a way to survive in and through the Roman empire and subsequent eras. And they did.

FIVE

Getting to
the Good Book:
History of the Bible

This only is denied to God: the power to
undo the past.

—AGATHON

The ancient Greek playwright Agathon observed the impossibility of
rewinding history. Unable to delete the past, can God nevertheless
rewrite it? To understand how the Bible came to be requires that we
suspend nearly everything we know about authorship and the business of books today. The Bible is wildly unique, yet it sits on modern bookshelves mum to its extravagant dissimilarity, with its modest
spine politely blending in—a book among other books. But it is not
like those other books. In considering how ancient texts developed
into the Bible as it appears today, here are a few crucial points to note
or simply to recall from discussions above:

1. The Bible comprises texts from a variety of times and places. A
conservative estimate for the Hebrew Bible is that it includes material from over 1,000 years, the earliest dating to around 1200 BCE (see

above concerning Judges 5) and the latest to about 165 BCE (the book of Daniel). Geographically, its sources are Mesopotamian (e.g., the Flood story), Canaanite (see especially Chapter 13, "God Names, Beings, and Doings"), and Egyptian (Prov 22–24 is nearly identical to the Instruction of Amenemope from 1100 BCE), spanning the Fertile Crescent of the ancient Near East. The New Testament is more limited, but not as limited as the few years and a single author that most books produced today involve. The texts of the New Testament concern events in the eastern Mediterranean and date from around 50 CE (Paul's earliest letters) to around 150 CE (Jude and 2 Peter).

2. The Bible includes different kinds of literature. It includes origin myths, devotional poetry, legal texts, biographies, pithy aphorisms, philosophical treatises, and letters both to individuals and to groups. It has songs and instructional narratives, humorous anecdotes, and stern sermons. And none of these was composed with an eye to becoming biblical, per se. Rather, the contents assumed authority over time within communities of faith, which only later compiled them into the Bible that we have today.[1]

3. During the period of the Hebrew Bible's development most people couldn't read or write. Those texts, then, were the product of an elite few who wrote either for their small band of academic colleagues or in an "oral" style (i.e., a style that lent itself to oral recitation) that the masses could use. By New Testament times, literacy was more common. Thus just as orality shaped much of the Old Testament, literacy shaped much of the New.

4. Authorship during the period of biblical development seldom meant the creative endeavor of an individual, whose words once written remained immutable. Nearly all of the Bible's literature is attributed to one person or another who did not actually write it. Most of the Bible (the Hebrew Bible in particular) is the product of the few, mostly anonymous people who could learn to read and write—scribes, schooled in the temple. They worked at least partly with existing traditions and

texts (e.g., oral narratives and poetry, royal annals and records, oracles preserved and passed down by a prophet's disciples), copying and editing as circumstances required and their theology dictated.

5. The literature that would come to be collected as "Bible" circulated in independent pieces, many of which took the form of scrolls, rather than in the page-bound codices that we think of as books today. One result is that their organization and order wasn't fixed.

The previous chapter began by noting the tough-to-overstate influence of the Babylonian exile on the development of the Bible. Add to that the Persian emperor's subsequent release of the exiles and encouragement for the returnees to codify a set of traditions and laws, and the Bible was off and running. Indeed, most scholars think that the first five books of the Bible took real shape during the exile and became truly authoritative among the Jewish community during the Persian period.

THE DOCUMENTARY HYPOTHESIS

The idea that Moses wrote the Bible's first five books has its roots in ancient traditions. Within the Hebrew Bible's latest books, Ezra-Nehemiah, Chronicles, and Daniel, as well as in New Testament texts, we read of the "torah of Moses" as God's instructions to the Israelites mediated by Moses.[2] Some traditionalists continue to maintain that a historical Moses wrote the entire Pentateuch—on the basis of key texts from Exodus, Numbers, and Deuteronomy, in which God commands Moses to write what God dictates.[3]

Yet even a casual reading of these books indicates a layered composition, and for centuries people have noted problems with the traditional belief of Mosaic authorship, despite the danger to one's reputation or even one's person that such a claim could elicit. Rabbi Ibn Ezra (c. 1090–1164) delicately noted that anachronisms within the Pentateuch suggest that at least a few texts do not seem to have been written by Moses.[4] In the seventeenth century, the philosopher

Thomas Hobbes, the Roman Catholic scholar Richard Simon, and the Jewish philosopher Baruch (Benedict) Spinoza were more outspoken in calling into question whether Moses could have written the entire Pentateuch. Principles of the Enlightenment, with its championing of reason, launched a new era in biblical studies, granting such investigation more credibility.

One long-standing approach to understanding the development of the Pentateuch is called the "documentary hypothesis." About 150 years ago, a German scholar, Julius Wellhausen, articulated an idea that had been hatching for some time. He posited four different literary sources (from different times and places) that were woven together over time to produce what we have today as the first five books of the Bible. Although details of the documentary hypothesis continue to be debated, its general ideas have stood the test of time. Observing different names for God and a constellation of vocabulary, perspective, and literary styles that attends those names gave the hypothesis its start.

For example, the first chapter of Genesis uses the name Elohim and portrays God as magnificently "other." It relates a story of universal creation in poetic repetition and orderly progression over six days accomplished with ease by the speech of God. In it, human beings were created simultaneously "male and female" in the image of God, and the whole project is said to be "very good."[5] By contrast, chapter 2 of Genesis uses the divine name Yahweh Elohim and portrays an earthy God who walks around and uses his hands to shape and plant a particular area and its creatures. In this story, God fashioned out of the soil a single human being. Then, judging that such solitude "isn't good," God divided the original human into "man" and "woman."[6] In effect, then, in the first few chapters of Genesis, we have two very different images of God, and two very different narratives about the creation of human beings, in two very different literary styles, combined into a yet larger narrative. This combination invites readers to connect the stories, yielding yet other interpretations than either text bears alone.

The literary sources that compose the Pentateuch don't appear in tidy and convenient blocks but are woven together, overlapping in some places and causing contradictions or disconnects in others.

Take a close look at the Flood story in Genesis 6:5–8:19. Just how many animals went on Noah's ark—two of every kind (6:19; 7:15), or seven pairs of every clean animal and one pair of every unclean animal (7:2–3)? How did the Flood come—by rain from above (7:4), or by an upsurge of water from the deep, or both (7:11)? And how long did it last—forty days (7:17; 8:6), or 150 days (7:24)? As in the case of chapters 1 and 2, considering stories in their final form, as they appear in the Bible today, readers may conclude that one source adds to or elaborates on details from another, producing a yet richer story. The texts invite such layered reading.

None of the four hypothetical literary sources was likely composed by an individual person; rather, the four represent both oral traditions and the writing of several parties, probably not together in one sitting, but over time. That is, each of the sources is built on other sources and reflects a process of transmission that allowed editing and change all along. And the final form reflects an intentional combination of received texts.

According to the documentary hypothesis, the earliest (but not the first) literary source in the Pentateuch prefers to use the divine name Yahweh. For that reason, it's called the Yahwist and abbreviated J (because Germans spell Yahweh with a J). It reflects especially the southern kingdom's interests and may date back to the tenth century BCE. This is the source responsible for the Adam and Eve creation story that begins in Genesis chapter 2.

The temporally next literary source prefers the divine name Elohim, and so is called the Elohist and abbreviated E. That source reflects especially the northern kingdom's interests and may date to the ninth century BCE. Together, J and E tell stories that may have been collected even before others began to write them down and add to them, editing or redacting along the way. That editorial group probably tweaked J and E or JE a bit while also adding its own material.

Contrary to what I wrote above, a third literary strand actually does appear as a block, according to this hypothesis. The Deuteronomist's work (D) is specific to the book of Deuteronomy. But that book also probably reflects at least three literary stages (preexilic and northern; seventh century BCE in the southern kingdom; and post-exilic).

Finally, according to the hypothesis, the group that edited J, E, and D worked during the period of exile to codify basics of belief and identity. They are called the Priestly writers (P) because they added material especially concerned with the workings of and reflecting ideas particular to the religious institution. The Priestly writers collected, arranged, and edited the material that we have fixed in the Pentateuch. They framed the work, adding new material as necessary.

For example, determined to address those questions that the exile posed, the Priestly writers, as a group or school, are thought to have composed the seven-day creation story that appears in Genesis chapter 1. With it, they demonstrated that God was not killed or defeated by the Babylonian god but rather is the creator of the entire universe. Not only that, but they described a God who has no image that could be manipulated or hurt but elegantly speaks an orderly world into being, and declares that it is good. This God, the story tells, is not bound by nation or temple but existed long before Israel and Israelite religion and is of cosmic proportion. The conclusion, and grand finale, is not the creation of human beings (simultaneously male and female in the image of God), but the creation of the Sabbath, a day dear to the Priestly writers as both sacred and an agent for maintaining the order of time.

According to the documentary hypothesis, the Adam and Eve story that begins in chapter 2 actually dates to an earlier time than the story in chapter 1. This can be confusing because modern readers are familiar with books composed as a single piece. Further complicating things, the content of the stories in the Pentateuch follows a chronological order, which is misleading because the beginning was not composed first, nor was the end composed last.

Finally, the documentary hypothesis is just that—a hypothesis. We do not have in a vault somewhere four disparate, individual documents signed by the Yahwist, Elohist, Deuteronomist, and Priestly writers that we can compare with the Pentateuch. The image of four discrete documents cut and pasted together is probably not entirely accurate, either, since there was a process of transmission and editing that made the traditions quite fluid over time—though not forever.

DATING *TANAKH*

The Babylonian exile prompted scribes not only to collect and codify oral and literary traditions but also to rework them in light of the theological challenges posed by the nation's spectacular destruction. When the Persian king Cyrus II conquered Babylon and allowed the exiles to return home, those traditions underwent yet further development.

Around 450 BCE, it appears that a learned priest and scribe by the name of Ezra was instructed by the Persian authorities to help his native people in Judah articulate the core of their beliefs and establish the law of the land.[7] This is the period most scholars assign to the finalization of the Pentateuch, when the "five books of Moses" became fixed and authoritative.

Finalization of the second section, the books of the prophets (including the historical books of Joshua, Judges, Samuel, and Kings), probably took place around 200 BCE, when the project of translating those Hebrew scriptures into Greek was under way. By around 100 BCE, the Septuagint was the Greek-speaking people's version of the Hebrew scriptures. Consequently, this was the Bible familiar to that Jewish sect of Jesus followers who would become the early Christian church, and its version served as the foundation for the New Testament.[8] Partly because of the Septuagint's growing popularity among Christians who continued to distance and distinguish themselves, traditional Jews abandoned this Greek rendering of the Hebrew Bible and renewed their commitment to a Hebrew version.

Following the Romans' destruction of the Jerusalem temple in 70 CE, Jews finalized their (Hebrew) Bible, ordering its books in a predominantly chronological manner, and setting Cyrus's call to return to Jerusalem and rebuild its temple as the final word. The third, "Writings," section and full canon of the Hebrew Bible was set around

130 CE,[9] but only books that met the criteria of having been composed by important people before about 450 BCE were included. Nothing deemed to postdate Ezra and Nehemiah was admitted as Bible into the Hebrew canon after that time. (Biblical books that were indeed composed later were admitted under the auspices of earlier authorship by important people—e.g., Daniel is set in the Babylonian period even though it was composed in the second century BCE; Ecclesiastes is attributed to Solomon, though it appears to come from the Hellenistic period following Alexander's conquest.) The books that were included had gained a standing and reputation of importance, and their traditions of authorship and antiquity made them eligible.

THE CHRISTIAN CANON

Development of the Christian canon is another story. Although its historical trajectory is much shorter than that of the Hebrew Bible (spanning a couple of hundred rather than a thousand years), its historical development has gotten a lot more attention lately, thanks in part to titillating stories of intrigue and power such as *The Da Vinci Code*. Indeed, understanding how the Christian bible took shape isn't as simple as tacking on to the standing Hebrew Bible a comprehensive collection of books about Jesus. For one thing, the Hebrew Bible that most of Jesus' followers used was neither Hebrew nor a Bible. They worked with Greek translations of Hebrew scrolls that hadn't yet achieved the status of an absolutely closed canon.

Furthermore, the early followers of Jesus were not all of one mind about who Jesus was, what he said and did, or the implications of his life. Jesus didn't write anything himself—at least nothing that we have. Rather, his followers and people who were convinced of his extraordinary nature wrote in his voice and about him. In the first couple of centuries, many people who identified themselves as Christian wrote texts that would be unrecognizable as Christian to us today.

Which books represented best the life, teachings, and implications of Jesus and what it meant to be a true Christian were hotly debated.

As with the Hebrew Bible, qualifying texts had to be old (the closer to Jesus the better) and attributed to Jesus' apostles or their close associates. Also as with the Hebrew Bible, the gradual process of a text's wide acceptance and use on the one hand, or neglect and attrition on the other (rather than definitive action by a single convening group of decision makers), accounts for what made it into the Bible and what did not. Other criteria for inclusion were that the texts needed to have broad application or relevance rather than be limited only to a particular individual or congregation and that they conform to accepted beliefs. It wasn't until 367 CE that we have the first mention of the definitive Christian canon.[10] That is a full 250 years after the latest of the books in the New Testament was written.

Many gospels were composed and circulated in the centuries after Jesus' death by his followers both before and after the New Testament was firmly established. Only four are included in the Bible. Of the others, some, such as the gospel of Thomas and the gospel of Peter, probably contain very early material (possibly from Jesus' time), even if their final form was later. The gospel of Thomas, consisting entirely of Jesus' sayings, may preserve some things that Jesus actually said, and may or may not predate similar sayings that appear in the canonical gospels. Scholars think that it dates to the end of the first century or the beginning of the second century CE. The gospel of Peter, from the mid-first century, concentrates its attention on the passion narrative, empty tomb and resurrection. It may actually have served as a source for the canonical gospels.

Among the many gospels other than the four that made it into the New Testament, several were produced late in the game—in the third and fourth centuries (and some even later than that). For this reason alone they would not have been eligible for inclusion. Some also reflected a particularly popular school of early Christian thought called gnosticism (because its adherents claim to have secret or special knowledge—Greek, *gnosis*), which was later deemed heretical (i.e., promoting false doctrine). The gospel of Judas is one such gnostic text. Discovered in the late twentieth century in Egypt, it seems to come from the fourth century CE but is probably a copy of a text originally from the second century CE. It relates in dialogues between Judas and Jesus a more sympathetic portrait of the infamous disciple than do the canonical gospels.[11] The third-century gnostic Gospel of Mary concerns Mary Magdalene and portrays her as a leader among the disciples, while the Gospel of the Birth of Mary, from the eighth or ninth century CE, tells about Mary the mother of Jesus. These and other noncanonical gospels provide a glimpse of the diverse faces of Christian belief and the variety of ways that Jesus and his inner circle were remembered in the light of disparate theologies.

As Jesus' followers accepted that his return might take a while, and as they coalesced into a community, they turned to literary traditions for worship, direction, and identity. Paul's letters were probably the earliest of the New Testament texts to be treated as authoritative. They were composed for particular congregations, so no single one was originally intended for every early Christian community; but with Paul's great reputation, the books quickly gained distinction as authoritative texts. The author of 2 Peter, probably writing around 150 CE, referred to them as scripture.[12] The church's earliest theologians and apologists (including Ignatius and Polycarp, Clement of Alexandria, Tertullian, and Irenaeus in the second century) also mention Paul's letters as normative Christian literature.

Matthew and Luke share a number of popular texts in common. Because of this, and a number of other stylistic indicators, biblical scholars have long supposed that Matthew and Luke appealed to a common source, besides the gospel of Mark, when developing their accounts of Jesus. We don't have a copy of that other source, and in scholarly lingo it is simply called Q, short for *Quelle*, which means "source" in German (German scholars proposed it). The theory is that Q was composed mostly of sayings of Jesus. Both Matthew and Luke drew from Q, drew from their precursor Mark, added some unique elements of their own, and voilà!—the canonical, synoptic gospels. Actually, they probably went through several permutations before arriving at the forms that we have today.

Because the ultimate authority among early Christians was not a body of texts but rather the person of Jesus, the gospels with their

biographical information were very popular. Likely built in part on
oral traditions, the written gospels weren't uniformly considered authoritative scripture until around 180 CE, when Irenaeus promoted
the four canonical gospels as a group.[13] It seems, then, that by the
second century CE, collections of Paul's letters were widely accepted,
the four gospels were gaining in status, 1 Peter and 1 John were well
known (though independent of any collection), and a number of other
texts enjoyed a strong reputation among Christian communities. The
so-called catholic epistles weren't widely adopted until the 300s CE;
and it seems that Acts and Revelation, each of which was popular and
widespread among early Christian communities, nevertheless also had
to wait until the fourth century to achieve canonical status.

SIX

What's the Best Translation?

> Translation it is that openeth the window, to let in the light.
>
> —MILES SMITH (preface to the first edition of the King James Version)

With this line, Miles Smith expresses optimism about the business of translation: it illuminates so that readers can understand the meaning and appreciate the craftsmanship and beauty of a text. Unless you can read ancient Hebrew, Aramaic, and koine Greek, you must depend on translations to read biblical texts,[1] but translation is a tricky business. There is no perfect system, no fail-safe method to follow. All translation involves interpretation on some level or other; and no translation can claim to be authoritative for all time, since our own language is always changing.

Umberto Eco wrote, "Translation is the art of failure," which sounds at first like a pessimistic rejection of Smith's sentiments; but it needn't be. In light of the impossibility of producing a timelessly perfect translation of any document, the work of translating is nevertheless an art. It's a creative task that demands of its practitioners skills born of training and practice, keen attention to the subject, and a kind of personal engagement with, even sympathy for, the subject. The result, if done well, illuminates—it lets in the light. Exactly what and how one sees, though, is up to the reader.

Translating the Bible is especially challenging for several reasons besides the difficulty of its original languages. One is that because the Bible is sacred text, people often feel a preconscious, emotional attachment to whatever version is most familiar to them. Anything different seems sacrilegious and is sometimes deemed frankly wrong, even if it is technically correct. Also, the Bible's original languages fell out of common use ages ago. In several cases, we have no way to know what a word or grammatical construction means except by the context of a single usage in the Bible, so even if you've gained facility in the ancient languages, limits to your knowledge still exist. What's more, the earliest biblical Hebrew had no vowels, making some words naturally open to several readings. Finally, and most important, even if one can read the biblical languages, there is no single original Bible from which to work. For that matter, we have no original manuscript of any individual biblical book, and the earliest manuscripts that we do have don't all agree or even always make sense.

ANCIENT AND GROUNDBREAKING TRANSLATIONS

Even before texts became biblical, many underwent translation, according to the Bible itself. A biblical story suggests that in Jerusalem around 450 BCE it was necessary for the great Jewish teacher Ezra to enlist translators to make the Hebrew Torah that he read aloud sensible to his Aramaic-speaking audience.[2] Aramaic, a language related to Hebrew, was the official language of the Persian empire, so when Judah and its people became subject to Persia, Aramaic became the common language.[3] People began to make interpretive translations into Aramaic, called the Targums, around this time.[4] As the tides of history went, so went translation. When the Greeks took over, Greek became the official language, though most people probably continued to speak Aramaic, too. Jewish scholars reacted to the increasing emphasis on Greek language and literature by translating their scriptures into Greek. As noted in Chapter 2, a legend about the translation of the Septuagint (LXX) is the basis for its name. The New Testament texts, composed during this Greek period, were written in the common, koine, Greek of the day.

When the Roman empire succeeded the Greeks, biblical texts, including those that would become the New Testament, were duly translated into Latin. When a biblical religion, Christianity, became for the first time the state religion, under the emperor Constantine (d. 337), there was nevertheless no standard for Latin translations. The proliferation of variations was disconcerting, so Church authorities commissioned the scholar Jerome to set a standard. He worked for a long time with existing Latin and Greek versions before turning directly, at the beginning of the fifth century, to manuscripts in the original ancient Hebrew and koine Greek. Although it took longer than his lifetime for people fully to embrace his translation, Jerome's "common version," the Vulgate, has endured as authoritative within the Roman Catholic Church to this day.

Following the invention of the printing press (1440 CE) and Martin Luther's famous efforts to break the Catholic Church's hold on scriptural interpretation, the business of biblical translation into a number of languages and versions of languages increased. Gutenberg's printing press liberated the process of producing Bibles from hand-copying them one by one, previously the labor of monks, to mechanically generating multiple identical copies. It was a propitious development, since the Protestant Reformation that Luther started in Germany naturally required Bibles in common languages that any average Joe or Jane could read. The coincidence of Gutenberg's invention in 1455 of movable type just down the road from Luther, ensured that this German bible indeed got out to the masses.

Nevertheless, it wasn't until fairly recently that Bibles in most of the world's languages became available. Compare: when Gutenberg printed the Vulgate in 1456, there were Bibles in thirty-three languages, most of them (twenty-two) European; by 1987, the Bible had been translated (at least in part) into 1,884 languages and dialects.[5] Today, the World Bible Translation Center advertises 50,000 "easy-to-read" Bibles in Awadhi, Vietnamese, Burmese, Bengali, Oriya, and Urdu, among other languages.[6]

WHERE TO START?

Many people are surprised to learn that no original Bible exists. The earliest complete Hebrew Bible that we have dates to the 900s CE, and the earliest complete New Testament to the 300s CE. It may be that the very idea of an original is wrong. Rather, stories were told, sayings recounted, things written down, and expectations and instructions accepted as authoritative for all sorts of reasons. These were retold, and copied (copied, copied, and copied), many times over and over a period of time—in some cases, many centuries. Along the way, things were respectfully altered, adapted to new historical realities and contradictory personal experience. And we know that sometimes mistakes were made in transmission, with corrections or explanatory notes added later.[7] What, then, does a translator translate from?

THE HEBREW BIBLE

In the case of the Hebrew Bible, the authoritative text has traditionally been a version called the Masoretic Text (MT), from *masorah*, "transmission." It was developed between approximately 700 and 900 CE. As with Jerome and Luther, most modern translations today are based primarily on the MT. Given that the earliest complete MT that we have dates to a time almost a millennium after the Hebrew Bible was finalized, scholars have taken consolation in knowing how scrupulously the Jewish scholars responsible for the MT approached the process of transmission. They were a meticulous bunch, even counting words and the individual letters of words to compare against each copy in order to guard against mistakes.

To help with reading and pronunciation, the Masoretes added vowels to the purely consonantal text that they received. Inevitably, of course, adding vowels reflects interpretation—something that translators have to keep in mind as they work out what exactly to translate. For example, think of the different ways that you might understand *s gd s th crtr*—"As good as the creature," or "So God is the creator," and so on.

We now know that there were Hebrew versions earlier than what the MT represents. Without wandering off too deeply into the thicket that is textual criticism (the science of figuring out the most original reading), suffice it to say that comparing ancient versions helps to determine what is the best, most accurate text to translate. A glance at Flanders's bookshelf in *The Simpsons*—the episode "Home Sweet Home: Diddly-Dum-Doodly"—shows a few versions. Although "The Thump Resistant Bible" and "Who Begat Whom" are clearly the product of the series writers' imagination, the Samaritan Pentateuch has a real historical basis. It is a version almost as valuable as the Septuagint and the Dead Sea Scrolls for determining the best, most accurate Hebrew Bible text to translate.[8]

In some cases, these ancient versions also signal the variety that existed before the Hebrew Bible was fixed in a single, final form. Sometimes they attest to a Hebrew text earlier than what is represented in the MT. For example, in certain places the Septuagint appears to reflect a Hebrew version that we no longer have, a version that predates the MT. The Septuagint version of Jeremiah is quite a bit shorter than the MT version. Because scribes were more inclined to add to than to delete sections of scripture, and based on the nature of the additions, most scholars conclude that the Septuagint's Jeremiah is based on a Hebrew text older than the MT's.[9] Adding to the intrigue, both versions are represented among a collection of texts discovered near the Dead Sea in what is now Israel.

DEAD SEA SCROLLS

The most important archaeological discovery for biblical studies is the Dead Sea Scrolls, found quite recently (1947–1956) in caves around the Dead Sea near the archaeological site of Qumran. More than 200

scrolls have come to light after being tucked away in caves and preserved in the harsh desert landscape. Included among them are at least
a scrap or two and occasionally a nearly complete manuscript of every
book in the Hebrew Bible except Esther. An entire scroll of Isaiah is
represented. Most of the Dead Sea Scrolls are Torah texts (especially
Deuteronomy), but there are also many copies of parts of Psalms and
Isaiah—favorites also among Jesus and his followers. These manuscripts have had a huge impact on biblical studies. For one thing, they
are the earliest by far (dating from as early as 250 BCE and into the
second century CE) of any versions available till their discovery, and
most are in Hebrew. Also, they have confirmed that the Bible's development is much more complicated than a linear system of handing
down fixed traditions and texts.

That said, the youngest biblical texts from the Dead Sea Scrolls
(dating from about 75–125 CE, discovered at Masada and in caves
where rebels of the first century CE hid) are remarkably similar to the
Masoretic Text. This suggests that by then, among the variations in
existence (such as those in the Septuagint, Peshittas, and Samaritan
Pentateuch), much of what would become the Masoretic Text had
become authoritative. Jewish scribes had established at least something resembling a standardized Hebrew Bible, a Bible that was then
transmitted with great care for exactitude through the centuries. Indeed, the present Masoretic Text is remarkably similar to those ancient
scrolls.

Although some of the Dead Sea Scrolls date to the first century
CE and include a number, or parts, of deuterocanonical books and
some nonbiblical texts as well as texts that would become the Hebrew
Bible, they include no New Testament texts, and no references to Jesus
and his disciples. Nevertheless, the collection and its circumstances
(coming from a breakaway ascetic Jewish community that fled from
Jerusalem and expected an apocalyptic involvement of God in human
affairs), do much to help us understand early Christianity.

THE NEW TESTAMENT

In the case of the New Testament, one would think that determining a hypothetical original is easier. After all, the books of the New Testament are much more recent than those of the Old Testament, and they were composed over a much shorter period of time (about 100 years, by comparison with the possibly 1,000 years over which the Hebrew Bible developed). But those advantages also present problems. Because the New Testament texts are much more recent, we have many more of them—thousands of manuscripts, quotations of biblical texts in the writings of early Christian theologians and lectionaries, and various early translations, including a number in Latin, Syriac, and Coptic, with hundreds of thousands of variant readings.

Although most of the differences are minor, some can be shocking to people accustomed to thinking of the Bible as fixed from the start and for all time. For example, one of the best-known gospel stories, the story of the woman caught in adultery and presented to Jesus for judgment, appears only in the gospel of John. Yet it is absent from the earliest versions that we have of that gospel, as are the last twelve verses of Mark's gospel.[10] The gospels themselves, written in the common Greek of the time, represent translations. That is, Jesus probably spoke Aramaic, in which case the gospels necessarily translated his sayings into Greek.

Trying to figure out the best, earliest version is daunting indeed. Thankfully, it's not a recent endeavor. As early as the second century CE, people such as Origen were already trying to determine the most authoritative New Testament text, and this work has continued to the present. Because there are so many variations of the New Testament, a practice based on what scholars call "eclectic" choosing among the existing possibilities is most common today. The most widely accepted eclectic version of a Greek New Testament is the Nestle-Aland, named for two people. It is regularly updated—as of this writing, it is in its twenty-seventh edition.

In sum, most scholars use the Masoretic Text of the Hebrew Bible to translate the Old Testament, and the Nestle-Aland to translate the

New Testament, appealing to ancient versions and variants to help understand, or even suggest alternatives to, particularly difficult words or passages.

CHOICES, CHOICES, CHOICES

Settling on a particular version or an "original" Hebrew or Greek "source text" from which to translate is only the first of many choices a translator makes. For one thing, no language has a perfect, one-to-one correspondence with any other language. Many words lend themselves to a variety of translations, and grammar and syntax multiply the possibilities. This is evident from the Bible's very first chapter. For example, the Hebrew word *ruach* in Gen 1:2 can mean "breath," "spirit," or "wind"; and *weruach elohim merachephet* can be translated "and the spirit of God was hovering" or "while a wind from God swept," among other possibilities.

Matters are complicated by the lack of punctuation and capitalization. As a case study, consider the following from Genesis 1–3, concerning the creation of human beings. The Hebrew word *adam* is a common, general term that can mean either "human being" (not gender-specific) or "man" (gender-specific), and it is sometimes translated as the proper noun: the name Adam. Because there is no capitalization in biblical Hebrew, translators have to figure out, on a case-by-case basis, whether or not *adam* should be understood as a proper noun or a general noun and capitalize (or not) accordingly. One helpful (but not foolproof) hint is whether or not the word appears with a definite noun marker. As in English, saying "The Adam" doesn't make much sense unless you're trying to distinguish between two Adams—say, "the Adam who" stole your cousin's heart and the one who walked into the new sliding glass doors at his friend's house-warming party. Reviewing how *adam* appears in Genesis chapters 1–2 illustrates the kinds of choices translators must make when faced with several options for a single word.

The Bible's very first story tells that God created *adam* on the sixth day of creation.[11] This *adam* comes without the definite article, hinting that it should be translated by the proper noun: the name Adam. However, the story immediately tells that this *adam* came in two varieties—male and female, created simultaneously.[12] When the word *adam* appears again, it is with the definite article, so most translations use the generic "man."[13] Because the story plays on words, saying that God formed the *adam* out of the *adamah*, meaning "earth" or "land," and because the Hebrew word *adam* is not necessarily gender-specific, one could translate it in this story as "earth creature,"[14] or simply "human" (out of humus).[15]

It is only at the point when God determines to make a corresponding helper for the human being *adam*[16] that the gender-specific Hebrew words for "man" (*ish*) and "woman" (*isha*) first appear. Reading this story strictly as an extrapolation on events narrated in chapter 1 could lead one to conclude that Adam in Gen 1:26–27 ("God said, 'Let us make *adam* in our image . . .'") was a hermaphrodite human ("so God created the *adam* . . . male and female"), whom God divided into one man and one woman (*ish* and *isha*, in chapter 2). But it's doubtful that the biblical writers and editors intended such literalism.

Translators also have to make choices about style. What is most faithful to the original? Is it the most literal, within the bounds of grammar and syntax; the one most true to the sound or structure (or both) of the original; or the one that captures the sense and evokes in readers the feel or tenor of the original? Seldom can a translator manage more than one of these styles. John Dryden, the rock star of *lettres* in seventeenth-century England laid out three categories in a preface to his translation of Ovid's *Epistles*. They are still helpful.[17]

The first, which he calls "metaphrase," fits what most people today mean by "literal." According to Dryden's evocative description, metaphrase involves "turning an author word by word, and line by line, from one language into another." This lovely description belies Dryden's ultimate dismissal of such a technique. The second he calls "paraphrase, or translation with latitude, where the author is kept in view by the translator, so as never to be lost, but his words are not so strictly followed as his sense; and that, too, is admitted to be amplified, but not altered." Paraphrase is Dryden's favorite, though he sees occasions also for using the third, "imitation, where the translator (if now he has not lost that name) assumes the liberty, not only to vary from the words and sense, but to forsake them both as he sees occasion; and taking only some general hints from the original, to run division on the groundwork as he pleases."

In the process of making such decisions, a translator also needs to figure out how accessibly to render the translation. In the case of the Bible, do you, as the translator, want to remind readers how unfamiliar the conditions of the original text would be to them, and so make the translation difficult—perhaps a little foreign? Do you choose archaic English words or awkward syntax to convey a sense of the Bible's sacred otherness? Or do you want to make the text sound as though it had been written immediately for your audience, to render it as familiar and available as celebrity gossip, pop songs, or a twentysomething's blog? It depends on what a translator wishes to accomplish.

In my book *Living Through Pain: Psalms and the Search for Wholeness*, I offered translations of each of the six psalms that I discussed in detail. In that case, I wanted readers to remember that the psalms come from a time and place far different from our own, yet from people who share a universal and timeless condition of suffering. So I tried to make my translations difficult in places where they are particular to the psalmist's context but immediately sensible where they describe the psalmist's condition. In that book, I was concerned, not necessarily about speaking from faith to people of faith, but rather about showing how this ancient religious poetry captures different aspects of the experience of pain, and how that may resonate with people in pain today.

By contrast, lately I've been working on a collaborative project to bring the Bible to a new generation of readers. It is a Christian project that strives, in part, to speak with an evangelical voice (it's actually called "The Voice"), inviting readers to embrace the biblical texts as part of their own faith journey. The aim of the Ecclesia Bible Society (sponsoring the project) and Thomas Nelson (publishing it) is to use the most familiar and contemporary language, complete with paraphrase and modern idioms, to capture the Bible's sense for today's Christian believers. Different projects, different translation goals.

Whatever the case, translation is not an anything-goes enterprise. Translators must wrestle with the sense, nuance, style, and context of the original text before making the kinds of decisions noted above. When it comes to the Bible, the implications can be enormous. For example, Michelangelo carved a stern and beach-buff Moses with a luxuriant beard, curly locks, and horns—little nubbins, but horns nonetheless. Jerome, the sainted translator of the Bible into Latin, opted to translate the Hebrew *qrn* as "horn" rather than as something else, such as "shine."[18] So in the Vulgate, Moses' face grew horns rather than being radiant. Michelangelo faithfully represented Jerome's reading, which is a sensible effort to deal with an odd case of *qrn*.[19]

By way of a New Testament example, there are at least three "original" Greek versions of a theologically charged phrase in John 1:18; and each contains a word that allows several translations: *monogenes theos*, "only God"; *ho monogenes theos*, "the only God"; and *ho monogenes huios*, "the only Son." Small linguistic differences, with huge theological implications. The King James Version translates *monogenes* as "only-begotten," reflected in several offshoot modern English translations. But a more accurate meaning of *monogenes* is "the only one of its kind," i.e., "unique," which is how the New English Translation, for example, renders it.

Sorting out how to translate *monogenes* isn't all, though. One also has to decide what the adjective modifies—(*theos*) "God" or (*huios*) "Son." Contrary to many translations, most scholars think that "God" is the best answer, because it (*theos*) is reflected in the earliest and most numerous manuscripts. Also, that is the most difficult and awkward reading; and when faced with a couple of different options, scholars of such textual issues argue that the most difficult is probably the earliest and most authentic, because people tended (then as now) to smooth things over with time. However, *huios* makes more sense in this particular context, and it is consistent with John's general theology.

THE BIBLE IN ENGLISH

Rendering the Bible into English was no gentle matter: instead stories of exile and intrigue, torture, piety, and corruption punctuate its account.[20] Although the Bible has now been translated into 97 percent of the world's languages, the English Bible has been the most influential in the course of human history to date. For nearly a millennium after its translation, the Latin Vulgate held sway, and with it church authorities exercised absolute control over their Christian subjects. After all, only the clergy could understand the Bible. As they grew more corrupt and oppressive, a revolution in biblical understanding was bound to happen.

That began not with Martin Luther (which would be a good guess, given his central role in the Reformation and passion for Bible translation), but with an English Christian by the name of John Wycliffe. At the end of the fourteenth century, Wycliffe led selected friends in developing the first English versions, in order to wrest control of biblical interpretation away from the largely corrupt ecclesiastical hierarchy, which was inseparable from the state. Wycliffe's were translations from the Latin Vulgate. Called the "John the Baptist of the Reformation," Wycliffe, like his biblical namesake, was subject to retaliation by the authorities, though not in as gruesome a way as one of his own followers, who was executed by being suspended from a gallows over a bonfire. Although Wycliffe himself died of natural causes, there was to be no R.I.P. for him. His remains were exhumed from the church graveyard, burned on a bridge, and then left to float away in the stream below.

In the sixteenth century, William Tyndale picked up Wycliffe's torch, though he had to run to Germany with it because he was suspected of spreading Lutheranism. Unlike Wycliffe (but like Martin Luther), Tyndale worked directly from the original languages, and he persevered despite Latin-loving critics who denied that English could be a respectable vehicle for the word of God. Tyndale countered their criticism by claiming, "They will say [the Bible] cannot be translated into our tongue, it is so rude. It is not so rude as they are false liars."

And he goes on to tell how both Greek and Hebrew work better in English than in Latin, any day.[21]

Tyndale didn't seem to be particularly committed to winning over the naysayers, or to conducting himself diplomatically for that matter, in his effort to make the Bible accessible to all England. In the face of ignorant clergy, and championing oppressed commoners, an exasperated Tyndale famously exclaimed to a priest, "I defy the Pope and all his laws. . . . I will cause a boy that driveth the plough shall know more of the Scriptures than thou doest!"[22] Meanwhile the infamous King Henry VIII and the reformer Martin Luther exchanged insults. To the young Henry, who wrote an anti-Reformation book, "In Defense of the Seven Sacraments," Luther was "the true serpent cast down from heaven." To Luther, Henry was a "swine of hell."

Committed to bringing the Bible to the masses, Tyndale worked in secret and on the lam until one day he was tricked, trapped, and shipped off to prison in England. In 1536, he was tried for heresy, strangled, and burned at the stake. He was forty-two years old. Although he never finished translating the entire Bible, Tyndale nevertheless remains its single most influential English translator. Many of his renderings have endured to the present time and have brought conventions of biblical Hebrew into common English speech, including "man of strength" (instead of "strong man)," "mercy seat," "a man after his own heart," and "apple of my eye." Without Tyndale, we wouldn't have the King James Version—but I'm getting ahead of myself.

First, love. And love changes everything. When Henry VIII fell head over heels for Anne Boleyn and got her pregnant, he wanted desperately to marry her. But he faced the pesky problem of being already married. He was able to divorce his first wife, Catherine of Aragon, only by a creative appeal to biblical texts, a process that effectively elevated biblical authority above the pope (and divorced the Church of England from Rome).[23] King Henry was ever more inclined, then, to make the Bible accessible to his countrymen, as the Bible became—in England, anyway—the paramount authority. His beloved Anne and his trusted advisers agreed, and Miles Coverdale was selected for the job.

This authorized English version of the Bible, also called the "Great Bible," was published in 1539, just three years after Tyndale died. It is the product of Miles Coverdale, whose sources included Tyndale's English translation, two Latin, and a German translation. Slightly earlier—in 1537—Tyndale's work received royal endorsement in yet another authorized version, under the editorship of John Rogers, who used the pseudonym Thomas Matthew. The "Matthews Bible," as it came to be called, made explicit reference of its debt to Tyndale. How the tides turn.

And turn they did. Although Henry VIII was first succeeded by his very Protestant son Edward VI, Edward was a frail child who died when he was only fifteen years old. In a dramatic reversal that would prove deadly for Protestant reformers, Henry's daughter, Mary (by Catherine of Aragon), once declared illegitimate and shunned by the authorities, became queen. Mary was an ardent Catholic, and promptly sought to rid England of the plague of Reformation. Her measures included persecuting and killing Protestants, and of course getting rid of those troublesome English translations of the Bible. Her tactics of terror backfired as people had grown to love their Bibles and were horrified by Mary's excesses of murder. In just three and a half years, before Mary finally died in 1558, some 400 people had been killed—many by torture, most at the stake. John Rogers (a.k.a Thomas Matthews) was among the first to die.

You can imagine the collective sigh of relief when Elizabeth, daughter of Anne Boleyn, succeeded Mary. Although Elizabeth had been raised as a Protestant, she nevertheless had a fondness for Catholic ritual—one example of her several correctives to senseless sectarianism. Indeed, Elizabeth scorned religious fanaticism and excess of any sort. During her tenure as queen, Elizabeth executed just four people—to Mary's 400. History has judged Elizabeth prudent, wise, practical, and balanced in her judgments, political and otherwise.

During her rule, the Geneva Bible's English translation with notes, the most accurate up to that time, was developed. Ironically, it was not a product of Elizabeth's reign, though, so much as of Mary's before her. Mary's terrible crackdown on the Protestants had driven many out of the country. Some found a new community of scholarship and faith in Calvin's Geneva. It was out of this community that the Geneva Bible grew and went on to become the version most commonly owned by English-speakers, including those back in (Elizabeth's) England. Shakespeare and the Puritans used this Geneva Bible, and some of its phrases continue to be favorites: "vanity of vanities," "Solomon in all his glory," and "a cloud of witnesses."

Its notes included significant rhetoric against Roman Catholicism, however. For example, the Geneva Bible explained the beast in Rev 11:7 as "the Pope which hath his power out of hell and cometh thence." The Catholics responded with a translation of their own. The Douay-Rheims Bible, purportedly based entirely on the Vulgate, nevertheless clearly made use of Hebrew and Greek sources as well as extant English translations. It was completed by the end of the sixteenth century.

THE KING JAMES VERSION

And this brings us finally to the grand and lofty King James Version—KJV for short. It is no mere serendipitous circumstance of history that King James is the name attached to the greatest English language translation of the Bible. For one thing, he wasn't the most obvious successor to the throne, but was quite deliberately selected, to the surprise of many. On her deathbed, Queen Elizabeth chose this son of her onetime rival, Mary Queen of Scots. He was well prepared, having served as King James VI of Scots for thirty-seven years before becoming King James I of England, France, and Ireland in 1603. James was extraordinarily well schooled, loved learning, and as a boy actually did some of his own Bible translating (from Latin). Thanks in part to his lovely wife, Anne, he knew how to party (their holiday revels at Hampton Court were said to be over the top)—not that this is a necessary qualification for Bible translators. Although his mother was Catholic, James was Protestant (a Presbyterian) and sought unity in the ranks of England's believers. He wasn't particularly keen on the Puritans, but he didn't dismiss them out of hand. As a matter of fact, it was the Puritans who first requested the new English translation, to which James agreed.

The project demonstrated James's efforts at unity: it was a group effort, but the group was no hodgepodge crew. Its fifty-four members included some of the brightest minds and the most learned academics and theologians, and not a few peculiar characters (among them a man of photographic memory, a penniless father of thirteen, and a man so handsome and charming that it seemed a shame for him to be so enamored of books). The arrangement like the holy Trinity, was tripartite, with two committees at each of three institutions. The names of those institutions still evoke awe of learning and theological leadership—Westminster (the "Crown's Cathedral"), Oxford University (with its significant attachment to ye olde High Church), and Cambridge University (the Birkenstock Berkeley of its time—known for its brilliant dissidents and rebels). This was a heady time, the time of Shakespeare, Sir Walter Raleigh, Cervantes, Galileo, and Kepler. Guy Fawkes tried to blow up Parliament (1604), and the colony of Virginia was founded (1607).

The King James translation project drew on the finest scholarship of the time, reflecting new developments in knowledge about biblical languages and culture, but the final product was not a unique creation, spontaneously generated. It had a genealogy. Going backward: the Bishop's Bible, on which the KJV was most immediately based, was a revision of the Great Bible (with help from Geneva), which was in turn indebted to Coverdale and Tyndale. And the translators conscientiously consulted every imaginable source as they strove for a clean, clear version as close to an original as they could figure. In its preface, "The Translators to the Readers," Miles Smith wrote, "We never thought to make a new translation, nor yet of a bad one to make a good one, but to make a good one better or out of many good ones, one principal good one." He was being modest. The KJV not only reflects the best scholarship available at the time but also sustains a tone that is at once lyrical and melodic—in a word, beautiful. That an academic committee could arrive at a literary product of such singular grace and majesty is enough to make the stoutest unbeliever proclaim the KJV to be the word of God.

Some favorite passages: Where Coverdale translated, "When the morning stars gave me praise, and when all the angels of God rejoiced," the KJV takes wing—"When the morning stars sang together, and all the sons of God shouted for joy."[24] Where Tyndale read, "How were the mighty overthrown," the KJV determined "How are the mighty fallen."[25] And where the Bishop's Bible rendered, "God is my shepherd, therefore I can lose nothing," the KJV translators gave "The LORD is my shepherd; I shall not want."[26] Commissioned by King James in 1604, the Bible was done in 1611. It soon became *the* bible for English-speaking Protestants. And it continues, centuries after its introduction, to have unparalleled authority. Still today, more of my students possess the King James Version than any other English translation.

But neither James nor his Bible was perfect. Early printings of the KJV suffered serious setbacks, numerous typos being the most glaring. The first running actually came to be called the "He" Bible because in a moment of gender confusion, instead of "she" in Ruth 3:15, it read, "he went into the city." Another edition failed to include the little word "not" in a particularly unfortunate context to read, "Thou shalt commit adultery." That edition came to be called the "Wicked Bible." As for James, he grew to hate the Puritans and eventually also banned Catholics from all manner of respectable work (including medicine and law). With precedent from Henry VIII and Elizabeth, James declared himself (and kings in general) to be appointed by God to do God's will.[27] The result had wide effects, the most obvious being a constitutional crisis that lasted long after James himself.

Indeed, his son and successor, Charles I, so angered a sizable portion of England's population (informed in part by their reading of the Bible) that civil war broke out. Charles lost the war, and his head, but was replaced by a different form of authoritative oppression under the civilian leadership of Oliver Cromwell, who got rid of the monarchy altogether. Cromwell's commonwealth didn't last. After his death, the

monarchy was restored with Charles's son, Charles II. He was succeeded by his brother, James II, who disappointed hopes that he would
be balanced and fair. James II elevated Catholics and repressed others
till his son-in-law, William of Orange (William III), put him in his
place—off the throne. William III favored Protestants, but went a
long way toward government by the people. (For example, he agreed
to be king only if Parliament determined it should be so, according to
a bill of rights.)

Of course, by this time, the American colonies were well on their
way, and the spirit of independence in government and thought that
would come to characterize the United States was also evident in biblical translation. My American background leads me to call the Bible
that King James sponsored the King James Version. In England, it
was called simply the Authorized Version (AV). It endured by those
names (KJV in the United States, AV in England) until the end of the
nineteenth century. By then, the original KJV's English had become
quite archaic, and biblical scholarship had undergone a revolution of
its own.

MODERN ENGLISH TRANSLATIONS

To reflect modern conventions of English and new discoveries, the
Revised Version was developed in England. (Revealing its Protestant
Christian roots, the first part revised was the New Testament; the
Old Testament came next, and then the Apocrypha.) As with its parent the KJV, this was a group effort, and one that involved disparate
points of view—English and American being the most, well, disparate. This situation ultimately resulted in two revised versions—the
English Revised Version (ERV) came out in 1881 (New Testament),
1884 (Old Testament), 1895 (Apocrypha); and an American Standard
Version (ASV), which incorporated the Americans' contributions (including the use of "Jehovah" for "LORD") came out in 1901. But both
the ERV and the ASV retained an increasingly awkward Elizabethan
English.

Meanwhile, biblical scholarship continued to blossom. It informed yet another revision—the Revised Standard Version (RSV), which was completed in 1957. The RSV strove to reflect its KJV roots; but it incorporated new information about the Bible as well as new conventions in English literature and speech. Perhaps in a kind of backlash, another revision of the ASV was developed in the 1960s. Translation in this New American Standard Bible (NASB) is much more literal and theologically conservative than in the RSV. Around this time, translation into English exploded. Twenty-six translations appeared between 1952 and 1990, when a *New* Revised Standard Version (NRSV) hit bookstands.

Although it was Protestant Christians who were especially interested in translating the Bible, and still today dominate translation efforts because of their particular emphasis on the authority of scripture, the mid-twentieth century saw important Jewish and Catholic translations develop. In 1985, the Jewish Publication Society (JPS) came out with its *Tanakh* as a revision of the first English-language Hebrew Bible (1917). The JPS has added to its Bible lineup a study bible (2004) that includes excellent articles, essays, and notes by leading scholars.

The first English translation for Catholics from the original biblical languages of Hebrew and Greek (rather than from the church-endorsed Latin Vulgate) was the RSV Catholic Edition. It was published by the same group that published the Protestant RSV. The Catholic Edition was essentially the RSV, but arranged so that the apocryphal books were incorporated into the Old Testament. In the New Testament, there were only sixty-seven differences between the Catholic Edition and the RSV. The first English translation *by* Catholics for Catholics and from the original biblical languages (with a little help from a French translation) was the Jerusalem Bible (1966), revised in 1985 as the New Jerusalem Bible. Another, the New American Bible, was developed by American Catholics in 1970.

Also a product of the 1960s and 1970s, and with broad appeal crossing sectarian lines, the Good News Bible or Good News Translation, also called Today's English Version (TEV), is designed for easy reading, and it's dramatic, too. For example, KJV's "darkness was upon the face of the deep" (Gen 1:2) is rendered in TEV as "the raging ocean that covered everything was engulfed in total darkness." Good News for Modern Man (1966) is the New Testament–only version of the TEV.

The most popular version of the Bible in America today is the New International Version (NIV), theologically conservative and highly readable in common English. It represents the work of more than 100 scholars from a variety of Protestant denominations. According to its preface, "the translators were united in their commitment to the authority and infallibility of the Bible as God's Word in written form." Soon, 31,173 Americans will have a chance to see their own handwriting in a unique, thirtieth-anniversary edition. Traveling across the country is a big blue RV with BibleAcrossAmerica.com emblazoned in red and white on its side. Along the way, two couples are slowly gathering, verse by verse, a completely handwritten NIV Bible. "Before the Gutenberg (the first Bible produced on a printing press), they were all handwritten," says Steve Sammons, a spokesman for the publisher, Zondervan. "In our digital age, we lose sight of what it means to have a tangible product we create by our hands. This will truly make the NIV America's Bible." [28]

Advances in technology and biblical scholarship over the past decades have hardly streamlined the possibilities for English language translations. On the contrary, translations have multiplied. There are upwards of 140 English versions available. Suffice it to say that in addition to those mentioned above (many of which continue to be used and occasionally revised and updated), a few others that are especially innovative, depart significantly from earlier translations, or simply strike me as unique, include the following.

Eugene Peterson's paraphrase, *The Message*, has sold millions of copies. Peterson, a professor, pastor, and writer, incorporated into his translation discoveries in biblical scholarship, modern ideas, and contemporary English idioms. For example, his translation of Gen 1:1–2 reads, "First this: God created the Heavens and Earth—all you see, all you don't see. Earth was a soup of nothingness, a bottomless emptiness, an inky blackness. God's Spirit brooded like a bird above the watery abyss." It reflects the fact that the biblical text doesn't describe creation out of nothing, that the Hebrew verb describing the Holy Spirit's activity is elsewhere associated with an eagle protecting its young, and it evokes images of primordial beginnings in deep space in a lively and accessible style.

Peterson wasn't the first to take on a translation paraphrase all by himself. In 1971, Kenneth Taylor produced a paraphrase titled *The Living Bible*, which became hugely popular and is regularly revised. It continues to be "the most widely read popular English version published by an individual."[29] Before Taylor, J. B. Phillips's *The New Testament in Modern English* was published in 1958. Phillips hewed more closely than either Peterson or Taylor to the principles of translation (rather than paraphrase). Clarence Jordan (d. 1969), who also founded Habitat for Humanity, translated the New Testament in fits and starts in what would become the *Cotton Patch Gospel* series. Jordan's goal was an interpretation of immediate relevance rather than a translation with precise linguistic accuracy. For example, the New Testament letter of Paul to the Romans became, in Jordan's hands, "The Letter to the Christians in Washington."

Today one can find a version of the Bible in non-copyrighted, electronic-only format—the *World English Bible* (*WEB*), which its creator claims to have undertaken not on the basis of credentials of academic biblical scholarship, but because "God called me to do this, and I willingly answered His call. God would not call me to do something without enabling me to do so."[30] Or one can peruse a dynamic Internet translation, *The Free Bible*, "the first Wiki translation of the Bible, so anybody is welcome to help—translating, and then correcting it for stylistic and exegetical errors."[31] *The Original Bible* (also called the *Transparent English Bible*) posts some of its translation in progress online, but aims to publish in a more traditional book format.[32] It is developed by some of today's leading biblical scholars with commentary and notes of high academic value. Graphic-novel-style bibles of all sorts have become wildly popular. There's the *Comic Book Bible* series for kids; the *Lion Graphic Bible* (also for kids); and the *Manga Bible* (for young adult—YA—and adult readers) by Siku, a British Christian comic book artist.

So what's an English-speaking, Bible-reading person to do? My recommendation: a bit of research and some soul-searching, too. Every translation started somewhere. Find out who is responsible—is it an individual or a group, and what are their credentials? Find out what the translation uses for its "original," source text—is it a Hebrew-Greek version or versions; and if so, which one or ones? Or is it the Latin Vulgate, other modern-language translations, or some combination thereof? And ask yourself what your goal is, what you want. Do you want a devotional guide with a particular theological slant; do you want an academic treatment, maybe one that includes notes, and hews as close to an "original" as possible; do you want an individual's "take" on sacred text; or do you want a creative interpretation that is easy to read? Whatever the case, I recommend getting a number of different translations and comparing them. Seeing where and how they differ can yield remarkable insights into the Bible's development, the richness of its original languages, and the variety of faith perspectives that people bring to the interpretive work that is translation.

SEVEN
We've Got Issues

Both read the Bible day and night, but thou readst
black where I read white.
—WILLIAM BLAKE

In Virginia only about 150 years ago, the Baptist minister Thorton Stringfellow published *Scriptural and Statistical Views in Favor of Slavery* (1856). In it, he declared, "I affirm . . . that Jesus Christ has not abolished slavery by a prohibitory command; and second, I affirm, he has introduced no new moral principle which can work its destruction, under the gospel dispensation; and that the principle relied on for this purpose, is a fundamental principle of the Mosaic law, under which slavery was instituted by Jehovah himself." Frederick Douglass, who earned an international reputation for oratory, served in the national government, and became a bank president and publisher, was born a slave. In his autobiography (1845) he recalls, "For of all the slaveholders with whom I have ever met, religious slaveholders are the worst. I have ever found them the meanest and basest, the most cruel and cowardly, of all others."

In as much as the Bible bolstered arguments in favor of slavery (and nowhere does it condemn slavery), it also served to undo that vile institution. Besides countless biblical passages, in both Testaments, commanding compassion and care for others, abolitionists appealed to specific biblical texts, such as this one, to support their cause: "Slaves who have escaped to you from their owners shall not be given back. They shall live with you and among you, . . . wherever they please; you shall not oppress them."[1] Ultimately, the abolitionists deemphasized the efficacy of appealing to particular biblical texts in the debate, though. Instead, they argued that slavery in their time was not biblically justifiable by noting differences in definition and context between ancient and modern slavery and especially by showing how the spirit, if not the words, of the Bible defied the slaveholders' arguments. Still today, at the heart of disagreements about what the Bible says on particular issues are often simply different ways of reading the Bible. For some persons of faith, appealing to biblical authority means seeking out and applying general precepts such as loving God and caring for others to specific issues that, in some cases, the word of the Bible may actually oppose. For others, specific texts trump such general ideas.

Like precocious teenagers, some biblical texts are especially prone to mischief and troublemaking. They mean well but have sometimes ended up doing great damage. Some are just little things; others are big bruisers. Some cause trouble in groups, clustered together by people who find that, combined, they justify or undermine a certain issue. Other passages are shocking zingers on their own. These troubled and troubling texts aren't confined to any particular book or to either Testament, for that matter, but rather crop up randomly throughout. Over time, some grow out of their inclination for mischief, such as those that were (ab)used to justify slavery in the United States. Others never seem to. For example, the patriarchal assumptions of the Sinai laws and pastoral epistles continue to generate disagreements about modern gender equality and the respective roles of women and men.

This chapter focuses on clusters of passages that show up these days when a particularly controversial issue is on the table. The issues include the Bible and science, particularly concerning the origins of the universe and people; homosexuality; abortion; poverty and prosperity; environmentalism; and anti-Semitism. A brief caveat: There is much more than can be (and is) said here about each of these texts.

Countless pages, websites, blogs, and volumes already exist on each topic. If we had a record of all the kitchen table arguments and tense cocktail party moments that each of these passages has engendered, there wouldn't be a gigabyte unit big enough to hold them. My goal here is simply to help readers understand the debate—to note how the Bible shows up in relation to these hot-button issues, the reasons why, and what is helpful or misleading about such uses of biblical texts.

Knowing about the Bible's origins—its history and development—goes a long way toward understanding why "the Bible says" isn't all there is. Stringfellow probably didn't know that in the ancient Near East slavery was not a function of race: anyone could become a slave through military defeat or economic misfortune. The Bible does not say that God established slavery but simply assumes its existence as a normalcy, just as it assumes that men have more rights and privileges than women. Understanding this context makes it easier to see why the biblical texts are concerned not with abolishing the practice altogether, but with how to handle specific issues about slavery. That does not make slavery right for our time.

The Bible represents diverse perspectives from different historical contexts. It says many things, some of which appear to be in stark opposition to others. Adding to the confusion, its texts are ancient, and we do not have an original *ur*-Bible. The copies of copies of copies that finally constitute our Bibles today contain references, idioms, and vocabulary that bewilder even the most careful and well-trained biblical scholars. The more one learns about the Bible the more one appreciates how difficult it is, finally, to say what "the Bible says." Yet at the same time, such learning also brings the Bible alive and helps to make sense of its disparate voices.

EVOLUTION AND CREATION

"In the beginning, God created the heavens and the earth" is the first sentence in the first book of the first part of the Bible. And it has set off quite an explosion of debate concerning the relationship of the Bible to modern science, especially theories about how the earth and living things came to be as they appear today. The biblical texts specifically at issue are the Bible's first eleven chapters, with their stories of God's creating the universe in seven days, Adam and Eve and the garden of Eden, Cain and Abel, the tower of Babel, and the great Flood. In other words, these are stories of beginnings, disobedience, catastrophe, and new beginnings, and in all of them God plays a crucial role.

In a survey released in August 2006, the Pew Research Center found that 42 percent of Americans believe that humans and other life-forms have existed only in the ways they appear today, despite the fact that this contradicts the most widely accepted scientific theory of life's origins and diversity by evolution through natural selection. And of the 51 percent who believe that life has evolved, only 26 percent of those surveyed agree with scientists that earth's life-forms evolved by natural selection. According to the survey, most white evangelical Christians (65 percent) find the scientific theory of evolution at odds with the Bible, throwing in their lot with a literal reading of Genesis.[2]

In May 2007, the much-anticipated $27 million Creation Museum in Petersburg, Kentucky, opened for business—and for what its supporters called education and its detractors called brainwashing. After only about six months, more than 300,000 people had already toured the site.[3] Roaring dinosaurs at the gate greet visitors, who then follow a series of displays that purport to tell the real history of the universe, earth, and the earth's inhabitants. Defending the images of a universe taking shape over seven days; life-size figures of a fit, attractive "first couple"; and children cavorting near dinosaurs, a spokesman avers, "No scientist alive today was present when life appeared on this planet. . . . We do, however, have the written account of the Creator Himself, who does not and cannot lie. Genesis 1–2 provides an accurate eyewitness account of the beginning of all things, according to God."[4]

Creationists claim that Genesis chapters 1–11 (and everything that follows) tell the history of the universe in a way that science corroborates. Some Christians with PhDs in geology, biology, chemistry, and physics argue that the world is only about 6,000 years old (their calculations follow the Bible); that the Grand Canyon was created by the receding waters of the Flood, which Noah survived; and that the extinction of dinosaurs is due to post-Flood circumstances that were simply unfavorable for the dinosaurs' continuance. These creationists note that other, scientific calculations about the age of the earth and some of Darwin's ideas about evolution have been changed or corrected, which they see as an indication that the science is faulty and that evolution is "just a theory."

Critics note, however, that science depends on a system of testing for verification of a hypothesis or falsification of its claims; when God is an ingredient, such testing is impossible. Evolutionary biologists, many of whom are themselves believers, explain that the very nature of science depends on a process of evaluation and reevaluation, and they emphasize that a theory in science is no small matter. Rather, a scientific theory is a means to explain a constellation of facts. It is the strongest description possible (for example, gravity is a theory), yet by definition it can be proved wrong but never proved correct.

According to the creationists, the stakes are high. In the words of Ken Ham, the president of Answers in Genesis (a group that, among other things conducts symposia and develops curricula for educators) and cofounder of the Creation Museum, "The Bible is true, . . . the Bible's history is true, therefore Christianity is true."[5] To these creationists, believing in God requires "taking God at His word," which they equate with reading the Bible literally. For Ham and others, to question the literal reading is to call into question God's trustworthiness, and that is not an option. For them, it would remove the very foundation from the edifice of Christian belief, collapsing faith and any true hope for the world.

Ironically, most biblical scholars who disagree with creationists' claims think that the first chapter of Genesis came into being under similar, theologically challenging circumstances—that the story of God's creating the entire universe in seven days, human beings in the image of God and all of it "good," probably got its start in the face of the threat of disbelief.[6] They think that the authors of Genesis 1 were determined to tell a different and deeper kind of truth than that of scientific origins—that theirs was not a provincial god bound by place or time, that human beings both male and female have inherent dignity and purpose, and that the world is good, sensible, and sacred.

The crux of this debate, and many others, is how to read the Bible. Although the stylistic and theological differences between the seven-day creation story in Genesis chapter 1 and the Adam and Eve story in chapters 2 and 3 contribute to the scholarly view that they have different origins and served different purposes, their arrangement side by side in a final narrative whole invites readers to consider them together.

Consequently, some people read the second story as expanding on the first, believe Adam and Eve to have been the first biologically human beings, and that human beings are unique among living things, unrelated and superior to all others. Creationists deny that evolution explains the emergence of humans, arguing instead that God formed the first human beings in the image of God, and out of the ground, exactly as written in chapters 1–3 of Genesis.[7]

This is not the only way that people of faith read those chapters, though. Some believers who do not find these stories to be at odds with evolutionary theory read them as narratives about how human beings should be (as God's coruler and caretaker of creation, for instance). Others believe that while the chapters illustrate ideals of responsibility and relationship that we should seek to attain, they also tell how human beings consistently fail in their charge and purpose, making the possibility of God's grace and mercy yet more meaningful.

Yet other people maintain that if the texts are freed from the necessity to conform to modern expectations about narrative and history, if they are not read "literally," then the Adam and Eve story can serve to tell truths about origins more metaphorically—for example, about a God deeply interested and intimately involved in the welfare of earth and the development of human beings, not as a species per se, but as personal and interpersonal beings. Many Christians accept evolutionary theory, understanding God to be an agent of change and God's creative activity to be an ongoing process; they believe humans have special responsibility but are ultimately one among other living beings that inhabit an evolving world.

Yet arguments continue to rage about science and the role of the Bible. The famous Scopes trial—or "monkey" trial—in 1925, dramatized in the 1960 film *Inherit the Wind*, determined that a biology teacher in Tennessee had broken the law by teaching evolution in a public classroom. Although the tables turned, it hardly put the issue to rest. At the end of 2004, Dover, Pennsylvania, became the first school district in the United States to require that intelligent design be taught alongside evolution in the science classroom. (This decision was later overturned.) In 2008, the National Center for Science Education reported that "at least nine county school boards in northern Florida" are resolved to teach evolution not as fact but as "one of several theories."[8] All these cases have their genesis in concerns that teaching evolution contradicts the Bible and undermines the trustworthiness of God. Efforts to block learning about evolution will continue as long as such learning is seen as a challenge to the integrity of God and God's purpose for people.[9]

HOMOSEXUALITY

In the elegant gold-and-crimson vestments befitting his high religious rank, and a bulletproof vest reflecting the furor over his appointment, Gene Robinson made history in 2003 as the first openly gay, noncelibate priest to be elected bishop in a line of succession going back to Jesus' first apostles. Years later, and still serving as the Episcopalian bishop of New Hampshire, Robinson gave the invocation that kicked off Obama's inauguration week. On Inauguration Day, though, the invocation was delivered by Rick Warren, an evangelical pastor and author of the best-selling *Purpose Driven Life*, who had earlier likened gay marriage to incest and pedophilia (though he later softened his language about it).[10] The controversy rages on, and it is political.

On one side are people who reject homosexuality as a sin, such as James Dobson, whose *Focus on the Family* radio program, magazines, and website reach millions; on the other side are people such as Lutherans Concerned/North America, whose members started "Reconciling in Christ," a movement of congregations that welcome people of any sexual orientation as equally acceptable to God. Many believers find themselves somewhere in the middle—uncomfortable equalizing homosexuality and heterosexuality but confident that all persons can and should somehow be part of God's community.

With all the attention that homosexuality gets, one might think the Bible is filled with commentary about it. However, the Bible says very little about homosexuality. It says nothing about lesbianism, specifically (with the arguable exception of Rom 1:26), and nowhere discusses homosexuality in the context of mutual love and respect between gay partners. The relevant texts, discussed below, are Gen 19:1–28; Lev 18:22 and 20:13; Rom 1:24–27; 1 Cor 6:9–10; and 1 Tim 1:10. (Of course, not everyone's bible has all those texts. The Jewish Bible doesn't include Romans, 1 Corinthians, or 1 Timothy.)

It's a slim list, and while this makes the modern debate more difficult (since there's so little to go on), some argue that it demonstrates that the people responsible for the Bible simply didn't care as much about the issue as we do. Indeed, in terms of word count alone, there is a great deal more in the Bible about adultery, eating right, and exercising justice. Nevertheless, even after discounting the texts that are of questionable relevance for modern debates about homosexuality and the Bible, the remaining passages seem to be unequivocal in their condemnation of gay sex.

Consequently, some conclude that God disapproves of, even despises, homosexuality and that the faithful must take this seriously as they make decisions about how to do God's will. At the same time, many others reach the opposite conclusion—that God accepts and loves homosexuals exactly as is. How can both sides be reading and reasoning from the Bible? In an effort to understand, I'll begin with those texts that are of questionable use in modern debates (from Genesis, Corinthians, and Timothy), and then discuss the most contentious texts (from Leviticus and Romans).

Genesis 19:1–28 focuses on the wickedness of Sodom. What exactly was the nature of that wickedness is at issue here. Sodom's towns-men sought to force Lot to send the men who were visiting him (and who readers know are actually messengers from God)[11] out so that the townsmen could "know them" sexually. That the crime involved men having sex with men leads some readers to conclude that the story describes gay sex as bad.[12] That the crime is more specifically told as an attempted gang rape of visitors leads other readers to conclude that the story condemns the violence and humiliation of this attempted crime as well as the gross rejection of ancient Near Eastern codes of hospitality, but that it has nothing to do with loving homosexual partnerships.

The texts in 1 Corinthians and 1 Timothy are also of arguable relevance for the modern debate, as they may be not a judgment of consensual gay sex but rather a condemnation of pedophilia. Both texts—1 Cor 6:9–10, with its list of ne'er-do-wells who will be de-nied the kingdom of God (including "the greedy" "slanderers," and "swindlers" as well as those engaged in illicit sex);[13] and 1 Tim 1:10, with its list of bad behaviors—are sometimes taken as strong critiques of homosexuality. However, the Greek term at issue, *arsenokoitai*, is difficult to translate.

Sometimes translated "perverts," "sodomites," "deviants," or "ho-mosexuals," it is, frankly, unclear to us today. While the word may in-deed have to do with homosexuality, a study of how it appears in other Greek texts from the same period suggests that it may refer specifically to the exploitation of young boys by economically and socially pow-erful older men. Nobody knows for certain. So, depending on how the word is translated, these texts sometimes do and sometimes do not weigh in on today's debates.[14]

The three remaining texts afford the strongest arguments against homosexuality in the Bible. Leviticus 18:22 is usually translated, "You shall not lie with a man as with a woman. It is an abomination"; and Lev 20:13 reads, "If a man lies with a male as with a woman, both of them have done what is abominable. They must definitely die; their blood is on them." These would seem to be quite clear-cut in saying that homosexuality is wrong, dead wrong. But there is more about them that readers should know, in order to understand how some people argue that even these are of questionable use in modern debates.

The Hebrew text that we have (for both Lev 18:22 and 20:13) doesn't actually make clear grammatical sense. That is, the phrase at issue, usually translated "as one [or "as a man"] lies with a woman" is an odd construction that literally means "lying downs of a woman." Its peculiarity demands of translators some interpretation in order to arrive at a sensible English translation.[15] That said, we can be fairly confident that the text judges reprehensible some kind of sexual interaction between two men.[16]

Leviticus is part of the Torah—the first five books of the Bible and the core of the Old Testament. Leviticus is filled with regulations concerning proper religious behavior, including the definition and qualities of a priest, instructions for sacrifice and other rituals, and how to observe sacred days in the religious calendar. It is especially concerned with holiness—because God is holy, the people need also to be holy, the logic goes. Holiness is set-apart-ness, with everything "according to its kind." No mixing is allowed. And so we read, sandwiched between the two texts that concern us here, such odd regulations as "You shall not let your animals breed with a different kind; you shall not sow your field with two kinds of seed; nor shall you put on a garment made of two different materials."[17]

Some argue that this logic of holiness through integrity actually renders those texts from Leviticus irrelevant for discussion about homosexuality. They argue that the priestly writers' concern about maintaining the distinction of "kinds" mandates that just as a man shouldn't act like a woman, it would be wrong for a homosexual person to behave as if he or she were straight. In other words, arguing that sexual orientation is itself a "kind"—heterosexual, homosexual, and bisexual—it would be unholy for a gay man to behave like a heterosexual man. This, of course, presumes that homosexuality and bisexuality are inalterable characteristics of a person—that a person is "born gay." However, the ancient authors of Leviticus do not provide any such nuance; and many people today maintain that homosexuality is purely a lifestyle decision.

Some who challenge the Bible's anti-homosexuality reputation suggest that the problem at issue in Leviticus was not homosexual sex per se, but rather its insult to God the creator, based on patriarchal assumptions of that time. A man who chose to behave like a woman scorned the God-given superiority of men. For a man to forsake his superior position to behave like an inferior woman was to spit in God's eye. Yet others suggest that the problem was really reproduction, since same-sex sex cannot produce offspring.[18] Ancient Israelite society indeed put a huge premium on reproduction, not least because the probable original audience of Leviticus (in Babylonian exile and during the postexilic readjustment) was sorely outnumbered by other people whose very otherness made them a threat. Still others say, assuming that these texts do indeed condemn homosexuality, that it isn't fair to apply select legal judgments from the Torah while ignoring so many others (such as properly observing the Sabbath, not eating pork, and so on).

The New Testament text in Rom 1:24–27, criticizing people who had become misled in their affections, also seems to be unequivocally antigay. It describes persons who, overcome with lust, made themselves impure with "degrading passions." "Women exchanged natural intercourse for unnatural, and in the same way men, giving up natural intercourse, were consumed with passion for one another." And it goes on in the following verses to warn of the social disruption and proliferation of crimes that follow such promiscuous homosexuality: "Because they [rejected God], . . . they were filled with every kind of wickedness, evil, covetousness, and malice."[19]

Some argue, however, that readers shouldn't be so quick to judge. For one thing, they warn that the admonition does not claim to come from God. Rather, it comes from Paul, who is not claiming to speak for God here but offers his understanding of what he deems to be best. In this particular passage, Paul criticizes how sexual indulgence compromises spiritual and religious orientation as well as social order— evidence of a God-forsaken life. They observe that elsewhere Paul considers sexual impulses of any kind as problematic to a properly spiritual life, counseling people to downplay such impulses in the interest of concentrating on preparation for the imminent return of Jesus.[20]

People who caution against concluding from Rom 1:24–27 that the Bible is antigay note that Paul doesn't say anything about mutually respectful, committed, and loving relationships between same-sex people. And like the authors of Leviticus, Paul assumed that what was "natural" was heterosexuality. Both sides note that the passage is followed by Paul's passionate denunciation of people who presume to judge others. "In passing judgment on another, you condemn yourself, because you, the judge, are doing the very same things."[21]

In 2007, the Sundance Film Festival nominated for its coveted Grand Jury Prize the documentary *For the Bible Tells Me So*, chronicling the lives of five American Christian families, each of whom wrestled with homosexuality. In the film, Dr. Laurence Keene, a Disciples of Christ minister, admits, "I have a soft spot in my heart for literalists because I used to be one. However, when someone says to me, 'This is what the Bible says,' my response to them is, 'No, that's what the Bible *reads*.' It is the struggle to understand context and language and culture and customs that helps us to understand the reading or what it is saying."[22]

By contrast, the official position paper on sexuality of the Southern Baptist Convention states simply, "We affirm God's plan for marriage and sexual intimacy—one man, and one woman, for life. Homosexuality is not a 'valid alternative lifestyle.' The Bible condemns it as sin. It is not, however, unforgivable sin. The same redemption available to all sinners is available to homosexuals. They, too, may become new creations in Christ."[23]

These days, issues of homosexuality are bound up with laws regarding marriage. Amendments to ban gay marriage are regular election fodder. They were on the ballots of eleven states in 2004; and on the ballots in Arizona, California, and Florida in 2008. Many people appeal to the Bible to argue that when it comes to marriage, the Bible is clear: from Adam and Eve on, marriage is between a man and a woman. Others, noting that the Bible doesn't mention Adam and Eve as being married, disagree.[24] Again, each group has the Bible on its side.

The Bible indeed assumes that marriage is between a man and a woman. At the same time, critics of its literal application note how culturally different its context was from ours today. That context—highly patriarchal, tribal, and underpopulated—has everything to do with what the Bible deems acceptable or not, and biblical marriage is arguably different from our ideas of marriage. According to some biblical texts, a man could marry several women;[25] marriage outside the faith was not ok,[26] or was at best problematic;[27] a man had to marry his brother's widow;[28] and female slaves could be forced to serve as surrogate mothers.[29] Marriage in the Bible is rarely described as a result of mutual love.[30] Paul adds that it's best not to marry at all.[31]

For those who maintain that the Bible condemns homosexuality, explanations such as those noted above represent the wishful thinking of people willing to twist the Bible's clear sense to a morally questionable purpose. Their detractors argue that the antihomosexuals are guilty of wishful thinking—they are looking for absolutes out of texts that actually are nuanced or simply ambiguous. Does the Bible include texts that condemn homosexual behavior? Yes. Does this mean that the Bible is antigay? Not necessarily.

Whether he was aware of it or not, Obama's choosing both Robinson and Warren as the face of faith on the occasion of his inauguration demonstrated the ambivalence that many earnest and thoughtful persons of faith admit they feel about how the church should treat the issue of homosexuality. Warren himself has protested that his condemnation of gay marriage as publicized was not accurate.[32] Seeking to be fair and just, to treat others with compassion and respect while taking the biblical texts seriously, many believers continue to wrestle with this issue. Brian McLaren, a prominent voice of the nondenominational emergent church movement, counsels equanimity and the need to take time—decades, even—to figure out how the faithful should manage this issue. In the meantime, he writes, "Being 'right' isn't enough. We also need to be wise. And loving. And patient. Perhaps nothing short of that should 'seem good to the Holy Spirit and us.' "[33]

Indeed, drawing conclusions about God from biblical texts is itself an act of interpretation in faith. Most folks on both sides agree that a powerful and well-represented biblical image of God is that God loves love—love of God, of course, but also love between people, love for others, love that is generous and kind. It's tough to argue with that.

ABORTION

As disproportionate as biblically based outrage against homosexuality is to the number of relevant biblical texts, when it comes to abortion the disproportion is even greater. Nowhere does the Bible explicitly address a woman's decision to end her pregnancy or otherwise require that she bring a pregnancy to term. Yet the Reverend Ron Johnson, Jr., of Living Stones Church in Crown Point, Indiana, was among pastors willing to risk losing their churches' tax-exempt status by telling parishioners not to vote for Barack Obama in 2008. He told them that the Democratic candidate's pro-choice position was "in direct opposition to God's truth as He has revealed it in the Scriptures."[34] The Bible is filled with concern for life—encouragement and exhortation to protect and celebrate life. What exactly that should mean for women facing an unwanted pregnancy today is the cause of great consternation.

The biblical texts that people argue oppose abortion include any that condemn killing, such as the seemingly unequivocal, "You shall not kill," which is one of the Ten Commandments.[35] Actually, the word translated as "kill" in these verses is one of several Hebrew words that mean ending a life. The word seems to be used most frequently to describe the kind of killing that is premeditated, what we call "murder." (Other kinds of killing, such as capital punishment and killing in warfare, are considered OK.) For many of the antiabortion faithful, this commandment is statement enough. They believe that abortion is murder and thus is expressly prohibited within the Ten Commandments and elsewhere. For them, no more needs to be said.

More technically specific to abortion is the law about reparation if someone should unintentionally cause a woman to miscarry: "If men are fighting and hurt a pregnant woman so that there is a miscarriage but no more harm than that, then the one responsible shall be fined what the woman's husband demands, paying as much as the judges determine."[36] While some claim that this shows the Bible's antipathy toward abortion, others observe that in this case, the woman's health (especially as it affects the husband) seems to be the main focus. The miscarried fetus gets little or no attention.[37]

Because legislation about abortion today includes language about when exactly life begins, people opposed to abortion note texts that suggest the personhood of a fetus, including God's response to Jeremiah's reluctance to be a prophet: "Before I formed you in the womb, I knew you; and before you were born, I sanctified you and determined that you would be a prophet to the nations."[38] Similarly, the Hebrew poet of Psalm 139 is delightedly awestruck at God's fashioning and knowing him or her before birth: "You formed my innards and covered me in my mother's womb. I praise you because you made me awesomely distinct, wonderfully crafted, I know it. My frame was not hidden from you, when I was made in secret, woven in the recesses of the earth."[39] In the New Testament gospel of Luke, there's a story of John the Baptist leaping in Elizabeth's womb when she met up with Mary, pregnant with Jesus at the time.[40] Many believe that these texts underscore how an immortal soul, capable of an afterlife, is present from the beginning, at conception. To end that ensouled life is a murderous crime.

Those who argue that the Bible does not forbid abortion point out that the Bible does not forbid abortion. Their opponents counter with the observation that medical processes like ours today were not possible then, to which pro-choice advocates retort that women in ancient times may have ended pregnancies in ways not recorded in the biblical texts. Concerning the texts cited above, some argue that abortion falls into the category of "killing" that is biblically acceptable. They argue that "You shall not kill" does not apply to abortion, just as it does not apply to warfare or capital punishment. They note that the law of reparation not only concerns an accidental abortion but also demonstrates a different social context from our own, in which not only were a woman and her children essentially the property of her husband, but also a woman's worth and security depended a great deal on her having children. Concerning texts that suggest the personhood of a fetus, pro-choice advocates note that these texts come from the metaphorical world of biblical language and poetry (and so should not be taken as directives), say nothing about compromising an immortal soul, and have nothing explicitly to do with abortion.

POVERTY AND PROSPERITY

If you do what is right in the eyes of God, worship only our particular God, and don't flirt with other gods and goddesses, then things will go well for you—you will enjoy prosperity and live long in the land. This is the message of the capstone to the Torah (the book of Deuteronomy). It is not confined to Deuteronomy, though, but crops up with some frequency throughout the Hebrew Bible, and it is echoed in the New Testament. It has found new resonance in recent years among proponents of the so-called prosperity gospel.

The Reverend Creflo Dollar preaches it with conviction. Given his own Learjet to speed him between a church in Atlanta near his mansion home and a church in Manhattan where Dollar owns a $2.4 million apartment, it seems to be working.[41] Dollar's World Changers International School of Prosperity is "designed to teach you how to fulfill your God-given destiny to be a blessing to others and by being His distribution center."[42] The first of five key points that a student can expect to learn is "why God wants you to be rich."[43] Dollar agrees, however, with Joel Osteen, the television evangelist and best-selling author, that prosperity need not be limited to financial well-being.[44] But money is definitely part of it. Osteen explains, "I think we should have a mind-set that God wants us to prosper in our relationships, our health, and our finances. God's desire is that we excel. And we see business leaders who are good strong Christians running [big] companies."[45] According to a poll taken by *Time* magazine and included in its cover article "Does God Want You to Be Rich?" 61 percent believe that God wants you to be prosperous; and 31 percent said that they believe that if you give money to God, God will give you more money.[46]

The specific biblical texts most frequently employed in support of this kind of thinking include the following: Moses' declaration in Deuteronomy, "Remember Yahweh your God because he gives you power to get wealth so that he may confirm his covenant that he swore to your ancestors, as he is doing today";[47] and Mal 3:10, "Bring the full tithe into the storehouses so that there may be food in my temple, and test me on this: see if I do not open the windows of heaven and pour out for you blessings to the very end." In the New Testament gospel of Mark, Jesus says, "So I tell you: whatever you pray for, believe that you have received it, and it will be yours."[48] And in John's gospel, Jesus declares, "I came that they may have life and have it abundantly";[49] and "If you ask anything in my name, I will do it."[50]

Critics of the prosperity gospel warn that interpretations require more nuance than simply applying specific biblical texts to modern circumstances. Here's a brief note about each in turn: The literary style of Moses' declarations in Deuteronomy speaks directly to readers (note the use of "today," and "you"), so it's easy to understand why people would apply it as immediately relevant for them today. Yet critics note that the message of wealth-getting as God's initiative and covenant fulfillment shouldn't be separated from the book's historical and literary context. Deuteronomy's literary position in the Bible makes it Moses' exhortations to the people before they entered the "land of milk and honey" that they understood to be promised to them by God. It sets this telling in the liminal space and time between wandering in the wilderness of Sinai and settling in Canaan. Yet it was probably composed and edited centuries later and interprets losses as all the good things that the people squandered by failing God. Deuteronomy provides justification for the destruction of Israel as the doing of a generous God who had properly warned them: if they didn't do what was right but worshipped other gods and goddesses, then they would lose the security and prosperity of the land that God had given to them.

Malachi comes from a much later time but nevertheless wrestles with a similar tragedy. After the loss of nation, temple, and king, and after a period of exile, some people returned and rebuilt Jerusalem. The situation was hard—economically they had little, and socially there was disagreement and unrest among the population. It was during this time that Malachi prophesied, urging the people to hang on and have faith. Even though it seemed that God had abandoned them or was ignoring them, Malachi promised that God would make good again. Both Deuteronomy and Malachi, then, aimed to stir up faith among people who had some serious doubts about God's goodness and ability to support them, people who faced terrible economic hardships. It's easy to imagine how modern readers facing similar uncertainty and financial strain may feel a special connection to these texts and read them as immediately applicable to their own lives.

Opposing the notion that God's purpose is to make his people financially wealthy, some people note that Mark 11:24 ("Whatever you ask for in prayer, believe it, and it is yours") is embedded in statements about the power of faith, not material acquisition. It follows Jesus' angry outburst in the temple, ironically (for the prosperity gospel) over using worship space for money matters. They also observe that John 10:10 ("I came that they might have life and have it abundantly") and 14:14 ("If you ask for anything in my name, I will do it") can be interpreted as being less about financial well-being and more about the power that Jesus wields as son to the Father God in looking out for his followers.

Against the prosperity gospel, many people have pointed out that the Bible is full of warnings that the business of acquisition and consumption is spiritually dangerous and socially destructive. They argue that Jesus sided with the underprivileged and poor, that Jesus himself had little to speak of, and that his promises of abundance shouldn't be taken as financial. Rick Warren finds the prosperity gospel preposterous: in a word, "baloney. It's creating a false idol. You don't measure your self-worth by your net worth. I can show you millions of faithful followers of Christ who live in poverty. Why isn't everyone in the church a millionaire?"[51] Within the Old Testament, too, are many texts that expressly challenge the logic of Deuteronomy, observing that frequently people who do the right thing suffer nonetheless and "the wicked prosper."[52]

Opposing the gospel of prosperity, people cite biblical critiques of wealth and social injustice (especially by prophets such as Amos and Micah), and Jesus' exhortations against looking for spiritual satisfaction in material goods. Matthew's Jesus teaches, "Do not store up for yourselves treasures on earth, where moth and rust consume and where thieves break in and steal; but store up for yourselves treasures in heaven. . . . For where your treasure is, there your heart will be also."[53] And Jesus instructs the rich young ruler, "If you wish to be perfect, go, sell your possessions, and give the money to the poor; and you will have treasure in heaven."[54] Jesus then explains to his disciples, "It is easier for a camel to go through the eye of a needle than for someone who is rich to enter the kingdom of God."[55] In Luke's Sermon on the Plain, Jesus blesses the poor and declares, "Yours is the kingdom of heaven."[56] By contrast to them he says, "Woe to you who are rich."[57] Some people opposed to the prosperity gospel declare, "Money is the root of all evil," which isn't actually in the Bible. "The love of money is the reason for all kinds of evil" is.[58]

ENVIRONMENTALISM

In our time and place, we see how human activity can have devastating environmental consequences. The biblical context was different. Back then, the planet's human population was far less, about 300 million people in Jesus' time; 2,000 years later, we've passed the 6 billion mark.[59] Production was slow and done by hand, fueled by bread, beans, and occasionally some meat—worlds different from the industrial machinery, technology, and speed that generate goods today. Transporting goods in biblical times meant carrying them on a donkey or camel at best, in distances measured by tens, not tens of thousands, of miles. Environmental concerns in the biblical world were defined more by managing severe natural constraints and challenges by small, local communities than preserving biodiversity and avoiding climate change. We shouldn't expect, then, to find in the Bible a twenty-first-century environmental ethic any more than we should expect biblical regulations about using cell phones in automobiles. Nevertheless, there are biblical texts that concern the relationship between human beings and the nonhuman natural world, just as there are texts that aim to regulate human interaction and potentially injurious behavior.

Against a biblically based environmental ethic are those who are not troubled by environmental degradation, because "this world is not our home" or who declare that God will set things right, so we don't need to. Many cite Gen 1:28—God's command to human beings to "be fruitful and multiply, and fill the earth and subdue it; and have dominion over the fish of the sea and over the birds of the air and over every living thing that moves upon the earth" as justification for limitless human reproduction and use of resources.[60]

On the other hand, in favor of a biblically based environmental ethic, people argue that because the earth and all that's in it are described as God's good creation, human beings have an obligation to take good care of it. These people read Gen 1:28 as a command for human beings to exercise their created-in-the-image-of-God power to take care of the planet. They also point to the next story of creation, in which the first human being—*adam* in Hebrew—is described as created out of *adamah* (the Hebrew word for soil) in a wordplay that underscores an intimate relationship of humans to the earth. In that story, *adam* is charged by God "to till and keep" the garden which God created and in which the human being lives.[61] The Hebrew verbs translated as "till" and "keep" bear a wider range of meanings that include the sense of "reverent service to" and "guarding the welfare of" . . . the garden, in this case. Together, then, these texts in Genesis can be interpreted as telling how human beings should exercise good stewardship of God's creation.

A lesser-known but relevant text comes from the prophet Hosea, who blames human violence and wrongdoing for the mourning and languishing of land, wildlife, birds, and fish.[62] Yet other texts declare that human beings would do well to listen to the natural world and its nonhuman inhabitants for they are vociferous witnesses to the greatness of God. "Ask the animals, and they will teach you; the birds, and they will tell you," Job says, while the psalmist writes, "The heavens are telling the glory of God."[63] Jesus declares that even the stones would announce his identity, if confessing persons were silenced.[64]

Jim Ball, president and CEO of the Evangelical Environmental Network, cites Col 1:15–20; John 1:1–4; and Heb 1:2–3 as the basis of his mission to "declare the Lordship of Christ over all creation."[65] He identifies fifty-eight biblical passages that led him to conclude that the environment—or nature—and human beings are inextricably connected as part of God's creation and that to care properly for God's creation means to care both for the environment and for people.[66] Bartholomew, the ecumenical patriarch of Constantinople, at present the most senior bishop of Orthodox Christianity, has earned the nickname "the Green Patriarch." He has gathered religious leaders of all the world's major religions at environmental hot spots around the globe to talk about how best to care for the earth. At a recent conference in Greenland, he said, "Preservation of the environment, promotion of sustainable development, and particular attention to climate change are matters of grave concern for the entire human family."[67]

Not all Christians agree, however, that human beings should be concerned with the welfare of the earth and its nonhuman inhabitants. The vice president of the National Association of Evangelicals, Richard Cizik, drew the ire of some other prominent Christian leaders (including James Dobson, Paul Weyrich, and Don Wildmon), who demanded in 2007 that Cizik be fired for his "creation care" stance.[68] In a sermon titled "The Myth of Global Warming" the evangelical Christian leader Jerry Falwell urged "all believers to refuse to be duped by these 'earthism' worshippers."[69] Although determined to take the debate over global warming "to a higher level . . . the Biblical perspective," Falwell cited only two biblical texts (without any attention to their literary or historical contexts). He quoted Ps 24:1–2, "The earth is the LORD's, and the fulness thereof; the world, and they that dwell therein. For he hath founded it upon the seas, and established it upon the Floods." And Gen 8:22, "While the earth remaineth, seedtime and harvest, and cold and heat, and summer and winter, and day and night shall not cease."[70] Just one year later, after his death, students at Falwell's Liberty University entered the RecycleMania Campaign 2008 "with the purpose of establishing a campus-wide recycling program and carrying forward the biblical concept of good steward-ship."[71] Many Christians seem able to reconcile good stewardship with the sense of an ultimate home elsewhere.

ANTI-SEMITISM[72]

It might seem absurd that although the Bible is first a Jewish product and although the foundational figure of Christianity was Jewish, the Bible has been one of the most deadly weapons used against Jews. Both the Hebrew Bible and the New Testament have general ideas and specific texts that have supported anti-Jewish attitudes over the past two millennia.

The Hebrew Bible developed over a long period of time and repre-sents ideas from the proto-Jewish, Hebrew-speaking people and from Judaism's early centuries in the Middle East. In an effort to articulate their identity and interpret historical events in light of particular ideas about God, this faithful people exonerated God rather than them-selves. The result is a collection of books with many stories about how God's chosen people failed God and suffered accordingly. If those stories are read as disinterested reporting of historical events (and if the Israelites are equated with Jews, as they often are), then the Jews come out looking really bad. Ironically, not only are the texts highly biased, by their own admission, but they were also actually written, collected, and edited by ancestors of the very people against whom they are used.

The same bias exists with the New Testament—composed, col-lected, and finalized by believers, not disinterested historians. Jesus, the central figure about whom the whole collection is concerned, was Jewish, as were most of its authors. But there were several kinds of Judaism in Jesus' time (as there are now, and just as there are today many kinds of Christianity). Not all Jews agreed with each other. Christianity began as a Jewish sect that broke with elements of tradi-tion and with ideas that some Jews deemed decisive. Only a small frac-tion of Jews agreed with Jesus' followers that he fulfilled prophecies about a coming Messiah, and they found claims of Jesus' divinity to be a heretical rejection of fundamental belief in the singularity of a God who could not be represented in any earthly form.

One specific text that has thrown oil on the fire of anti-Semitism made for a dramatic scene in Mel Gibson's movie *The Passion*. It appears in Matthew's gospel, where a crowd of Jews demand that Pilate crucify Jesus. They say, "His blood be on us and on our children."[73] Ever since, Jews have been accused of deicide—murdering God—and the results have been horrific. The Holocaust (and its denial today) is, sadly, only one of many historic examples whereby Jews have been judged to be a faulted and failing people with evil intent who should be converted, persecuted, or killed.

In John's gospel, especially, Jesus is portrayed as regularly at odds with "the Jews"[74] who accuse him of breaking the law and even of being possessed by demons. There is still disagreement about just whom John meant by the term "Jews" in his gospel. Was it all the people who lived in Judea, in general? Was it specifically the Jewish authorities (and not your regular Jewish Joe), or was it all those who identified themselves as Jewish by race and religion? Whatever the answer, the ways in which John's gospel disparages "the Jews" as quarrelsome, scheming, and bloodthirsty have strained Christian-Jewish relations ever since.

Paul (who was raised a devout Jew and became a follower of Jesus after Jesus' death) was ambivalent about the Jews. More accurately, in his letters—which dominate the New Testament after the gospels—Paul said both good and bad things about the Jews. For example, in Romans, he declares on one hand, "the Jews are entrusted with the oracles of God";[75] and on the other, "Being ignorant of the righteousness that comes from God, and seeking to establish their own, they have not submitted to God's righteousness."[76] Paul points to "my kindred according to the flesh . . . to whom belong the adoption, the glory, the covenants," but despairs that they cannot be saved without submitting to Jesus.[77] Paul's conviction that only by faith in Jesus could a person be right with God informs his judgment about Jews.

Jesus is remembered for challenging some of the leaders of his day, taking them to task for hypocrisy and arrogance. Naturally, he criticized the leaders of his own Jewish community. Consider, for example, how the gospels remember Jesus' critiques of the Sadducees and Pharisees, the temple and scribal leaders of his day.[78] (Among the most memorable is his rant against them, repeating "Woe to you, hypocrites!" in a full chapter of Matthew's gospel.)[79] It's a different thing to maintain that he claimed the Jews were bad, wrong, or otherwise should be silenced. He was one!

The biblical records that we have about Jesus portray him as a thoughtfully observant and deeply religious Jew. About his own role, the gospels remember him as saying, "I have come not to abolish the law but to fulfill it."[80] They also portray Jesus as regularly appealing to his Jewish scriptures for reference and self-identification. For example, he understood his role in terms of the Hebrew prophet half a millennium before him who said that God had appointed him "to bring good news to the downtrodden, to bandage the broken-hearted, to declare release for the captives and an opening to those who are shut in."[81] Although he clashed with religious authorities distinguishing the spirit of the law from its literal application, Jesus observed the Jewish traditions of Passover[82] and appealed to Jewish biblical poetry at his death.[83]

Finding anti-Jewish rhetoric in the Bible is easy, but that is so because the Hebrew Bible is a collection of Jewish literature concerned to make sense of history and human experience in light of particular ideas about God. Those ideas about God require that when God's power, justice, or goodness is at stake, the people, rather than God, take the fall. And the New Testament is a collection of Christian literature concerned with portraying the Jew, Jesus, as the son of God in terms that were ultimately unacceptable to traditional Judaism. Consequently, it reflects its Jewish context particularly in the ways that it broke with Judaism. For most first-century Jews, the integrity of their faith, with its foundational belief in the unity of a singular God who defies physical representation, disqualified belief in Jesus as the embodiment of God. Ironically (and tragically), then, both testaments can fuel anti-Jewish sentiment.

EIGHT
Quotes and Misquotes

No man ever believes that the Bible means what
it says; he is always convinced that it says what
he means.

—GEORGE BERNARD SHAW

"Moses died before he ever reached Canada. Then Joshua led the Hebrews in the Battle of Geritol." "When Mary heard she was the mother
of Jesus, she sang the Magna Carta." "Paul cavorted to Christianity
and preached holy acrimony, which is another name for marriage."
You may have heard or seen these and other side-splitting misquotes
by children. They're a hoot. They're also instructive, telling us something about how we hear and understand—that we make sense based
on what we know, our expectations, and our perception of the world.
The tricky thing about biblical texts is that while many are familiar
and seem immediately sensible, they're nevertheless ancient and foreign.

There's a canon within the canon that is the Bible. That is, there
are certain biblical texts that get a whole lot more attention than others, and for good reason. The Bible is a treasure trove of inspiration,
comfort, counsel, and praise. Many beloved or at least oft-quoted texts
show up well outside the purview of believers and have become the
stock in trade of casual conversation, too. This chapter covers several
of the most popular and also some problematic or puzzling quotations

from the Bible, not just by citing them, but by providing a bit of context and explanation. That way, you can appreciate and evaluate for yourself how they're used today.

SOME OLD TESTAMENT INSTRUCTIONS

In her recent novel *My Sister's Keeper*, Jodi Picoult explores the world of love, conflict, and self-definition of a girl conceived in order to provide the genetically matched blood, bone, and tissue on which her critically ill sister's life depends. The title plays on the first human question posed in the Bible (God asks several questions before this). When God asks Cain where his brother Abel (whom Cain has murdered) is, Cain asks in return, "Am I my brother's keeper"?[1] It's a poignant question that I've argued elsewhere actually indicts readers, when considered in the greater narrative of Genesis 2–4.[2] By answering "yes" for Cain, readers are implicated in a complex responsibility, for and with other people and the earth itself, in relationships that mediate the presence of God. Barack Obama appealed to this text in his acceptance speech at the Democratic National Convention in August 2008, saying that "we are responsible for ourselves, but . . . we also rise or fall as one nation. . . . I am my brother's keeper; I am my sister's keeper."

The next couple of texts—"An eye for an eye . . ." and the Ten Commandments—come from a body of legal material in Exodus. They're part of Torah, a word that is often translated as "law," but whose etymology and use suggest that "instruction" is more accurate. This is important in part because these texts did seem in the ancient world to function at least as much to teach people generally about how to be in relation to each other, to the greater world, and to God as to apply in the strictly legal manner that our laws do today. "Eye for eye, tooth for tooth" in Exod 21:24 (and again in Lev 24:20 and Deut 19:21) may not have actually been carried out to the letter; rather, it may have simply instructed against unbalanced and chaotic retaliatory violence in a more general sense.

Gandhi, made famous by his revolutionary nonviolent resistance in India, said, memorably, "An eye for an eye makes the whole world blind." It is an important corrective from a wise and courageous man, but he wasn't exactly right. An eye for an eye leaves two people with partial sight. Not optimal, but not as absolutely destructive as he suggests, though he probably didn't mean to be so literal about it. Reading the biblical text less literally, its own revolutionary suggestion declares a limit to violence, not restricted to body parts. This *lex talionis*—"law of retaliation"—taught that responding to violence must be strictly controlled and operate on the principle of equity. If one's house is attacked, it isn't right to respond by destroying the attacker's entire town. We could certainly argue the merits of nonviolence against the use of violent punishment, but that's another book. The point here is that this particular biblical quote need not promote, but rather limits, damage.

The Ten Commandments (a.k.a. "Decalogue") appear, like "an eye for an eye," in both Exodus and Deuteronomy. That is, there are two sets of Ten Commandments; three, if you count the replacement set that God made after Moses smashed the first ones. Confusing matters, the replacement tablets, spelled out in Exod 34:10–28, are not exactly like the originals of a few chapters earlier (Exod 20:2–17), and while the replacements are explicitly called the Ten Commandments (in Hebrew, literally "ten words" or "ten matters"), the other sets are not—they're identified simply as "words; matters."

Comparing the most famous—Exod 20:2–17 and Deut 5:6–21—shows that although they are not identical, they have more in common than not. In both cases, they have no conditions, but rather are absolute: "Thou shalt not . . . ," no ifs, ands, or buts. This recognizable form has given rise to oodles of modern "commandments." The title of a recent article in Slate.com was "The Facebook Commandments," including "Thou shalt not friend promiscuously."[3] Then, there are the Vatican's "Ten Commandments of Driving," including #1: You shall not kill.[4]

One of the first difficulties with the biblical Ten Commandments is defining exactly where they begin and how to count them. Not everybody agrees. Most Jews take the first "matter" to be God's byline in Exod 20:2, "I the LORD am your God, who brought you out of the land of Egypt, out of the site of slavery." Most Christians consider what follows, "You shall have no other gods before me," to be the first commandment. Some count all of verses 3–6 as a single commandment. Others take verse 4 (no idol-making and its description through verse 6) to be a commandment distinct from verse 3 (no other gods). Some count the "coveting" commandments in verse 17 as one, others as two.[5]

The "Thou shalt not kill" commandment has puzzled generations of English readers, not least because so much killing is sanctioned, even commanded, in the Bible. It helps to remember that the Hebrew word translated "kill" in this verse seems to be specific to murder. At any rate, it is a different word from the killing done in war or as punishment.[6]

The Sabbath-keeping commandment is the one that differs most between the Exodus and Deuteronomy versions. They give different reasons for observing this day of rest. In Exodus, the justification reflects Genesis chapter 1—the creation of the world in six days followed by a day of (Sabbath) rest. In Deuteronomy, the justification reflects a historical event—God's liberating the Hebrew people from slavery in Egypt. The implications are different.

In Exodus, rest and creation are paired. Not only does this recollect the greatness of God's universal, creative activity as narrated in Genesis 1, but it also suggests that human rest is inseparable from the creativity of our working lives. Extrapolating a bit, we could say that the Sabbath commandment in Exodus, with its link to Genesis 1 presumes that human work be defined (like that of God's in whose image Genesis 1 says that humans are made) by creative acts of bringing order and goodness out of chaos. Sabbath rest rewards and facilitates this work.

In Deuteronomy, by contrast, rest is paired with liberation. The implications of this may fit more closely with the experience most of us have of work, as a kind of bondage. Sabbath rest, according to Deuteronomy, should recall God's activity in human affairs as the author of ancient Israel's freedom. This is related to another difference between the Ten Commandments of Exodus and those of Deuteronomy. Deuteronomy extends the benefits of the Sabbath a little further, spelling out the oxen and donkeys who should be allowed to rest, too, and repeating "your male and female slaves," stressing (again) that they should be able to rest as well, "just like you."

For high-minded people intending to read every word of the Bible straight through, if the second half of Exodus, with its detailed instructions for behavior and also for building the tabernacle (a portable shrine), tests their resolve, then Leviticus often breaks it. Filled with line-by-line instructions about proper religious personnel, garb, preparation, and behavior, and with hundreds of highly specific laws, only the most determined or anthropologically curious get through Leviticus without some kind of introduction to the book in advance. Yet it is in Leviticus and only in Leviticus of all the Hebrew Bible, that we find the command to "love your neighbor as yourself."[7] Jesus, for whom the Hebrew scriptures were the whole Bible, singled out this commandment to pair with the command to love God as the greatest of all the hundreds of commandments.[8]

If that is the most important thing to do, the most important thing to say is found in Deut 6:4, which immediately precedes the command to love God that Jesus cited, with love of one's neighbor, as the greatest. Deuteronomy 6:4 begins, "Hear, O Israel," and is sometimes called the Shema, because its first word is *shema*, which means "hear." This text is the closest Judaism comes to having a creed. It is a declaration of faith in one and only one God, and although it's brief, it is rich and powerful. I say "rich" because there is no single way to translate the Hebrew that covers all its meanings; and "powerful" because it is clear, elegant, and direct. While Christians have a body of creeds and confessions of faith, the Shema, consisting of only six Hebrew words, is the central declaration of faith for Jews. The Hebrew word that follows the command "Hear, O Israel" is a four-letter name for God transliterated YHWH, frequently represented as LORD (capital "L," small caps "ORD"). Reading a proper name for God here makes "our God" in the succeeding clause sensible, since the four-letter name of God distinguishes YHWH from other gods.

There are occasions when the grammar of biblical Hebrew assumes the verb "to be" without spelling it out, and this is one, so we can translate the first few words as either "Hear, O Israel, the LORD our God," or "Hear, O Israel, the LORD is our God." In any case, this is a perfectly distilled confession of allegiance to a particular god, the LORD, rather than to any other god. Then it repeats the four-letter name of God and follows that with the word for "one," lending translations: ". . . is one LORD," "the LORD is one," or ". . . the LORD alone," thus declaring the singularity of the LORD either as a single entity or as the singular God of the people reciting the Shema.

HEBREW PROPHETS AND KINGS

Out of the Pentateuch and into the historical books that follow, we find several popular phrases associated with David, the most celebrated king of Israel. One of these—"God doesn't see things the way people do; people look on the outward appearance, but the LORD looks on the heart"[9]—appears in the story of David's secret anointing. Little David, the youngest of his family, was absent when the prophet Samuel came by to select Israel's future king. As each of his seven brothers was trotted out, God told Samuel, "No. No. And no." Since none of the young men were suitable in God's eyes, Samuel asked their father, Jesse, if there were any others. Jesse acknowledged that there was indeed one more, David, who was out looking after their sheep. When David arrived, the first thing the narrator tells us is what he looked like: "ruddy, with beautiful eyes, and good-looking," and God immediately said, "He's the one!"[10] So much for God's indifference to external appearance, when it comes to kings, anyway.

Another familiar phrase associated with David was spoken by him. "How the mighty have fallen!" is an exclamation heard today in contexts ranging from politics to baseball, Hollywood to Wall Street. It usually refers to a sudden plummeting from power and prestige to impotence or disgrace. It has a nice ring to it for such a purpose, but its original biblical use was a grief-stricken cry of mourning. David exclaimed and repeated it in a poetic dirge over the dead bodies of his king, Saul, and best friend, Jonathan.[11] This poem is the culmination of a drama that played out over the course of many chapters leading to it. In short: the triangle of David, Saul, and Jonathan was fraught with competing loyalties; and Saul had sought David's death for quite some time. Nevertheless, when David learned that Saul and Jonathan had been killed in battle, he sang this song of lamentation, praising their greatness, forbidding any celebration over their death, and declaring great love for Jonathan. The song also includes a line about the father and son that appears today on many family grave markers: "In life and death they were not divided."[12]

Isaiah and Micah have an identical passage in common: "They shall beat their swords into plowshares and their spears into pruning hooks; nation shall not lift up sword against nation, and they shall practice war no more."[13] It comes at the end of verses describing a future time, when Jerusalem will be restored after destruction and will be an international center of wisdom, justice, and peace. The passage in Isaiah ends with this image of the transformation of violent weapons into peaceful agricultural tools; the rural prophet Micah tacks on a pastoral idyll: "They shall all sit under their own vines and under their own fig trees, and no one shall make them afraid."[14]

Few peace-loving people who cite this text know that its exact opposite is in the Bible, too. The prophet Joel, who came along much later than Isaiah and Micah and who made significant use of earlier prophecies, told his audience that a time is coming to "beat your plowshares into swords, and your pruning-hooks into spears."[15] Context makes all the difference, of course. Joel turned those words around to use them against Israel's abusers, calling them to prepare for the wrathful onslaught of God's vindicating Israel in battle.

Another peace-lovers' quote, "The lion shall lie down with the lamb," is the subject of numerous paintings, and was recently emblazoned on T-shirts and even tattooed on teen fans of the vampire *Twilight* saga, whose website is called "Lion and Lamb Love."[16] The contemporary novelist Martin Amis may have been correct in more ways than he intended when he wrote, "Only in art will the lion lie down with the lamb," because that exact phrase is not actually in the Bible. It is a paraphrase of Isa 11:6 (and reiterated in Isa 65:25), in which the prophet foretells a time when predator and prey coexist peacefully, when "they will not hurt or destroy on all my holy mountain."[17] In the biblical imagery, a wolf is paired with the lamb, a leopard with a baby goat, and a calf with a lion. In recent years, a Kenyan lioness named Larsens has made international news (and her sanctuary home a lot of money) by adopting and protecting a series of baby oryx antelope. The story is regularly told as an example of this "peaceful kingdom" imagery, and Larsens has been renamed Kamunyak, "the blessed one."[18]

Micah is also the source of a celebrated call for social justice. In reference to it, someone in my town is driving a car with the license plate MIC66-8. Beginning with the question, "With what shall I come before the LORD?" and followed by listing ritual gifts of valuable sacrifices as a possible answer, the text concludes: "He has told you, human being, what is good and what the LORD requires from you, namely: to do justice, love kindness, and walk humbly with your God."

Like Micah, the prophet Amos also distills proper worship down to acts of social justice. Martin Luther King, Jr., famously repeated

Amos: "Let justice roll down like waters, and righteousness like an ever-flowing stream!"[19] These timeless texts ring with a message frequently recurring within the Bible: that one's relationship to God is not limited to a one-to-one, me 'n God thing but is inseparable from one's relationships to others and to the world around. Doing right by others, the prophets declare, is to do right by God.

That was hardly the modus operandi of *Pulp Fiction*'s murderous hit man Jules (played by Samuel Jackson), who claimed to have memorized Ezek 25:17, and recited it three times. Yet the movie did introduce a lot of people to this wacky Hebrew prophet. The passage is an obscure one, and Jackson's character doesn't have it quite right, though the second and third recitations are closer. For one thing, Ezek 25:17 isn't nearly as long as Jackson's speech, and it doesn't have anything to do with being "his brother's keeper" (from Genesis 4) or the "finder of lost children."[20] That didn't prevent it from being voted the fourth best movie speech of all time in a 2004 poll cited by the BBC.[21]

Better known from the book of Ezekiel is the "valley of dry bones" speech, full of hope and promise.[22] It appears in the book after Ezekiel got the fateful news that Jerusalem had fallen to the Babylonians. At that point, Ezekiel changed his focus from God's judgment and destruction of Judah to its coming restoration. Part of the message of restoration comes in the form of Ezekiel's vision, in which the spirit of God took him to a valley scattered with dry human bones and told him to prophesy to them that God would make them live again. A popular spiritual recounts, "The foot bone connected to the ankle bone and the ankle bone connected to the leg bone and the leg bone connected to the hipbone; now, hear the word of the Lord!" Although many people think that the story tells about the resurrection of the dead, in the text, God explained to Ezekiel that the bones are the community of Israel who thought that they'd been utterly decimated, never to be a people again. The image conveys hope that even though it seemed impossible at the time, God would make ancient Israel a distinct people with their own land again.

A much more obscure text from Ezekiel has become familiar to diet-conscious, health food folks today. A company called Food for Life produces "Ezekiel 4:9" breads and cereals "inspired by the Holy Scripture verse: 'Take unto thee Wheat and Barley and Beans and Lentils and Millet and Spelt and put them in one vessel and make bread of it.'" They are delicious products, but I dearly hope they are not produced as biblically intended. Ezekiel was commanded by God to make this bread as a disgusting sign of the unclean conditions of exile that the sinful nation had to endure. That is, it was supposed to communicate *dis*taste, at the least.

Ezekiel was a priest as well as a prophet, so he knew and observed the laws that forbade mixing unlike things. To mix all these different things—different grains and legumes—into one loaf and to eat it was an abomination to Ezekiel. What's more, the text continues with God commanding Ezekiel to bake the bread on human feces, giving the message of ritual uncleanness nauseating clarity. But Ezekiel protested, and God conceded to allow him to bake it on cow patties instead. I suspect that Food for Life departs from scripture at this point and bakes its products in a conventional oven.

OLD TESTAMENT POETRY AND
UNIVERSAL WISDOM

"The LORD is my shepherd . . ." begins Psalm 23. It is a psalm of comfort and assurance that in the face of danger, God has got you covered. George W. Bush cited this psalm in his first speech after September 11, 2001. Specifically, he cited part of verse 4: "Even though I walk through the valley of the shadow of death, I fear no evil, for you are with me." It's a powerful psalm. Interestingly, Bush chose not to continue with the next verse, "You spread a table before me in the presence of my enemies," a curious line that could be taken in a few different ways. God's preparing such a table for the psalmist (and bestowing the good things that are described next) in front of the psalmist's enemies could be a kind of snub—see what God is doing for me but doesn't do for you. Or it could be understood as a radical kind of peace—to eat with others is a conciliatory act. Or it could be simply a further expression of God's protection in danger, in this case eating safely in the midst of people whose aim is hurtful.

I recall a pastel picture in a little book of psalms given to me as a child, in which a brown-haired man, dressed in a long beige robe, stood holding a staff near a stream. It was for Psalm 23 of course—"The LORD is my Shepherd . . ."—and I figured that the man was Lord Jesus, the Good Shepherd (like the name of our church—the Lutheran Church of the Good Shepherd). That is one interpretation, and an image supported by the gospels;[23] but of course Psalm 23 wasn't originally written with Jesus in mind (and who was centuries from being born), and the "LORD" that begins the psalm represents the Hebrew YHWH. Nevertheless, no matter how Psalm 23 is interpreted, it has comforted and emboldened countless Jews and Christians over the millennia with its surety of God's guidance and protection during even the most uncertain and terrifying times.

Psalms is full of uplifting aphorisms that have found their way into common speech and contemporary thought—"The heavens declare the glory of God";[24] "Weeping may endure for a night, but joy comes in the morning";[25] "from strength to strength";[26] "Your word is a lamp unto my feet and a light unto my path."[27] So, too, is the book of Proverbs. You may have seen the little green or orange Bibles that the Gideons give away for free. Maybe you have one. They are actually abbreviated Christian bibles, emphasizing the New Testament. The only Old Testament books they include are Psalms and Proverbs—understandably, since those books contain much that transcends time and place and feel immediately relevant, even to modern people.

Both books have the iconic phrase of so-called biblical wisdom literature: "The fear of the LORD is the beginning of wisdom."[28] Wisdom literature does not require a shared set of laws or rituals for readers to feel that it speaks for and to them. Indeed, Proverbs is full of advice for a general audience, including the popular "Trust in the LORD with all your heart; and don't lean on your own understanding."[29] Strikingly, however, the book of Proverbs is full of instruction about how to have understanding and, with that knowledge, how to succeed in the world. In such a context, the proverb just quoted is not a facile championing of ignorance. Rather, the book resolutely urges readers to seek wisdom everywhere and always, and to be wary of stupidity, both of which are personified as women—Woman Wisdom and Woman Folly, who vie for the affections of the (male) reader.

Ecclesiastes is another book of biblical wisdom literature. But it is far less optimistic than Proverbs, which considers success to be straightforward—simply a matter of being smart and responsible (and failure as the product of stupidity and ignorance). Ecclesiastes is instead dominated by the sentiment that begins the book: "Vanity of vanities, . . . all is vanity," or at least that's how the King James translation reads. That translation can be misleading because King James's "vanity" is not exactly the same as our "vanity" today. The Hebrew word, *hevel*, translated "vanity" means something like "breath" or "vapor."[30] It describes something transient, something that cannot be held and kept but rather evaporates and disappears. It's the same word as Abel's name, a name that tells Hebrew readers of Gen 4:1–16 that Abel is not going to be in the story for long. (Indeed, he's murdered within a few verses.) So Ecclesiastes does not mean to suggest that everything is self-absorbed in a "you're-so-vain" sort of way. Instead, the book is preoccupied with the transient nature of life, success, and happiness.

Similar to its observation of the ever-changing nature of things, the book repeats that there is "nothing new under the sun." Everything is cyclical—it's been done before and will be so again. Ernest Hemingway's title *The Sun Also Rises* comes from the King James translation of Ecc 1:5, "The sun also ariseth and the sun goeth and hasteth to his place where he arose." It's in Ecclesiastes that we find the lyrics to Pete

Seeger's "Turn, Turn, Turn (To Everything There Is a Season)," which has been sung by numerous performers, and round many a campfire. It was made especially popular by the Byrds and by Forrest Gump, too.[31] Depending on your mood, the song can be an optimistic open-armed embrace of all that is, each in its appropriate time—mourning and dancing, crying and laughing, keeping and releasing, war and peace, love and hate—or it can be a pessimistic observation that there's little point in going after anything, since anything goes.

The Song of Songs, also called the Song of Solomon or Canticles (reflecting the Latin), disagrees. The speakers in that book throw in their lot with love—erotic, sensuous, physical love. There you can find great wedding material: "your love is better than wine,"[32] "set me as a seal upon your heart, as a seal upon your arm, for love is strong as death, passion fierce as the grave."[33] It looks to the natural world for illustration and meaning, and every sense—sight, smell, hearing, taste, and touch—is brought to bear on the quest for and delight in love. In an effort to explain how such a saucy book made it into the Bible, different faith groups have interpreted the book as describing the love of God for Israel or Jesus for the church. But many recognize the book for its celebration of the sensuous and embrace of physical love. Book22.com is a Christian website that sells sex toys. Its name refers to the Song of Solomon, the twenty-second book in the Bible, according to a Christian ordering and numbering of books.[34]

Speaking of great wedding material, how many times have you heard "Where you go, I will go; where you lodge, I will lodge; your people shall be my people; and your God will be my God" while two lovers stand at the front of a church or synagogue? It's a beautiful passage of fidelity and love, perfect for the occasion of a wedding, though its biblical context is a passionate though platonic conversation between two women (in-laws, no less).[35] Ruth said these words to her mother-in-law, Naomi, after Naomi's sons, including Ruth's husband, had died and Naomi was heading back to her native Bethlehem. The foreigner, Ruth, was a native of Moab, yet she was determined to stick with Naomi despite the bleak future a couple of widows would have faced in the patriarchal ancient Mediterranean world. It was not the most prudent choice for Ruth, but her *chesed*, her loving-kindness-plus-loyalty, makes her the heroine in this charming biblical novella.

To date, when I've asked my students which biblical character said, "I know that my redeemer lives," not a single one has gotten it right. The answer is Job, the Old Testament character known for enduring terrible suffering that he didn't deserve.[36] Nearly everybody guesses that it must be in the New Testament somewhere, and that "my redeemer" is necessarily Jesus. The spirit of the exclamation fits Christian theology to a T; but it actually comes from a character who is not even portrayed as an Israelite. This man, Job, was driven to rail against both his friends and God as he sought some justification for and relief from his torment. Ironically, just before declaring, "I know that my redeemer lives," Job said, "If only someone would write all this down so that my words would last forever!"[37] Job punctuated his suffering with this exclamation of faith, confident that "even after my skin is gone, yet in my flesh I will see God." The sentiment has struck a chord, giving rise over the years to countless songs—classical, pop, liturgical hymns, Christian rock, and more.

According to the postexilic books of Esther and Daniel, those Babylonians were quite the partyers, and we all know (if not firsthand) that strong drink can make a person do stupid things. Dan 5:1–31 tells how King Belshazzar, deep in his cups with a crowd of rowdy revelers, decided that drinking out of the sacred vessels pillaged from the Jerusalem temple sounded like a good idea. When they then toasted the greatness of their idol gods, a human hand emerged out of thin air and began to write on the wall in front of them. Utterly terrified by the apparition, and by the words, which even his magicians could not decipher, Belshazzar called in the Jewish exile Daniel to see what he could make of it. After chastising Belshazzar for his haughtiness, Daniel translated with ease the writing on the wall, *mene mene tekel parsin* (Aramaic words for specific denominations of weight or currency),[38] as meaning that God would soon end Belshazzar's rule and kingdom, that the king himself was judged to be a light-weight, and that his kingdom would be divided between the Medes and the Persians. Today, "the writing is on the wall" still sounds the ominous note of a done deal—a fait accompli.

NEW TESTAMENT: THE BABY JESUS

Every time, and I mean every time, that I see the *Peanuts* Christmas special, I get choked up when Linus takes the stage. He answers Charlie Brown's angst-ridden exclamation, "Doesn't anyone know what Christmas is all about?!" with a lisped, "Sure, Charlie Brown, I can tell you what Christmas is all about." Linus turns abruptly and, blanket in tow, wanders purposefully onto a theater's stage where Lucy, Snoopy, and the other children are gathered. "Lights, please?" Then with a few demonstrative gestures and an occasional smile, and absent any background music or sound, Linus faces the empty theater and says simply, "And there were in the same country, shepherds abiding in the field keeping watch over their flock by night. Lo, an angel of the Lord came upon them, and the glory of the Lord shown round about them, and [hands to mouth] they were sore afraid. And the angel said unto them [a little smile], 'Fear not. For behold, I bring you tidings of great joy [clasping his hands to his chest and smiling]. For unto you is born this day in the city of David, a savior [shuts his eyes briefly, arms out] which is Christ the Lord. And this shall be a sign unto you: you shall find the babe wrapped in swaddling clothes, lying in a manger. Suddenly, there was with the angel a multitude of the heavenly host praising God saying, 'Glory to God in the highest, and on earth, peace, goodwill toward men.'" Then he picks up his blanket and toddles out of the spotlight and off the stage, where he says, "That's what Christmas is all about, Charlie Brown." It gets me every time. The passage comes from Luke's gospel,[39] and it is the most recited of the gospels' different birth narratives.[40]

NEW TESTAMENT: THE TEACHING JESUS

Andrew Carnegie, who worked his way out of poverty and into a grand fortune, gave away a great deal of money, not least to build beautiful public libraries throughout the United States and the United Kingdom, because he said that "man does not live by bread alone. . . . It is the mind that makes the body rich."[41] Many people credit Jesus with the statement "One does not live by bread alone"; but Jesus was actually quoting from his Hebrew scriptures, in which Moses reminded the Israelites of how God looked after them in the wilderness, providing manna when they were hungry, and instructed them that "a person does not live by bread alone, but by every word that comes from the mouth of the LORD."[42] The phrase has come to describe how human beings have cultural and spiritual needs beyond the physical needs for food and water.

The beatitudes (from a Latin word meaning "blessed" or "happy") is a title given to a series of blessings-statements ("Blessed are the . . .") that Jesus makes in both Matthew's and Luke's gospels. Matthew's Jesus, a new Moses, goes up and holds forth from a mountain, so these beatitudes are part of what people refer to as the Sermon on the Mount. In Luke, Jesus "stood in a level place," hence the Sermon on the Plain. The Bible itself does not use the terms "beatitudes," "sermon on the mount," or "sermon on the plain." These descriptions are a modern convention. Some Bible editors embed them in the text to help guide today's readers.

The beatitudes are not exactly the same in Matthew and Luke. In keeping with the overall differences, Matthew is more abstract or general and emphasizes spiritual matters; Luke is more personal and emphasizes social and economic matters. For example, in Matthew,

Jesus says, "Blessed are the poor in spirit, for theirs is the kingdom of heaven;[43] while Luke's Jesus says, "Blessed are *you* who are poor, for yours is the kingdom of God."[44] In Matthew, Jesus says, "Blessed are those who hunger and thirst for righteousness, for they will be filled;[45] while Luke's Jesus says, "Blessed are you who are hungry *now*, for you will be filled."[46] A 1980s rock band, the Police sang, "They say the meek shall inherit the earth." Simon and Garfunkel's "Blessed" (1978) adds several beatitudes, such as "blessed are the penny rookers, cheap hookers, groovy lookers," that don't appear anywhere in the gospels. "Blessed are the peacemakers" was the motto of King James I of England (and of the King James Version of the Bible), and is quoted ironically in *The Godfather, Part 3.*

In both Matthew's Sermon on the Mount and Luke's Sermon on the Plain, Jesus states the Golden Rule, "the most common moral maxim in the world's religions"[47]—"Do to others as you would have them do to you."[48] This New Testament text is often confused with the Old Testament text from Leviticus that I cited above (to "love your neighbor as yourself"). George W. Bush made such a mistake in an October 2000 presidential debate with Al Gore, saying that Americans should appeal to the "larger law" to "Love your neighbor like you would like to be loved yourself."[49] There is a slight, characteristic difference between Matthew's Golden Rule and Luke's: Matthew, concerned with showing Jesus as fulfilling the Hebrew scriptures, adds, "for this is the law and the prophets"; Luke, whose message is consistently more universal and directed toward the gentiles, doesn't.

It's quite possible that Jesus adopted and adapted the Golden Rule from the famous teaching of Hillel, a revered Jewish teacher of the first century BCE. (This is the Hillel for whom the Hillel House on your local college campus is named.) There is a story that a man came to Shammai (another revered Jewish teacher, of the century before Jesus) declaring that if Shammai could teach him the whole Torah while he stood on one foot, then he would be converted. Incensed at what seemed to him to be gross ignorance and disrespect for the complexity and nuances of God's instruction, Shammai slammed the door, sending the man away.

The man went next to Hillel and proposed the same challenge. Hillel's response was to say, "That's easy. Do not do to others what you would not have them do to you. That is the whole Torah. All the rest is commentary. Now go and learn it." Hillel's is a negative representation of the Golden Rule—"Do *not* do . . . what you would *not* have . . ."—wherein restraint is the key, and it emphasizes the importance of learning and study. Practicing the restraint that he advises is not the end. Learning the directive's nuances in the context of the rest of the scriptures and studying the ways that sages have sought to understand and follow the rule is crucial.

In Matthew's Sermon on the Mount, Jesus extrapolates on instructions from the Hebrew scriptures that would have been authoritative for his Jewish audience. He embraces the law and adds to it—"sees and raises" the ante. So it is in Matthew that Jesus says things such as, "You have heard it said that you shall not commit adultery"—one of the Ten Commandments—"but I say to you that everyone who looks at a woman with lust has already committed adultery with her in his heart." [50] Americans of a certain age who were subject to Bill Clinton's Lewinsky scandal recall with nostalgia Jimmy Carter's earnest confession, in an interview with *Playboy* (1976), of having looked lustfully at women and so, according to the Bible, had committed adultery in his heart.

It is in Matthew that Jesus takes the Torah sentiment of "an eye for an eye, and a tooth for a tooth" and turns it on its head, saying, "If anyone strikes you on the right cheek, turn the other also." [51] "Turning the other cheek" has come to mean any act of passivity in the face of threat or violence. The Russian novelist Leo Tolstoy took this commandment of nonresistance at face value in the book that maps his definition of a Christian society, *The Kingdom of God Is within You* (1894).

★ ★ ★

Today, the Lord's Prayer is frequently recited aloud in a congregational setting, with everyone joining in; but it almost always creates a few moments of anxiety, because despite the prayer's familiarity, not everyone says exactly the same thing. If yours is the minority voice declaring a discordant version, it can be embarrassing. Truth is, the multiplicity is actually very biblical.

The Lord's Prayer (which actually doesn't have that or any title in the Bible) appears in Matthew's Sermon on the Mount but not in Luke's Sermon on the Plain. Mark and John don't have it at all. Matthew's Jesus introduces his instructions for this short and sweet prayer by contrasting it with verbose gentile prayers (to pagan gods).[52] Luke makes the prayer even shorter, and leaves out the critique of other people's prayers.[53]

Not only are Matthew's and Luke's versions different, but each also appears in different forms. For example, some ancient versions of Matthew's gospel include a clause, "For the kingdom and the power and the glory are yours forever. Amen." But other ancient versions end with "deliver (or rescue) us from evil (or from the evil one)." Some ancient versions of Luke's Lord's Prayer begin, "Father," and others "Our Father in heaven." Some versions such as the one that appears in the *Book of Common Prayer*, use "trespasses" where others use "debts."

My parents' church in northern Minnesota has one version etched in stone in huge letters from floor to ceiling behind the altar. That helps.

A couple of other popular Jesus sayings common to Matthew and Luke (and part of Matthew's Sermon on the Mount but not Luke's Sermon on the Plain) include "Consider the lilies . . ." and "Ask and it shall be given to you . . ."[54] The full texts, too long to quote here, both give poetic assurance that God looks out for his own. Each one includes three elements: don't worry; strive for God's kingdom; and

God will give you what you need or ask for. Both of them have been used in discussions for and against the "prosperity gospel," for obvious reasons.

An interesting counterpoint is the literary context of "For human beings, it is impossible, but for God all things are possible," which we find in all the synoptic gospels—Matthew, Mark, and Luke.[55] The gist of the lesson preceding this statement seems to be that material wealth precludes experiencing the kingdom of God. Jesus likened a wealthy person's chances of entering the kingdom of God to a camel squeezing through the eye of a needle. When the disciples exclaimed that this is impossible, Jesus responded with the statement that with God all things are possible. Such a context would seem to suggest that God can give a wealthy person access to the kingdom of God, and can push a camel through the eye of a needle. Incidentally, "With God all things are possible" is the state motto of Ohio.

Back to the eye of the needle for a moment, because it's a phrase that appears quite a bit today, and there are several different explanations of its origins floating around out there. One is that the Greek word translated as "camel" is actually "rope"—the difference between *kamelos*, and *kamilos*, respectively. But the end result is the same. That is, it's only a little less extraordinary to push a rope through a needle's eye than to push a camel; both are impossible.[56] Another popular theory is that there was a gate in Jerusalem called the Needle's Eye, through which a camel could pass only if it was relieved of its burden and crawled through on its knees. But there's no evidence for this.

Immediately after the beatitudes, Matthew's Jesus tells his audience, "You are the salt of the earth."[57] Lest his audience feel smug about this and grow complacent, Matthew's Jesus goes on to warn that if salt loses its savor, it's good for nothing and should be tossed out and trampled on. "Salt of the earth" has come to be associated with honest, hardworking, usually blue-collar folk—the kind of people who do not enjoy privilege or high standing but on whom whole economies and communities depend.

In the mid-twentieth century, when communism was on the minds of many people, it became fashionable among some left-wing scholars to show how "red" Jesus appears to be in the synoptic gospels. Indeed, the economic critiques of Jesus regularly favor the poor and promote a social system of common possessions. *Salt of the Earth* is the title of a film that was so controversial when it was first released that it was denounced by the U.S. House of Representatives, its financing was investigated by the FBI, and it was widely boycotted—only a dozen theaters in the entire country were willing to screen it. Produced in 1954 using only a handful of professional actors, it tells the story of a mining strike that challenged not only economic but also ethnic and gender inequities. It has become a cult classic, and in 1992 the U.S. Library of Congress included *Salt of the Earth* in its National Film Registry because of the movie's cultural significance.

Stories about Jesus reflect his everyday context: ordinary and hard-working laborers; salt, fish, and bread. In November 2007, the Republican presidential candidate Mike Huckabee credited his surge of popularity to "the same power that helped a little boy with two fish and five loaves feed a crowd of 5,000 people." When the NPR correspondent Barbara Bradley Hagerty asked a woman waiting to visit the Washington Monument if she knew this reference, the woman responded, "That's when Moses . . . had to feed all the people, the multitude of people that left Egypt, that's what it was?"[58] No. But the question wasn't entirely fair. After all, only John's version of the story includes a boy, and it's a bit part, anyway. Jesus was not a little boy, according to the story; but then, neither was Moses when he led the people out of Egypt.

Huckabee meant to refer to the only miracle that appears in all four of the gospels.[59] Both Matthew and Mark include two such stories,[60] which may be either similar occurrences or different versions of the same event. In one case, Jesus told his disciples to give the 5,000 people who had followed him something to eat. His disciples protested that they had only five loaves of bread and two fish. Nevertheless, after Jesus blessed the meager food and divided it, the narrators explain that "all ate and were satisfied." In the other story, 4,000 people are fed with seven loaves and "a few small fish," with food left over. Today, there are countless "loaves and fishes" charitable food programs all around the world.

NEW TESTAMENT: REMEMBERING JESUS

Historians of Christianity think that one of the earliest rituals among followers of Jesus after his death was the common meal of remembrance with its symbolic bread and wine. Called Holy Communion, the Lord's Supper, or the Eucharist today, the ritual continues to be fundamental for Christians of all kinds. Matthew, Mark, and Luke each have stories of the last supper that Jesus shared with his disciples.[61] The synoptic gospels say that at this common meal, specifically the Jewish celebration of Passover, Jesus instituted the practice that would become the Eucharist. And where Jesus said, "Everyone who wants to be in the picture, get on this side of the table." OK, no. That's not really in the Bible.

The words recited at this meal, "the words of institution," are reflected in all three of the synoptic gospels. Again, though, they are not identical. Mark, the earliest gospel, has the leanest account: "While they were eating, he took a loaf of bread, and after blessing it he broke it, gave it to them, and said, 'Take; this is my body.' Then he took a cup, and after giving thanks he gave it to them, and all of them drank from it. He said to them, 'This is my blood of the [new] covenant, which is poured out for many. Truly I tell you, I will never again drink of the fruit of the vine until that day when I drink it new in the kingdom of God.'"[62] All the synoptic gospels include Jesus' description of his blood as the covenant, and some ancient versions of those gospels add "new" to "covenant." Only Matthew specifies that Jesus' blood was shed "for the forgiveness of sins," [63] and only Luke adds the command to "do this in remembrance of me." [64]

Each of the synoptic gospels includes some reference to Jesus' not drinking again "until . . ." But they do so differently. Mark's Jesus declares that he "shall not drink again of the fruit of the vine until that day when I drink it new in the kingdom of God"; [65] Matthew's Jesus adds "with you" and makes it "my Father's kingdom"; [66] and Luke's Jesus won't drink again until "the kingdom of God comes." [67]

The early Christian Church was conflicted about who should and should not be allowed to take Holy Communion. In the context of this debate, Matthew's comment about throwing "pearls before swine" [68] was reinterpreted by early Jewish Christians to disallow non-Jews from partaking of the Eucharist. [69] Ironically, its literary context follows Jesus' warning against judging others and precedes illustrations of God's great generosity. Today "pearls before swine" has a more general application, meaning a gift of great value that is utterly unappreciated by someone too ignorant or backward to understand it.

While celebrating the Eucharist was one of the earliest practices among the nascent Christian community, one of its earliest hymns, scholars think, appears in Paul's letter to the Philippians. [70] The hymn itself probably predates Paul and may come directly from Jesus' first followers. It declares belief in Jesus as the humble incarnation of God, an incarnation that led even to death, for which God exalted Jesus so that "at the name of Jesus every knee should bow . . . and every tongue confess that Jesus Christ is Lord, to the glory of God the Father."

This phrase has motivated people throughout the centuries to do both noble and awful things, as Christians have taken it as a clarion call to mission. Ironically (when Christians seek to proselytize Jews), its origins are in part the Old Testament book of Isaiah, wherein Yahweh (the LORD) declared, "There is no god beside me, a righteous God and a savior. . . . To me every knee shall bow and every tongue will confess/swear" (this is the same word in the Greek of Philippians as in the Greek Septuagint). [71] In his letter to the Romans, Paul repeats the ancient text from Isaiah, but reinterprets it in light of his own understanding of Jesus. Paul says, "It is written, 'As I live,' says the Lord, 'every knee shall bow to me and every tongue shall give praise to God.'"[72]

ALPHA AND OMEGA, THE EVER-LOVIN' JESUS

The author of the book of Revelation reports that God declared, "I am the alpha and omega."[73] Referring to the first and last letters of the Greek alphabet in this way is to claim that God is everything, A to Z, beginning to end. This section notes biblical quotations about Jesus' presence at the cosmic beginning and apocalyptic end, plus famous quotations about love from the New Testament. They come from "the Johns"—gospel, letters, and Revelation, and from Paul, too.

John's gospel is strikingly unlike the other three gospels. "In the beginning was the Word and the Word was with God and the Word was God" is how it begins. And this suffices for a nativity story. In John, there is no baby Jesus in the manger; rather, there is a powerful force of divinity that is already present at the creation of the universe and that infuses the whole created order with life and light, power and glory, grace and truth. John's Jesus is the incarnation of this force, the Word—"he was in the world, and the world was made by him, yet the world did not know him."[74] The gospel is committed to addressing this ignorance. Unlike the Jesus of the synoptic gospels, John's Jesus teaches about himself in particular, and that self is radically unique.

At the beginning of his gospel, John equates Jesus with "the Word," which is how most English translations render the Greek *logos*.[75] *Logos*, though, can mean far more than what we think of as a word—represented by particular sounds or by letters on a page such as the string that you're reading right now. It also connotes reason, sense, meaning, idea. (It's behind the English word "logic.") It can mean account, a full message, or matter. In any case, it reflects John's prioritizing mind over body. John's Jesus is a thinking, spiritual man, far less affected by his embodiment than the Jesus of the synoptic gospels, and far more given to lengthy discourse than in the others. So the emphasis on Jesus as *logos* that begins this fourth gospel is paradigmatic.

With this beginning, John reaches back to the first words of the Hebrew scriptures and transforms the beginning of the creation story narrated in Genesis chapter 1 to make Jesus an integral part of the origins and order of the universe. Jesus becomes the creative act ("All things came into being through him"), without beginning, and eternally existent in the world. Incidentally, the philosophical notion of God's purposeful thinking permeating the world is not unique to John. In the book of Proverbs, which predates John's gospel by centuries, we meet wisdom, the Hebrew *hokmah*, personified and animated, described as present with God at the beginning of creation.[76] All the wisdom literature of the Old Testament assumes that the world is a reflection of God's ideas and purpose. Applying oneself to understand it is a sacred pursuit.

The gospel of John promotes understanding Jesus in order to understand God. So it's in John's gospel and no other that we find statements such as "You will know the truth and the truth will make you free";[77] "I am the way, the truth, and the life; no one comes to the Father except by me";[78] "I am in the Father and the Father is in me."[79] And it is from the gospel of John—namely Jerome's Latin translation of it—that we get *ecce homo*—"behold the man." The context is Jesus' trial. After the Roman soldiers placed a crown of thorns on his head and a purple robe around his shoulders, mocking him as "king of the Jews," Pilate presented Jesus to the crowd. Although Pilate would have spoken Greek, and the gospel was written in Greek, Jerome's Latin translation of Pilate's declaration is remembered best: *ecce homo*. John's gospel then reports that the chief priests cried out, "Crucify him!"[80]

John's Jesus is the personification of abstract principles identified with God, not the least of which is love. This love, John explains, is contagious and circular—God's love for the world and for Jesus is manifest in Jesus, who loves others; and these others are commanded to love each other, the world, and God and Jesus in return. Early in John's gospel we find the verse that Max Lucado calls the "Hope Diamond of scripture" and that serves as the title of a series of Lucado's highly popular modern books, *3:16*. "For God so loved the world that he gave his only begotten Son that whoever believes in him would not die but have eternal life" is from the gospel of John's third chapter, sixteenth verse—hence "John 3:16." The cover art for Lucado's books and DVDs represents the colon between chapter and verse as antique nail heads, connoting the nails that fatally fixed Jesus to a cross. According to John, and foundational to Christianity, Jesus' sacrificial death on the cross is evidence of God's love for the world, as it effects eternal life for believers.

Newt Gingrich quoted from the gospel of John when he told James Dobson (of Focus on the Family) that because of his own marital infidelities he couldn't "cast the first stone" when other Republicans attacked Bill Clinton for his sexual dalliance with Monica Lewinsky.[81] One of the most famous "sinners saved" stories about Jesus concerns a woman caught in the act of adultery.[82] Jewish leaders brought her before Jesus and exclaimed that according to the law (of Moses from God), she should be stoned to death. Smoothly sidestepping the trap of either breaking the law or breaking his own standards of love and forgiveness, Jesus famously responded, "Whoever is without sin among you, let him cast the first stone." That diffused the crowd. Jesus then released the woman with the words, "Neither do I condemn you. Now go, and sin no more." This story appears only in John's gospel; but it is not in the earliest versions we have of that gospel. It was added at a later date.[83]

It is also in John's gospel that Jesus declares, "As the Father has loved me, so I love you. Abide in my love";[84] and, "This is my commandment: that you love one another as I have loved you."[85] The book known as 1 John was written some time after the gospel and probably not by the same person, yet its name reflects the fact that it is clearly modeled on the fourth gospel. In part, we see this in 1 John's association of Jesus with God's love: "Beloved, let us love one another, because love is of God, and everyone who loves is born of God and knows God. Whoever does not love, does not know God because God is love."[86]

Speaking of love, although Ruth's declaration of devotion and loyalty to Naomi is certainly popular at weddings, 1 Corinthians 13 is even more so. "Love is patient and kind, and envies no one. Love is never boastful nor conceited, nor rude, never selfish nor quick to take offense . . ." This meditation on love concludes, "Three things endure: faith, hope, and love; but the greatest of them is love." Jesus didn't say this. Paul did. And as far as we know, Paul was never married. But, then, I've heard it said, "I was a much better parent before I had children." Despite his single status, Paul certainly understood love.

Like weddings, funerals bring disparate people together in a religious setting, so it makes sense that, just as for weddings, certain biblical texts are especially popular for funerals. For Jews, whose emphasis generally is less on life after death than on life as it is presently lived, texts that matter-of-factly note our natural mortality,[87] that counsel the living to respect the dead (for instance, Abraham's care for his deceased wife, Sarah),[88] and that demonstrate compassion for the bereaved are sensible and comforting. Especially characteristic, though, are texts that remind mourners of God's righteousness and justice.[89]

For Christians, whose emphasis at funerals is predominantly on life after death, biblical references often include the New Testament texts "In the twinkling of an eye . . . the dead will be raised imperishable, and we will be changed";[90] and "The Lamb will guide them to springs of living water, and God will wipe away every tear from their eyes."[91] The KJV's "in the twinkling of an eye" has firmly established itself in the western literary canon as meaning "in a moment," and appears in Darwin and Dickens, *Moby-Dick*, Anne Brontë, four of Shakespeare's works, and seven of Joseph Conrad's, among others. Although the original Greek word connotes not the twinkle of a light but instead something that happens super-quickly, nearly all English translations nevertheless continue to use "twinkling." But judging from the way the phrase appears in other places, the idea of rapid movement hasn't been lost. Besides, it has a lovely lilt as it rolls off the tongue.

The texts from Revelation are apocalyptic, describing mystical things "revealed" about what's to come. The Shepherd or Lamb is Jesus, who ushers in a new age, in which those who have been persecuted will be vindicated and those who have died "in the blood of the Lamb" will live again. Like other apocalyptic literature, Revelation looks forward to a time when present conditions will be turned upside down (and morally righted). Notice, for example, how blood whitens and the sheep is also the shepherd.[92] It gives hope that the world will be radically changed by the immediate action of God, and the righteous who have endured great suffering and tribulation will enjoy abundant rewards. The New Testament apocalyptic writing looks beyond this world to a new age inaugurated by God's intervention and ruled by Jesus.

The author of Revelation reached back to the latest prophecies in the Old Testament book of Isaiah, which declare "new heavens and a new earth,"[93] and reinterpreted and reshaped them for his new apocalyptic context. "God . . . will wipe every tear from their eyes. Death will be no more; mourning and crying and pain will be no more."[94] It's easy to see why such texts are so popular at Christian funerals.

NOT SO BIBLICAL, AFTER ALL

This is only a smattering of the biblical references that crop up in contemporary culture, sometimes in the most unexpected places. I would be remiss, though, if I didn't mention briefly some popular phrases commonly attributed to the Bible that simply aren't there. "This too shall pass" is not in the Bible. Neither is "To thine own self be true";[95] "Spare the rod, spoil the child";[96] "God works in mysterious ways"; "God helps those who help themselves"; and "Cleanliness is next to godliness." Nancy Pelosi meant well when she declared in her 2008 Earth Day speech, "The Bible tells us in the Old Testament, 'To minister to the needs of God's creation is an act of worship. To ignore those needs is to dishonor the God who made us.'" Although the general sense of her biblical reference is an acceptable interpretation of some biblical ideas and texts, she seemed to suggest that she was quoting; but no such text exists, and she caught a lot of heat for it.

NINE

Men, Famous and Infamous

My ancestors wandered lost in the wilderness for
forty years because even in biblical times, men
would not stop to ask for directions.

—ELAYNE BOOSLER

From adulterers to dreamers, prophets, murderers, kings, philosophers
and mystics, pranksters and preachers, the chaste and the chastened,
saviors and the damned, the Bible's male characters are as diverse
as can be imagined. Some are clearly villains and others are heroes.
Many have ambiguous morals, misstep, or succumb to weakness, even
in the midst of doing great things. Some seem blind to their purpose,
and others proceed with laser-sharp ambition. It's no wonder that this
cast has inspired countless remakes over the centuries. References to
Adam alone—much less to Jesus—in art, literature, music, movies,
and more, are beyond measure. What follows is a brief description of
some biblical men who turn up regularly outside the Bible.

BEGINNINGS, OR MR. UNIVERSAL

The stories and characters of the first several chapters in Genesis are universal. Adam and Eve, Cain and Abel, Noah and his family are not Jewish, Christian, pagan, or otherwise identified by religion. Neither are they described by race or class or any other human category that makes for "us versus them" discourse. Their stories aren't bounded by the particularities that would limit their references, relevance, or application to only a specific people or group; and each has something to do with beginnings.

Adam—the first man, Man, or not? Depending on how one reads the Bible and translates its Hebrew text, Adam is the first male human being, the first human being, paradigmatic of human beings, or some combination thereof. Adam gets surprisingly little attention in the Bible, yet apart from Jesus, he probably has the best name recognition.

After Gen 1:26, the next time that *adam* should be read as the proper name Adam is Gen 5:1–2, which echoes 1:26–27 by also using the word as an umbrella term for the "male and female" human beings that God created in his own likeness. The text goes on, though, to a brief genealogy of Adam the individual man (his son Seth was born "in his likeness . . . and image"), and to an obituary (dead at age 930).[1] The only other reference to Adam in the Old Testament is at the beginning of Chronicles, where he is named as the first human being.

Later deuterocanonical and New Testament writers understood him unambiguously as Adam, the first man.[2] Luke refers to Adam in taking Jesus' genealogy back to this *ur*-man and universal ancestor.[3] For Paul, Adam is a paradigmatic, fallible, mortal human being, in contrast to Jesus, a life-giving second Adam.[4] In a rant against allowing women leadership roles within the church, the author of 1 Timothy laid the groundwork for what has become the dominant interpretation of Gen 2–3: that Adam was made before Eve, and that "Adam was not deceived"—it was all Eve's fault.[5]

In the account in Genesis, Cain and Abel were the first people to be born. They were the sons of Adam and Eve and were the first to make sacrifices to God; and they also were the first to know murder. In Robert Ludlum's novel *The Bourne Identity* (though not in the movie series), Jason Bourne, a trained assassin, has an alias—Cain. The name fits his vocation. Like cocaine (for which "cain" is slang), he was a killer.[6] As the biblical story goes, God looked favorably on Abel's sacrifice but didn't care so much for Cain's, which made Cain upset. Rivers of ink have been spilled explaining just how Cain's offering was inferior and why it deserved the divine silent treament,[7] but the fact is that the Bible doesn't say why God shunned it. Instead, the focus is on what Cain will do or not do about it. Rather than getting hold of his anger as God counseled him, Cain killed Abel. When confronted by God, Cain delivered the famous "Am I my brother's keeper?" line.

God expelled Cain from that place, making him a nomad, but not before mercifully giving him a mysterious mark designed to protect him from other murderous people. (Ironically the name of the place, Nod, where Cain comes to dwell means, in Hebrew, "wandering.")[8] This brief biblical story narrated in Gen 4:1–16 of family, resentment, passion, danger, and sorrow served as the inspiration for John Steinbeck's great American novel *East of Eden*, a title that reflects the biblical story's setting. *East of Eden* was adapted for the screen in a 1955 release that catapulted James Dean to stardom.

It is surely not a coincidence that the acronym NOAH is used by such organizations as the National Office for Animal Health and Nurturing Orphans of AIDS for Humanity. In the Bible, Noah is a savior of sorts for animals and people alike. The narrator of Genesis explains that after the episode of Cain and Abel, violence increased on the earth until God, seeing how terribly bad people are, regretted ever having made them at all. God confided in Noah (a "righteous man" and presumably the only person good enough to merit God's salvation), and directed him to build an ark on which his family as well as representative birds and beasts would survive the coming Flood.

Noah is very like Utnapishtim, the hero of a Mesopotamian flood story narrated in the epic of *Gilgamesh*, which circulated in different versions throughout the Near and Middle East at around the time that the stories of Genesis began to be told. *Gilgamesh* includes different gods, monsters, and extraordinary happenings, but it also tells about a faithful human being who was spared devastating floods by an angry God, saved sample critters, and tested post-flood conditions by sending birds out of the ark. The Bible notes that after smelling the delicious odors of Noah's post-flood sacrifice, God allowed meat eating and promised never to destroy the earth by flood again, a promise symbolized by the rainbow.[9]

Noah also gives us the first story of grape growing, wine making, and the inevitable result: drunkenness.[10] In the story, however, Noah's drunkenness was not an object lesson in overindulgence but rather served as justification for slavery. The story does not blame Noah for his drunken stupor. It blames his youngest son, Ham, for seeing him naked. Noah then cursed Ham's son, Canaan, for some unreported but presumably terrible crime that Ham committed against his father in Noah's drunken nakedness (though the crime may simply have been not looking away); and Canaan was condemned to be "lowest of slaves to his brothers."[11] Ham became associated with Egypt and by extension Africa; therefore, a twisted logic goes, African people are singled out in the Bible for slavery.

THE BOSOM OF ABRAHAM

Whether or not the "bosom of Abraham," which appears in one New Testament story,[12] reflects the Greco-Roman practice of reclining at a banquet in a kind of staggered spooning or to a child's comfort and security in his or her parent's lap, it is described as a happy place to be—a kind of heavenly Paradise for the faithful after death. Elvis introduced the traditional gospel song "Rock-a My Soul," or "Bosom of Abraham," to a whole new audience. Abraham is remembered not only as the first ancestor of the Jewish people but also as the father of all the faithful; Christians and Muslims claim him as an ancestor, too. Beginning with Abraham, the Genesis story focuses on a particular family.

Originally called Abram (his name, like others', changed after close encounters with God), Abraham left his hometown, Ur, in immediate response to God's command to get up and go. It was just the first of many times that Abraham would unquestioningly obey apparently random, radical instructions from God. On account of this trait, Abraham is sometimes called the "father of faith." Protestants love him for that—faith, not works but Abraham did some works, too. Not least was his agreeing, as a sign of God's covenant with Abraham's clan, to circumcise himself at the ripe old age of ninety-nine, and to circumcise all his male descendants, too—to the present day.[13] With this agreement, God singled Abraham out for a special blood-brothers relationship and promised to Abraham significant perks besides. The terms of the covenant are repeated several times in Genesis, with Abraham and with his successors. They include God's promise of having many descendants ("a great nation") and a land of their own (hence, the "Promised Land"), and of being the means by which other nations would bless themselves (it's this awkward in the Hebrew).

Although Abraham is considered a father for Jews, Christians, and Muslims (the Abrahamic faiths), Abraham wasn't the father of anybody for many, many years, according to the Bible. Abraham and his wife Sarah had trouble conceiving a child, so Abraham sired a son with their slave Hagar. The boy, Ishmael, was so named because "God heard" (*El ishma*, more or less) Hagar's cries after Sarah discarded her and her son in the wilderness. Herman Melville's biblically saturated *Moby-Dick* begins with the sentence, "Call me Ishmael." The name, reflected in that novel and elsewhere, evokes alienation and exile. Eventually, the biblical Ishmael became associated with the Arab people, and it's his life and family line that the Qur'an is most interested in.

Sarah finally did conceive and bore Abraham's son, Isaac. Despite Ishmael's status as the elder, God assured Abraham that Isaac would be the one "of the promise," that is, the one who would inherit the covenant God had made with Abraham. But in a nail-biting turn of events, known as the *akedah*, the "binding of Isaac," God required that Abraham sacrifice Isaac. This is probably the most famous Abraham story. At the last minute, a divine messenger stopped Abraham from killing Isaac, and God praised Abraham for his willingness to carry out such a horrifying command.[14] Although this is remembered as another demonstration of Abraham's tremendous faith, the story never explains how Sarah or Isaac felt about it. In succeeding stories, Isaac deteriorates rapidly into a nearly blind, doddering old man. Nevertheless, Isaac did carry on the line and the promise God made to Abraham's family.

The Abraham of the Bible is a friend of God's. In another famous Abraham story, God confided in Abraham about God's plan to destroy the wicked cities of Sodom and Gomorrah. After hearing God out, Abraham offered his own thoughts. It seemed unfair to wipe out whole cities when only a few (or even many) of its inhabitants are bad, so Abraham challenged God's reasoning with "Shouldn't the judge of all the earth do what is just?"[15] In fear and trepidation, Abraham nevertheless negotiated: if there are fifty righteous people, wouldn't it be unjust to destroy them along with the others? God agreed. How about forty-five? God agreed again—no destruction if forty-five good people reside there. And so their bargaining went until Abraham got to ten. And God agreed. Nine or less, we don't know. God destroyed them all.

One of God's biblical taglines, "the God of Abraham, Isaac, and Jacob," situates him in relation to the "Patriarchs," the leading men of the family that God tapped out of all others to be the Chosen People. By contrast to Abraham, the stories about his son Isaac focus on Isaac's youth (near-sacrifice by his dad) and his old age. Isaac simply doesn't do much in the Bible.[16] Even the famous story of how Isaac was tricked into giving his younger son the elder's blessing is more about his son Jacob than it is about Isaac.

Jacob, on the other hand, rivals his grandfather Abraham in the amount of biblical press he garnered. But Jacob was the baseball cap and sagging "see my underwear" pants to Abraham's fedora and neat wool suit. Jacob was a trickster, most famously tricking his older brother Esau out of Esau's eldest-son status—first by trading lentils for Esau's birthright and then by pulling the wool, so to speak, over Isaac's milky-white eyes to gain the one and only eldest-son blessing.

This blessing, which passed on not only family leadership but also the covenant torch of God's promise, was confirmed for Jacob in one of his fantastic, otherworldly night experiences. Alone, and with a rock for a pillow, Jacob dreamed of a ladder reaching to heaven on which angels were climbing up and down. God talked to him in the dream, reiterating the family promise plus assurance of God's presence. When Jacob woke up, he was understandably flustered, figured that this must be a sacred space, named the place "God's House" (Hebrew *Bethel*), and marked it with the pillow rock. But he was no Abraham. Even after this divine affirmation, Jacob added a list of conditions (God's presence, food, clothes, safe travel home) that must be met by God in order for Jacob to sign on.[17]

Another of Jacob's famously unusual nocturnal experiences left him with a limp and a new name, Israel. It happened after Jacob had acquired quite a large family—a couple of wives, a couple of concubines, eleven sons, and a daughter. In this particular incident, Jacob was again sleeping alone, when "a man wrestled with him until dawn." The Bible can be exasperatingly tightfisted with details, relating extraordinary events in a matter-of-fact style that belies the questionable nature of what's happening. That's true here. Jacob's opponent is described with the Hebrew word *ish*, "man," and that's all. Whoever he was, as they wrestled into the night, it was an even match, with no clear winner. By the end, though, Jacob had been renamed "Israel" and secured a blessing. Although the narrator doesn't tell the identity of the night man, Jacob interpreted him as none other than God and presumed to name that place Penuel (or Peniel), meaning "Face of God," because, he exclaimed, "I have seen God face to face, and lived."[18]

It is this Jacob, renamed Israel, whose twelve sons became the eponymous ancestors of the nation of Israel. One of those, Judah, gave rise to the tribe associated with the southern kingdom. Judah was an ancestor of David, with whom God made a royal covenant, and through whom Jesus' genealogy must be traced, based on the Hebrew scriptures' messianic traditions. So Judah's a big deal. Another of Jacob's sons, Joseph, became associated with the northern kingdom, particularly through his sons Ephraim and Manasseh. (This is a different Joseph from Jesus' "father," discussed below.)

Joseph's story dominates the end of Genesis (chapters 37–50) and is retold in Andrew Lloyd Webber's musical *Joseph and the Amazing Technicolor Dreamcoat*. Indeed, Joseph is remembered as a dreamer whose receipt of a coat that marked Jacob's favoritism toward him made him vulnerable to the machinations of his jealous brothers. Having tricked Jacob (touché), they dispensed with Joseph, first by leaving him in a pit, and then (discovering that they could make some money) by selling him off to some traders passing through on the way to Egypt. Consequently, Joseph began his tenure in Egypt as a slave, but after some dramatic ups and downs during which he demonstrated his dream-interpreting abilities (and because God was looking out for him), Joseph was promoted to a position something like prime minister—second only to the pharaoh. When famine struck at home, Joseph was able to help his family (and reconcile with his brothers), settling them with him in Egypt. Genesis ends with these descendants of Abraham comfortably settled as VIPs in Egypt.

NEW BEGINNINGS: FREEDOM FROM, FREEDOM TO

The next book, Exodus, immediately explains that circumstances had changed, and it is into these new circumstances that one of the most influential Old Testament figures comes: Moses, prophet par excellence, liberator, and law giver. Moses first enters the scene as a baby, a baby who escaped the pharaoh's genocidal plot to have all male Hebrew infants murdered at birth. It's a great story of female heroics, between the midwives, who wouldn't comply with the pharaoh's evil scheme; the pharaoh's daughter (ironically), who rescued the orphaned Moses from his river-going basket; and Moses' sister (a relationship unbeknownst to the princess), who volunteered Moses' mother (also unbeknownst to the princess) to serve as his wet nurse until he could be weaned. The young adult Moses murdered an Egyptian who was beating a Hebrew slave, and had to flee. On the lam, Moses married Zipporah and became a shepherd for her father, alternately called Reuel and Jethro. (All this is narrated within the first two chapters of Exodus.)

Moses is the one whom God tapped to liberate the Hebrew people from Egypt, to tell the pharaoh, "Let my people go." The brief commissioning story is packed with memorable moments—God spoke to Moses from a burning bush that didn't burn up; God revealed God's "name"; and Moses is portrayed as a man of self-doubt and poor public-speaking skills, willing to argue with God.[19]

It was Moses who confronted the pharaoh, led the fleeing Israelites out of Egypt, parted the intervening waters that they might cross (and the Egyptians drown), and brought them on toward Sinai and the Promised Land. Moses is also known as the great law giver, because he mediated a new covenant between God and the Hebrew people. The terms of this agreement—the detailed regulations, ordinances, and instructions—would become the heart of the Torah and Jewish identity. In scholarly circles, this covenant is sometimes called the Mosaic or Sinaitic covenant because it was transmitted at Mount Sinai. There Moses received from God the Ten Commandments, and then some.[20]

Afterward, Moses led the band on, through the desert wilderness toward the Promised Land. The narrator explains that because of the people's persistent whining, their generally ungrateful attitude, and especially their failure to fully trust God, God determined that none of this generation would see the Promised Land.[21] Even Moses was denied entry into the "land of milk and honey."[22] Nevertheless, he got mighty close. Moses pulled up at the edge of the land, on the plains of Moab, and proceeded to deliver sage advice and reiteration of the finer points of God's instruction. Deuteronomy purports to be Moses' final words to the Israelites before they entered Canaan, and before he died . . . which he did at the end of that book.

The civil rights leader Martin Luther King, Jr.'s, stirring "I've Been to the Mountaintop" speech, delivered in Memphis on April 3, 1968, is remembered best for its conclusion. There, King likens himself to Moses, leading people out of their wilderness and into a new place and time of prosperity and peace. Despite his own suspicion that, like Moses, he would die before experiencing that situation himself, King declared with prophetic hope, "[God]'s allowed me to go up to the mountain. And I've looked over. And I've seen the Promised Land. I may not get there with you. But I want you to know tonight, that we, as a people, will get to the Promised Land!"[23]

It is difficult to overstate Moses' importance in the Bible and in religious tradition. He is the main character, the leading man, in 80 percent of the Pentateuch or Torah. Sometimes also called the "Five Books of Moses," tradition credits him with their authorship. Most people remember the baby Moses in the bulrushes story, and his many glorious exploits as an adult. His murderous act, which set the course of his adult life, is seldom noted. Moses casts a long shadow over much of the Old Testament and into the New. He is remembered as the great liberator, a friend of God's, an exemplary prophet, and an epitome of the reluctant but great leader. He is the prototype for his successor Joshua (who also leads the Israelites through a liminal body of water), for Elijah (a prophet who also meets God on Mount Sinai or Horeb), and for Jesus (who goes into and out of Egypt and delivers a sermon "on the mount").

Joshua was Moses' successor as leader of the Israelites, but he wasn't Moses' son.[24] Joshua is described several times as Moses' assistant, and he is the only one (other than Caleb) of "that generation" who was allowed to enter the Promised Land. He served under Moses as a kind of military general, acolyte, right-hand man, and scout throughout the years of wilderness wandering, so he was an obvious choice. The biblical book of Joshua tells about how, as a military general and religious leader, he led the Israelites into the Promised Land and violently took it from the Canaanite peoples who inhabited the land. So it was Joshua who "fit de battle of Jericho," and Joshua who divvied up the territory among the Israelite tribes. Before he died, Joshua gathered all the Israelites together, in a covenant renewal ceremony to determine whether or not they would continue to follow the instructions of God. With rather transparent rhetoric, Joshua basically said, "It's up to you, of course. But as for me and mine, we'll keep the covenant."

The narrator explains that the rest of the people said they would, too.[25] Joshua's death pretty much ends the book.

After the Israelites had settled, they seem to have operated in predominantly tribal groups, with leaders cropping up every now and then to remind and reconfirm the people's religious loyalty and (not unrelated) to defeat whatever Canaanite group was causing them the most grief. These "judges" were defined less by judicial than by military and religious leadership. A judge became so because God raised him or her (there is one female biblical judge) up at a particular historical moment to deliver the Israelites. Judgeship was not an elected or hereditary position. The most well known of these judges is Samson, who is also described as a "nazirite" (sometimes capitalized in English translations). This was not a requirement for judgeship. His nazirite condition set him apart from others, and was marked by leaving his hair uncut and abstaining from alcohol. Although Samson is far from the greatest or most upstanding of the judges (he failed or is otherwise morally suspect in nearly every way), he takes up the most space of any in the book.[26] Samson is larger-than-life—a party boy, hotheaded, a philanderer, and a smart aleck. He's remembered most for his extraordinary strength and sexual dalliance. Samson fought a lion mano a mano, or hand to paw, as the case may be, and won with ease. He killed 1,000 men with "the jawbone of an ass," and later carried off a Philistine city's gates and gateposts. Samson tangled with the Philistines not only because they were the enemy du jour but also because he found their women irresistible—a fateful combination.

His famous undoing came at the hands of a foreign woman, Delilah, who sweet-talked him into telling her the secret of his strength (his long hair) and that was the end of it, his hair, that is. The bald Samson was easily overcome by his enemies, who took out his eyes, sent him to prison, and put him to work. They neglected regular shearings, though, so when his hair grew long enough again, in a dramatic curtain-dropping act, Samson turned what the Philistines hoped would be a spectacle of his humiliation at their temple celebration into the greatest bloodletting of his life. He pushed down the pillars that supported the structure so that its massive tumbling crushed more

Philistines that day than Samson had killed in his entire life, the narrator exclaims.[27]

In 1991, the Pulitzer Prize–winning journalist Seymour Hersh published a controversial best-seller titled *The Samson Option*, concerning the nuclear capabilities and intentions of the modern state of Israel. Hersh argued that like the biblical Samson, Israel would use its nuclear weapons to self-destruct if it were overrun by its enemies. In another military reference to Samson, the 1995 Oslo Accords led to Israel's disbanding its special forces "Samson Unit," designed to infiltrate Gaza.

BUILDING A KINGDOM

Despite the biblical Samson's heroics, the Philistines continued to be Israel's archenemies. Because of this enduring threat, according to one line of biblical thinking, the Israelite tribes clamored for a bona fide national king to replace the scattershot system of judges. The man who would negotiate this transition is Samuel, and his story is tangled up with Saul's and David's. Like many of the biblical greats, Samuel was born only after his mother, Hannah, had despaired of ever having children. When she finally bore Samuel, Hannah sang a song which Luke's gospel tells us that Mary, the mother of Jesus, repeated generations later—her "Magnificat."[28]

Samuel served as a prophet, judge, priest, and kingmaker in the transition from tribes to nation and from judges to king. Although he was grooming his good-for-nothing sons to succeed him (in blatant contradiction to the nonhereditary nature of judgeships), God directed him to anoint Saul to serve as (the first) king.[29] Samuel continued to work as an adviser and priest during Saul's reign, but when things went south (so to speak) with Saul,[30] who was abandoned by God and deteriorated into spells of madness, Samuel secretly anointed David to succeed Saul as king after Saul's death. Samuel is the only biblical character, apart from Jesus, to come back from the dead in order to give counsel to the living. With the help of a kind and conscientious witch, Saul summoned Samuel, who was not happy about it. Samuel told Saul that he would lose to the Philistines. In the series *Battlestar Galactica*, Saul Tigh is the ship *Galactica*'s executive officer. Like the biblical Saul, he is a tormented leader who fears that he is losing his sanity.[31]

When the biblical narrative describes the Philistines' army, it adds that David was among them—and not as an Israelite spy. But the Philistines became worried about David's loyalty and ditched him. This can be quite confusing, since David would become the single most important Israelite king. Nevertheless, he spent some of his pre-king years hanging out with lawless men, even serving in the army of Israel's archrival, of all things. In a word, here are the best-known things about or most commonly associated with David (in roughly chronological order): music, Goliath, Jonathan, Jerusalem, eternal covenant, Bathsheba, Absalom, and Solomon.

To take them briefly, one at a time: After Saul lost favor with God (a tragic story, if there ever was one), God commissioned Samuel to anoint the next king, even though Saul was still king. In a narrative with admirable tension, God directed Samuel to anoint the new king from among Jesse the Bethlehemite's sons. After David was anointed, but in a completely unrelated turn of events, he was brought into Saul's court to provide music therapy for the manic-depressive Saul. David's reputation as a musician was so good that the biblical book of songs (Psalms) is attributed to him, and he may actually have written some of its pieces.

The narrator explains that Saul "loved David very much and David became his armor-bearer."[32] This is odd because in the next episode, the David vs. Goliath story, Saul is portrayed as never having met David.[33] Again—different literary sources, woven together, and not always seamlessly. In that episode, the narrator shows the Israelite army in a terrible predicament. It stood face to face with the Philistine army. If one of the Israelite warriors fought and won a man-to-man battle against one of the Philistines, then the whole enemy army would consider itself defeated. The Philistine representative was a monster of a man, a giant champion warrior named Goliath, so no one stepped up. Goliath reissued his challenge, without answer from the Israelites, for forty days. Then, David just happened to hear him. The narrator explains that David was only a child and was usually busy tending the family sheep. On this day, though, he was visiting his eldest brothers, who were in the army. When David heard the challenge, he persuaded Saul—by explaining his shepherding defense skills and God's protection of him—to let him fight Goliath. Rather than go toe to toe with the monster-man, David finessed a single slingshot strike to nail Goliath fatally with a stone between the eyes. "And he fell facedown on the ground."[34]

When people refer to David and Goliath today in a nonbiblical context, they usually mean to convey the idea of a gross imbalance of power between rivals. For example, an editorial in the *New York Times* concerning online music piracy was titled "When David Steals Goliath's Music,"[35] and when a Saskatchewan farmer was sued by Monsanto for having genetically modified canola in his fields without paying for the seeds, a journalist called the case "Biotech's David and Goliath."[36]

Saul's son, Jonathan, was smitten with David after the incident with Goliath. The rest of David's young adulthood is filled with romance and adventure. Jonathan became his best friend, and David's popularity soared among the people on account of his continued military successes. Saul's daughter, Michal, also fell in love with David. And Saul grew ever more bitter. Saul agreed to let Michal marry David for the gruesome price of 100 Philistine foreskins (thinking that David would die trying). David brought him the stinking penis parts, and the lovers married; but Saul became David's enemy. In separate incidents, both Jonathan and Michal saved David from their father's murderous intent. Finally David simply had to flee. That's how he ended up, an ancient Robin Hood, with his band of lawless men, occasionally signing on as a mercenary soldier. Ultimately, though, he didn't fight against his own people, and the narrators tell that he never disrespected Saul, "God's anointed."

After Saul died, David became king; and after some years he established Jerusalem as the nation's capital. David clinched the loyalty of all Israelite tribes when he brought the sacred Ark of the Covenant into this "City of David." Yet when David determined to build a proper temple for God and to house this important religious object, his court prophet and religious adviser, Nathan, told him that God had other plans for David. Namely, that God would build David a house, in a sense, with an unconditional, eternal covenant.[37] That is, God would build up David's family and reputation so that even if he or his descendants did wrong, someone from David's line would always be king. Indeed, David is remembered as the greatest king of Israel, with a special connection to God, "a man after his own heart,"[38] and any future king would necessarily come from his line.

The part about God's punishing for wrongdoing but not taking away the throne was put to the test soon enough. When the narrator explains that the season for kings to go to war had come but that David stayed in Jerusalem, we know that something will go wrong.[39] Sure enough, David spied the beautiful Bathsheba, took her, slept with her, and got her pregnant (all in about three verses). He was in a bind, though, because she was already married. In the face of her husband's upstanding righteousness, David orchestrated the husband's death and married Bathsheba.

God was not happy and promised trouble and discord within David's house. And so it was that soon afterward, one son (Amnon) raped his half sister, Tamar, and was subsequently murdered by another son (Tamar's full brother), Absalom. Absalom went on to instigate a revolt against his father and succeeded in routing David from Jerusalem. In the ensuing power struggle, Absalom was killed, and David was heartbroken. When David was old and infirm, yet another son (Adonijah) rebelled against him by presuming to be king, before Bathsheba successfully lobbied for one of her sons, Solomon, to become David's successor. All this drama is excluded from another biblical book's bio of David: Chronicles includes no mention of David's working for the Philistines, his adultery, or his domestic troubles. In those books, David is squeaky-clean, and Solomon smoothly succeeds him to build the temple that, Chronicles explains, David had prepared with great forethought down to its finest detail.

Solomon proved to be a fine successor, following the trajectory of nation-building from Saul's initial efforts at tribal unity to David's clinching that unity and establishing a capital city. Solomon expanded the nation and the court; developed international alliances; and took on significant architectural projects, of which the most ambitious and celebrated is the temple in Jerusalem.

Solomon is remembered not only for this awesome house of God but also for wisdom, wealth, and women. In one of his parables, Jesus referred to Solomon's rich finery.[40] Solomon demonstrated the first trait early in his monarchy, when called upon to judge a particularly knotty case. Two prostitutes each laid claim to the same baby. Solomon said that he would cut the baby in half and give them each a share. Woman A said, "That sounds fair"; Woman B said, "That sounds awful. Give the baby to Woman A." So it was that wise Solomon determined that Woman B must be the mother.[41] Proverbs and Ecclesiastes, with their sage advice and philosophy, are attributed to Solomon. His reputation as a lover is reflected in the fact that the erotic poetry in the Song of Songs is also attributed to him (and is sometimes called the Song of Solomon).

The country prospered under Solomon's rule. The narrator says, "Judah and Israel were as numerous as the sand by the sea; they ate and drank and were happy."[42] During his reign, Solomon married many women (and took many more concubines), ostensibly to secure international partnerships. The trouble, the narrators note, is that the charming and hospitable Solomon built those foreign women temples of their own, a grave temptation to the Israelites to worship other gods and goddesses. This was the Achilles' heel of the nation.

The temple that Solomon built in Jerusalem was one illustration of Israel's wealth gained during his monarchy. Its elegant architecture and detailed floor plan facilitated its function as the site of sacrifice and a reminder both of God's holiness and of God's choosing to be specially present to these, God's chosen people. After the Ark of the Covenant was solemnly brought into the temple, Solomon prayed a dedication of the temple to God, and God responded with a reiteration of the Davidic covenant. This time, though, God added conditions: "If you . . . then I; but if you . . . , then I will cut Israel off from the land ... and this house will become a heap of ruins."[43] In the Bible's interpretation of history, those other temples would prove to be problematic. Solomon's successor lost hold of the united nation, and a couple of hundred years later, the northern kingdom (Israel) was taken by the Assyrians. Nearly 150 years after that, the southern kingdom (Judah) was defeated by the Babylonians.

PROPHETS: SPOKESMEN FOR GOD

With the advent of a monarchy came a number of prophets—people who functioned as spokesmen for God (and for or against the state). Some, such as Nathan (David's court prophet), appear as characters within a greater narrative. Other prophets, such as Amos, have books named after them. For our grand overview purposes here, I'll discuss briefly a few of the most important Old Testament prophets: Elijah and Elisha, Isaiah, Jeremiah, Ezekiel, Jonah, and Daniel (though in the arrangement of the Hebrew Bible, Daniel is not counted among the prophets). Among them, Elijah (a freelance loner of a prophet in the northern kingdom of Israel) and his successor, Elisha, fall into the first camp—prophets who appear in narratives about them and their times. The others all have books named after them and are mostly remembered for what they said.

Two people didn't die normal, human deaths in the Old Testament. They are Enoch, who instead "walked with God; then was no more, because God took him away,"[44] and Elijah. There isn't much in the Bible about Enoch, but there is a lot about Elijah. Because Elijah didn't die and get buried, some believe(d) that he will return. He is mentioned at the end of Malachi, the final book of the Old Testament prophets, as coming back in the end-time.[45] Every year, during the Passover dinner, one cup of wine is left untouched, and the door is briefly opened, for this prophet, who is expected to return and herald the Messiah's coming. In the New Testament, John the Baptist, who behaved a bit like a prophet, was suspected by some, as he laid the groundwork for Jesus' ministry, to be none other than Elijah returned.

Elijah was a prophet in the northern kingdom around 850 BCE. His greatest challenge, it seems, was reminding the Israelites of their promise to worship only their one God and to avoid the gods of the other people around them. Remember those temples that Solomon built for the gods of his foreign wives? Not good, the Bible says. Elijah made a name for himself as a burr in the side of the Israelites, especially of their king Ahab, who had married the foreigner Jezebel. The trouble, as far as the biblical narrators saw it, was that these imported queens imported their own gods and goddesses into Israelite religious practice.

When Elijah's cloak fell during his dramatic exit from earth into heaven in a fiery chariot in the midst of a whirlwind, Elisha picked up the mantle and carried on Elijah's work as a prophet in the northern kingdom. (Elijah "passed the mantle," in other words.) Whatever wonders Elijah accomplished, Elisha also did . . . and then some. Elisha is probably best known, however, for consigning a pack of disrespectful youths to bear-mauled deaths after they teased him for being bald. I am not kidding (2 Kings 2:23–25).

Isaiah was a prophet in Judah from about 740 to 700 BCE. Because he was consulted by kings and had access to the innermost part of the Jerusalem temple, it's safe to assume that he was a respected man with considerable political as well as religious power. His name is given to the whole book of Isaiah, but the whole book does not come from him, as it contains sections from the exilic and postexilic periods (including references to Cyrus II, for example).[46] Isaiah claims to have volunteered to serve as a prophet when he overheard God ask the divine council, "Whom shall I send?" Isaiah said, "Here I am, send me."[47]

This is in striking contrast to Jeremiah, who did not want to be a prophet. Like Moses, he protested that he had trouble with public speaking. As with Moses, God would not be deterred.[48] Jeremiah is another Old Testament prophet with a book named after him; most of this book may be his prophetic words, but some of it is surely not. Jeremiah prophesied for decades, from about 640 BCE up through the fall of Jerusalem to the Babylonians in 587 BCE. The burden of prophesying a harsh message over and over again took its toll on Jeremiah, and his book is punctuated with poignant complaints. He is sometimes called the "weeping prophet." The whole book of Lamentations is attributed to him. We have a word whose origin is the name of this unfortunate yet eloquent prophet: "jeremiad," which describes a sorrowful or angry expression—a complaint.

Ezekiel, the third of the "big three" Old Testament prophets, seemed to be quite satisfied with his lot as a prophet. He ate a scroll on which were the words he was to prophesy, "words of lamentation, mourning, and woe"; but they were "as sweet as honey" to his tongue.[49] He worked during the Babylonian captivity from 597 BCE (he was among the first set of exiles taken ten years before Judah fell) until sometime past 587 BCE.

Ezekiel "saw d'wheel, way up in the middle of the air," in the words of a popular spiritual. Indeed, he had many fantastic visions. At the beginning of the book, Ezekiel describes a fantastic and highly detailed vision of God's chariot, accompanied by winged creatures, with wheels inside wheels, and eyes all around. The Jewish Talmud warns against a young person's studying this passage, because of the dangers it could pose to one's mental health. There is a variety of mysticism called *merkavah*, from the Hebrew word for "chariot," that focuses on Ezekiel's chariot vision; and kabbalah and Hasidic philosophy give a great deal of attention to the mind-expanding possibilities of its interpretation. In another vision, a spirit took Ezekiel by the hair and dragged him flying through the sky from Babylon (in present-day Iraq) to Jerusalem to see all the wicked things that were going on in the temple (and that ultimately justified its destruction, from this biblical perspective).[50] In another, Ezekiel saw human bones re-form themselves into people in response to God's word that Israel would be a vital people again.[51]

By contrast, Jonah could hardly have been more prosaic. The only one of the "minor prophets" that I'll discuss in this chapter, Jonah deserves attention because of his episode with the whale. Besides, he's quite a character. When Jonah was called to prophesy against Nineveh, the capital city of Israel's nemesis Assyria, he caught a ship going in the opposite direction. To correct him and get him on the right track, God caused a storm to come up. Jonah was thrown overboard, and a big fish swallowed him. Three days later it spat Jonah up, back where he had started. This time, he headed to Nineveh, as instructed. The book is a neat little story with anti-xenophobic implications. Jonah is not an admirable prophet. For one thing, he prophesies only once, and it's only a single sentence. (This, by comparison to the pages and pages and pages of prophecies issued by other biblical prophets.) Also, in contrast to Jonah's disobedience, his Ninevite audience immediately took the prophecy to heart and repented, from the king on down to the last person. Even all the Ninevite animals wore the sackcloth of repentance. This infuriated Jonah, who pouted and complained to God. Jonah's character is, finally, a humorous one, though the book conveys a sober corrective message: that God's care and concern extend well beyond the individual or special group. Indeed, its concluding statement suggests that God loves even the enemy foreigners, and (we animal lovers are happy to hear) cows, too.

Daniel—prophet, or not a prophet? Daniel is not among the Hebrew Bible prophets, but he is among the Old Testament prophets for reasons of both character and canon. The book of Daniel is not part of the Prophets section of the *Tanakh*. Rather, it is part of the Writings section, probably because it was composed and accepted into the canon relatively late.[52] Also, the character Daniel acts less like a prophet than like an apocalyptic visionary. For example, God didn't speak directly to him with a message for Daniel's contemporaries; rather, Daniel had symbols-rich visions about the future. Nevertheless, Daniel did tell what was to come, satisfying later ideas of what constitutes a prophet. So generally speaking, Daniel is considered a prophet by Christians but not by Jews.

The biblical Daniel is described as a Jewish man in exile in Babylon who stood out by refusing to compromise his faith and worship like the Babylonians. He thrived on a meager but strictly kosher diet and miraculously survived being thrown into a lion's den because God was with him. In a truly apocalyptic style, he related visions of powerful nations rising and falling and of a time when God would finally make things right again. Like Joseph long before him (Daniel's character may be modeled in part on Joseph's), Daniel interpreted dreams and rose to a position of considerable prominence in the country of his exile. Unlike Joseph or any other man in the Old Testament, however, Daniel described an idea that had become popular during the time that his book was written (around 164 BCE)—resurrection from the dead.

It is in the book of Daniel that Michael, Israel's guardian and chief of the angelic princes, inaugurates a resurrection. Daniel is told that when Michael arises and earthly tensions reach fever pitch, "Many of those who sleep in the dust of the earth shall awake, some to everlasting life, and some to shame and everlasting contempt."[53] Michael is the champion of the faithful in another apocalyptic battle narrated in Revelation.[54] The great archangel, Gabriel, also appears in the book of Daniel, explaining about the end-time. Gabriel appears again in Luke's gospel to announce to the "highly favored one," Mary, that she has been chosen to bear God's son, Jesus. There are countless visual representations of this awesome exchange, titled the Annunciation.

THE PATIENCE OF JOB

Job (pronounced like Joe with a b on the end) also has a book named after him. Job is popularly known for his patience, his suffering, and his righteousness. "The patience of Job" is supposed to be quite remarkable, saintly even. Googling the phrase yields about 101,000 hits. Shakespeare's character Falstaff declares, "I am as poor as Job, my Lord, but not so patient."[55] This patience is understood as Job's response to suffering, demonstrating his righteousness, but that's like saying Caribbean food is known for its heat: There's so much more to it than that—and it's not even entirely accurate. Job suffered, but he hardly fits the popular model of patience.[56] And what the book identifies as his righteousness is not the product of graciously accepting in stoic silence the misfortune that (God in) life doles out; on the contrary.

In the biblical story, Job, a man from Uz (not necessarily Jewish), was considered by none other than God to be upstanding, blameless, and righteous in every way. He was then subjected to terrible affliction—mental, physical, and spiritual—because of a wager God made with the *satan*[57] to prove whether Job was God-fearing for the sake of being God-fearing or because God did and could give Job so much.

Job did not suffer in silence. As a matter of fact, the rather large biblical book of Job is composed of lots of talk, and much of it is Job's complaints. Job complained about his trouble, he complained about the companions who talk with him, and he complained about God. So Job's righteousness and patience should not be understood as those of some hangdog abuse victim who whimpers about deserving the pain and abuse he suffers. Rather, Job shook his fist at God, demanded justification or at least some explanation, and berated his "friends" for encouraging him to fess up and admit that he simply couldn't be perfect and must somehow have brought on these terrible experiences. Job consistently maintained his innocence in the face of suffering, and he wrestled with the silence of God.

At the end, after a monologue from God about God's greatness and the intricacies of the natural world that has seemingly nothing to do with the rest of the book (why the innocent Job was suffering), Job stopped talking. Job's final words were to say that he had said too much. Many translations render Job saying something like, "I despise myself and repent in dust and ashes."[58] This is certainly one valid translation, but the Hebrew is very rich. The word translated as "despise" needn't mean "despise" or "hate" with a kind of distaste. Rather, it connotes the "refusing," or "rejecting" of setting something aside. The word translated as "repent" is one that in Hebrew can bear the sense of "comfort" or "consolation" as well as being sorry, changing one's mind, or recanting. It's a very different word from the one the prophets regularly use to get people to repent and turn from their sinful ways. Although the verse can certainly be read in its traditional sense of an awed and chastened Job, its translation possibilities also yield the paradoxical sense of setting Self aside to discover exactly who one is—a discovery that lends comfort and consolation.

Add to that the nature of God's speech, "out of the whirlwind," and one finds a Zen-like moment—a koan followed by the possibility of aha enlightenment. God's speech is radically different from what we expect after reading the rest of the book. In it, God says nothing about Job's suffering, nothing about reward and punishment, nothing about justice. Rather, God describes in remarkable, poetic detail knowledge and control of the nonhuman natural world, from its beginnings, "when the morning stars sang together," to "the gates of death," from the "springs of the sea" to the constellations above, and from the care and feeding of baby ravens to the midwifery of wild goats. It could be that, like a Zen koan, God's speech invites a radical shift of thinking and being that takes Job outside himself to look categorically differently on the world and his place in it. Job's response, then, is not necessarily to say that he is puny and worthless; but he recognizes deeply and profoundly exactly who and how he is, and this is a comfort.

As if in confirmation, God wraps up the story by declaring that Job has spoken about God what is right, in contrast to Job's companions who had tried so desperately to justify and exonerate God. Job's righteousness, then, is inseparable from his protestation. His patience is as much a refusal to compromise his integrity as it is his endurance through suffering. The narrator ends by saying that God gave Job more children and restored his wealth.

JESUS: THE REASON FOR THE
ENTIRE NEW TESTAMENT

Up to this point, everyone we've described appears in the Hebrew Bible Old Testament. After this point, everyone appears in the New Testament. To claim an exhaustive description of Jesus here would be folly at best, heresy at worst. For our purposes, in ten words or less: Jesus is *the* guy of the New Testament. What is not a description of his birth, life, death, and resurrection is a description of their implications. Consequently, I discuss much of the information associated with Jesus (for example, the Marys, Bethlehem, the cross) more fully in other chapters. Although there are countless volumes and a whole ongoing seminar devoted to determining what is and is not "historical" about Jesus, I will treat him here as I've treated the people described above—as a biblical character. Because Jesus is distinct from those other people, though, by the fact that he is also considered divine, I will discuss him again in Chapter 13, "God Names, Beings, and Doings."

"Christ" is not Jesus' name, first or last. It is the Greek translation (*christos*) of the Hebrew word *meshiach*, meaning "anointed one," and it serves as a title, a description of how believers interpret Jesus' role and significance (as a messiah). "Jesus" is a good Jewish name. In his time, it was an updated version of Joshua, meaning something like "the one who saves." Indeed, Jesus the biblical character is a Jewish man whom New Testament writers believed to be the incarnation of God sent by God (this can be confusing)—God's son—to save people from their sins.

Depending on whom you ask, the Bible portrays Jesus as a radical pacifist, a militant religious reformer, a political gadfly, a wise sage and teacher, a social justice activist, a miracle worker, a healer, an animal lover, a feminist, and so on. The gospels support each of these profiles and more. As we've seen, there are four biographies of Jesus in the New Testament. That is, there is no single description of Jesus in the Bible; rather, there are several different ones. They are all written not by disinterested observers but by people who believed that he was extraordinary, somehow divine, and the one who fulfilled "the scriptures." They also agree in portraying Jesus as a Jewish man from first-century Palestine (specifically, the Galilean region) whose person, teachings, and actions inspired people to follow him, who, though innocent, died a criminal death and then came to life again. It is through these four evangelists, the four gospels, the letters of Paul, and several anonymous authors that we have the material to describe Jesus as a figure in the Bible. Jesus himself didn't write any of it.

The bulk of the gospels concerns the three years or so of Jesus' public ministry. Only Matthew and Luke include stories about his birth and infancy. Luke also includes a brief mention of Jesus' circumcision, accompanied by an auspicious blessing, and followed by a story demonstrating a precocious Jesus at twelve years old engaged in wise discourse with Jewish sages in the temple.[59] Although the gospel of John is not explicit about Jesus being baptized, it agrees with the other gospels that, in the context of baptism, the Holy Spirit, like a dove, descended from heaven upon Jesus, marking him as the unique Son of God.[60] This launched his adult ministry of teaching, preaching, and healing. During this three-year period, Jesus amassed a following, including a core group of disciples—twelve men, in particular.

Toward the end of this period, the synoptic gospels reiterate God's baptismal declaration (and the uniqueness) of Jesus as "my chosen/ beloved son" in an episode called the Transfiguration. Witnessed by three disciples, Jesus was dazzlingly transfigured on a mountain in the company of the Old Testament greats Moses and Elijah, who spoke with him.[61] All four gospels further develop the special nature of Jesus' role by narrating his celebratory entrance into Jerusalem at Passover. The crowd joyfully announced Jesus with monarchal imagery, "Hosanna!" (meaning "Save!"), and as the one "who comes in the name of the Lord," thereby starting the events that would lead to his death.[62] In addition to the general characteristics noted above, the gospels all agree that Jesus was crucified in Jerusalem during the Passover season.[63] Despite his death, the New Testament writers also agree that, unlike any other person, Jesus came to life again, even though his resurrected form wasn't always immediately recognizable to his friends and disciples.

It was out of their belief in the extraordinary nature of Jesus' capacity to reconcile humanity to God that the New Testament writers composed their biographies (the gospels); church history (Acts); and letters of advice, instruction, and encouragement (the rest)—"so that," the author of John's gospel writes, "you may believe that Jesus is the Christ, the son of God, and that by believing, you may have life in his name."[64] On the basis of such New Testament texts, Christians believe that Jesus is the incarnation of God and that because he was a uniquely sinless human being who sought with divine love to redeem people to God, he could choose to die as an ultimate sacrifice for human sin so that those who believe in him would be forgiven and enjoy eternal life with God.

Jesus is not a character, per se, in much of the New Testament apart from the gospels. The *implications* of Jesus, what Jesus *means*, are what preoccupy Paul and the others responsible for all the other books of the New Testament—except Revelation. In a few verses of Revelation, the apocalyptic book that closes the canon, Jesus is envisioned during the end-time, both in heaven (as a lamb with seven horns and seven eyes, who opens the seven seals of a cosmic scroll) and on earth (when Jesus will return and stand on Mount Zion).

CHARACTERS FROM JESUS' EARLY YEARS

For most New Testament writers, belief in Jesus as the son of God precluded an ordinary conception and birth. Nevertheless, Jesus has a genealogy that includes human parents—Mary and Joseph. Although Jesus was understood to be conceived by the Holy Spirit, not by Joseph, his genealogy is traced through Joseph, whose lineage (according to both Matthew and Luke—the ones that tell about Jesus' birth) goes back through David's line. In other words, thanks to his surrogate father, Joseph, Jesus is part of David's family. As we've already seen, it is very important politically and theologically that this be so.

Joseph's name, of course, reflects his far distant uncle, Joseph the son of Jacob. The New Testament Joseph, stepfather of Jesus, is described as a carpenter by trade, something that he taught to Jesus. What little is said of Joseph the "father" of Jesus in the Bible is complimentary, willingly going along with the divine plan despite his apparent cuckoldedness. We don't actually know how things were for Joseph given this unprecedented state of affairs, but it couldn't have been easy.

John the Baptist gets more press than Joseph in the New Testament and is more consistently represented across the four gospels. John the Baptist (who is different from the authors of the gospel, the letters, and Revelation) is portrayed as a reformer, a radical loner who called for change. He lived in the wilderness desert, as a kind of wild man, clothed in animal skins and living on locusts and wild honey. He preached repentance and performed baptisms, in preparation for a new time that God would soon bring about. John the Baptist is interpreted by each of the gospels in light of an Old Testament prophecy from Isaiah.[65] In every gospel, John is depicted as inaugurating Jesus' ministry by baptizing him. During the early days of Barack Obama's presidential campaign, an Iowan observed Oprah Winfrey's public support and called her "John the Baptist," effectively summarizing the extraordinary hopes many Americans pinned on Obama.[66]

Only Matthew and Mark tell about John's gruesome death, another favorite theme of Renaissance painters. According to the story, John's acerbic critique knew no limits; it included an attack on the sex lives of Jewish royalty, which landed him in prison. When the king promised anything to the girl (variously identified as the king's wife or wife's daughter) who danced at his birthday party, she asked for John's head on a platter. Done.[67] Paul never mentions John the Baptist.

It can be confusing to learn that the King Herod who ordered John's execution was not really a king, per se, nor the only Herod of New Testament importance. Because the Jews were under Roman control during this period, their political leaders weren't autonomous monarchs but were granted authority, with Roman oversight. The Herod who ordered John's execution was Herod Antipas, one of three Herods (the others were Archelaus and Philip II), all sons of Herod the Great, the half Jew described in Chapter 4. In a messy web of alliances and desire, Herod Antipas married his brother's wife, very confusingly named Herodias. It was this marriage that incited the righteous ire of John the Baptist.

GOOD-GUY, BAD-GUY DISCIPLES: PETER AND JUDAS

Among Jesus' twelve disciples (a number evoking association with the twelve tribes of Israel), the most famous and infamous, respectively, are Peter and Judas. We read most about them in the gospels. Matthew favors Peter and describes him as Jesus' right-hand man, the one Jesus called "the rock [on whom] I'll build my church,"[68] and to whom

Jesus gave the "keys of kingdom."[69] Consequently, we get both the tradition of Peter as gatekeeper of heaven and the tradition of Roman Catholic popes, who claim lineage back to Peter. Peter's name means "rock" in Greek; it's Cephas in Aramaic, and Simon or Simeon in Hebrew. He goes by all these names in the New Testament. Peter is also a prominent character in the book of Acts, which follows the gospels. There, we see Peter as instrumental, especially among Jews in Jerusalem, in developing the community that would be called Christians. Matthew portrays Peter as walking on water . . . till he realized what he was doing and sank.[70] All four gospels poignantly describe Peter during the night of Jesus' arrest denying three times any association with Jesus.

Peter's fame is matched by Judas's infamy. Judas, called Judas Iscariot to distinguish him from other Judases of the time, is portrayed in the biblical gospels as a traitor who betrayed Jesus to the authorities, ultimately leading to Jesus' crucifixion. Each of the four biblical gospels, as well as the book of Acts (the only other biblical book in which Judas appears) always adds this bio when his name comes up, and Judas is always the last name in gospel lists of the disciples.

Details about Judas are not exactly the same in every gospel. For example, the tradition of Judas receiving thirty pieces of silver from the Romans for leading them to arrest Jesus is found only in Matthew's gospel.[71] And only there is the story of Judas's feeling bad about what he'd done—seeing "that Jesus was condemned, he repented"; when the authorities refused to take back the money they'd paid Judas, he threw it down and "went and hanged himself."[72] Mark hardly mentions Judas at all—Judas simply serves the purpose of handing Jesus over to the authorities.[73] Luke adds Satan to the story, driving Judas through demon possession to commit his traitorous act.[74] John's gospel intensifies the association—in John, Judas is associated with the dark side immediately and consistently (described as "of the devil").[75] Acts' brief mention of Judas is in the context of Peter's efforts to determine whom to appoint as a replacement to retain the important number of twelve disciples. Acts' description of Judas as the betrayer concentrates on his death (either the means—by falling and splitting open, against Matthew's account of Judas hanging himself; or as a gruesome result— his body swelling up and splitting open, possibly after hanging for a while) and cites a couple of psalms as prophecy.[76] Paul, whose writings predate the gospels, doesn't mention Judas at all.

Judas has maintained a powerful hold in popular imagination. From the biblical stories about him, we get the ominous "thirty pieces of silver," also called "blood money" (the amount the authorities paid Judas to bring them to Jesus), which, Matthew explains, fulfills an Old Testament prophecy.[77] Judas is associated with perhaps the second most infamous biblical question: "Is it I, Lord?" when Jesus predicted at the Last Supper that one would betray him.[78] Finally, Judas identified Jesus to the Roman officers by kissing him. A "Judas kiss" has come to refer today to any act of betrayal. Judas has fueled the awful engine of anti-Semitism, not least because his name is a Greek form of Judah, from which we get "Jew." At a concert in 1966, when Bob Dylan took his folk music electric, a fan summed up the crowd's displeasure by calling out, "Judas!" Dylan responded, "I don't believe you. You're a liar."[79] Some people cite this as a watershed moment in Dylan's career, and for popular music in general.

Judas has come down through the ages as a complicated figure— one of Jesus' select group of intimates who nevertheless proved fatal to Jesus. In Judas, the dilemmas of free will and divine predestination crash together. The result is countless stories, poems, musical pieces, artworks, sermons, and films that explore the enigma of this dark disciple.

Recently, a new translation of an ancient text, discovered in Egypt, has added to our fascination with Judas.[80] The *Gospel of Judas* relates things from Judas's perspective and claims that he acted as perhaps the most *loyal* disciple, obeying Jesus' command to do what was necessary in order for Jesus to fulfill his destiny as the sacrificial son of God. It suggests that Judas, portrayed as a favorite of Jesus', was entrusted by Jesus with the distasteful task of handing him over to the authorities, and that Judas knew that he would be excoriated and condemned throughout history for it.

OTHER MEN OF THE NEW TESTAMENT

There are a couple of unnamed men in the New Testament who are nevertheless quite well known. One is the Good Samaritan. He appears in a (gospel of Luke only) teaching story that Jesus tells, as the model of a man who breaks with convention to do a shockingly good deed.[81] I say "shocking" because the Samaritan not only was kind, caring, and generous when others were not, but he was also the paradigmatic archenemy of the one he helped.[82] Jesus' parable—following the question, "Who is my neighbor that I should love him as myself?"—tells about a man attacked, beaten, and robbed by bandits who left him for dead. Two people whose vocational identity should have dictated that they help the man passed him by. By contrast, the Samaritan, whose identity would dictate at least ignoring if not killing the victim, went out of his way both literally and figuratively to make sure the victim was OK, even cared for.

Although few people today appreciate the enmity between first-century Jews and Samaritans, the phrase "Good Samaritan" still denotes a person who gives help to a stranger. "Good Samaritan laws" have been developed in the United States and Canada to protect people who might otherwise be sued for misadventures during their efforts to help. In 2006, Republican legislators drafted a bill that would make it a federal crime to offer aid to illegal immigrants. In a sharp critique, Senator Hillary Clinton quipped, "This bill would literally criminalize the Good Samaritan."[83]

Jesus' story of the Prodigal Son,[84] another anonymous yet famous New Testament character, is the essence of Christianity, Tim Keller maintains in his book *The Prodigal God*.[85] For most of us, this is the only context in which we've heard the word "prodigal." (It means extravagant to the point of wastefulness.) The parable tells about a man who had two sons. One of them went off and blew all his money, got homesick, repented, and returned. Rather than taking him to task for his profligate wastefulness, his father ran to meet him, "killed the fatted calf," and threw a tremendous party. The other brother, responsible and hardworking, was understandably dismayed, and thoroughly ticked off. At which point their father delivers the poignant directive: "Son, you are always with me, and everything I have is yours. Now we should be happy. For this brother of yours was dead, yet is alive again; he was lost, but is now found."

The only parable protagonist with a name is Lazarus. Confusingly, he's not the best-known New Testament Lazarus. In other words, there are two Lazaruses in the New Testament. The best-known Lazarus appears only in John's gospel, where Jesus brings him back from the dead.[86] In light of this, there is a category of creatures called the Lazarus taxon that share the characteristic of reappearance after a break (suggesting extinction) in the fossil record. *A Lazarus Taxon* is now also the name of a box set of music by the rock group Tortoise. The "Lazarus phenomenon" refers to the medically baffling occurrence of a person's "waking up again" after all vital signs are gone.

Jesus must have really been fond of Lazarus, because the shortest verse in the Bible, "Jesus wept," is associated with Lazarus's death (or sympathy with Lazarus's grieving sisters).[87] After Lazarus had been dead for days, in a dramatic moment, Jesus called to him at the door of the tomb, and Lazarus walked out, still wrapped like a mummy.

The other Lazarus, the one from the parable,[88] is a poor man who begged at the gates of a rich man's house. Jesus teaches that after they died, Lazarus was taken to the comfortable "bosom of Abraham," and the rich man was consigned to Hades (sometimes translated "hell"), from where he envied Lazarus's good situation. The rich man begged Abraham to send Lazarus back to warn his family, but Abraham said that if they didn't recognize the authority and take to heart the teachings of Moses and the prophets, then they wouldn't alter their behavior—not even if someone came back from the dead to tell them. So there may be more than an incidental connection between the two Lazaruses, after all.

THE "ONE UNTIMELY BORN": PAUL

Finally, Paul (né Saul). It is entirely possible that without Paul, we'd have no form of Christianity recognizable to us today, or maybe even any Christianity at all. Paul's letters are the earliest of any New Testament texts (this can be confusing, because the gospels are arranged before Paul's letters), and they inspired a number of other letters by other Christians, some of which are also included in the New Testament. Originally from Tarsus, Paul/Saul, seems to have been very much a man of his times—well educated in the ways of Greco-Roman culture (Paul is a Greco-Roman name), but also very much a Jew (Saul is a Jewish name). By his own report, he was passionate about his faith, became a member of the learned sect of Pharisees, and persecuted Christians—until one day, which changed everything.

On the road to Damascus, Paul underwent a dramatic conversion experience. He heard Jesus calling, "Saul, Saul, why do you persecute me?"[89] Revealing himself as the object of Paul's persecution, Jesus told Paul to go into the city, where he would receive further instructions. Paul was blinded until he received those instructions, which specified that he was to preach about Jesus to the gentiles. At that point, "something like scales fell from his eyes,"[90] and Paul could see again. This personal exchange with the risen Jesus compelled Paul to identify himself as an apostle (one "sent forth"), even though he was not a disciple and had not known Jesus before Jesus was crucified. Because Paul had never met the man Jesus, he describes himself as "one untimely born."[91]

After his conversion, Paul became passionately committed to teaching whoever would listen about Jesus. Trained as a tent maker, Paul traveled throughout Asia Minor, preaching the gospel especially to non-Jews. It's tough to know exactly what Jesus' surviving disciples thought of Paul, though there is record, especially in Paul's letter to the Galatians, of sometimes heated exchange between them.[92]

Paul actually spent very little time, energy, or ink telling about Jesus' life and teachings. Rather, he concentrated his teaching and preaching on what he understood to be the radically unique divine-human nature of Jesus and on what the resurrection means for those who believe. Paul interpreted the Jesus Event as far greater than the greatness of a charismatic healer and teacher or preacher simply to be emulated. He preached faith in Jesus, the resurrected Messiah, as the single most important thing, not specific behavior or compliance with social norms. He took his gospel message, "the power of God for salvation to everyone who has faith,"[93] out into the Mediterranean world, starting and nurturing new Christian churches all along the way.

Paul wrote letters to congregations he visited and to groups he intended to visit in order to address particular issues, problems, and questions as he anticipated them or as they arose. These letters include considerable theology and explanation of his understanding of how Jesus' unique humanity-divinity should affect people's lives and thoughts. They demonstrate and are informed by Paul's expectation of the imminent return of Jesus, something that never happened in the immediate way he imagined, but that Christians believe will still occur in the future. Some of those letters, such as Romans, 1 and 2 Corinthians, Galatians, and others, are now books in the Bible. All of them have profoundly influenced the shape of Christianity to a degree inseparable from the religion itself.

TEN

Lovely (and Not So) Ladies

Howiver, I'm not denyin' the women are foolish:
God Almighty made 'em to match the men.

—GEORGE ELIOT, *Adam Bede*

Some time ago, my parents were in the post office waiting to send a Christmas package, while a young woman in front of them was deciding on a style of stamps. The postal worker asked if she'd like the "Madonna with child stamps," and the young woman exclaimed, "Does Madonna have a kid?" Women in the Bible get relatively little attention in the texts themselves, yet they've had enormous influence ever since. From rock stars to halfway houses for recovering prostitutes, the names of biblical women have found their way into our time and place. In recent decades, some of their influence has been due, paradoxically, to the fact that they get so much less attention in the Bible than men. There is burgeoning interest in the whys and wherefores of biblical silences and exclusion, and feminist scholarship has come bearing rich fruit. Although this chapter, like the one before, concentrates on the best-known biblical characters, it also includes discussion of women in the biblical world, in general, and briefly describes some of the results, possibilities, and problems of feminist research in biblical studies.

BEGINNINGS, OR "MOTHER OF ALL LIVING"

In *Wall-E*, a futuristic animated movie released in 2008, a lovely egg-shaped robot is tasked with finding evidence of plant life on Earth. Success would mean that human beings could return and survive again on the planet. The robot's name, an acronym for Extra-terrestrial Vegetation Evaluator, is EVE. The biblical name Eve comes from a play on the Hebrew word for "life" or "living." This Eve is the first human mother in the Bible.

When her name first appears, it is late and bittersweet. After the Garden of Eden story relates how the woman and the man ate the forbidden fruit, it shows a breakdown in relationships—the people became estranged from God, from the nonhuman natural world, and from each other. Then, after God issued critical judgments on each responsible party (the serpent, the woman, and the man), "the man" (*adam*) named "his woman." The process of naming is an act of dominance, which reflects God's earlier judgment on the woman—that "her man" would rule over her—and it reflects a breakdown in what the story suggests had been a relationship of equity. But the name itself is hopeful, expansive, and powerful—Eve, the story glosses, "is the mother of all living."[1]

Although Eve isn't named until the end of the story, it supposes that she is the woman created when God performed extractive surgery on *adam*, and the one who first ate the fruit that God had forbidden. At that point in the narrative, the man and woman realized that they were naked; God came around, asked what they'd done, and issued "curses" against them. The story does not call them curses (although the serpent is cursed in the process), though. Neither does it describe them as God's punishment for sin. The gist of the statements tells of breaks in relationships and shows a certain perspective on "the way things are"—snakes crawl on their bellies and are dangerous to humans; women suffer pain in childbirth yet desire men, who rule over them; and men labor against the land to grow food and ultimately die and decay in the ground.[2]

Nevertheless some subsequent readers have taken them to be descriptive of timeless truths, prescriptive for all time . . . at least in the case of women. That is, this text has been used to justify an enduring hierarchy: God over man over woman over animals. It has been used to counsel a woman who suffers abuse at the hands of her husband to go home and take it, because "God says your husband should rule over you." It has also been used to argue against providing pain relief for women during childbirth.[3] (By contrast, arguments that men must physically labor against thorns and thistles to grow food, live off that vegetarian diet until they die, and then be disposed of in such a way as to decay in the ground haven't gotten very far.)

Reflecting such sentiment as the bumper sticker "Eve Was Framed," some feminist scholars have sought to exonerate Eve by noting that she wasn't even around until after God had told Adam not to eat that particular fruit. They note that Eve engaged in contemplation and thoughtful debate with the serpent, appreciated the tree's goodness, and observed its benefits—by comparison with Adam, of whom the narrator says only that he was "with her, and he ate."[4] Before Eve, there was no birth, no new human life born as a product of human love. According to the story, it was Eve's desire for wisdom that led her to eat the forbidden fruit. Yet it is as the guilty party and temptress to misbehavior that Eve has been most commonly remembered.

Finally, though, like Adam, Eve gets very little mention in the Bible. She is named only one more time in the Old Testament (when she bears Cain), once in the Apocrypha (Tob 8:6, where Eve is identified as Adam's good partner), and only twice in the New Testament (2 Cor 11:3, in a passing reference likening Eve's deception by the serpent to the dangers of false teachers; and 1 Tim 2:13–15). Nevertheless, Paul's interpretation of Genesis chapters 2–3, together with the even later New Testament writer responsible for 1 Timothy, led to a line of thinking that has been used against women ever since.

Although in his letter to the Romans, Paul explains that "just as

sin came into the world through one man . . . so one man's righteousness leads to justification and life for all"; and in 1 Corinthians, he
writes, "As all die in Adam, so all will be made alive in Christ," it
didn't take long before Adam's sin was blamed on Eve (she gave him
the fruit, after all, so the thinking goes) and described as "The Fall
of Man." The author of 1 Timothy is explicit about this and justifies
all sorts of restrictions for women, including silence and subservience
to men, based on this story. It's from 1 Timothy that we get the ideas
that Adam was formed first and so is better, that "the woman" was
deceived and sinned (not Adam), and that her pain in childbirth is
supposed to pay off some of her sinner's debt.[5]

MATRIARCHS: MOTHERS OF A PEOPLE

Couples trying to conceive may do well to pray to Sarah, the patron
saint of infertility. The Roma (Gypsy) people also venerate a Saint
Sara in France who is, whatever her origins, the namesake of the biblical Sarah and protector of those who take to the road.[6] The biblical
Sarah was the wife of Abraham, so when God called Abraham to go,
Sarah went, too. Like her husband, Sarah underwent a name change in
association with a special divine assignment/relationship—from Sarai
to Sarah. Both names mean "princess." With Abraham, Sarah traveled from Mesopotamia to Canaan, from Canaan to Egypt, and from
Egypt back to Canaan again.

When readers first meet Sarah, she was in her mid-sixties and still
didn't have any children. Sarah was, as they say, barren.[7] Yet as Abraham's wife, she was instrumental in the struggle to fulfill one part of
God's promise to Abraham—that he would have many descendants.
Every part of Sarah's story is tied to that dilemma and expectation.

Even though the Bible represents centuries (perhaps millennia) of
stories, poems, and religious development, from its earliest oral influences to the latest additions and editorial input, a consistent influence is its patriarchal worldview. Add to that a context in which it
was really hard to survive, and fertility became the issue that defined
women. From this vantage, readers may find it remarkable that the

Bible includes any other information about women than what is associated with their having children. Yet there are some remarkable women. Sarah is one of them. Nevertheless, we do well to remember that Sarah's story, like every other biblical women's, is inevitably informed by the patriarchal context of the Bible's authorship and transmission.

Sarah's childlessness in the face of God's promise of many descendants creates dramatic tension that builds throughout the middle chapters of Genesis. At one point, Sarah ended up in the Egyptian pharaoh's harem because Abraham, fearing for his life, passed her off as his sister (technically, this was half true) to save his neck should the pharaoh want to take her. (Abraham and the Egyptians agreed that she was very beautiful. Never mind that she had to be at least seventy years old at this point.) [8]

In desperation, Sarah determined that God might not be such a literalist—that she herself didn't actually have to conceive and bear a descendant. Rather, Sarah gave her Egyptian slave Hagar to Abraham with the understanding that if Hagar had a baby, it would count as Sarah's. But the heart is not so readily swayed. When Hagar did conceive, she grew contemptuous, and Sarah got mad. Sarah threw Hagar out, and God confirmed that it was through Sarah (now about ninety years old) that Abraham's line would become great and numerous. When God's messengers came for a visit and announced to Abraham Sarah's impending pregnancy, it seemed so absurd that Sarah, eavesdropping on their conversation, laughed at the idea of it. Called out on it, though, she said, "Did not." The divine messenger said, "Did too." Then, after another wife-as-sister, Sarah-restored episode, Sarah finally did become pregnant with Isaac, named "he laughs." [9]

The biblical Sarah is only half a character without her counterpart, slave yet rival, Hagar. The two women are painfully connected in the biblical narrative. We don't know anything about Hagar's past except that she was Egyptian. We don't know how old she was in the story, or what she looked like, but thanks to the biblical narrative, we can imagine, with pity and sympathy, her plight. Although the Bible champions God's chosen through the line of Abraham and Sarah, it doesn't spare a scathing portrait of Sarah as cruel and abusive under the pressure of fulfilling God's promise. In that context, readers are privy to Hagar's character and condition, too.

When Sarah first threw her out, Hagar despaired of surviving. But a messenger of God visited her, explained that she would indeed bear a son who would survive and earn his own reputation, and told her to return . . . to Sarah's harsh treatment. Hagar is the only woman— and a slave, at that—who was visited by God with a descendants promise of her own, and she is the only woman who named God. In her relief, she called God "El-Roi," which means "God of seeing," because God saw her plight and helped her.[10] When she returned to Sarah, she bore Ishmael. At that point in the narrative, he was Abraham's one and only son.

After Sarah bore Isaac, though, the tension increased until Sarah threw Hagar out again, this time with Ishmael. Again Hagar despaired of surviving, and again an angel comforted her. Hagar and Ishmael found water, and that's the last we hear of them. Hagar does show up again in the Christian bible, but only where Paul uses her story to symbolize the old Sinai covenant that enslaves, in contrast to the new promise through Jesus' death in Jerusalem that liberates.[11]

The last we hear of Sarah is of her death. It follows immediately the story of Isaac's near-sacrifice at the hands of his father, Abraham. Coincidence? After all those years, the trials and tribulations, she finally bore a son, making possible the fulfillment of God's promise of many descendants. Then God required Abraham to kill him. Some say that even though the sacrifice didn't happen (Isaac and Abraham both came, safe and sound, back down from the mountain), Sarah couldn't get over the shock of it all. The Bible doesn't say. After Sarah satisfied her procreative role, the Bible tells us only that she died, 127 years old.

If Eve is the mythopoeic "mother of all living," Sarah is the flesh-and-blood mother of the God-fearing faithful. The fictional mother of the hope for humanity in the TV series *Terminator: The Sarah Connor Chronicles* is named Sarah. She faces the daunting task of raising her

son John to save humankind and avert the nuclear disaster they refer
to as "Judgment Day."

The biblical Sarah was a contemporary of Lot's wife, who is infamous for having disregarded a warning not to turn back and look at
the destruction of Sodom. She did, and turned into a pillar of salt.[12]
Learning this, a man in an adult Bible study class said, "That's not so
bad. Just yesterday, coming back from the store, my wife turned into
a telephone pole." Jesus used the biblical story to warn against getting
caught looking back when the end-time comes. "Remember Lot's
wife," he exclaimed.[13] A rock-salt pillar formation near the Dead Sea
in Israel is called Lot's Wife, as is an uninhabitable, pillar-shaped vol-
canic island off the coast of Tokyo.

Lot's two daughters aren't portrayed in an especially positive light,
either.[14] A bit provincial in their thinking, they assumed that with
Sodom and Gomorrah gone, there were absolutely no eligible bach-
elors left to have sex with. ("There is not a man on earth to come into
us," they said.) So, the narrator explains, determined to preserve all
humanity, they got their dad drunk and, unbeknownst to him, slept
with him—one daughter on one night, and the other on a second
night. The story's concluding comment that this is the origin of the
Ammonite and Moabite peoples certainly suggests the biblical writers' antipathy toward (or at least ambivalence about) these neighbors
of Israel.

Isaac's wife, Rebekah, is the most outstanding woman of the next
generation. She is really the one who drives the action and the plot.
Like Sarah, she is first described as "barren,"[15] but immediately after
telling us this, the narrator says that God fixed things so that she became the mother of twins—Esau and Jacob. Also like Sarah, Rebekah
is described as so beautiful that her husband had to take the precaution
of passing her off as his sister (unlike Sarah, she wasn't), but God got
her back. To appreciate her character—as with other biblical women—
requires digging more deeply into the stories to interpret her words
and actions. Rebekah is portrayed as polite and kind (she greeted
Abraham's envoy and gave him and his camels water), brave and ad-

venturous (she agreed to return with the envoy to Abraham's place and marry Isaac), resourceful and smart (she tricked Isaac into giving her favorite son, Jacob, the blessing that marked him as the bearer of God's intergenerational promise), and desirous of a proper daughter-in-law (she is disgruntled with Esau's choice in Canaanite wives and set it up for Jacob to visit her brother, where Jacob falls in love).

Even though it was the lovely Rachel that Jacob fell for, he ended up marrying her sister Leah first. Jacob's tricky father-in-law explained, after switching the girls on the wedding night, that Leah was older, after all. In a brothers Grimm style moment, Jacob promised another seven years of work to earn Rachel's hand, and finally got it. But (perhaps not surprisingly) Rachel "was barren."[16] By contrast, Leah was the picture of fertility. Again, this childbearing business is front and center. Rachel finally did bear a son—Joseph, Jacob's favorite, and the one who ended up in Egypt. Between Leah, Rachel, and their two slave women (Zilpah and Bilhah), Jacob had twelve sons and one daughter.

That daughter, born to Leah after Leah had had seven sons (and right before Rachel finally had a baby), was Dinah. In the Bible, Dinah plays a minor but intriguing role that fired the imagination of the novelist Anita Diamant, who built her international best-seller, *The Red Tent*, around Dinah's character. The biblical narrator tells us that once, when Dinah went out to visit the women of the region, a local hotshot spied her and raped her; he also immediately fell in love with her "and spoke tenderly to her."[17] Shechem's desire to marry Dinah, in good faith, set off a chain of events that left all the men of his town dead. To facilitate the intermarriage, they had agreed to be circumcised, but when they were laid up and sore from the surgery, Dinah's brothers killed them all. Her brothers then made off with Dinah, and that was the end of it. How did Dinah feel about all this? The narrator doesn't say.

Another racy story of Jacob's children involves his granddaughter-in-law Tamar, who was married to the eldest of Judah's sons, who promptly died. Her story is a well-crafted drama with plenty of innuendo and suggestion. Tamar was swiftly widowed again when God killed her second husband, Judah's second son, for refusing to get her pregnant. She was sent away "until the youngest son" was old enough to marry her; but Judah failed to actually set them up, "for he feared that he too would die, like his brothers."[18] Tamar took matters into her own hands, dressed as a prostitute, and waylaid Judah himself. Judah discovered that she was pregnant; she revealed that he himself was the father, and so it was that Perez, the great(x7) grandfather of David, was born.

MARGINALIZED BUT NOT MARGINAL

Among this list of women made famous by sex in some way or other, Miriam stands out. Described as Moses' sister, she was not a famous mother or otherwise married or slept her way into the Bible. Maybe because of this the narrator has little to say about her. We don't even know for sure if Miriam was the sister who facilitated Moses' rescue when he was a baby.[19] For that matter, we don't even know for sure if a historical Miriam was Moses' sister (the biblical association may reflect a late tradition). Whatever the case, Miriam must have been an outstanding woman to be included at all (even more so if she wasn't Moses' sister). She is described as the first to celebrate victory after the Hebrew people escaped the Egyptians, leading the community in song and dance.[20] Many scholars think that Miriam's song is the earliest piece of literature in the Bible. It's a toss-up between that and the song of Deborah (see below). Miriam is called a prophetess, and she had access to the tent of meeting. In other words, she had access to the presence of God, the same as Aaron and Moses, her brothers. When she and Aaron angered God by criticizing Moses for marrying an African woman, though, Miriam was struck with leprosy, while Aaron got away scot-free. Only after Moses prayed for her healing did God relent, but she was exiled from the community for seven days.[21] The prophet Micah remembers Miriam, with Aaron and Moses, as the triumvirate that led the people out of Egypt.[22] The popular New Testament name Mary comes from the Hebrew Miriam by way of its Greek equivalent, Mariam.

Rahab, whose name means "wide" or "broad," was a prostitute who gets almost as much biblical press as Miriam. She was every prostitute cliche—good-hearted, deceitful, scheming—plus she recognized the biblical God as the God of heaven and earth. Rahab was a native of Jericho who cleverly sheltered and planned the escape of Joshua's spies in return for the protection of her family. She became an Israelite after Joshua and company made good on their promise of saving her when they destroyed the rest of Jericho.[23]

In the New Testament, Matthew remembers Rahab in his genealogy of Jesus, noting that she was the mother of Boaz, who married Ruth, who became the great-grandmother of David.[24] The author of Hebrews uses Rahab as an example of justification by faith;[25] while the author of James uses her as an example of justification by works.[26] It would seem that she is, finally, in the context of the canon, whoever you want her to be. Incidentally, in English translations, Rahab appears to be the name of another biblical character, chaos in creaturely form; but the Hebrew words are different.[27]

The name Deborah also refers to two different biblical characters, three if we count the deuterocanonical/apocryphal book of Tobit. One is Rebekah's nurse. Although she is referred to by name only when she dies, it's remarkable that she is named at all.[28] The other Deborah has a much higher profile. She is of Miriam's caliber and shares with Miriam the unusual quality for a biblical woman of fame without sex. Like Miriam, she was a leader within the community of Israel. Deborah is described as a prophetess and a judge. That is, she was one of the military and religious leaders of the people in the period before they had kings. Deborah appears early in the book of Judges and is portrayed as a competent and confident leader. The victory over Sisera that Deborah masterminded and another woman, Jael, finally executed, is related in both prose and poetic form in the book of Judges.[29] This poem is tied with Miriam's song for the award of Quite Possibly the Earliest Biblical Text. In the book of Tobit (possibly from around 250 BCE), Deborah is the name of the loving grandmother who raised and taught Tobit. The hero declares loyalty to "the law of Moses and the instructions of Deborah."[30]

Delilah stands in stark contrast to Deborah within the book of Judges. Whereas Deborah is an Israelite judge, Delilah disables an Israelite judge; whereas Deborah strengthens the man in her control, Delilah weakens him; and whereas Deborah's power has nothing to do with her sexuality, Delilah's power is inextricable from it. Delilah's name may mean something like "flirt" or "loose hair," both of which are on full display in the one story where she appears.[31]

Unlike Deborah, Delilah has fired the imagination of creative artists through the centuries. Handel's oratorio *Samson* reflects Milton's *Samson Agonistes*; and Saint-Saëns composed a whole opera based on this biblical story. Tom Jones's version of "Delilah" quickly became a hit in the 1960s and has been remade many times. Leonard Cohen sings about Delilah in "Hallelujah," as does Bob Dylan in "Tombstone Blues." The story is at the heart of songs by the Grateful Dead, PJ Harvey, and the Gershwin brothers. Regina Spektor's song "Samson" puts the story in a modern setting, adding, "The Bible didn't mention us, not even once."

In the Bible, Delilah is described as a foreign love interest of Samson, the famously philandering Israelite judge. Using her womanly wiles, Delilah persuaded the rather doltish Samson to tell her the true secret of his strength—his long hair. (He had lied to her about it previously a couple of times, and she betrayed him then, too—makes readers wonder about Samson's judgment.) Then she promptly spilled the beans to his enemies, the Philistines, because they offered to pay her lots of money, and that's the last we hear of Delilah. Depending on whom you ask or how you read, the literary character of Delilah is a crude product of androcentric (male-centered) thinking, or she undermines exactly that. Either Delilah is the distasteful stereotype of misogynistic fantasy—a gold-digging, treasonous liar whose beauty is a trap, a lover who cannot be trusted—*or* she reveals the rotten underbelly of patriarchy wherein a grossly incapable man is stripped of his authority only by a resourceful woman who is able to get things done despite the severe limitations of her culture. Perhaps it's a little of both.

However she is judged, Delilah clearly seduced. Bathsheba did not.

Yet Bathsheba is regularly portrayed as inviting David's attention—complicit in, if not responsible for, his adultery. After an introduction that hints of trouble ahead (the narrator says that David did not go off to war as kings should do),[32] his impropriety is made starkly clear in a breathless rush of narration: David spied the beautiful Bathsheba bathing, learned that she was married, "sent messengers to get her, she came to him, and he lay with her."[33] The text's brevity conveys David's impulsive lust . . . and its consequences: the very next statement is Bathsheba's declaration to David that she had become pregnant.

Whatever the biblical narrative has revealed about Bathsheba by this point is positive: she was beautiful, obedient (she came when the king sent for her), religiously observant (specifically, she took care to follow the purity laws), and she told the truth (immediately after the narrator tells us that she conceived, she told David). However, people frequently dilute David's guilt by making Bathsheba out to be some kind of temptress—she was bathing in the open, after all. But the architecture of houses in the ancient Near East, reflecting both climate and culture, makes it likely that she was in the courtyard of her house, a not uncommon place to bathe.

After David dispatched Bathsheba's husband and married her, she bore the baby, who immediately died, in partial fulfillment of God's punishment of David. We are told nothing about her feelings or response. Bathsheba appears again in the biblical narrative only much later, when David was so old that he was sexually uninterested in the beautiful young virgin Abishag, and two of his sons were jockeying for the throne. At that point, we learn that Bathsheba was (the adult) Solomon's mother.

Through her intervention with David on behalf of Solomon, Solomon succeeded David as king. Her last narrated act is another of intervention, this time on behalf of Solomon's brother and former rival, who asked for Abishag as a consolation prize. Solomon was incensed (probably because sleeping with the king's women was considered tantamount to taking the throne) and had the offending brother killed. Bathsheba isn't mentioned at all in the books of Chronicles, with their image of David as unfailingly honorable. Although nowhere in the biblical text is Bathsheba described as bathing naked, nearly every artistic representation of her takes the opportunity to paint/draw/sketch/woodcut/photo-shoot a female nude.

The biblical narrators give us a much richer portrait of another, later queen—Jezebel.[34] A Phoenician-born (hence foreign) princess, Jezebel was married to Ahab, king in the northern kingdom of Israel some decades after the split of the twelve-tribe kingdom into northern Israel and southern Judah. Ahab has the dubious distinction of doing "more to provoke the anger of Yahweh, the God of Israel, than had all the kings of Israel before him."[35] This is partly due to Ahab's efforts to keep Jezebel happy.

Jezebel is portrayed not only as infecting the nation with the temptation to worship deities other than the LORD (namely Baal and Asherah), but also for her fiery temper, unscrupulous behavior, and manipulation of the king. By all accounts, she had Ahab by the balls, as they say. After the prophet Elijah single-handedly slew the 450 prophets of Baal, he ran in fear of Jezebel. Jezebel was the mastermind behind Ahab's seizing land he had no business taking; and Jezebel is blamed by the biblical narrator for instigating Ahab's wickedness, wickedness that contributed to the downfall of the entire nation.

When Jezebel scolded Ahab for wimping out on seizing a particularly lovely vineyard because it was wrong to do so, and told him to buck up and use his kingliness to kill the owner and take it anyway, she brought down on herself a gruesome prophecy.[36] Sure enough in the midst of a dramatic coup, she went into a tower, dolled herself up, and confronted the man who would be king. At his invitation, eunuchs threw her down, where she was trampled by horses and then eaten by dogs, thus fulfilling the prophecy.

Jezebel's idolatry, feistiness, and proud beauty have made her a favorite, especially for criticism. As of this writing, there are sixty-six "cultural references" to Jezebel listed in her Wikipedia entry.[37] Jezebel appears again in the Bible only once—in the New Testament book of Revelation. There, Jezebel is a metonym for a female opponent of Revelation's author. It is only the first of many subsequent descriptions of any misbehaving woman as "a Jezebel." The narrative in 1 Kings sets the stage for associations of Jezebel not only with idolatry and compromising the strength or integrity of others but also with illicit sex. Although modern interpretations sometimes characterize her as "loose" (and Jezebel is a line of lingerie), the narrative doesn't describe her as such except through the slanderous words of other characters.[38] Bette Davis portrays Jezebel as a difficult and unpleasant woman in the film of that name.

By contrast, some modern references to Jezebel embrace what they see as her strength and style. For example, *Jezebel* is the name of a magazine whose aim is to define, describe, and promote "Atlanta Luxury Living." And it is also the name of a popular blog directed at women. Sade sings about Jezebel as a resourceful and ambitious young woman, and the novelists Isaac Asimov and Tom Robbins portray Jezebel sympathetically in *Caves of Steel* and *Skinny Legs and All*, respectively.

WOMEN WITH TITLES

One story that graciously challenges the assumption that all foreign women are bad is Ruth's. The narrator describes Ruth as a native of Moab, so she starts with two counts against her: not only was Ruth a foreigner, but she was also associated with a people who traced their ancestry back to the incestuous liaison of Lot and his daughters.[39] Yet Ruth is portrayed in the Bible as a model of fidelity, kindness, and love.

As the story goes, Ruth stuck with her mother-in-law, Naomi, even after all the men in the family died and Naomi decided to return to her hometown of Bethlehem. Much of the story's tension derives from the patriarchal culture it supposes—without men, the women have nothing. Despite this cultural truth, Ruth famously determined to stay with Naomi. As a result, she met the shining white knight— the gracious, wealthy landholder Boaz, who was fortuitously in a position to marry her. Ruth is one of only four women identified in Jesus' genealogy[40]—the only place that she appears outside the book that bears her name.

Although Ruth is nearly always recollected in positive terms,

Amy-Jill Levine, professor of New Testament at Vanderbilt University, notes the narrator's profound ambivalence toward her—crediting Ruth with continuing the family line leading to King David while also denying her full entry into the family that is Israel (she continued to be "the Moabitess"); she was virtuous, but with a hint of sexual aggression (following Naomi's plan, Ruth initiated the delicate exchange, which the narrator hints was intercourse, with a buzzed Boaz on the threshing floor); she is a dream daughter-in-law who was also taken for granted, even ignored, at key moments by her mother-in-law: Naomi, ironically, claimed to have nothing when returning to Bethlehem (what was Ruth, chopped liver?!), and Ruth's newborn became the "son . . . born to Naomi."[41]

Esther, who also has a book in her name, is portrayed as a heroine who preserved Israel by means of her sexuality. Esther's story takes place centuries later than Ruth's—after the rise and fall of the Davidic monarchy; after the enemy, Babylon, was destroyed; and during the Persian period of Cyrus's successors. While the character Ruth seldom invoked God (by comparison with the other women in her story), the Hebrew heroine Esther never did. For that matter, God is glaringly absent from the entire Hebrew book of Esther. The book probably comes from the early years of the Hellenistic period (around 300 BCE). Later Greek additions to the book, preserved in the Septuagint, maintain the overall plot but make the heroine and her story more religious, with many references to God.

Esther's name reflects her foreign context, probably derived from Ishtar, the Babylonian goddess of love; it may come from the Persian *stara*, "star." In the story, Esther was an undercover Jew (née Hadassah), selected as substitute queen after Vashti lost her position by refusing the humiliation of entertaining (presumably naked) the king and his guests at a long, raucous party. Esther was so beautiful and charming that she won the Miss Persia contest for the crown. Meanwhile a member of the court, Haman, who harbored a personal grudge against Esther's stubborn uncle, plotted to kill all the Jews. Only after Esther agreed, under some duress, to Uncle Mordechai's counterplot was her own identity as a Jew revealed. She risked the king's wrath but succeeded in not only foiling Haman's genocidal plot but also affecting its reversal (the literary structure of the story is built on such reversals). Consequently, Esther is remembered as a great heroine of Israel, and as one model of the dangers and challenges of Jewish life in the Diaspora.

Although the overtly religious version of Esther is found only in the Septuagint, Esther is nevertheless part of the Hebrew Bible. Not so for Judith. Judith does not appear in the Jewish or Protestant Christian canon. The entire book of Judith only appears in the Septuagint and thus in the Roman Catholic and Greek Orthodox Old Testaments. Like Esther's, Judith's story is set long before it was actually written, and it contains such glaring historical inaccuracies that many people think its authors purposely included them so that it would be taken as fiction.

Judith doesn't appear until well into the story, but then she certainly stirs things up. Judith (or "Jewess") was rich, beautiful, smart, pious . . . and recently widowed (her husband had died of sunstroke). When their town was besieged and all hope seemed lost, she worked her way into the good graces of the powers that be, in this case the commander of the Assyrian army, Holofernes. When the drunken Holofernes took her to bed, she decapitated him. Back in town, she produced his head from her maid's lunchbag, and made sure to announce that they had never had sex. Virtue intact, Judith went on to lead the Israelites to victory against the Assyrians and lived happily single ever after. Apart from that, Judith shares much in common with several biblical characters, and (given the late date of the book's composition) she is probably an intentional composite of them all.

ABSTRACT WOMEN

"The queen of heaven," as a title referring to several different entities, has had a tumultuous history, from harsh dismissal as an idol (by the Old Testament prophet Jeremiah) and as a personification of evil (by some controversial Protestant Christians) to passionate embrace as God's mother (by Catholic and Orthodox Christians). She is represented in iconography as old as any that we have, and is still venerated by millions today. For just as long, people have disagreed about exactly who she was or is and what she did or does.

Toward the end of his career, after he had been taken to Egypt following Judah's defeat in 587 BCE, Jeremiah continued to prophesy against the worship of any deity other than Yahweh. He was troubled by the propensity of his fellow exiles to worship the "queen of heaven,"[42] make cakes for her, and fashion figures in her likeness. Writings from Egypt dating to the fifth century BCE attest to the worship of a goddess named Anat-Yahu ("Anat of Yahweh").[43] Maybe Jeremiah was attacking this practice.

"Queen of heaven" as Catholic and Orthodox Christians use the term refers to someone else—Mary, the mother of Jesus. Believing that she was taken up into heaven and can serve as an intercessor to God, Catholic and Orthodox Christians have venerated Mary—this "queen mother," who humbly bore the "king of kings"—as the "queen of heaven" for centuries. In 2006, Pope Benedict XVI reiterated the belief that "Christ crowned [Mary] Queen of heaven and earth."[44]

Yet another interpretation casts Mary in a dim light. Although many evangelical and fundamentalist Christians disavow it, some Protestant churches are involved in a network movement called Third Wave, committed to waging spiritual warfare against demons before the end-time, when believers will take over the earth on God's behalf. They are convinced that the Orthodox veneration of Mary, the mother of Jesus, Jeremiah's "queen of heaven," and the "whore of Babylon" are all one and the same and must be exorcised.[45]

The "whore of Babylon" makes quite a splash in Revelation, where she is depicted as all decked out and carrying a golden cup filled to the brim with the filth of her wickedness, drunk with saints' blood. On her forehead is tattooed "mother of whores and earthly abominations."[46] To clarify: the phrase does not refer to a woman in Babylon whose vocation was prostitution; rather, it is a personification of the city or nation of Babylon itself. Places in the Bible are regularly referred to as female. Consequently, they (and by extension, their citizens) are subject to the same kinds of criticism as women in the Bible.

One particularly rich metaphor for biblical writers and editors is of Yahweh or God as husband to the people of Israel as wife. (Almost the entire book of Hosea is built on this metaphor.) The Sinai covenant, renewed with Moses in Deuteronomy[47] and again with Joshua,[48] is remembered throughout the Bible as binding the parties to each other, like a marriage contract binds husband and wife. Since Israel promised fidelity to this one God and God promised surety for them in the land, religious idolatry was likened to sexual promiscuity. Metaphorically, Israel's worship of other deities was adultery, which terminated the contract and God's promise that they would keep the land.[49]

Babylon, being not only foreign but also Israel's captor, came in for exceptional criticism. Babylon was not God's adulterous wife or even a loose woman but a full-fledged whore in the biblical imagination— her people worshipped all sorts of deities. By the time Revelation was being written, many centuries after Babylon's heyday, "Babylon" had become synonymous with the heart of evil earthly power. So the term "whore of Babylon" lent itself symbolically not only to Rome but also, throughout subsequent millennia, to the Roman Catholic Church, the United States, and the Soviet Union, depending on the interpreter, of course.

In Proverbs, the abstract principles—wisdom and folly—are also personified as women. The readers are counseled to seek out wisdom, for "Her ways are pleasant, and all her paths are peace; she is a tree of life and [source of happiness]."[50] Wisdom acts and speaks as a woman, calling to the young men who are Proverbs' audience to come to her and listen closely. "By me princes rule . . . and with me are riches and honor," she says.[51] And she warns against the temptation to follow Woman Folly, who says, "Stolen water is sweet, and bread eaten in secret is delicious" but whose ways lead to ruin and despair.[52]

WOMEN IN THE NEW TESTAMENT: THE MARYS

The first women to appear in the New Testament do so in Matthew's genealogy of Jesus (through Joseph's side of the family).[53] Although the list begins way back with Abraham, it includes only five women:

Tamar, Rahab, Ruth, Bathsheba—and Mary. They are notable because each one has a questionable sexual past. Bathsheba is not named but rather called "the wife of Uriah," underscoring the issue. Situating Mary in this company of women immediately disarms arguments about her part in God's plan based on suspicion about her virtue. Although each of these women have eyebrow-raising biographies, they nevertheless served crucial roles in the furtherance of Israel.

Matthew explains that Mary was pregnant not by Joseph or any other human man but "from the Holy Spirit." Matthew's Jewish scriptures were in Greek translation, and that Greek translation rendered a biblical prophecy from Isaiah as "a virgin shall conceive, . . ."[54] though the corresponding Hebrew word means simply "young woman." Interpreting his scriptures in light of how he understood Jesus, the author of Matthew applied this Greek translation of an ancient Hebrew prophecy to Mary.[55]

For nearly all Christians, the virginity of Jesus' mother is a key characteristic. Orthodox Christians maintain a doctrine of "perpetual virginity," i.e., that Mary was a virgin until she died. Others understand biblical references to Jesus' brothers and sisters as evidence that after bearing Jesus, she went on to have children naturally with Joseph. For Roman Catholics, Mary was uniquely pure from the moment of her own conception (the Immaculate Conception), so she was never tainted by original sin. Although there is no biblical reference to Mary's ascending to heaven at her death, except by interpretation of symbolism in Revelation 12, the "assumption of Mary" has become dogma for Roman Catholics. Some Christians (though not Protestants) venerate Mary and pray to her as an intercessor—extraordinary but not equal to God.

The combination of Mary's humanity, femininity, maternal nature, and unique relationship to God through Jesus and the Holy Spirit make it easy to understand how she could be especially and universally beloved. La Virgen Morena ("the brown-skinned virgin"), also called Our Lady of Guadalupe, is the patron saint of Mexico and inseparable from Mexican identity. The Italian term *madonna*, meaning "my lady," has come to be understood primarily as referring to Mary the mother of Jesus. "Black madonnas" are a common representation of Mary in Europe. The origin of their color is disputed, but they have become understandably popular among people of African descent.

Accounts of Mary sightings have occurred all over the globe, wherever there is a Christian, especially a Catholic, presence. Our Lady of Lourdes (France), Our Lady of Fatima (Portugal), Our Lady of Zeitoun (Egypt), and Our Lady of Sorrows (Rwanda) are just a few such manifestations. Incidentally, while the Beatles' "Mother Mary" in "Let It Be" is evocative of the biblical Mary, Paul McCartney has explained that she refers to his real mother, who died when he was fourteen years old. McCartney says that during a particularly stressful time with the band, she comforted him in a dream, saying, "It will be all right. Just let it be." [56]

The earliest biblical references to Mary do not seem familiar with the doctrine of virginity; but they don't explicitly contradict it, either. Paul, the earliest source of New Testament texts, wrote very little about Mary, and never by name. He comes closest to mentioning her in the following: contrasting Jesus' mortal and immortal natures, Paul writes of Jesus as "born of the seed of David according to the flesh," [57] and "born of a woman." [58] The only references to Jesus' mother Mary occur in the gospels, yet Mark, the earliest gospel, does not include a birth narrative at all. When this gospel first refers to Mary, it is un-complimentary: When Jesus was told that his "mother and brothers" had arrived to see him, Jesus rejected them and substituted the "fam-ily" of his followers instead. [59] Mark describes the townspeople's efforts to identify Jesus by asking if he wasn't "Mary's son and the brother of . . ." [60] Jesus' mother is never mentioned by name in the gospel of John.

It is from Matthew and Luke that we get the birth stories that define popular images of Jesus' mother—the young virgin (Matthew, Luke) to whom an angel announced the conception (Luke), who trav-eled (Luke) with her fiancé to Bethlehem, where she bore Jesus (Mat-thew, Luke) in a stable (Luke) and was visited by shepherds (Luke) or by the magi (Matthew), fled to Egypt (Matthew), and returned and settled in Nazareth (Matthew). Although Mel Gibson makes much of the presence of a nunlike (anachronistic by at least 1,000 years) mother Mary in *The Passion of the Christ*, there is precious little reference to her presence at Jesus' trial, crucifixion, and burial. One would suppose that she would have been there—all able Jews would have been in Jerusalem for Passover, and she was his mother, after all. Yet only John (otherwise the least concerned with prosaic historical reportage) refers to her presence at the cross. The author of Acts mentions Mary as present among the disciples after Jesus' assumption into heaven.[61] The only other appearance of Mary, the mother of Jesus, within the gospels is John's description of her part (she is unnamed) in Jesus' miracle of turning water into wine at the wedding in Cana.[62]

There are half a dozen important Marys in the New Testament, and this can be confusing. Mary, the mother of Jesus, is also described as Mary of Nazareth because that Galilean town was her home. She is distinguished, then, from Mary of Bethany and Mary of Magdala. And she is distinguished from other Marys similarly described as "mother of James," "mother of John," or "wife of Clopas."[63]

The number of "Mary and Martha" homes and service programs in operation today, such as a maternity home for unwed mothers in California, a day care and nursing home service in Washington, and an emergency shelter in Tampa, Florida, attest to the enduring image of domestic comfort and security these friends of Jesus provided. True to life, their situation was not without conflict. According to the gospels, Mary of Bethany defied the traditional system, to the chagrin of her hardworking sister, Martha, by forgoing housework in order to sit at Jesus' feet and learn from him. It's hard not to sympathize with Martha when she complained to Jesus that she was stuck with all the food prep and serving while Mary just sat soaking up the conversation: "Tell her to help me!"[64] Yet it is Martha whom Jesus gently scolded, maintaining that Mary had found what is crucial and enduring.

Nevertheless, John describes both women as loved by Jesus—and they are the only women to be so described in the gospels. There certainly is a comfortable familiarity among them—Martha conscientious and a little bossy; Mary sweet and endearing; Jesus not only an object of adoration but also a friend. One can hear an edge of criticism in Martha's voice when she told Jesus that if he'd just been with them (and they did call for him, but he delayed), their brother Lazarus wouldn't have died. (Mary said the same thing later.) But Martha also held nothing back in professing her faith in his being the "Christ, the son of God, who has come in to the world."[65]

These sisters, Mary and Martha, clearly recognized Jesus' importance. When Jesus came to visit them, a week before Passover (and his death), Mary again ignored social mores. She not only let down her hair in the presence of this man unrelated to her, but she boldly covered his feet with it. Scolded again, this time by Judas, Mary of Bethany nevertheless proceeded to massage Jesus' feet with her hair, using very expensive perfumed ointment. And Jesus again defended her actions.[66] Because another, unnamed woman is described as doing something similar,[67] Mary of Bethany is occasionally mixed up with her, but many things about the stories indicate that they are two different women. The contexts and points of the two accounts are very different, and the unnamed woman's distinguishing characteristic is her sinfulness.

Speaking of confusion, Mary Magdalene takes the cake. In the popular imagination, she has been conflated with all of these women, and more. The misunderstandings abound. For one thing, Magdalene is not her last name but a reference to her town of origin. Magdala (like Nazareth) was in the Galilean region. This identification should immediately distinguish her from Mary of Bethany, since Bethany is in a completely different area (not far from Jerusalem). Many people are most surprised to learn that nowhere in the Bible is Mary Magdalene described as a prostitute. Her reputation as a reformed prostitute has no explicit biblical support, but it does have support in the Church. Pope Gregory I (d. 604) gave this misinterpretation legs by delivering a sermon that equated Mary Magdalene with both Mary of Bethany and the anonymous sinner who washed Jesus' feet. This portrait also absorbed the story of the unnamed woman caught in adultery, combining to make the popular image of Mary Magdalene quite different from the biblical depiction.

Indeed, since then, more often than not, Mary of Magdala has been represented as a prostitute who gave up her wicked ways to follow the forgiving Jesus—sometimes to powerfully positive effect. For example, the creative and successful Magdalene community, begun by Becca Stevens in Nashville, aims to help women recovering from drug addiction, prostitution, and abuse. Because Mary Magdalene is so depicted also in the twentieth-century blockbusters *Jesus Christ Superstar, The Last Temptation of Christ*, and *The Passion of the Christ*, it's no wonder that few people (besides you, now) know that the Bible doesn't describe her in this way. In Dan Brown's popular and controversial novel *The Da Vinci Code*, Mary Magdalene is the disciple to Jesus' right in Leonardo da Vinci's mural *The Last Supper* and was Jesus' pregnant wife when he was crucified.

Although the prostitute riff on Mary Magdalene is titillating, equally intriguing but seldom appreciated are the implications of her actual presence in the gospels. For one thing, ironically, we can be more confident about a real, historical basis for her character than for any of the other women in the gospels. More than any other, Mary Magdalene appears consistently in every one of the four gospels, and she does so as witness to the most christologically significant moments. The gospels are in remarkable agreement about her presence at the death, burial, and resurrection of Jesus. Not only that, but according to the longer ending of Mark and to John's gospel, it is to this Mary *alone*, out of all his followers, that the resurrected Jesus appears first.[68]

Elsewhere, we know that resurrection appearances lent authority to the witnesses and confirmed their legitimacy as leaders in the early Christian community.[69] Some suspect, then, that Mary Magdalene's role may have been more significant than simply that of a devoted follower. She may have been a bona fide leader, with authority over even some of Jesus' male followers. The discovery of the gnostic gospel of Mary further supports such a conclusion. In this gospel—which did not become part of the Bible, in part because it represents a kind of thinking deemed heretical by the early church—Mary's claim to have seen the risen Jesus was called into question by Peter (who, some think, represented orthodox Christianity). But lest we think that this is a feminist-friendly tract, note that in good gnostic style, Mary is described as thrilled that Jesus liberated her by making her into a man.[70]

Scholars debate the role of women among the first generation of Jesus' followers, since it would seem that women served as leaders in the community, alongside men. Jesus' inclusion of women among his followers and supporters, his contact with them regardless of their ritual state (the hemorrhaging woman)[71] or social mores (Mary's hair), his redefinition of the family from biological to faith, and his favoring a woman's learning over household service (Mary and Martha) demonstrate a radical break with patriarchal convention; yet he did not overturn that convention.

After Jesus' death, it would seem that women continued to be influential within the early Christian community. Note, for example, the women included in Paul's greeting to the Romans.[72] However, they also continued to be subject to the conditions of their social context. For example, note Paul's counsel that a woman accept a subservient identity even while she "prays or prophesies."[73] One evangelical biblical scholar and professor of the New Testament, Ben Witherington III, explains the situation of women among Jesus' and the early Christian community's "family of faith" as one of "reformation" rather than "repudiation." Women gained new roles and status within, not radically distinct from, the generally patriarchal system.[74] When Jesus' second coming didn't happen immediately as expected, women's roles became ever more subject to the patriarchy of their time and place.

FEMINIST SCHOLARSHIP AND THE
HERMENEUTICS OF SUSPICION

Feminist scholarship has contributed a great deal to our understanding of biblical texts. For one thing, it has reminded us of the inevitability of interpretation. No text makes sense or can be applied without interpretation, and the biblical texts that we have are themselves interpretations. Within the Bible itself, for example, Paul interprets the story of the creation of human beings narrated in Genesis chapters 2–3 to understand woman as created second, reflecting (or being the "glory" of) man, though this is not explicit in the Genesis text. Paul reasons, then, that women should comport themselves accordingly.[75]

Hermeneutics is a fancy word that refers to the science of interpretation. In the 1970s, the French philosopher Paul Ricoeur noted the importance of accounting for the possibility that the surface meaning of a text masks political interests, prejudices, and the narrow perspectives of social location. To make sense of texts, then, it makes sense to investigate the influences behind them as well as simply to read them at face value. Ricoeur called this process of listening and questioning a "hermeneutics of suspicion."[76] Because the Bible comes from cultures dominated by patriarchal structures and ways of thinking, making sense of its texts requires taking into account the assumptions and motives of authors under such an influence. For example, interpreting relevant texts within the context of the developing church, we can understand why the new "family of faith" would be organized in keeping with social convention. It shouldn't surprise us, then, to read "Wives, be subject to your husbands . . . obey,"[77] immediately following a similar exhortation for "slaves" to be "subject to your masters," no matter how cruel those masters may be.[78]

Recognizing that interpretation is inevitable, identifying how biblical texts interpret earlier texts, and appreciating how a text's social and historical context affects interpretation can modify the impulse to pluck out particular passages and plop them down without reflection as prescriptive today. Methods of biblical scholarship informed by the feminist principle that women should be afforded the same dignity, value, and potential as men have put the hermeneutics of suspicion to good use.

Feminist scholarship has also brought to our attention the relative lack of attention to women in biblical stories, laws, and accounts. It has taught us to read for the silences, to note what is *not said*, to note who is *not present*, and to ask why and how. This is not to suggest that feminist scholars speak with one voice or are motivated by a single aim, however. Some seek to rehabilitate female characters, to fill out their roles on the basis of subtle clues in the text or nonbiblical information about a text's particular time and place of origin. Others name and note how biblical texts have been used in hurtful ways, and some conclude that women should look elsewhere than to the Bible for religious authority and spiritual direction. Some find hope and an exhortation for equality in the Exodus story of liberation; in women movers and shakers such as Deborah, Esther, and Mary of Bethany; in the inclusion of women among Jesus' followers and early church leaders; and in Paul's instruction that in Christ there is "no longer male and female."[79]

Although many biblical scholars who apply methods of feminist criticism to the Bible are women, not all of them are. And not all women who read the Bible use a feminist critical methodology. Furthermore, different women read the Bible differently, depending on their personal experience with the text, their cultural contexts, and the myriad mysterious qualities that compose any individual human being.

Nevertheless, there are a few issues that any woman faces in reading the Bible and that may well (though not necessarily) result in some application of feminist critical methodology (wittingly or not).[80] One is the Bible's inclusion of texts that are undeniably oppressive for women. A second is its exclusion of voices from minority women (even by ancient Near Eastern standards). Nearly all the women represented in the Bible come from the dominant culture of their time and place. It is not unusual for women, where they are second-class citizens themselves, to side with the dominant culture against their even lower-class minority sisters. The story of Sarah's cruel treatment of Hagar is a glaring example. Third is the Bible's assumption that men are the norm. This has powerful implications for theology. That is, despite numerous protestations that God resists representation by human means in any form, God is portrayed in the Bible almost exclusively in masculine imagery and terms. Nevertheless, there is no single name or image for God in the Bible, a topic addressed in this book's final chapter.

ELEVEN

Flora, Fauna, Etcetera

Some people see things that are and ask, Why?
Some people dream of things that never were
and ask, Why not? Some people have to go to
work and don't have time for all that.

—GEORGE CARLIN

Contrary to popular belief, the snake in the Garden of Eden story as Genesis tells it, is not the devil, Satan, or Beelzebub. It is a cunning, talking snake—weird, but just a snake, nonetheless. This chapter discusses some biblical things—creatures and objects—that have taken on postbiblical lives elsewhere. How did Satan sneak into Genesis? What is the Ark of the Covenant, and where is it now? Why is a baby gift of myrrh so sinister? How can the holy grail be understood as a goblet on the one hand and a woman on the other? And what is the Bible's personification of evil? In this chapter, I have tried to identify the most popular and sometimes misunderstood biblical things so that readers can appreciate and judge for themselves how they show up in contexts outside the Bible, too.

TALKING SNAKES, HYBRID GODS, AND OTHER FANTASTIC THINGS

To quote the snake experts at herper.com, who made a study of it, "Does the Bible state that snakes are evil? Nope."[1] Nevertheless, even after citing and examining each case of snakes in the Bible, they write, "In Genesis, after Satan shows up in the guise of a reptile . . ." The snake in Genesis chapters 2–3 is definitely problematic, but nowhere in that story is it identified as Satan or even called "evil." On the contrary, the biblical narrator introduces the snake to readers as "the most clever" of all the animals,[2] and cleverness was considered a laudable attribute.[3] Some say that the snake became a troublemaker because he was bitter. After all, God had told all creatures to multiply; but the snake is just an adder. Buh dum bum.

In the biblical story, the snake, with its half-truths, sowed doubt in the woman's mind that led her and the man with her to disobey God's directive. In the process, the narrator sows doubt in readers' minds about who is closer to the truth—God or the snake. After all, Adam and Eve did not die "on the day" that they ate, as God had said they would.[4] Rather, God confirms verbatim what the snake said: they became like God, knowing good and evil.[5] Yet, although the serpent said, without qualification, "You will not die," Adam and Eve did indeed die (albeit centuries later).

The idea that the snake in the garden was Satan in disguise developed centuries after the story had become scripture, after Satan had become a bona fide, stand-alone personification of evil (starting in the final years BCE). A noncanonical Jewish text (*The Apocalypse of Moses*), probably from the first century CE, extrapolating on the Genesis narrative, portrays Satan as speaking through the serpent.[6] This idea was reflected also in the popular *Life of Adam and Eve*, a Jewish text roughly contemporary with and related to *The Apocalypse of Moses*; it told how Eve was deceived (again) by Satan.

Nowhere does the Bible equate the Eden serpent with Satan, but the following New Testament texts have justified the equation through their shared reputations for deception. Paul's concern that other people might mislead his Corinthian congregation in the same way that "the serpent deceived Eve by its craftiness," together with his description of Satan as deceptive and tempting, supports the Satan = snake computation.[7] Revelation also tells of "Satan . . . the devil who deceived" people in the final days; and suggestively adds "ancient"—"that ancient serpent, who is called the Devil and Satan, the deceiver of the whole world."[8]

The third-century Christian theologian Origen formalized the equation of the Genesis serpent with Satan in Christian theology. It is Origen and the other early "Church Fathers" whose influence John Milton cites to introduce *Paradise Lost*, which launched the snake-as-Satan imagery into an even more popular sphere.

Most biblical references to snakes concern their natural threat to people, but they are not portrayed as *evil* per se. Moses' serpent on a stick was actually an agent of healing.[9] This bronze serpent, called the *nehushtan* (from the Hebrew word *nahash* for "snake"), was a form of first aid for the wandering Israelites. Someone who was bitten by a poisonous snake needed only to look at the *nehushtan*, and he or she would be fine.[10] Centuries later, in a pique of religious fanaticism, King Hezekiah destroyed the image, fearing that it had become an idol in and of itself.[11] Archaeological discoveries showing the prevalence of serpents in images of gods and goddesses, and even bronze serpent images from the Israelite Canaanite region, suggest that the *nehushtan* may have been an object of worship (or at least that it was associated with a deity) from the start.[12]

The snake handlers of Appalachia today don't worship the snakes but rather use them to demonstrate their belief in Jesus. Appealing to Jesus' declaration that "in my name . . . they shall pick up serpents . . . and it will not hurt them," people such as Junior G. McCormick treat snake handling as a divine commandment.[13] This religious practice, particular to a small group of Christians, doesn't have anything to do with the serpent in Genesis or Numbers. Rather, these Pentecostal Christians take literally Jesus' statements in the gospel of Mark that true believers have nothing to fear. They won't be hurt even by something as injurious as a biting snake, and handling such snakes will be a sign of their belief.[14] Although this part of Mark appears to be a late addition (some question its authority), Luke's Jesus also promises to protect his followers from biting snakes and scorpions.[15]

If Satan isn't in the Garden of Eden story, then what about the apple? After all where does our Adam's apple come from, if not Genesis? But the apple is not there either. Not exactly anyway. What Adam and Eve ate is simply called by the generic Hebrew word for "fruit." Many years ago the English word "apple" was used in the same way— like we use "Kleenex" to refer to any facial tissue. Translating the Hebrew story into English, then, made the word "apple" a good choice. Over time, though, "apple" came to mean only the particular fruit that we know in varieties such as Red Delicious and McIntosh, and so readers imagined the first couple indulging in a crisp bite. Although the story lacks the detail about exactly what type of fruit Adam and Eve ate, people nevertheless have posited more historically and culturally likely options. Pomegranates lead the running.[16] Meanwhile, the authors of the story have moved on. For one thing, the trees themselves have greater priority in the narrative.

Exactly how many forbidden trees were there? Early in the story, the narrator explains that among Eden's many trees were two: "the tree of life . . . and the tree of the knowledge of good and evil."[17] Then God forbade *adam* to eat from one tree: "the tree of the knowledge of good and evil, for in the day that you eat of it you shall die."[18] Apparently because they did eat it, God kicked Adam and Eve out of the garden before they had a chance to "take also from the tree of life, and eat, and live forever."[19] In other words, the tree of life became off-limits only after Adam and Eve ate from the knowledge-granting one that had been forbidden.

If you thought the talking snake in Genesis 3 was weird, just wait till you get to the part about the hybrid god-humans. The *nephilim*, as they're called in Hebrew, are the offspring of frisky gods mating with human women. In the ABC miniseries *The Fallen*, which is full of biblical references, the Nephilim play a central role, as the offspring of fallen angels consigned to earth, where they are hunted down by the "Powers"—angel warriors.

The biblical *nephilim* get the most press in Genesis but appear also in Numbers. In Genesis, they are described as famous, mighty men of old.[20] That they predate the Flood (and would presumably have been destroyed) makes their appearance in Numbers a little puzzling. Nevertheless, there they are, and in Numbers they cause considerable angst.[21] When the Hebrews saw that the *nephilim* occupied Canaan (which the Hebrews planned to take as Israel), they despaired, because by comparison to the gigantic stature of the *nephilim*, "we seemed like grasshoppers." Probably because of this description, the *nephilim* are sometimes called a "race of giants." Indeed, the Greek translation of this Hebrew word is *gigantes*.

The Hebrew *nephilim* seems related to a word meaning "to fall." Its etymology probably refers to "falling" in the sense of a military defeat.[22] Yet in New Testament texts, centuries later, the term took on the mythic sense of falling from grace or from heaven. In a couple of the latest New Testament books are two references to fallen angels that appear, by their context if not character, to have the *nephilim* in mind.[23] According to those texts, God threw them out of heaven to be kept chained in hell until the Judgment Day.

This New Testament understanding is probably based on literature such as *1 Enoch*, an originally Aramaic text (fragments exist among the Dead Sea Scrolls) that was part of Jewish tradition in the last centuries before the Common Era but did not become biblical. Chapters 6–19 of *1 Enoch* tell how the "watchers of heaven" left their heavenly abode to sleep with human women (to whom they also taught magic). Their offspring took everything from the human beings and then killed and ate them, and generally wreaked havoc on the earth. Needless to say, according to *1 Enoch*, God was not happy. He ordered the righteous angels (including such favorites as Michael and Gabriel) to bind up the wicked ringleaders, who eventually ended up in a fiery abyss of torment.

According to the Bible, the ten plagues were real-world torments that demonstrated the power of Yahweh over the powers of Egypt.[24] These "signs and wonders," as the Old Testament Exodus narrative describes them, weren't designed simply to show Yahweh's authority. They also served to liberate. They ultimately persuaded the king of Egypt to let the Hebrew captives—Yahweh's people Israel—go free. In the process, they also demonstrated the Egyptian king's failure to maintain order in the cosmos, thus undermining his supposed divinity.

In the story, the plagues are never identified by number, though each is preceded by the phrase "Then the LORD said to Moses." They are narrated in groups of three, with the tenth plague being a unique climax. They are: (1) water turning to blood and killing the fish, (2) frogs, (3) biting insects, (4) flies, (5) sickening livestock, (6) boils, (7) thunderstorm with hail, (8) locusts, (9) darkness, (10) death of the firstborn.

Whether or not they really happened is a question we cannot answer for certain. There is no reference to such events in Egyptian sources, and, as noted above, historical accuracy did not seem to be the biblical authors' primary aim. Although two psalms also list the plagues, they do so in a different order and each includes only seven (possibly reflecting a liturgical function), but not exactly the same seven.[25]

One of the most convincing theories of how these events may have transpired presumes a seasonal situation gone bad.[26] Flagellate organisms from Lake Tana worked their way into the Nile during the annual flooding period and sucked up all the oxygen, killing the fish. Frogs migrated out of the flooded river as they normally would but were infected by bacteria, *Bacillus anthracis*, possibly exacerbated by the decomposing fish.[27]

The biting insects should probably be understood as mosquitoes—not "gnats," as in many translations. They would have reached unbearable numbers as the high floodwaters receded. As for the flies, well, just imagine all those decomposing critters. It's possible that at this point, the livestock, which had been safely secured some distance from the floodwaters, became infected with the same anthrax as the frogs. According to Greta Hort, it was transmitted by the fly *Stomoxys calcitrans*, which bites people and animals alike—perhaps explaining the "boils." As for the storm, such weather isn't common in Egypt, but it isn't unheard of, either. Swarming locusts are more common, and the occasional khamsin (Arabic for an intense sandstorm) would have made the day seem as dark as night. The most likely period for these events would have been August to May, a bit longer than the narrative suggests. The biblical story isn't explicit about duration.

If these nine plagues really did happen in a manner that can be explained as natural events, the tenth cannot. Try as we might (and there are some imaginative theories out there), the tenth and final plague, the death of the firstborn, defies natural explanation. In the story, God instructs the Hebrew people to slaughter a lamb and spread its blood on their doorways before roasting and eating it. That would mark which households to spare as the LORD passed through Egypt, killing firstborn children and even firstborn animals. "Whoa, it's like creeping death!" thought the bass player for Metallica while watching Cecil B. DeMille's *Ten Commandments*.[28] "Creeping Death" became the title of one of their most popular songs, which retells the Exodus story.[29] Horror movies such as *The Reaping* and *The Mummy* also picked up on the biblical subject.

Avoiding this tenth plague initiated Passover, an annual Jewish festival commemorating God's liberating the Hebrew people from slavery in Egypt. One of my Jewish colleagues explains that all Jewish festivals reflect the same three-part pattern: they tried to kill us, we survived, now let's eat! Although all of the plagues are narrated as God's wondrous actions on behalf of his people and undermining Egyptian power, this tenth plague emphasizes the degree to which God can alter even natural events to suit God's purpose. No one has been able to provide a satisfactory natural explanation for such an event or otherwise proved that the tenth plague actually happened exactly as narrated, at some historical time and place.

THINGS THAT DAMN AND THINGS THAT SAVE

This emphasis on God's extraordinary activity on behalf of the Hebrew people makes the story of the "golden calf" especially appalling—at least, that was probably the effect the biblical writers were aiming for. According to the narrative, only a short time after the LORD liberated them from slavery, the people began worshipping a golden calf.[30] They had grown tired of waiting for Moses to return from his mountaintop meeting with God, and they clamored for a replacement. (They suspected that Moses and God had run off and abandoned them, the story explains.) Moses' brother Aaron instructed the people to hand over all their gold earrings; they did, and subsequently melted the jewelry down to refashion the gold as (voilà!) a god. Aaron introduced the calf-shaped image with the declaration, "These are the gods, O Israel, who brought you out of Egypt!"

The Hebrew plural suggests that this story borrowed from an earlier narrative, which appears later in the Bible—the story of how Jeroboam, the first king of the northern kingdom (after the great schism), set up two altars, rivaling Jerusalem's, in the towns of Dan and Bethel. Those altars were graced by calf figurines, which the king declared were the gods that had brought Israel out of Egypt.[31] Needless to say, the biblical writers didn't smile on any of these calf deities. For one thing, back at Sinai, Moses had to talk God out of obliterating the stiff-necked lot, and then Moses punished them himself. (God followed up with a plague.) In the case of Jeroboam, the northern kingdom is criticized over and over again for engaging in the kind of illicit worship that brought the wrath of God down upon them (in the shape of the Assyrian army).

The Dutch answer to the Academy Awards is the Golden Calf Award. Winners walk away with a gold-colored calf image, which a former jury member explained is a kind of "wink. . . . Other countries have golden lions and golden bears. We have a golden calf, which moreover is sinful to worship."[32] Mooby the Golden Calf shows up in the movie *Dogma* as the basis for a highly successful fictional corporation with a fast-food restaurant and Mooby paraphernalia. *Dogma*'s main characters, a couple of fallen angels, take the corporation's board to task for making Mooby a false idol.

A recent, real-world example of a (literal) golden calf was created by Damien Hirst, the wealthiest artist in England, who took a dead bull, covered its horns and hooves in gold, and stood it up in a gold-plated tank of formaldehyde with a golden disk on its head.[33] Of course, the biblical calf was purely a sculpture, not a real animal covered in gold like Hirst's.

Today, a "golden calf" is anything that elicits an inappropriate degree of attention and affection. Combine that sense with the "golden," reference, and it's easy to see why people sometimes confuse the story of the golden calf with Jesus' God-versus-Mammon teaching. Mammon, meaning "wealth" or "money," is personified as a rival deity by Jesus who explains that no one can serve two masters—"You cannot serve both God and Mammon."[34] The sense in both cases is of worshipping the wrong thing—Mammon makes the wrong thing money, in particular.

Two other biblical creatures—a substitute goat and a red heifer—are saviors of a sort. Both appear in detailed instructions about religious formalities. The goat is part of a ritual of atonement to get rid of the community's accumulated sins.[35] The biblical book of Leviticus instructs a priest to symbolically transfer those sins onto a goat chosen for this purpose. According to the priestly instructions, the goat was to be cast out into the desert, taking the community's wrongdoing with it. Leviticus doesn't say explicitly that the goat must die; rather, it is "as an" or "to" (the meaning of prepositions is notoriously tricky to pin down) *azazel*, which remains a mystery.

The theory that Azazel was a wilderness demon continues to hold sway, since it came from biblical scholars with considerable clout; but there is, finally, little justification for that interpretation. It's tough to know the best way to understand this Hebrew word.[36] In modern versions, *azazel* is frequently translated "scapegoat," following the lead of the KJV translators who were actually as puzzled as we still are. They probably simply defaulted to rendering it an (e)scapegoat. Yet while scholars debate the meaning of *azazel*, "scapegoat" is the word that's come down to us. Part of common speech, it's now used to refer to a fall guy, "[some] one that is made to bear the blame of others."[37] Early Christians identified Jesus with the goat of atonement in Leviticus. The New Testament book of Hebrews, all of which looks back to reimagine rituals from the Hebrew Bible in light of the high priest Jesus, compares both the scapegoat and the red heifer to Jesus.

The red heifer is another purifying animal in the Old Testament that has taken on new significance today. According to the Torah, the ashes of an unblemished purely red cow that has done no work (hence the interpretation that it must be young, a "heifer") can ritually purify a person.[38] The biblical ritual has come to be associated with rebuilding the holy temple in Jerusalem because only ritually pure men can officiate as priests. This has joined the interests of some Orthodox Jews with those of Christians eager for the end-time. In 1989, it occurred to Clyde Lott, a Pentecostal preacher who also raised cattle, that he should help, because he believed that before the long-awaited return of Jesus, when the righteous will be taken up into heaven, the Jerusalem temple's sacrificial system must be restored.[39] For that, a red heifer was needed, so Lott set about getting one.[40] In April 2002, the Israeli rabbi Chaim Richman, whose Temple Institute partnered with Lott on this project, declared that finally a perfectly red heifer had been born. It was disqualified in November that same year, illustrating how rare such animals are.[41]

The references to and stories about the golden calf, scapegoat, and red heifer all take place in the context of the Hebrew people's sojourn at Mount Sinai, where Moses received from God the instructions that would define this people's relationship to God. Indiana Jones's quest for the "lost ark" was a quest to find the container in which those instructions were kept.[42] One of the Bible's holiest objects, the Ark of the Covenant was more than simply a wooden chest that housed the commandments. The Ark was God's sacred ottoman.[43] Where it went, God went. Instructions for building the Ark, decorating it, carrying it, and situating it are detailed in the book of Exodus, which also goes to great lengths to describe the tabernacle (a.k.a. tent of meeting) that housed the Ark.[44] (God met with Moses and was present to the journeying Hebrews in this tent.) The great number and kind of details imply that this is no ordinary box but a mysteriously powerful extension of God's very presence. Indeed, this is part of what makes it so attractive to the parties vying for its control in *Raiders of the Lost Ark*. Ironically, one of those parties is the Nazis, infamous for their hatred of the Jews. In synagogues today, the most important item is the Ark, which houses the sacred Torah scroll.

In the biblical narrative, the original Ark traveled with the Hebrew people on their journey through the desert wilderness between Egypt and Canaan. In addition to holding back the Jordan River so that the people could access the Promised Land[45] and ensuring dramatic success in their military exploits,[46] it could also be terribly dangerous. When the Israelites' archenemies, the Philistines, captured the Ark, not only did their god's image keep toppling over in front of it, but they also got so sick that they sent the Ark back to the Israelites—along with gold in the shape of the objects that portrayed the nature of their afflictions—hemorrhoids and mice.[47] On its way into Jerusalem, an Israelite was struck dead on the spot for spontaneously touching the Ark when he acted to keep it from falling. This irked David, who nevertheless eventually brought the Ark into Jerusalem with much fanfare.[48] After the temple was built, the Ark was kept in the temple's innermost holy place.

Where in the world is this fantastic object? Indiana Jones aside, real people are still looking. The last we hear of the Ark in the Bible is that it enjoyed pride of place in the Jerusalem temple's most holy (and inaccessible) spot. When the Babylonians destroyed the temple in 587 BCE, they took a number of its more valuable objects away with them, but the Ark isn't mentioned among the items taken.[49] Nevertheless, it's likely that if they could have gotten their hands on it, the Babylonian invaders would have taken it. But then what? When Cyrus took over in 538 BCE, he let the Jews return and bring their things with them. The Ark's mention is conspicuously absent, and it wasn't reintroduced after the second temple was built, either.

The Ark's whereabouts is no mystery to some Ethiopian Christians. They believe that when Menelek (son of the queen of Sheba and ancestor of Haile Selassie) traveled to Judah to visit his father, Solomon, Menelek returned with Israelite nobles—and (unbeknownst to him) the Ark of the Covenant. Because nothing untoward happened to them, when he discovered the theft, Menelek reasoned that God must have wanted them to have the Ark. At any rate, today these Old Testament-abiding Christians believe that the Ark is in the town of Arum, where it has been guarded by a succession of virgin monks for millennia, and occasionally hidden as necessary to protect it. Only the single living guardian is allowed to see it.[50]

Tudor Parfitt, a professor at the School of Oriental and African Studies in London, begs to differ. He claims that there is a genetic link between the Lemba people of Africa and ancient priests of the Jerusalem temple, a claim which was later corroborated by DNA. Now Parfitt thinks that he's found the Ark, in a Zimbabwean museum—or at least a part of the Ark. It was rebuilt in a drum shape after it self-destructed 400 years ago, according to his theory.[51]

Others beg to differ with both. Some believe that the Ark made its way to Europe thanks to the Templars of the Crusades,[52] and others believe that it never left Jerusalem.[53] The New Testament book of Revelation confidently declares that its narrator saw in a vision the Ark safely ensconced in God's heavenly temple.[54] The Qur'an tells that the Ark will come as a sign to faithful Muslims from God when the time is right.[55]

GOD'S PETS

In the Hebrew Bible, "apple" is to "fruit" (in Genesis) as "whale" is to "big fish" (in Jonah). In other words, in biblical Hebrew, Jonah's whale is not exactly a "whale," but a generic "big fish"—a big *dag* (pronounced "dog"—not to add confusion about the creature's identity).[56] In the biblical story, told in the brief book of Jonah, God sent this fish to swallow the stubborn and disobedient prophet—not to kill Jonah, but to teach him a lesson before vomiting him up on land to start afresh (figuratively speaking). The three days that Jonah spent in the fish's dark belly prefigure the three days that Christians believe Jesus spent between his burial and resurrection.

In modern Hebrew (and *Moby-Dick*), it's the word *leviathan* that means "whale." The most extended biblical description of Leviathan is in the book of Job, where it's preceded by a description of another great beast, Behemoth.[57] The jury is still out on whether or not these two monsters are modeled on real animals. Some "young earth" creationists think that they are biblical references to dinosaurs.[58] Because Behemoth is described as eating grass like an ox and living in marshy areas, it seems like a hippopotamus; others say it's a crocodile because the poetry declares, "It moves its tail like a cedar." Truth is, the Bible doesn't clarify this. Rather, what's important seems to be the creature's awesome strength and intimidating presence; and the main point is that God created Behemoth, and God alone can master it. Today, of course, a "behemoth" is any huge or unwieldy thing. Recently, the *New York Times* described ESPN as a behemoth that nevertheless remains in its tiny town of origin, and an article in the *Los Angeles Times* tells how Bank of America grew to be a behemoth in the financial industry.[59]

In the Bible, Leviathan is described as a great sea creature that terrifies even the gods, except the LORD.[60] God's speech about Leviathan in Job, a whole chapter's worth of description, virtually gushes about the monster's grand wildness and terrifying presence. The rhetorical questions suggest that only the boundless strength and far-reaching dominance of God can control Leviathan. Although Job gives Leviathan the most attention and detail, two psalms and one verse in Isaiah also mention Leviathan as a great monster subject to God's mastery.[61] Mythological poetry from the Canaanite city of Ugarit (predating the biblical) describes a tyrannous, many-headed serpent creature called *ltn*, whom the god Baal defeated in a cosmic struggle.[62] In the much later deuterocanonical book of 2 Esdras (first century CE), Behemoth and Leviathan are described as early (fifth-day) creations of God assigned to different parts of the world—Behemoth to the dry land, and Leviathan to the waters.[63]

The British philosopher Thomas Hobbes initiated a new paradigm in western thought with his book *Leviathan* (published in 1651), in which he developed the "social contract" theory that lies at the foundation of democracy. The name and its associations in the Bible and through Hobbes's philosophy have inspired films, music, novels, and games. Although the biblical Leviathan is associated with chaos—a threat to world order—the creature is not described as evil per se. Nevertheless, the "Leviathan number" in mathematics is $(10^{666})!$. The exclamation point shouldn't be taken here as a grammatical exclamation; rather, it's a technical mathematical symbol that represents a factorial. (The parentheses are part of the number, too.) The Leviathan number, pictured as an O with horns, plays on the "mark of the beast."[64]

REPRESENTATIONS OF EVIL IN NUMBER AND PERSON

The "mark of the beast" comes from the apocalyptic New Testament book of Revelation, which relies heavily on Old Testament references and imagery. A vision related in Rev 13:1–10 combines the four beasts of Dan 7:3–28 into one sea beast that represents the Roman empire. The author of Revelation tells how in the end-time, which many early Christians believed was their own time, this beast will deceive a great many people into following its lead and worshipping it. They will bear the mark of the beast on their heads or hands, and that mark is the number of the beast. On June 6, 2006, various groups of Christians gathered together all over the world to try to ward off what they were concerned would be an outpouring of evil on that day.[65]

Most English translations (including the KJV) render the number as 666; but among the early variant manuscripts, it is sometimes 616. The discrepancy may be explained if one considers that the number(s) originally meant to refer cryptically to the Roman emperor Nero (feared and despised for his torture of Christians).[66] The sum of the Hebrew consonants (each letter is given a numerical value) transliterated from the Greek *Neron Kaiser* is 666. Transliterated into Hebrew from the Latin *Nero Caesar*, it is 616. Other explanations for associating 666 with evil note that it is the sum of numbers 1 to 36, and 36 is the sum of 1 to 8, so it's a "double triangular number," unfavorably contrasting with the square numbers 144 (for the heavenly city in Rev 21:17) and 144,000 (for the martyrs in Rev 7:4). Another such symbolic interpretation observes that 7 is a perfect number and 777 absolutely perfect; 888 is the sum of Jesus' Greek name, so 666 is as evil as Jesus is good.[67] None of these explanations are completely satisfying.

Because of the highly symbolic nature of Revelation, the end-time beast has been interpreted and reinterpreted throughout the ages. A number (pardon the pun) of people, nations, and supernatural powers have been associated with "the beast" and its number. Most people today assume that the number is 666 (rather than 616) and identify it with the Antichrist, the devil, or Satan. Despite *The Da Vinci Code's* suggestion that the glass pyramid at the Louvre's entrance has 666 panes of glass, it does not. Quentin Tarantino's film *Pulp Fiction* prominently features a black suitcase whose combination is 666 and whose contents glow when it's opened. The fear of 666 even has a name: hexakosioihexekontahexaphobia.

Today, some people interpret Rev 13:16 to mean that bearing the mark of the beast is involuntary—people will be forced to bear it. According to the biblical prophecy, people will need the mark in order to participate in the economy. Consequently, what it means to have the mark has expanded to include bearing a Social Security number.[68] Some people believe that there is something sinister at work in the bar codes that are ubiquitous retail symbols.[69] Some even see the microchipping of animals to be a sign of tribulation to come, when the Antichrist gains power over the earth, as noted in this book's introduction.

ANGELS AND DEMONS

Angels and demons as we think of them reflect diverse biblical references and ideas that evolved over time. The English word "angel" derives from the Greek *angelos*, which is the Septuagint's favorite way to translate the Hebrew *malak*, meaning simply "messenger." ("Malachi," the name of the prophet, means "my messenger.") Both *angelos* and *malak* are used of ordinary human messengers as well as of God's supernatural messengers.[70] Occasionally they are actually bad.[71]

When it comes to identifying supernatural beings who do God's bidding, *malak* is the term used most often in the Old Testament.

That said, the Old Testament shows little interest in defining or otherwise describing these *malaks*, even when the context suggests that they should be understood as divine or quasi-divine. They show up, do their task (besides delivering messages, sometimes they direct a person's actions, provide protection, or execute punishment), and that's that.[72]

Another way that the Old Testament identifies divine beings is generally as the *bene elohim*, literally "sons of God" (sometimes translated "heavenly beings"), which can include the *malak* messenger-angels described above. In Hebrew, the word that means "sons of" can also mean "those who belong to the category of."[73] However one interprets it, "sons of God" here refers to the divine beings who compose the divine assembly over which God presides and whom God often directs. The most well-developed biblical portrait of such an assembly is found in the story about the prophet Micaiah ben Imlah (not to be confused with the prophet Micah) in 1 Kings 22:19–22.

Other beings sometimes translated in English as "angels" are identified in the Old Testament as "men" who have inhuman characteristics or abilities. Ezekiel describes both a manlike spirit who serves as a vision guide, and "men" whom God instructed to carry out judgment in ways that conform to modern ideas about angels.[74] Likewise, Zechariah was led by a being called both a "man" and *malak YHWH* to see and understand the message he was to prophesy.[75] By the time when Daniel was composed (in the mid-second century BCE), ideas about angels were much more developed and detailed. Some angels, such as Gabriel (who looked "like a man" but flew swiftly and helped Daniel interpret signs) and Michael (identified by a Hebrew term for an "official," "leader," or "prince"), are distinguished in Daniel as individuals with personal names.[76]

Other supernatural beings that appear in the Hebrew Bible, such as the seraphim and cherubim (Hebrew plurals for "seraph" and "cherub," respectively) are less "angels" as we think of them than, say, fauna of the otherworldly sphere. They aren't intermediaries between heaven and earth; nor do they otherwise deal much with human beings. Rather, they act as guardians and protectors of the divine (in the case of the hybrid, animal-humanoid cherubim) and may serve to proclaim the holiness of God (in the case of the winged serpentine seraphim).[77] Seraphim appear also as agents of God's anger against the Israelites—as fiery snakes whose bite could be lethal (the Hebrew word *srp* has to do with fire).[78]

In the New Testament the supernatural *angelos* not only continue to serve as messengers, guides, and intermediaries, like the *malak* of the Hebrew Bible, but also appear more frequently and with more significant roles than in the Old Testament. One of the most distinctive developments in the New Testament in terms of angels is as guardians of human beings, both individual persons and communities (such as the seven churches in Revelation chapters 2–3, each of which has an assigned protective angel). They are a significant part of Jesus' life, ministering to him from the beginning to the end of his life; and they help with judgment, both immediate (e.g., Acts tells that angels killed Herod)[79] and ultimate (e.g., "weeding out" evildoers, destined for punishment in the last days).[80]

Moving from good to bad, consider that just as God might send divine "messengers" to do his good work on earth, God is said in the Hebrew Bible also to be responsible for sending a *ruach ra'a*, literally translated as an "evil/harmful spirit." The most famous such spirit is the one that tormented King Saul with anxiety and distress.[81] Not the same as autonomous beings that work against God (what we might call demons), these spirits are always identified as coming from (or as "of") God. They don't appear very often, though, making it difficult to confidently detail their characteristics.[82]

In the Old Testament, there is no single, specific term that is obviously equivalent to the English "demon." One of the Hebrew terms (*shedim*) that is translated in the Septuagint as *daimonion* and in English as "demon" applies to the "not-God" gods that Israelites wrongly worshipped; this word is rare, appearing only twice.[83] Some people think that unnaturally peculiar animals such as Leviathan or Behemoth might be considered Old Testament demons. Destructive natural phenomena or plagues, if personified, might also qualify as demons.[84] Lilith, a Hebrew word that appears only once in the Hebrew

Bible, does so as a feminine noun in the context of a list of scary wild creatures that took over the deserted territory of Israel's enemy.[85] Later Jewish interpreters developed the portrait of (proper noun) Lilith as a child-snatching demon. Similarly, the scapegoat of Leviticus 16 later became a name, Azazel, and was thought to be a demon that inhabited the wilderness areas.

Finally, there is simply very little in the Hebrew Bible about demons as we think of them. Our concept of demons is informed much more by intertestamental and New Testament texts. In the New Testament, the Greek term *daimon* or some variation of it (often in the diminutive form *daimonion*) appears more than sixty times.[86] Although the word in Greek doesn't necessarily denote a nefarious supernatural being, in the Bible it usually refers to what we would think of as a "demon." Spirits (from the Greek *pneuma*) of a malevolent variety also sometimes instigate or are otherwise implicated in troublesome acts.

Illnesses and disabilities—physical, mental, and spiritual—are frequently identified as the doing of demons who have somehow insinuated themselves into a person. Consequently, among Jesus' many healing acts is the exorcising of demons. In one of the more dramatic examples, demons begged Jesus not simply to drive them out of the man they were afflicting but to let them inhabit a herd of swine. He agreed, and the pigs promptly ran off a bank and drowned.[87] Enormously important to the synoptic gospels, such exorcisms signaled to early audiences that the kingdom of God had broken into the human domain to take on and defeat the powers of evil. Demons are less concrete and immediate characters per se (though no less problematic) in the rest of the New Testament, where they are evident more by the moral and spiritual troubles that they incite.

SATAN

If Satan is not in the snake or in the Genesis story at all except by interpretation and inference, then where in the Bible does he come from? The word comes from the Hebrew *satan* (the accent is on the second syllable), which apparently didn't originally refer to an individual (whose name we might then capitalize) at all. Rather, it is used in the Hebrew Bible as a general noun or verb to connote "accusation, betrayal, adversity." The word appears only thirty-three times in the Old Testament (including its use as a verb), and fourteen of its occurrences are in the prose story at the beginning of Job. In only one case does the noun identify an adversary of God: 1 Chron 21:1, where it also appears without a definite article, indicating that it should be translated there as a proper noun—the name Satan. By contrast, the worldview of the New Testament emphasized the personification of evil, and so the Hebrew term appears there as the name of an autonomous evil entity, Satan.

Concerning the Old Testament: as a noun, *satan* is used to describe ordinary human beings as well as supernatural adversaries (not necessarily evil). Its canonically first use associates David with such adversarial characteristics. When Saul was still king, and David was serving as a mercenary in the Philistine army, the Philistines were concerned that in the impending battle with the Israelites David might "become a *satan* to us."[88] Later, in the course of shifting national power into his own hands, David called one of his own supporters a *satan* for suggesting that he execute a man who once had bad-mouthed David but then recanted.[89] Solomon used the noun *satan* to refer to national military threats.[90]

There are only four cases in the Hebrew Bible of supernatural *satans* (in Numbers, Zechariah, 1 Chronicles, and Job). Their literary and historical contexts suggest that they were originally understood as distinct beings, rather than as different manifestations of a single individual. In three of them, the *satan* serves as an accuser, an adversary, something like a prosecuting attorney. Only in 1 Chronicles, probably the latest of these texts, does the noun refer to Satan, a personified adversary of God.

In Numbers, the word *satan* refers to a messenger angel sent by God to prevent an attack against Israel and correct a case of animal abuse. Specifically, the foreign prophet Balaam, who was supposed to curse the Israelites, was halted in his path by this *satan*, this adversary.[91] Balaam's donkey saw the angel and refused to go forward, but Balaam couldn't see the angel, so he beat his donkey until the donkey said something like, "Why do you keep hitting me? I've always been obedient. Don't you think that there must be some good reason for me not to go forward?"[92] And the angel, finally revealing itself to Balaam, said something like, "Why are you being so hard on your donkey? I came as a *satan* to stop you from cursing the Israelites. That donkey actually saved your life."[93]

In the apocalyptic book of Zechariah, the prophet relates a vision in which a *satan* (noun) makes a brief appearance to *satan*ize (verb): "the high priest Joshua standing before the LORD's angel, and the accuser (*satan*) standing at his right to accuse (*satan*) him."[94] In the next verse, God rebukes the *satan*, presumably because he is getting ready to hector the high priest. This may illustrate a development of the idea of a *satan* from playing the role of an accuser (who helps God to assay righteousness) into an autonomous force, separate from and opposing God.

The noun *satan* is most prominent in the book of Job, where it describes a character in the prose prologue. In Job, the *satan* fits the image of an adversary or accuser—problematic, but not a pure personification of evil, who challenges but is not the antithesis of God. Described as among the divine beings that report to God in the heavens, he also was free to roam the earth, and this is how Job's troubles began. The *satan* posed a challenge to God, requiring that Job suffer. God agreed to it, and Job's torment then becomes the focus of the book. (The *satan* does not appear again in the prose section that concludes Job.)

Although Zechariah's *satan* is scolded by God, and Job's *satan* instigates great suffering, the only instance where the Hebrew *satan* might be considered a supernatural personification of evil opposite God is at the end of 1 Chronicles—a retelling of the same story that concludes 2 Samuel. It's an odd episode in which David took a census that angered God, who sent a plague. In 2 Sam 24:1, it is God who incited David to take the census; in 1 Chron 21:1 it is Satan who does so. It's a weird story, any way you read it. For our purposes here, suffice it to say that this case, in which Satan's substitution exonerates God, is the only instance in the Old Testament of an evil Satan.

Given the increase in personal names applied to demons in later, intertestamental literature, it seems that shifting worldviews (likely influenced first by the dualism of Persia's Zoroastrianism) allowed for the development of a devil such as we would recognize.[95] Later Jewish commentary on the Hebrew scriptures, during the intertestamental rabbinic period, attributes much more evil to (proper noun) Satan. By the time the books of the New Testament were composed, Satan had become identified with a full-fledged source of evil *distinct from* God. While the *satan* of the Old Testament always operated in some sense under the purview of God and only against humans (with the possible exception of 1 Chron 21:1), the Satan of the New Testament is another creature altogether. Indeed, by the first century CE, Satan had come to be understood as an adversary of God, and as such was much more of a preoccupation. The Hebrew *satan*, translated in the Septuagint as the Greek *diabolos*, was thus transformed into Satan, the devil.

Satan appears by name in the New Testament thirty-five times. As the personification of evil, he goes by titles such as "prince of this world," "prince of demons," "evil one," and "father of lies."[96] Satan is also called *diabolos*, "devil," in the New Testament (about thirty times). For example, while Mark says that Satan tempted Jesus in the wilderness, in Luke it is "the devil."[97] Revelation makes this connection explicit, adding "that ancient serpent" and "the great dragon" as one great personification of evil,[98] and so contributing to the popular equation of the snake in Eden (as well as Job's Leviathan and the dragon Rahab) with Satan.

The idea of Satan as a fallen angel named Lucifer is not made explicit in the Bible, but likely developed from a couple of biblical references. In Luke 10:18 Jesus says, "I saw Satan fall like lightning from heaven," probably reflecting an interpretation of the Old Testament prophet Isaiah's exclamation, "How you have fallen, morning star of dawn!—you who once brought nations down are [yourself] cast down to earth."[99] To give some context: the prophecy in Isaiah tells how one particular star aspired to climb higher than God's stars to sit among God's divine assembly and become like the highest God; but Isaiah declares that instead it would be reduced lower than earth.[100] As with most poetry, it works on several levels. Introduced as symbolic of the Babylonian king (described as "a man" in verse 16), it nevertheless also evokes and consequently condemns Babylonian and Canaanite astral theologies.

By the beginning of the second century, the Christian theologians Origen and Tertullian associated that Isaiah prophecy with Satan; and soon afterward, when it was translated into Latin, the Hebrew word *helel,* "morning star," was interpreted as "the light bringer," *lucifer.*[101] The English King James Version retained Jerome's Latin *lucifer,* and rendered it as a proper name, making the association complete, where it crystallized in the popular imagination.

Besides Lucifer, other biblical names for the personification of evil include Beelzebub, from the Hebrew *Baal zebub,* whom readers meet in the Old Testament book of 2 Kings. According to the biblical story, after the Israelite king suffered a bone-shattering fall, he sought a prognosis not from Yahweh, as he should have but from this Philistine god, *Baal zebub.*[102] The name means literally "Lord of the flies," and that is also how the Septuagint renders it (*Baal muian,* in Greek). William Golding's novel *Lord of the Flies* tragically reveals evil as inherent in human beings, not something that can be killed like some "beastie."[103] By the time of the New Testament, Beelzebub had become equated with Satan.[104]

BRIEF NOTE ON A NUMBER OF NUMBERS

The number 7 makes its debut in the very first chapter of the Bible: Genesis chapter 1, the story of God's creating the world in seven days. The seventh and final day, the culmination of creation in this story, is the Sabbath. God blessed and sanctified that day. Seven seems to have connoted completeness, wholeness. The writers responsible for the priestly matters enumerated in Leviticus (possibly the same who wrote Genesis 1) described specific observances for the seventh year and the seventh seventh year (also called the Jubilee). In addition to many other scriptural examples, the last book of the Christian bible, Revelation, is filled with 7s. The narrator explains that the revelation is for "the seven churches that are in Asia." The churches numbered many more than seven; but appealing to that number of completeness, John's audience would have understood that he meant the message to be for all of them. John also explains "the mystery of the seven stars . . . and the seven golden lampstands: the seven stars are the angels of the seven churches; and the seven lampstands are the seven churches."[105] The most famous 7s in the book of Revelation are the seven visions that follow the opening of the seven seals, accompanied by seven trumpets. Ingmar Bergman's iconic existentialist film *The Seventh Seal* (1957) pits a knight whose faith is faltering against the personification of Death in the context of chess. The popular film *The Seventh Sign* (1988) is preoccupied with apocalyptic signs of the end-time.

Jews and Christians have both extrapolated on the significance of the number 7 in contemporary religious practice. For example, Jews observe shivah, a mourning period of seven days. The word *shivah* means "seven." Some Christian traditions enumerate seven virtues and seven deadly sins to help define a godly life. In J. K. Rowling's *Harry Potter* series, the number 7 trumps all others in power.

The number 12 is another biblically significant number. In Genesis, Jacob has twelve sons, whose descendants compose the twelve tribes of Israel. It is no coincidence, then, that the disciples of the Jewish Jesus would number twelve. Just as the tribes always number twelve (though Ephraim and Manasseh sometimes stand in for Levi and Joseph), an additional disciple (Matthias) was selected to replace Judas after he betrayed Jesus, to preserve the number of disciples as twelve. John Milton's epic poem *Paradise Lost* is divided into twelve books. In *Battlestar Galactica* the Twelve Colonies of Man/Kobol represent all of humanity. In a bit of religious turnabout (or confusion?) Cyndi Lauper released an album in 1994 of earlier favorites. It's titled *The Twelve Deadly Cyns . . . and Then Some.*

HERALDING THE MESSIAH

At the end of Genesis, Judah the man is described in monarchal terms
and called a lion.[106] According to the biblical narrative, it is from Judah's line that David would eventually come and establish the kingdom of Israel. Still today, the Israeli coat of arms for Jerusalem features
a fearsome lion against the backdrop of a wall (the Western Wall),
flanked by olive branches. Revelation picks up this imagery, portraying "the lion of the tribe of Judah" as the one who is worthy to unlock
the book of God's plans.[107] As Revelation continues, the Lion is also
said to be the slain and resurrected Lamb—the crucified messiah.[108]
So for Christians, Jesus is the ultimate fulfillment of Judah's royal
lineage.

According to Ethiopian tradition, the lion of Judah's family tree
sprouted another branch with Solomon. As the legend goes, after the
African queen of Sheba visited the famous king Solomon, she went
home bearing new ideas, gifts, and a baby, too. In the late nineteenth
century, Emperor Menelek I claimed descent from this famous pair
and developed a flag to show it. Against green, yellow, and red stripes
(recalling the rainbow of God's promise after the Flood) strides the
Lion of Judah, wearing a gold crown and holding a standard (reflecting more imagery from the same passage—Genesis 49:8–12).

Haile Selassie, emperor of Ethiopia in the mid-twentieth century,
adopted this imagery, and the flag continued to bear the Lion of Judah
emblem until 1975. Rastafarians carried Haile Selassie's identification
with the tribe of Judah yet further, as a divine messiah. They believe
him to be God incarnate, "Lord of lords," "Jah." The great reggae musician Bob Marley brought these traditions to a wider public. Today,
Lion of Judah, Ras Judah, and Tribe of Judah (tagline "anointed reggae band") are names of reggae music groups.

The star of Bethlehem is a reference from Jesus' birth story, and it
appears only in Matthew's gospel, perhaps based on a prophecy from
the book of Numbers. This prophecy, that a "star would come out of
Jacob, and a scepter rise out of Israel" (the poetic parallelism suggests
monarchal imagery)[109] had taken on new meaning in the Roman-

ruled years between the testaments. The Near East saw an increase in messianic hopes during the centuries straddling the Common Era, and people were on the lookout for signs. According to Matthew's story, a bright star hovered over the place where Jesus was born, enabling the oriental wise men to locate him and give him their gifts.[110] No search for a historical celestial event that would meet the criteria of Matthew's story has yielded a wholly convincing physical explanation, yet some people are certain that the star existed.[111] People flock to planetariums at Christmastime to learn more about the skies above Bethlehem at the turn of the era, and to consider the options, including a comet, a meteor, a nova, or a subtle heavenly sign (a massing of planets, for example) that only highly trained astronomers such as the magi might have seen as significant.[112] "Star of Bethlehem" is also the name of a plant.

Matthew's gospel reports that magi astronomers from the East brought gifts to the newborn Jesus. Although the Bible never gives the number of "wise men" (or their names), most people assume that there were three, probably because the Bible does note their three gifts—gold, frankincense, and myrrh. Ancient readers would have understood these gifts to bear significance beyond the thoughtful gesture. While the gold and frankincense are fitting gifts for a king, the myrrh carries a dark and sinister message, giving "You shouldn't have!" new meaning. First, a word about gold and frankincense.

These two luxury items were mentioned in a prophecy of Isaiah, in a poignant poem of restoration, when the people of Israel, who had been living in the land of their Babylonian conquerors, return home. The poem describes in evocative detail the newly polished reputation of Israel, eliciting foreign gifts as God brings the people back. "Arise, shine, for your light has come," Isaiah declares; and: "the abundance of the sea shall come to you . . . all those from Sheba shall come. They shall bring gold and frankincense. . . . Nations shall bring you their wealth, with their kings led in procession."[113]

As far as gifts go, gold is an obvious choice—a material of considerable timeless value, gold doesn't just symbolize but actually is wealth. In the ancient Near East, frankincense, too, communicated wealth, and it added an element of luxury, since it was (and still is) used primarily in makeup and perfume. The stuff itself comes weeping from the scored bark of particular trees that can be found in Oman, Yemen, and Somalia. The resin hardens into chunks called "tears." Its color varies in shades of warm yellow, and it can be burned for aromatherapy[114] (and the black residue serves as kohl for eyeliner), or combined in perfume. Frankincense continues to serve as an ingredient in the incense burned today in Roman Catholic churches.[115] The tree itself is a romantic image of value bled from adversity and sacrifice. The scrubby trees grow in harsh, dry climates and have remarkably strong roots. Able to survive in poor, shallow soils, they seem to grow right out of stone.[116] Given the value of frankincense, it makes sense that it was an integral part of Israelite sacrifice.[117] Sometimes in the ancient Near East it was burned at funerals.[118]

The hint of death in rich perfume is even stronger for myrrh. Myrrh, which rivaled frankincense in value in the ancient Near East as another heady perfume, was also used for embalming. Like frankincense, myrrh is a resin from a tree native to the same region. After the magi's appearance at Jesus' birth, myrrh appears in the gospels again only in the context of Jesus' death. Mark tells that Jesus was offered a sip of wine mixed with myrrh as he hung dying on the cross.[119] While some people think that such a mixture would have dulled Jesus' pain, others note that adding myrrh would have made the wine bitter and undrinkable and so exacerbated the torture.[120] Because only Mark tells this bit and does so following a clear reference to the Psalms,[121] the wine and myrrh may also be meant to evoke a psalmic complaint—"They gave me poison for food, and for my thirst they gave me vinegar to drink."[122] At any rate, Jesus rejected it. The gospel of John tells how the wealthy Nicodemus generously brought myrrh and aloe to accompany Joseph of Arimathea in getting and entombing Jesus' dead body.[123]

Myrrh gets the most biblical mention in the erotic love poetry of the Song of Solomon. There it appears with frankincense in a bouquet of the "lover's perfume" (literally or figuratively the smell of sex) and is a metaphor for the lovers themselves. Myrrh also infused the anointing oil that God commanded Moses to concoct for the priests, and it shows up again wafting from the king's robes in the poetry of Psalms.[124] You'll remember that the Hebrew word translated as "anoint" is the one from which we get "messiah." Not insignificant, then, these gifts that Matthew reports were highly suggestive of how Matthew understood the infant Jesus.

JESUS' DEATH AND THE END THAT IS A BEGINNING

Indeed, for Matthew and others, Jesus was a new kind of priest and king, preaching reinterpretation of Jewish scripture and reformation of tradition. His followers believed that Jesus was the "king of kings," God incarnate. Thus the trajectory of Jesus' life inevitably led to clashes with religious authorities and the political power of Rome. Yet according to the New Testament writers, his death was not the tragic ending of an exemplary life, but the demonstration of exceeding divine love in a cosmic, vicarious atonement for human sin that would grant the faithful eternal life. So it's with a sense of irony that the gospel writers tell how Jesus' Roman tormentors planted a "crown of thorns" on his head and mocked him as the "King of the Jews."[125]

Today, "Crown of Thorns" is also the name of a hard-rock band, a spiny starfish, an evergreen relative of the poinsettia, and a racehorse that ran for the 2008 Triple Crown. Michael Gerson, former speechwriter for G. W. Bush, described the brutality and devastation of "Congo's crown of thorns" in an opinion piece for the *New York Sun*.[126] Meanwhile, it continues to be significant for Christians as a symbol of Jesus' suffering. Several places, including Notre Dame in France, Stonyhurst College in England, and the Basilica di Santa Croce in Gerusalemme in Italy,[127] claim to possess a genuine relic. None of these relics can be confirmed as historical with absolute certainty.

The search for material remains associated especially with Jesus' passion (his suffering and death) is big business, in part because so many of the faithful venerate these relics; but the possibility of real physical evidence associated with these powerful stories fascinates nonbelievers, too. In this, the crown of thorns, the fabric that was used to wipe Jesus' face (a claim for the Shroud of Turin), and remnants of the "true cross" all pale in comparison with the holy grail. For centuries it was the search for this relic that preoccupied people more than any other.

It seems that the grail was originally believed to be Jesus' Last Supper dishware (used to institute the Eucharist). Most people focused on the cup, in particular. Although the word's Latin origins in *gredalis* suggest dishware, a new etymology developed in the Middle Ages, from the French *sang réal*, "holy blood"; to *san gréal*, "holy grail"; and finally to *sangréal*.[128] Early stories also linked Joseph of Arimathea with the grail, claiming that the resurrected Jesus gave it to Joseph. A later legend said that Joseph caught some of Jesus' blood in a cup during the process of burial, making that cup the holy grail. Either way, Joseph was said to have entrusted the grail to folks who brought it to England. The legend of the grail and the quixotic quest for it is woven throughout the King Arthur stories.

Although some churches claim to have the holy grail (in these cases, it is usually represented as a chalice), questions about its identity, power, and whereabouts continue to occupy the imagination. Works of fiction and poetry include nineteenth-century Tennyson's *Idylls of the King* and twenty-first-century Bernard Cornwell's *Grail Quest* series; fantasy (*The War Hound and the World's Pain* by Moorcock); science fiction (*Nova* by Samuel R. Delany); and Peter David's *Knight* trilogy, which sets King Arthur in modern New York City. The grail has showed up in movies both serious and hilarious (*Excalibur, Indiana Jones and the Last Crusade, The Fisher King*, and *Monty Python and the Holy Grail*), in Wagner's opera *Parsifal*, and in the television show *Stargate SG-1*. The most controversial grail idea in recent years, suggested in the nonfiction book *Holy Blood, Holy Grail* and popularized by Dan Brown's novel *The Da Vinci Code*, is that the grail was a woman's womb—Mary Magdalene's with whom Jesus had children.[129] That the grail's definition has always been debatable has kept open the window of possibility for this captivating thesis.

However, it is not a crown of thorns or the grail that Christians first choose to signify their belief in the deeds and divinity of Jesus. It is the cross. From the simple intersection of one long vertical and one short horizontal line or bar favored by Protestants to the Celtic addition of a circle at the joint, from the Rosicrucians' rose-centered cross to the highly filigreed decorative crosses of some Orthodox Christians, this symbol of death signifies belief in Jesus as the incarnation of God whose sacrificial death redeemed humanity from sin and promises eternal life for believers. As of this writing, the Wikipedia "Christian Cross" entry cites nearly forty different styles of crosses, each with a particular history and nuance of meaning.[130]

The New Testament voices are unanimous in telling that Jesus died by the Roman method of execution by crucifixion. The technique was hardly unique.[131] Hundreds of people deemed criminals or enemies of Rome in first-century Palestine were crucified. In the case of Jesus, however, his followers believed that unlike anyone else before or after, Jesus was God, who atoned for human sin and conquered death. They claim that they saw him again, alive as ever, before he ascended into heaven. Consequently, the cross is a crucial symbol of Christian faith.

Christians hang crosses around their necks, affix them to their cars, tattoo them into their skin, mount them above beds and doors and kitchen tables, and gesture its sign before and after prayer. When the body of Jesus is represented on a cross, it's called a crucifix. Roman Catholic and Orthodox Christians often choose the crucifix over an empty cross in order to emphasize the sacrificial nature of Jesus' death, while most Protestant Christians favor the empty cross, because of their focus on the resurrection.[132]

The idea that Jesus will return and take the faithful up into heaven at some dramatic moment in the world's last days has captured the imagination of thousands of fundamentalist, evangelical, and nondenominational Christians. "Rapture," the term used to describe this event, is not actually in the Bible. Bible-based Jews, Catholics, Orthodox Christians, and many other Christian denominations do not accept the premise, yet Tim LeHaye and Jerry B. Jenkins's creative depiction of the rapture in the *Left Behind* series has clearly struck a chord. Tens of millions of these books have sold since the first was released in 1995, and several have become popular movies.

Ironically, it's the faithful who are described by the term "left behind," in the rapture proponents' central biblical text—1 Thess 4:16–17. Paul wrote that passage to assure people that their loved ones who had died before Jesus' return would not be overlooked. Those who were dead, Paul wrote, will rise first, and then the living (the ones who were left behind) will join them, "caught up in the clouds . . . to meet the Lord in the air; and so we will be with the Lord forever." The Greek word *arpazo,* translated "caught up," is *raptus* in Latin—the basis of the English "rapture." Of course, what LeHaye and others mean by the people "left behind" is those who are not caught up at all.

Although the rapture as it's popularly understood has little biblical support, the idea that Jesus will return is prominently represented. Sometimes called the Parousia (reflecting its Greek root in "presence, coming"), the expectation of Jesus' returning to earth to initiate a new age permeates the New Testament, and it is a central feature of Christian doctrine and theology today. Even though the Bible strongly maintains that people cannot predict exactly when Jesus will return, people try anyway. Hal Lindsey wrote *The Late Great Planet Earth* (1970), fairly certain that his was the end-time (specifically, the 1980s). Not everyone who believes in a coming rapture agrees about its chronological relationship to other end-time events, but they share the certainty that it will happen. Then, as a popular bumper sticker warns, "In case of rapture, this car will be unmanned"—to which unbelieving humorists respond with the bumper sticker, "Come the rapture, can I have your car?" In a curious twist, the Rapture Ready Index recommends that you "fasten your seatbelts" when the number measuring end-time-like world events indicates the speedy approach of the rapture.[133]

TWELVE
Sites to Be Seen

One's destination is never a place but rather a new
way of looking at things.

—HENRY MILLER

I am embarrassed to admit how long it was before I finally realized
that Canaan and Israel are different names for the same general territory, and it's really no comfort to find that a lot of churchgoing,
Bible-reading folk don't know that either. This chapter aims to dispel
the vague unrest that comes from feeling you *should* know where, say,
Zion is relative to Jerusalem, or Judah is to Israel, but can't quite say
for certain or why it matters. Truth is, questions such as these really
are more complicated than simply determining a site's location. In
some ways, Canaan and Israel are different places; Zion *is* Jerusalem;
and depending on what part of the Bible you're reading, Judah is either
part of Israel or a nation at odds with it. While it's important simply
to know where on a map these places are or were, this chapter also
describes how they function in the narrative as a whole. Inasmuch as
they may have distinct geographical locations, these places are even
more significant in their interpretation—as sites where the dramas of
creation and destruction, nation building and demise, passion, miracle, and mystery transpired.

BEGINNINGS, OR BEFORE PLACES WERE LOCATED

"Eden," a simple transliteration of the Hebrew place-name, is the first
locality mentioned in the Bible—where God created Adam and Eve.
Its site is described in some detail, so people ever since have tried to
pinpoint just where on earth it is . . . or was. Some people think Eden
was in Scotland; others think it was in the middle of Africa; the Mormons believe Eden is in Jackson County, Missouri. Most people use
the familiar geographical markers in the biblical text to situate Eden
in modern Iraq.

The desire for Paradise and nostalgia for a perfect time and place
drive the quest to find Eden as much as efforts to corroborate biblical
claims with historical and geographical fact. The biblical description
itself flirts with both fact and fiction. It tells that four rivers originate
in Eden.[1] Two have real-world reference today: the Tigris and the
Euphrates. But the other two rivers—the Gihon and Pishon—defy
geographical pinpointing. The Gihon has no Mesopotamian referent;
in this particular biblical story, it probably refers instead to a famous
Gihon spring in Jerusalem, the source of water that made Jerusalem
habitable in the first place. Together with the Pishon, which has also
stumped efforts to locate it geographically, but is figuratively described
elsewhere as overflowing with wisdom,[2] these rivers imagine an ideal
Jerusalem, of sorts, as the center of an ideal world. The Genesis story
associates three territories with the rivers' courses: Cush (usually interpreted as Ethiopia), Assyria (along the Tigris in northern Mesopotamia), and Havilah (probably southern Saudia Arabia, though we
can't say for certain).

The story adds another point of orientation. It tells that Eden is
miqeddem, a word usually translated "in the east." But the word could
also have a temporal sense: "from antiquity" or "in ancient times."
Indeed, for all its geographical specificity, the story tells a universal
tale of creation in harmony, disruption, and then new beginnings in
tougher, more ambiguous circumstances. In other words, although
the story is situated in the Middle East (as we would expect, knowing
what we do about the Bible's authorship), Eden is also an ancient state

of being, not a place that one can find with a GPS. The combination
of references in Genesis locating Eden invites readers to imagine an
ideal place only just out of reach. Often equated with Paradise, Eden
represents a condition of new creation when everything was bright and
good, before human beings disobeyed God and were evicted. Incidentally, "Paradise" is not mentioned in the Hebrew text of Genesis—or
anywhere in the Old Testament, for that matter. That is, however,
how the Septuagint translated Eden. "Paradise" may come from a Persian word describing a walled garden, so that by the time the Hebrew
story was translated into Greek, *paradeisos* was a sensible translation for
the Hebrew *gan*, described in Genesis 2–3.

In the story, the narrator took pains to call the place *gan*, a Hebrew
word that means "garden," in particular, and to describe it as something that God actually "planted" with beautiful and delicious trees.
Adam was assigned to tend it. The story takes place at the beginning
of creation, before the human being (*adam*) was divided into "man"
and "woman." After God had planted this garden (arguably more an
orchard, given its description here), and after its lengthy description,
the narrator tells that God put the human being into it in order to take
care of it. The economy of the text and the limits of English translation belie the rich potential of this statement's meaning.[3]

For one thing, the specific Hebrew word for God's putting the
human being in the garden connotes the ah-relief-rest of being settled, like the way my hound stretches out on the carpet at the end of
the day (or any time, actually) and sighs deeply before sleep. Ironically,
the word is attached to work, in this case, tilling and keeping. Or
maybe it's not so ironic. After all, as noted above, those Hebrew words
translated "till" and "keep" are more nuanced. This tiny sentence can
rather mean that God's purpose for the human being was that *adam*
serve the garden with reverent care, watchfully guarding its welfare.
What's more, far from being burdensome, that activity afforded the
human being satisfaction and repose. Eden was, then, a place of harmony and satisfaction amid lush fecundity.[4]

Is it any wonder that we smile and sigh nostalgically for the garden
of Eden, or that we'd buy products that evoke such well-being? Eden

Organic foods, Eden Body Works for hair and skin, Eden Springs water, and Bono's Edun line of socially and environmentally conscious clothing are a few examples. The first album by the popular British musical duo Everything But the Girl was titled *Eden*, and international star soprano Sarah Brightman also cut an album with that title. The Eden Project, a series of greenhouse domes in England, strives to remind people of their connection to nature.

When Adam and Eve ate from the tree of the knowledge of good and evil, which God had forbidden, they launched a series of events that led to their expulsion from the garden. At the garden's eastern edge, the biblical narrator explains, God set winged creatures[5] and a flaming sword to keep the human beings from eating the fruit of the other forbidden tree, the tree of life. The Garden of Eden has come to be associated with a perfectly lovely condition of harmony between human beings, the natural order, and God. Its roots lie in the stories of creation that begin the Bible, and it has fed popular imagination ever since. People long to return to Eden, but the biblical story of humanity immediately following tells of increasing discord, beginning with a first-generation murder, and the subsequent proliferation of violence that led God to despair at having made people in the first place.

According to the Bible, Noah's ark parked on the Ararat mountains.[6] Though no single peak is mentioned, modern explorers motivated by a desire to corroborate the biblical story with real-world evidence, such as Ron Wyatt of Wyatt Archaeological Research, have looked to Mount Ararat, the highest peak in Turkey. In the 1980s, Wyatt declared that he had found a piece of the ark, following the hint of a ship-shaped object spied by an Air Force pilot in 1949; but the mainstream archaeological community rejects his claims, and leading proponents of creation science consider them to be fraudulent.[7] A 1977 documentary, "In Search of Noah's Ark," repurposed for release on national television in 1993, also claimed evidence for the ark on Mount Ararat. Embarrassingly for CBS, the show was found to be based on a hoax.[8] In 2004, a Christian businessman, Daniel McGivern, started an expedition in the area, to the tune of nearly $1 million, to explore what satellite images suggested to him might be the ark's remains, but he was unable to get a climbing permit.[9] The Bible Archaeology Search and Exploration Institute of Colorado Springs claimed in 2006 to have found petrified ark remains in Iran, but the findings have not been corroborated by outside agencies.[10] The search continues.

Our next stop on this Fateful Sites Tour is Babel, where people again trod dangerously close to divine territory. The story of how people tried to build a tower to the heavens appears just a few short chapters after the Flood story. By this time, the narrator explains, Noah's descendants had multiplied, yet "the whole earth had one language and the same words."[11] The story begins by explaining that the people had all migrated to and settled in Shinar—an area of Babylonia in lower Mesopotamia. There the people planned to build a city with a great tower and a name for themselves to preserve their unity. This upset God, who reasoned that if they kept this up, people would be able to do anything. So God proposed, "Let us go down and confuse their language so that they can't understand each other's speech."[12] God scattered them, and they quit building. The narrator explains that because God "confused" their language and scattered the people, the place is called Babel.

"Babel" is a play on the Hebrew word *balal*, "to confuse," and is the Hebrew name of Israel's nemesis, Babylon. Although the story is usually interpreted as God's correcting an act of profound hubris, it also serves the polemical purpose of God's judgment on Babylon, whose name in Akkadian (the Babylonian language), *Bab-ilu*, means "Gate of God."

Babel has come to be associated with an inability to communicate (though it's probably not etymologically related to "babble"), as portrayed recently in a movie by that name. After its release in the autumn of 2006, *Babel* rocked the film world, eventually winning the Golden Globe Award for best motion picture and being nominated for seven Academy Awards (it won one). Its story shows how the lives of four families, living across the world from each other, are connected. In the process, the film demonstrates a human longing for relationship, inevitable misunderstandings, and consequent tragedies and triumphs. Ironically, as of this writing, the United States is embroiled in a war predicated in part on deep cultural misunderstandings in the region of the biblical Babel—a poignant commentary on the human condition.

MESOPOTAMIA AND EGYPT: NEITHER HERE NOR THERE

Mesopotamia, the "land between rivers" (the Tigris and Euphrates rivers, specifically), provided a backdrop for the origin stories of Eden, Ararat, and Babel; but none of those biblical places has been determined to have a definitive geographical location. With Abraham, we're on more solid ground. That is, his story and the others that follow are, for the most part, situated in locations that we can pinpoint with confidence on a map.

Indeed, the most dramatic turning points in the biblical stories of the human relationship to God take place. In other words, the sites of the stories are crucial. Comings and goings, promise and peril, exile and home drive the Bible's plot and define people's relationship to God. Abraham accepts God's charge to go from Ur to Canaan. Jacob's family settles in Egypt where they go from power to slavery. The Hebrew people journey through Sinai and into the Promised Land. A nation under God splits in two—north and south—and each part is destroyed by foreign powers. The northern tribes are scattered within the Assyrian empire, and Judahites are exiled to Babylon. The return to Israel brings restoration and rebuilding. A Jew from Galilee, killed in Jerusalem, is believed to be none other than God's son, resurrected and promising new life for all. His followers fan out into the world to spread the good news. Some believe that Jesus will return, at the end of the world, to Jerusalem. Each event, a fulcrum of divine-human relationship, is geographically situated. And nearly all of them are located within the S-shaped region of Egypt, Israel, and the Fertile Crescent of Mesopotamia.[13]

The story begins in Mesopotamia. Abraham's family hailed from Ur of the Chaldees in the southern part of Mesopotamia.[14] That city made my city's news on the Fourth of July, 2008, when a local man returned home for a couple of weeks' rest before returning to his army unit posted near Ur.[15] According to the biblical narrative Abraham's father, Terah, led the family from Ur toward Canaan, stopping and settling in Haran located in what is now Syria; but it doesn't say why. It does, however, tell why Abraham later left Haran: God called him to do so—to depart "from your country, your kin, and your father's house."[16] Abraham did, but that is not the last that his family saw of Mesopotamia.

Like Mesopotamia, Egypt developed a highly sophisticated culture long before Israel became a nation. Unlike Mesopotamia, Egypt's environment was predictable, dominated by the regular ebb and flow of the Nile River, which left rich deposits of silty soil along its banks. It's no surprise, then, that the first mention of Egypt in the Bible is as a destination of relief from famine. Abraham went there to escape famine "in the land" (Canaan/Israel).[17] Generations later, similarly dire circumstances led Jacob's family to reunite with Joseph in Egypt. After the Hebrew tribes became political nations, Egypt sometimes proved to be an important and valuable ally. Indeed, after the Babylonians conquered the nation of Judah, and after the governor whom they had appointed in Jerusalem was assassinated, it was to Egypt that the people fled. After the rise and fall of the Babylonian and Persian empires, and after the death of Alexander, Israel spent some time under the control of the Egyptian Ptolemies,[18] who promoted Alexandria as a beacon of cosmopolitan learning and ideas. Alexandria in Egypt was the site where Jewish scholars began translating their Hebrew scriptures into Greek.

But the biblical Egypt was not all emergency aid, political posse, and intellectual brilliance. Joseph was taken as so much chattel into Egypt, after his brothers abandoned him in a pit. Although Joseph rose in stature from a slave to second in command, subsequent generations of Hebrews became enslaved there. Indeed, Egypt is best remembered in the Bible for Hebrew captivity, from which Moses dramatically led the escape. Over and over again, the definition of God's character is tied to liberation from Egypt. God repeatedly declares, "I am the one who brought you out of Egypt."[19] Although Egypt was sometimes an ally, such alliance came at a cost—literally. In the eighth century BCE, Israel paid financial tribute to Egypt and fatally ticked off Assyria,[20] and in 609 BCE, it was Pharaoh Neco who killed the beloved and righteous Josiah, king of Judah.

In the New Testament, Egypt doesn't get much attention except to remember the Exodus and God's saving action of liberation. One other instance is worth mention. The gospel of Matthew, concerned as it is to situate Jesus in line with the Old Testament and underscore his Jewish origins, tells a story commemorated in countless "Flight into Egypt," paintings.[21] In that infancy story, Jesus is a new Moses: threatened along with other baby boys by Herod (as Moses was by the pharaoh), the savior is nevertheless spared in Egypt, from where he is called out by God to serve. None of the other gospels include this story.

Mount Sinai is neither here nor there. That is, Mount Sinai is betwixt and between Egypt and Israel, slavery and the Promised Land. Like many of the Bible's geographical sites, it transcends the physical in significance and meaning. Thus it's possible for Judith Plaskow to write *Standing Again at Sinai: Judaism from a Feminist Perspective* and for modern entrepreneurs of romance to name an online Jewish dating site SawYouAtSinai.com. According to the biblical narrative, after the Exodus from Egypt, the Hebrew people made their way through the desert wilderness, stopping for a time at the same mountain where Moses met God, in the burning-but-not-burning-up bush. You may protest that that mountain was called Horeb. True: same mountain, different names.[22]

It was on the top of Mount Sinai that God gave Moses the terms of a new covenant with Israel—the instructions and commandments that would define the Israelites and bind them to God. In a word: the Torah. Mount Sinai, then, is the earthly location for a paradigm-shifting brush with heaven. The biblical story tells how the mountain shook, clouds covered it, and lightning, thunder, and fire awed the people gathered at its base.[23] It is difficult to overestimate the importance of Sinai for God's relationship to the people. Affairs at Sinai occupy the second half of the book of Exodus, all of Leviticus, and the beginning of the book of Numbers.

Where exactly the biblical Mount Sinai is continues to be a matter of debate. At least a dozen possibilities exist. Because the biblical narrative situates the event between Egypt and Israel, most people figure that Mount Sinai must be somewhere on the Sinai peninsula (in which case the identical names are not coincidence). In the sixth century CE, a church that later grew to become the monastery of Saint Catherine was built at the base of Mount Catherine, thought by some to be the historical Sinai because of its great height.[24] But the nomadic bedouin people of that area call an adjacent mountain Jabal Musa, "Moses' Mountain." The History Channel's *Exodus Decoded* (2006) follows a different path of wilderness wandering to conclude that Mount Sinai is modern Hashem el-Tarif in the northeastern part of the Sinai peninsula. That conclusion and many other of the show's claims have gotten far more criticism than support from the scholarly community.[25]

WILDERNESS

Mount Sinai was a stopover on the road to Canaan. The journey as a whole, from Egypt to the Promised Land is remembered as the forty years of wandering in the wilderness. We read about this journey in the book of Numbers, whose Hebrew title is *Bemidbar*, which does not actually mean "numbers" but rather "in the wilderness."[26]

Wild spaces shape us. They push and test us. Wild spaces surprise us, fuel the imagination, and go to work on our innermost selves. They confront us with our limits and stretch our sense of possibilities. Wild places blow the mind. The biblical *midbar* is no different. When the Israelites left Egypt, they immediately began to complain about how difficult it was. They missed the comforts and predictability of urban life, never mind their subservient status. So persistent were the people in pestering Moses and God that God got fed up and determined that no one from that generation (except two—Caleb and Joshua) would get to enter the Promised Land, and forty years is a generation. They

were consigned to wander, then, till the Exodus generation had died
away.

Despite the people's rebelling, the wilderness tempered Israel like
fire tempers metal. Without a lot of external influences and distrac-
tions, the people bonded with each other and with God. God provided
for them, and they survived. After forty years, the people descended
from Abraham and liberated from slavery in Egypt had become a community that survived into a new generation with a shared sense of religious and cultural identity, confirmed with Moses in Deuteronomy.
The Sinai covenant, a binding agreement that God would be their
God and they would be God's people, gained depth and meaning, and
the wilderness is remembered by some, such as Hosea and Jeremiah,
as a honeymoon. Not quite the Bahamas or a Tuscan tour but a honeymoon just the same, when no one and nothing stood between or
distracted from the relationship of the bridegroom—God—and lovely
(if a bit snippy) Israel.

Years later, the prophet Elijah retreated to a different wilderness
after defeating the prophets of Baal. In a clear riff on the story of Moses
and the Israelites in the wilderness, God provided food and water for
Elijah before the prophet trekked "forty days and forty nights" to
Mount Horeb (a.k.a. Sinai). There he experienced a close encounter
with God, the mirror opposite of Moses' storm-studded one.[27] The
narrator explains that Yahweh was not in the great wind, the earth-
quake, or the fire that passed by, but after the fire was a "still, small
voice" (as the KJV translates it). Then Elijah talked with God and
gained a new commission.

The biblical wilderness reconfigures and defines relationships to
God in other stories, too. Isaiah prophesied a wilderness transformed
by God to enable a second Exodus, this time from Babylon back to
Israel. John the Baptist preached in the wilderness a message of repentance to prepare for a new form of connection to God. And Jesus,
immediately after he was baptized, took off into the wilderness, compelled by the Spirit of God. All the synoptic gospels include this episode, and all explain it as a forty-day period of testing. Wild places
call our purest selves, like shy animals from their hidden places, to

account. It's not always pretty, but it's authentic, and from there it's good to grow. Henry David Thoreau declared, "In wildness is the preservation of the world." He may be right.

CANAAN ET AL.

Canaan is a name the Bible uses for that stretch of land at the eastern edge of the Mediterranean between modern Turkey and the Sinai peninsula that has been the object of tug-of-wars (heavy on the "war") for as long as we can tell. It's not the only name for this general tract of land, though. From a biblical perspective, the land is called Canaan when it belongs to "them" and Israel when it belongs to "us." The native inhabitants, whose worship of other gods and goddesses threatened Israelite well-being, are called Canaanites. At the same time, Canaan was also understood by the biblical authors as the place that God promised them, beginning with Abraham (even while Abraham was living in it). The goal of those forty years in the wilderness was to reach it. Canaan, then, was the Promised Land, "the land of milk and honey,"[28] home. Frequently, it's called simply "the land."

From a history-in-the-Bible perspective, it's appropriate to call this land "Israel" after Joshua led the twelve Hebrew tribes in a military and religious rout to oust the native peoples and settle there. Indeed, the designation Canaan nearly drops out of the Bible altogether after the people settle in the land. Then the people became nationally, religiously, and politically "Israelites," and understood themselves to be descendants of Jacob/Israel, himself descended from Abraham, whose family God had chosen to be in a special relationship with God. The Israelites trace their collective history back through Mount Sinai, where Moses brokered the agreement with God that determined the stipulations of their relationship.[29]

"Israel" is a multifaceted name, too. Not only is it an alternative name for the patriarch Jacob, but it is also the name for two different chunks of land. On the one hand, Israel covers roughly the same geographical territory as Canaan; but it is also the name given to the northern kingdom after the united Israel split into two nations. It was distinct from the southern nation of Judah. (Together, then, this new northern kingdom of Israel plus Judah equaled the old united kingdom of Israel.)

Judah, one of Jacob's sons, is the eponymous ancestor of that tribe and also the name of the southern kingdom. It's quite possible, though, given the archaeological record and what we know about the Bible's development, that this chronology is backward. In other words, many people think that the place-name predates the tribe, which may predate the stories about Judah, son of Jacob. However it happened, Judah became the name associated with the southern kingdom after the united Israel split into two. David is inextricably connected to Judah. It is from the tribe of Judah that this most celebrated king came and the nation of Judah saw itself as the nation of David, God's anointed. The word "Judah" is related to Judea, Judaism, Jew, Judith, and Judas. During the Persian period, the territory of Judah came to be called Yehud. Judea is its Greek name, and so was its designation through the Hellenistic and Roman periods that followed; and the people were sometimes called Judeans. However, because of their cultural and religious inheritance, they were also called Israelites.

Two other biblical place-names whose geographies overlap Canaan are Phoenicia and Philistia. Neither was a nation per se; rather, each was a group of towns occupied by people sharing a cultural and ethnic history. The towns of Phoenicia lay in the northern part of Canaan on the Mediterranean coast; the towns of Philistia lay in the southern part of Canaan, also on the Mediterranean coast. Some of the coastal miles between them were controlled by Israel (as the united and later northern kingdom). Given their locations, it is not surprising that both the Phoenicians and the Philistines were known for international trade—red dyed stuffs from Phoenicia (the name means red dyed stuffs) and iron from Philistia. Although both peoples were religiously suspect to, even abhorred by, the biblical writers, Israel enjoyed friendlier relations with Phoenicia than with Philistia. The Phoenician king Hiram (of the city of Tyre) was an associate of both David and Solomon. The Bible tells that he provided construction materials for David's palace and for the temple in Jerusalem. Imagine that—a Canaanite responsible for a crucial contribution to the most significant religious site in Israelite history.

The Philistines, by contrast to the Phoenicians, have a much darker reputation in the Bible. Among the so-called Sea Peoples,[30] they went marauding down the Mediterranean coastline in the mid-second millennium BCE until the Egyptians brought them under control around 1200 BCE and settled them on the southeast shore. The Philistines threw off their Egyptian yoke but stayed put and established a five-city confederation. They are blamed for (or credited with, depending on which biblical perspective one takes) providing the impetus to develop a monarchy in Israel that could efficiently meet the Philistine military threat. And they gained a reputation for boorish behavior. Still today, a buffoon of a person lacking culture and tact is called a "philistine." Modern archaeology shows, however, that the Philistines actually had a much more sophisticated material culture than Israel. And it's thanks to the Philistines, by way of the ancient Greek historian Herodotus, that we have yet another name for Canaan—"Palestine."

CAPITAL CAPITALS

After the united Israel divided into Israel and Judah, the northern kingdom Israel established its capital city in Samaria. "Samaria" is used for both the city itself and its general region. Jesus's parable about the good Samaritan assumes that by his time, Samaritans were reviled by the Jews. This can be confusing, since Samaria was the capital city of Jewish ancestors. But what happens over nearly a millennium can make all the difference. After Samaria and the northern kingdom of Israel were defeated and many people deported in 722 BCE, the Assyrians also imported other defeated peoples and settled them with the remaining natives in the former Israel. Mixed marriage inevitably followed, and many scholars believe that the Samaritans are the result. That was the position of Josephus, and a recent DNA study seems to corroborate it.[31] Perhaps the reputation of Samaritans as having some foreign blood contributed to the Israelites' antipathy. Whatever their ancestry, the Samaritans of Jesus' time had also developed somewhat different religious practices, and they had a rival temple on Mount Gerizim. (The proper temple for Jesus and other Jews was, of course, the temple in Jerusalem.)

It's tough to say if such associations lie behind John's story of Jesus meeting a Samaritan woman at a well (a site the Bible identifies with forthcoming nuptials), but noting that she had had five husbands certainly doesn't elevate her status.[32] Kim Ki-Duk's 2004 movie *Samaria*, about a girl who prostitutes herself, shows the shady reputation of the biblical Samaritan woman. Given the movie's line, "He who is without sin, throw the first stone," one wonders if Ki-Duk has conflated the Samaritan woman with the woman caught in adultery.[33]

No city in the Bible equals Jerusalem in importance and timeless significance. Jerusalem became the capital city of the united Israel when David was king, and David brought the holiest item, the Ark of the Covenant, there. It was in Jerusalem that David's son Solomon built the celebrated temple that further unified the people under God. When Solomon dedicated the temple, God reiterated the covenant made with David but added a crucial condition—if the king (and consequently the people) failed to maintain allegiance to God, then God would remove his protection.[34] Then, the temple would be destroyed and the nation would be subject to defeat. After Israel split into Israel and Judah, Jerusalem continued to be the capital city of Judah, and the biblical editors considered its temple to have the only official altar.

Jerusalem, then, was the place where God determined to be present to his people in a special way. The temple, some biblical writers said, is where God put God's Name (i.e., his particular self) to dwell. Because of its unique status associated with God's presence, the temple and Jerusalem had an extra obligation to be worthy. Lest God's name (and thereby reputation) be sullied, it was crucial in the thinking of biblical sources such as Isaiah that Jerusalem be above reproach. Because God would settle for nothing less, sometimes Jerusalem comes under especially critical fire. The Bible interprets any assault on Jerusalem as God's doing. For example, many biblical writers claim that Jerusalem's defeat by Babylon in 587 BCE was a necessary and deserved punishment that God caused to happen.

Jerusalem, with its Davidic throne and temple (both constant reminders of God's commitment to Israel), was a meeting place of heaven and earth. God had promised that someone from David's line would reign from Jerusalem forever, as "God's anointed," commissioned to execute justice and peace, and that his very presence would be made real to the people from the temple that Solomon built in Jerusalem. Consequently, that particular place, on a limestone plateau along a mountain ridge, with the Judean desert slipping away behind it on one side and the hill country rolling away to the other, is greater in the biblical imagination than its geographical site.

The term "Zion" captures this "greater than" sense of Jerusalem, the place and its people, infused with the power and mystery of God. The poetry in Psalms sings of Zion, "the perfection of beauty out of which God shines,"[35] and the exiles wept when they "remembered Zion."[36] Over and over again, the prophet Isaiah tells of Zion, which the LORD founded,[37] where the LORD of hosts dwells,[38] and whose destiny is to be a universal center of learning and peace.[39] The New Testament author of Hebrews makes it even more explicit, calling "Mount Zion . . . the Heavenly Jerusalem, city of the living God."[40]

Salem, Mount Moriah, and Beulah land are also names associated with Jerusalem. Although Salem, Massachusetts, took its God-fearing down an ugly and divisive witch-hunting path in the seventeenth century, Salem means "peace." Salem first shows up in the Bible when Abraham received a blessing from the local king—Melchizedek of Salem, "priest of the Most High God."[41] Psalm 76 equates it with Zion, and consequently with Jerusalem. The story of Abraham's near sacrifice of Isaac took place on Mount Moriah, which the Bible associates with the Jerusalem site where Solomon built the temple.[42] Because the King James Version transliterated a description of the restored Jerusalem as "Beulah," Beulah land has become synonymous with a spiritual, heavenly Jerusalem. The word in Hebrew means "to be taken in marriage," and its context in Isa 62:4 is of God's taking Jerusalem back as his beloved after destruction and exile.

Yerushalayim, al-Quds, the "Holy City," continues to be enormously important. It is sacred not only to Jews, going back to David, and to Christians as the site of Jesus' passion and resurrection, but also to Muslims as the place where Muhammad ascended into heaven. As you read this, chances are good that Jews are milling about at the Western Wall in Jerusalem's Old City, pushing paper scraps of prayer between the stones of the (second) temple's remaining fragment; Christian pilgrims are winding their way through the cobblestone streets following the Via Dolorosa and locating the stations of the cross; and Muslims are praying, their foreheads against a mosaic of rugs, in submission to Allah at the Al-Aqsa mosque near the Dome of the Rock. In a few minutes those disparate peoples will brush shoulders and nod as they pass each other in the narrow streets.

"Jerusalem syndrome" (mentioned in *The X-Files* and the name of a Belgian band) is an actual mental condition in which a person develops religious obsessions after or about visiting Jerusalem. William Blake's poem about Jerusalem, "And did those feet in ancient time," has been reworked and refashioned and interpreted yet again by several musical groups, including Billy Bragg and Emerson, Lake & Palmer. "Jerusalem" is the title of songs by Sinead O'Connor, Anouk, and Black Sabbath. The Jerusalem artichoke, on the other hand, in contrast to these and countless other contemporary uses of "Jerusalem," actually has nothing to do with either artichokes or Jerusalem. Rather, it is an American sunflower whose tuberous roots are edible. The Italian word *girosole*, meaning "sunflower," is where the "Jerusalem" part mistakenly comes from.

GREAT ENEMIES AND PLACES OF ILL REPUTE

Assyria, a nation based in the northeastern arc of the Fertile Crescent, grew to be a huge empire in the eighth century BCE, when Israel and Judah were two small kingdoms at the eastern end of the Mediterranean. Assyria came to dominate the entire Fertile Crescent, in a territory extending along the Tigris and Euphrates rivers from the Persian Gulf up into modern Turkey and sweeping down through Israel and Judah as far as Egypt. Assyria ultimately conquered the northern kingdom of Israel in 722 BCE and scattered Israel's people among the greater empire. Assyria's cruelty in war was legendary, so the fall of its capital, Nineveh, in 612 BCE was reason for such jubilation that a whole biblical book, Nahum, is devoted to celebrating Nineveh's demise. It's not surprising that the prophet Jonah should be commissioned to preach against that city; he declared that unless it mended its ways, God would destroy it. The surprising thing is that this biblical book ultimately portrays Nineveh and other non-Israelites so well (and Jonah so badly). Most scholars think that the book of Jonah was written centuries after 612 BCE as a corrective to the xenophobia evident in other biblical texts that demonized "the other" and cast them outside God's reach.

Jeremiah, prophesying in Judah toward the end of Assyria's dominance, regularly identified trouble as coming from the north, whence the Assyrians came. Indeed, even though the next big threat, Babylonia, lay directly east, it also attacked from the north, in part because going in a straight line would have required traversing the huge, barren Arabian Desert. (Babylonia lay just north of the Persian Gulf, where the Tigris and Euphrates rivers run parallel.) Besides, the Babylonians first gobbled up Assyria to *their* north and continued to absorb the former Assyrian empire, including the former northern kingdom of Israel, into their own. As far as the Bible is concerned, the Babylonians accomplished what the Assyrians fell short of because they conquered and destroyed the southern kingdom of Judah (587 BCE). They then took Jerusalem's elite back to the empire's capital city, Babylon, and settled the exiles there. The Bible recalls this period as a dark and depressing time of captivity.

The Babylonian empire prospered and developed, and conditions for at least some of the exiles were pretty good. They settled in, had children, and many of them adapted to life in Babylon. Indeed, Babylon was culturally sophisticated, stimulating, dynamic, and wealthy. "Babylon Revisited," F. Scott Fitzgerald's most celebrated short story—a tale of alcoholism, alienation, and spiritual poverty—alludes to this reputation of Babylon as a place of both great wealth and terrific sorrow. Long after the empire had disintegrated and the exiles could return to the land (if not the nation) of Judah, Babylon continued to be a vigorous region for Jewish life and thought. In other words, not everyone elected to return.[43] Nevertheless, in biblical memory, Babylon achieved mythic proportions as the Great Satan of its time. In later, apocalyptic literature such as Daniel and Revelation, Babylon symbolizes everything that's wrong about humans—their arrogance and greed, and their striving for power, wealth, and prestige.[44]

Babylon's reputation as the site of cataclysmic events is reflected in some contemporary uses of the name. *Babylon 5* is the title of a science fiction television series of the 1990s, in which characters living on a space station, many of whom are deeply religious, promote peace and fight evil. The 2008 movie *Babylon A.D.* is also a work of science fiction with religious implications. Its plot is driven by the fact that the pregnant charge of a mercenary may be carrying twin messiahs. To Rastafarians, "Babylon" represents conventional thinking and oppressive systems contrary to the better, more harmonious, mystical sensibility that they champion. Today, Babylon's ruins are situated in and around Baghdad. Consequently, the U.S. invasion and subsequent occupation not only has been politically controversial but also has caused considerable anxiety among archaeologists and historians concerned about damage to the ancient sites and artifacts.

Like Babylon, the Bible casts Rome—metonym for the Roman empire (as Babylon was for the Babylonian empire)—in a less than favorable light. Consider: it was the Romans who crucified Jesus around 33 CE and who destroyed the Jewish temple in Jerusalem in 70 CE (possibly the catalyst for the earliest gospel). Yet Rome's postbiblical history is very different from Babylon's. Thanks mostly to Constantine's history-shaping adoption of Christianity as the national religion of his Roman empire (313 CE), Rome has become the undisputed capital of western orthodox Christianity.[45] It is the site of the Vatican—the pope lives there, after all.

Despite its enormous historical significance, Rome as a place gets little attention in the Bible by comparison with Egypt, Assyria, and Babylonia. This is probably because nearly all of the Old Testament was composed before Rome became a seat of power, and few biblical events or stories are set there. In the Bible, Rome is best-known from

Paul's letter to its Christian community. That book is the most elegant biblical representation of Paul's influential theology. The last we hear of Paul is his preaching in Rome. The Bible doesn't say, but it seems that he died there.

Paul probably wrote his letter to the Romans from the Greek city of Corinth, another place that he put on the biblical map with his letters to its citizens canonized as biblical books (1 and 2 Corinthians). Corinth is not mentioned in the Old Testament at all. Like modern Australia, Corinth experienced a boom in population when it served as a dumping ground for the Roman empire's unwanted people. Just as the British destination for criminals and troublesome Irish developed into a beacon of civilization, Corinth, which got the Romans' former slaves and disenfranchised farmers, became a bustling cosmopolitan commercial center. The particular language and themes of 1 Corinthians reflect characteristics (and challenges) of that vibrant place—spiritual ecstasy and charisma, unorthodox sex, religious diversity, and the self-satisfaction of the nouveaux riches. Two women featured prominently among the Corinthian Christian leadership, Prisca (a.k.a. Priscilla—"little Prisca") and Phoebe.

HOLY WATER: THE DEAD SEA, THE JORDAN RIVER, AND THE SEA OF GALILEE

The situation for Jews and Christians under Roman control was tenuous and tumultuous. It was probably under such conditions that the Dead Sea became a site of considerable religious activity. Corinth, a seaport at the hub of international trade, like San Francisco or New Orleans, was a place one might simply end up, and quite happily at that. The Dead Sea, by contrast, sits surrounded by a stark and barren landscape. More like Ruby Ridge, Idaho, it was a place where the few and piously proud went to get away from everyone and everything else and to await the imminent end of the world. During the period between Testaments, from about 150 BCE to 68 CE, an ascetic community of Jews settled near the Dead Sea. They went there to live a carefully circumscribed religious life, in contrast to what they considered corruptions perpetrated by the Jerusalem temple establishment and by mainstream Judaism. These people, a Jewish sect called the Essenes, are probably responsible for the scrolls that made the Dead Sea region so famous in our time.

Although the Dead Sea is just thirteen miles east of Jerusalem, its almost lunar landscape and the "sea" itself (so saline that no fish, saltwater or freshwater, can survive in it) make it seem worlds away. People seeking to identify a site for the ill-fated cities of Sodom and Gomorrah look to the area around the Dead Sea, and David hid from Saul near there. Some think that John the Baptist spent time among the Essenes in the desert wilderness of the Dead Sea, but we have no proof of it. These days, there is mounting concern that the Dead Sea will soon be a sea in name only. It is rapidly receding because Israel and Jordan are drinking up its only tributary, the Jordan River. (The resulting sinkholes pose science-fiction style threats to livestock, cars, and people.)

The Jordan River is no longer as "deep and wide" as the American spirituals "Michael Row Your Boat Ashore" and "We Are Crossing Jordan River" claim, yet its symbolic association with freedom remains. The Jordan River marked the boundary between the wilderness wandering and settlement in the Promised Land, so it also became an ideological symbol of God's keeping his promise, and of coming home. After Moses died, Joshua led the Israelite tribes across the Jordan River in a manner evocative of Moses' parting the Red Sea—priests holding the Ark of the Covenant stepped into the rushing river, its waters stopped and parted, and the people crossed on dry ground.[46] It was in the Jordan River that John the Baptist baptized Jesus. Indeed, if you follow the Jordan River from the Dead Sea, upstream north ("Jordan" comes from the Hebrew word "to descend"), you'll run into the Sea of Galilee, near where Jesus was raised and conducted much of his adult ministry.

The Sea of Galilee is actually a freshwater lake. Because it's quite shallow (its average depth is only about 84 feet) and because it sits in a valley, storms come fast and the waves are impressive. It's a good place for fishing, and Jesus recruited a number of his disciples from its shores to become "fishers of men." Jesus' miracles include calming a threatening storm on the Sea of Galilee. On its banks, Jesus fed 5,000 people with only five loaves of bread and two fish, and it's on the surface of Galilee that Jesus was said to walk. (His star disciple Peter, too, until Peter lost nerve.) Today, people say of someone who can do no wrong that he or she "walks on water."

In the Old Testament, the Sea of Galilee is called Chinnereth, meaning "lyre-shaped." Luke's gospel and the deuterocanonical 1 Maccabees pick up this moniker, calling the place Gennesaret.[47] Galilee is also the name of the region around the sea. In the Old Testament, references to the sea of Chinnereth and to the region of Galilee are few (three and six, respectively). Only one, and that disputably, shows up in the context of a prophecy that could be associated with Jesus. Its disputed sense is evident in the different ways that it's enumerated in the Jewish and Christian bibles. The Jewish Hebrew Bible considers it to be the final verse of a chapter describing an area that God will restore to Israel; the Christian Old Testament makes it the first verse of a chapter that describes a new ruler who will initiate victory, justice, and peace.[48]

JESUS SLEPT HERE

In the Old Testament, Bethlehem became associated with messianic hopes. There, Ruth married Boaz, whose union led, generations later, to the birth of David. When things went bad, people remembered King David's special place in God's heart and looked expectantly for God's chosen savior-ruler to come from David's line, as promised. Not only was David's tribe, Judah, from the area that includes Bethlehem, but the small-town rural prophet Micah declared in the eighth century BCE, in the face of Assyria's terror, that "you O Bethlehem of Ephrathah, who are one of the little clans of Judah, from you shall come forth for me one who is to rule in Israel, whose origin is from of old, from ancient days."[49]

Thus, even though Jesus was from the northern part of Israel, from the Galilee region, messianic expectations necessitated that he be associated with David's Judah and the town of Bethlehem. A crowd in John's gospel sees this as a real problem. They say: How can Jesus be the messiah? He's from Galilee, but the Bible says that the messiah will come from Bethlehem.[50] The issue isn't resolved in John's gospel. Matthew and Luke, on the other hand, situate Jesus' birth there. Matthew's simple report that Jesus was born in Bethlehem satisfies Micah's prophecy, whereas in Luke, Mary and Joseph traveled to Bethlehem to fulfill census obligations. Beyond these two birth stories, Bethlehem plays no role in the New Testament.

By contrast, Nazareth is regularly identified as Jesus' hometown, the village of Mary and Joseph. All four gospels plus Acts identify Jesus as "from/of Nazareth" (about twenty times). The place lies about fifteen miles west of the Sea of Galilee and seems to have had the reputation of being a bit of a hick town in Jesus' day. One of Jesus' disciples-to-be exclaims rhetorically, "Can anything good come out of Nazareth?"[51]

Nazareth is never mentioned in the Hebrew Bible, but some think that its association with Jesus shouldn't be understood only geographically—rather, Jesus should be understood as a Nazirite, a person set apart by God for special service. But the Hebrew *nazirite* is not represented as such in Greek, suggesting that although they look similar to our English-reading eyes, *nazirite* (appearing only in the Hebrew Bible) has no relationship to Nazareth (appearing only in the New Testament). The one possible exception is a passage wherein Matthew claims that Jesus came from Nazareth to fulfill a prophecy that he would be "called a Nazarene."[52] There is no such prophecy in the Bible as it has come down to us. However, Matthew may have had in mind the Hebrew Nazirite tradition. Or perhaps he was using a bit of wordplay to associate the "branch" (*nezer*, in Hebrew) of Jesse's family tree in a messianic prophecy with Jesus.[53]

There are towns all over the world—e.g., in Mexico, Peru, India, South Africa, Belgium, and Indonesia—named after Jesus' biblical home. Nazareth is a band from Scotland that took its name from a line in The Band's hit song "The Weight": "I pulled into Nazareth, was feelin' about half past dead." Although the song's Nazareth refers to a Pennsylvania town, its lyrics are heavily influenced by biblical language and thought.

The gospels all agree that Jesus taught, healed, and preached in the Galilee region but that he died in Jerusalem, where Judaism's religious and political center was firmly ensconced. Consequently the Mount of Olives, the Upper Room, and Golgotha, sites that feature prominently in Jesus' last days, are all in or around Jerusalem.

The Mount of Olives (a.k.a. Mount Olivet, or simply Olivet) is not technically much of a mountain. It's a hill just shy of 3,000 feet, separated from the Old City of Jerusalem (with its own Temple "Mount") by a valley (the Kidron Valley). From it, one has a great view of Jerusalem to the west; looking east, one can see the Jordan Valley and Dead Sea; and to the south is the seemingly endless rolling wilderness of the Judean Desert. There are still today a few olive trees, some possibly almost 2,000 years old, of the sort that gave the mountain its name.

Although Jesus' passion[54] accounts for much of its fame, Olivet is first mentioned in the Bible when David climbed it, weeping and weeping, in poignant retreat after his son Absalom revolted and claimed the throne.[55] The Mount of Olives is also mentioned by the Old Testament prophet Zechariah, who tells of an end-of-days time when God will stand in cosmic battle on the Mount of Olives, and it will split in two.[56] Those are the only two occasions in the Old Testament when the Mount of Olives is mentioned by name. Nevertheless, those traditions of grief and of a coming "day of the LORD" are reflected in the enduring popularity of the Mount of Olives as a Jewish cemetery. Though historically questionable, the supposed tombs of Absalom and Zechariah are on the Mount of Olives.

The shrines that dot its peak and slopes today mostly attest to Olivet's association with Jesus, especially his last days. The New Testament makes several references to the site. It was from the Mount of Olives that Jesus' disciples secured the animal or animals that Jesus rode into Jerusalem to great "Hosanna!" acclaim at the beginning of the week that would end with his death.[57] This moment is celebrated annually as Palm Sunday, which begins Holy Week in the Christian calendar.

Jesus likely stayed with Mary and Martha in Bethany on the Mount of Olives during that week, and he retreated to the Mount of Olives for anguished meditation and prayer in the garden of Gethsemane before he was handed over to the authorities, setting in motion events leading to the cross. Today, the beautiful Church of All Nations maintains the garden of Gethsemane; Dominus Flavit Church recalls Jesus' weeping over Jerusalem; and the Dome of the Ascension claims to be the last earthly place where Jesus stepped before he ascended to heaven.

Golgotha is a transliteration of the Hebrew name, which the gospels (except Luke) explain means "the place of a skull." As the site of Jesus' crucifixion, and mentioned nowhere else, it is fittingly macabre. When Jesus died, Golgotha was just outside Jerusalem's city walls; soon afterward, it was part of territory annexed to the city. Jesus' body was laid in a new cave tomb there. Archaeologists have worked long and hard to determine if the traditional site, in today's Old City Church of the Holy Sepulcher, is the historical Golgotha. The jury is still out, though that's incidental to the devout who crowd the church, passionately identifying it with Jesus' death and resurrection.

The church is a colorful stage of interdenominational dynamics. The Greek Orthodox, Roman Catholic, Armenian Apostolic as well as Ethiopian, Coptic, and Syriac Orthodox all share in its maintenance and administration, though not always peacefully. For example, in April 2008, the Greek and Armenian faithful got into a fistfight on Palm Sunday after a Greek priest was kicked out. Police who came to break up the melee were themselves attacked by worshippers with palm fronds.[58] A few months later, during a commemoration of the discovery of what some people believe to be Jesus' cross, they were at it again. Greek Orthodox monks took umbrage at what they feared was an Armenian effort to wrest control of a key part of the site by having a processional without a Greek representative present. Israeli police broke up the brawl and made two arrests.[59]

HEAVEN, HELL, AND THE END OF DAYS

Armageddon gets only one brief mention in the Bible,[60] yet it has captured the imagination of millions. Its name appears in everything from video games (e.g. Mortal Kombat), to movies (among several, the *Armageddon* of 1998, starring Bruce Willis), from graphic novels (DC Comics published *Armageddon 2001*) to rap music (one rapper's name is Armageddon). The Marvel Comics *X-Men* series includes a character named Armageddon. In an unusual demonstration of biblical literacy (or maybe a lucky guess), he's described there as the son of Apocalypse. (Because the biblical book of Revelation is the clearest example of apocalyptic literature that we have, one could argue that Armageddon is the product, or son, of apocalyptic thinking.) In contrast to the comic book character, though, the biblical Armageddon is a place, not a person. According to Revelation, it's a Hebrew name for the place where the world's final battle will take place, but where is this place? Dealing as it does with larger-than-life, end-time scenarios, Revelation is famously rich in symbolic details and poor in concrete facts. In this case, Revelation probably meant to evoke an Old Testament site and elevate it to a cosmic mountain.

That is, the author of Revelation probably had in mind Meggido, northern Israel's site of great historical battles including the epic battle of Deborah and Barak against Sisera, as narrated in Judges.[61] Megiddo is also the place where good King Josiah, from Judah, tried to intercept the Egyptians on their way to Assyria and was killed.[62] "Armageddon" combines the Hebrew word for "mountain," *har*, with a word that looks a lot like "Megiddo." There is no mountain of Megiddo, but there are mountains in the region, and it wouldn't be surprising for the author to think that any cosmic battle should involve a mountain, mythic or otherwise.

Which brings us to hell. Well, not exactly, but an overview of biblical places would hardly be complete without some mention of heaven and hell, and heaven seems better to end on. The Bible gives little attention to hell in either the Old or the New Testament. For one thing, the word "hell" only appears in the Bible by way of translation. The word probably comes from the pre-Christian Norse *hel*—goddess of an underworld by the same name—or it may have roots in an Old High German term meaning "to conceal."

The Hebrew Bible doesn't say much at all about what happens after death. When it does, it's usually in the context of *sheol*, sometimes translated as "the grave," though it has the sense of "land of the dead." No one knows for sure what exactly *sheol* means etymologically, and the word never appears as such in the New Testament, but all agree that it is down below. Probably because of its subterranean nature, one synonym for *sheol* is *bor*, often translated "the Pit." Although we might come up with a general definition and description of Sheol (this is how the term appears in English) from the collective references, different biblical writers disagreed with each other on the details. For example, some assume that after death everyone goes to Sheol, where they are cut off from God, and from which there is no return. Job says, "As a cloud dissipates and goes away, so those who go down to Sheol do not come up again,"[63] and in Isaiah we find "Those who go down to the Pit cannot hope for [God's] security."[64] By contrast, the song of Hannah suggests that people can come back from Sheol—"the LORD kills and brings to life; he brings down to Sheol and raises up"[65]—and a psalmist sings, "Bless the LORD, . . . who redeems your life from the Pit."[66] Jonah praises God for bringing him back from the Pit.[67] Although Sheol is hardly a happy place, neither is it the site of eternal torment, like modern ideas of hell.

A synonym for Sheol is "Abaddon," related to a Hebrew word that means perishing or destruction; it appears in half a dozen or so Old Testament references. Abaddon appears only once in the New Testament, where it is personified as an angel king of the bottomless pit of death.[68] There, the author explains that Abaddon is the same as "Apollyon" in Greek (a word that means "the destroyer"). Some Christians naturally identify this Abaddon with Satan, presiding over hell.[69]

The Septuagint translates *sheol* as *hades*, a word that appears ten times in the New Testament.[70] In Revelation, Hades is not only a place for the dead, but also an agent who could cause death and destruction but who would finally be thrown, at the end of time, into a fiery lake (along with Death).[71] This may reflect the author of Revelation's familiarity with ancient Greek mythology, in which Hades, the brother of Zeus and Poseidon, is ruler of the underworld.

Eventually, Judaism did develop a more detailed idea of hell, around the same time as and similar in nature to that of the early Christians. For Jews, the place is usually called Gehenna. This Greek word, translated as "hell" in English New Testaments (and never appearing as such in the Old Testament), is a transliteration from the Aramaic *ge-hinnom*, which is associated with a real place: the Hinnom Valley, just south of Jerusalem. Sometimes called the valley of "the son of Hinnom," it is remembered as the infamous site where worshippers of Molech sacrificed children by fire.[72] For Jews, Gehenna took on a more mythical cast, to become the place where sinners go after death; the pious go to Paradise.

In the New Testament, Jesus used the term in this way several times, suggesting that his opponents are murderers and charging, "How will you escape being condemned to Gehenna?"[73] There are finally only a dozen occurrences of the word in the Bible, most of them in Matthew.[74] None gives much description, except to suggest that it's a place where sinners go and is to be avoided, even at the cost of limb or life.[75] A few references associate Gehenna, like the infamous Hinnom Valley sacrifices, with fire.[76] The Greek term "Tartaros," also translated "hell," appears once: in 2 Peter, an apocalyptic letter in Greek rhetorical style.[77] Many people interpret other references to afterlife torment as taking place in hell, but such texts do not specify the site. Nevertheless, "fiery furnace," "outer darkness," and "gnashing of teeth," all in Matthew's gospel, are some terms that have come to be associated with hell.[78]

Popular ideas of hell as a place of eternal punishment by fire where horned demons torment and the devil rules mostly reflect images that developed during the intertestamental period. Detailed in deuterocanonical texts and pre-Christian mythologies (such as the noncanonical apocalyptic books of *1–2 Enoch*, whose ideas are reflected in some biblical texts), these references aroused renewed interest and attention in the medieval Christian imagination. The few references to Gehenna in the New Testament, Revelation's Abaddon, and Jude's mention of uppity angels chained "in deepest darkness," plus "a punishment of eternal fire"[79] contribute, but much we owe to later Christian theology.

Similarly, popular ideas of heaven are informed primarily by late biblical (and nonbiblical) references. The most common word for "heaven" in the Old Testament is the Hebrew word *shamayim*. It appears well over 200 times, but not as a paradisiacal afterlife location. Sometimes translated as "sky," it can refer to whatever material is above (i.e., the physical skies, where the sun and stars are set, and whence come rain and snow), and it also describes the abode of God and the divine beings.[80] The Septuagint translates *shamayim* as *ouranos*, which also appears in numerous New Testament references, translated into English as "heaven."

Heaven does not take on the meaning of a place of reward or life after death until quite late in the Bible's development. The book of Daniel (from around 165 BCE) has the first explicit reference to resurrection, judgment, and an afterlife, though it doesn't mention heaven: "At that time . . . many of those who sleep in the earth's dust will awake, some to everlasting life, others to shame and everlasting abhorrence."[81] Although the Old Testament says virtually nothing about heaven as the place of such reckoning and reward, intertestamental literature such as *1–2 Enoch*, the *Testament of Abraham*, and *3 Baruch* (from around 300 BCE to 100 CE) shows considerable interest in what the heavens look like (many passages describe levels, usually seven), who occupies them (divine beings as well as the dead), and what happens there (events including judgment and the revelation of secrets).

By the time the New Testament was being written, the idea of heaven as a place one went after death for judgment and eternal reward seems to have been well established. Although only Luke tells specifically of Jesus' ascension to heaven,[82] that event was understood by the early Christian community to be the model of resurrection (through the sky and into heaven) that its members would follow. Paul tells the Thessalonians that when Jesus returns, "the dead in Christ shall rise first, then we who are alive will join them in the clouds . . . and be forever with the Lord."[83] In heaven, they would be rewarded and enjoy communion with God, Jesus, and all believers. Jesus exhorts those persecuted for the sake of righteousness to "rejoice and be glad, because your reward in heaven is great"; and, without naming heaven explicitly, he says, "In my Father's house are many rooms. . . . I go to prepare a place for you, I will come again and take you to myself."[84] The author of Revelation relates a vision in which the righteous dead stand before the divine (heavenly) throne and are assured of an everlasting life of comfort and joy with Jesus.[85]

"The kingdom of heaven," is a phrase exclusive to Matthew. Because parallel texts in the other canonical gospels use "kingdom of God" instead,[86] it's possible that Matthew simply substituted "heaven" to avoid using the name "God." Some texts assume that it is the site of reward. ("Not everyone who says to me, 'Lord, Lord' will enter the kingdom of heaven, but only those who do the will of my Father who is in heaven.")[87] Others suggest that it's a quality or way of being. ("The kingdom of heaven is like yeast—a little affects the whole loaf"[88]—or like a tiny mustard seed that grows into a lush plant.)[89] So important are Jesus' teachings about the kingdom of heaven/God (the phrase appears about 100 times), that defining it is central to his entire ministry.

The 2005 movie *The Kingdom of Heaven* ostensibly concerns the crusades of Christians in the twelfth century to reclaim the Holy Land, particularly the city of Jerusalem, from Muslims led by Saladin. The main character's goal of an exemplary place where Christians and Muslims live together in peace, aiding the powerless and generally doing the right thing, shares commonalty with biblical ideals for the kingdom of heaven/God. The movie generated considerable controversy, not least because of its questionable telling of history, but its linking the "kingdom of heaven" with Jerusalem has biblical precedent.

Given Jerusalem's peerless significance in the Bible, it's easy to understand the eschatological hope for a "new Jerusalem" that transcends ordinary human history to become a kind of heaven, in and of itself.

After the crisis of exile, Isaiah prophesies "the new heavens and new earth" in which Jerusalem will become a central site of worship for the whole world.[90] In the New Testament, Revelation picks up on this, and adds that a "new Jerusalem" will come down from heaven.[91] Images of pearly gates and streets paved in gold come from Revelation's detailed description of this new Jerusalem, lowered from heaven in the final days, sparkling with jewels and gold, where "the twelve gates were twelve pearls . . . and the street . . . is pure gold."[92] Peter's role as the celestial gatekeeper derives from an interpretation of a passage that appears only in Matthew's gospel, in which Jesus gave Peter the keys to the kingdom of heaven, and charged him, saying, "Whatever you bind on earth will be bound in heaven, and whatever you loose on earth will be loosed in heaven."[93] In Galatians, Paul contrasts the present Jerusalem, as a condition of slavery imposed by the Sinai covenant, with a future Jerusalem "above," which he defines as ultimately representing liberation in Christ.[94]

By contrast to the infrequent explicit references to hell, the Greek word *ouranos*, translated as "heaven," appears many times in the New Testament—almost 150 times in the gospels alone and nearly 100 times elsewhere. Most references share ideas with the Old Testament about heaven as a place above earth, where God and divine beings dwell, and as the source of good things ("a person can receive only what is given from heaven").[95] In the New Testament, however, heaven is also an object of hopeful expectation, where believers will be rewarded with everlasting life and communion with the other faithful who have preceded them in death, and with God the Father, Jesus, and the Holy Spirit.

THIRTEEN

God Names, Beings, and Doings

The feeling remains that God is on the
journey, too.

—SAINT TERESA OF AVILA

Elohim, Yahweh, El Shaddai, Theos, Logos, El Elyon, and more—all
serve to name God in the Bible. Why so many? Why not simply El
and Theos, the generic Hebrew and Greek words for "God"? The
answer is due at least in part to the fact that the Bible did not emerge
in one piece, all together at one time. Rather, it developed over a
long period, reflecting disparate conditions and ideas, all of which
ultimately contributed to a richly layered theology. Because the final
form of the Bible (whichever Bible one has) is a single book, these different images and names of God are in conversation with one another.
For the faithful who seek a definitive, comprehensive portrait of God
that takes into equal account all of these disparate references, it can be
downright confounding. They're in good company, though—witness
the tomes of theology written during each century.

This chapter does not aim to do such theology or to tell readers what to believe (or not) about God. Rather, it simply and briefly
explains different names for God in the Bible, from the Hebrew

Bible to the Septuagint and the New Testament. That leaves room
to note, briefly, other beings referred to as deities, such as Baal and
Asherah, who show up in ways that inform ideas of God; and to address general matters, such as how the Bible's cultural contexts and
grammatical peculiarities inform ideas about the gender and character
of God.

ELOHIM AND THE ELOHIM

When readers open the Bible, the very first God name that they encounter is Elohim. This is the God who "In the beginning . . . created
the heavens and the earth."[1] Yet the Hebrew word *elohim* is a plural
form of *el*. So although *elohim* sometimes refers to a single God, it also
means "gods." (Remember also that Hebrew doesn't distinguish between uppercase and lowercase letters. They're all the same size.) Another peculiarity of Hebrew grammar helps translators decide which
meaning to use: verbs indicate the number, person, and gender of their
subjects. The verb in Gen 1:1 indicates that *elohim* should be read as a
singular noun, so we can be confident that "God" is the best translation there.

The Hebrew Bible uses *elohim* both ways—as both "God" and
"gods." In fact, sometimes the single God, Elohim, appears to admit
the existence of, even company with, other gods (*elohim*). At the top
of the Ten Commandments, for example, we read, "You shall have no
other gods before me," indicating an assumption that there are indeed
other gods out there.[2] The "sons of god" inhabit the heavens in Job,[3]
and the psalmist declares that "the LORD is a great God, . . . above all
gods."[4] The poetry of Psalm 82 may represent a transitional theology,
telling how the gods were reduced to mortality after failing to execute
justice, protect the vulnerable, and maintain order.[5]

In that first chapter of Genesis, when Elohim determined to create
human beings, God spoke as if to other gods, saying, "Let us make
humankind in our image";[6] in the next story, God was concerned that
"the human being has become like one of us";[7] and Isaiah tells how
God asked from the divine throne, "Who shall go for us?"[8] Some

people interpret such references as functioning like the royal "we," in which a (singular) monarch speaks of himself or herself in the plural. Others suggest that this is a reference to the Trinity. Both are interpretations from a later context or reflect Jewish or Christian theologies. The ancient historical context of these verses and other similar Hebrew Bible references led scholars to conclude that they originally reflected the assumption that Elohim ("God") presided over a divine council of elohim ("gods").

Although the Hebrew Bible finally of course promotes monotheism, some of the earliest biblical texts apparently reflect henotheism—the worship of only one God while allowing that other gods may exist, too. This is in keeping with ancient Near Eastern cosmology, which assumed that each nation had its own particular god. In the Bible, the Israelites' God is nevertheless portrayed in many texts as superior to the others, sometimes unseating them or even revealing them to be worthless not-gods.[9] Indeed, appealing to other biblical texts that critique other gods as nothing more than idols—objects or ideas to which people wrongly attribute power and supernatural characteristics—some interpreters understand all such references to other gods in this way.[10]

EL-PLUS

Besides the plural-form name Elohim, the Hebrew Bible also uses the singular form *el* (though not nearly as frequently as it uses *elohim*). *El* is the generic word meaning "god," shared by ancient Hebrew with others in its family of northwest Semitic languages.[11] When *el* appears in this singular form, it is usually attached to other words specifying a particular quality or characteristic of God. Sometimes it refers to a revelatory experience—Hagar called God El Roi (the God who sees), for example. In other cases, *el* is associated with a particular place, such as El-Bethel (God of Bethel); and sometimes it is used to convey something about God's intrinsic nature: e.g., El Elyon (literally "the God of Gods," i.e., the highest God) or El Olam (Everlasting God).

Probably the most familiar, though, is El Shaddai. Although it's sometimes translated "God Almighty" (following the Septuagint and Vulgate), what exactly El Shaddai means in Hebrew is still up for grabs. The closest contenders are "God of the mountain (ranges)," "God of the plains," and "God of, or with, breasts."[12] None of these are certain. In Genesis, the name El Shaddai almost always appears in the context of fertility. For example, El Shaddai promised the ninety-nine-year-old Abram that he would have many descendants; and Isaac invoked El Shaddai to bless Jacob with fertility, which God reiterated, saying to Jacob, "I am El Shaddai. Be fruitful and multiply."[13] Given that, it's ironic that this is Job's favorite name for God, since Job suffered such tremendous losses. In the book of Job, "El Shaddai" appears more frequently than in all other biblical instances combined.

Recent discoveries in modern Syria reveal that El was also the name of a Canaanite god just north of ancient Israel. Beginning in 1928 and over subsequent years, a rich trove of cuneiform tablets and cultural artifacts was unearthed.[14] Written in Ugaritic, a language related to ancient Hebrew, and dating to the 1400s BCE, the tablets include stories about gods and goddesses including Baal and Asherah that, until this discovery, had been known primarily by biblical references excoriating their worship.

One Ugaritic god name that escapes biblical condemnation, however, is El. In the Canaanite tablets, El is the name of the high god. He is described as "the Kind, Compassionate" and "Father of humankind," a powerful and wise old patriarch who sat enthroned amid the clouds, presided over a divine council, and created everything. Despite their similarities, images of the Canaanite and biblical Els are hardly identical. For example, one story of the Ugaritic El tells how he got falling-down drunk at a banquet—quite different from images of the biblical El.[15] If the biblical writers adopted existing language and imagery to describe God, they also adapted it in light of their distinct experiences and ideas about the nature and quality of God while strongly criticizing the worship of other deities. The Canaanite El is sometimes referred to as Bull El, suggesting that some of the condemnation against calf worship in ancient Israel may originally have critiqued worship of the "wrong" El. The resulting effect is of a biblical God unique to ancient Israel.

YHWH

The god name YHWH does not appear at all in the Ugaritic texts; yet it is crucial to the Hebrew Bible, where it occurs more than 6,000 times.[16] Indeed, it's hard to overestimate the importance to ancient Israelite religion and biblical theology of this four-letter name for God. Transliterated YHWH, because those letters are our Roman alphabet's equivalents of the Hebrew letters יהוה (*yod he vav he*—Hebrew is read from right to left), it is sometimes called the tetragrammaton (and sometimes with a capital T). As I'll describe in more detail below, this is the word rendered LORD in most English translations and is sometimes vocalized today as Yahweh.

While other divine names simply appear in the Bible without explanation, Exodus includes a story of how Israel came to know the name YHWH.[17] When God commissioned Moses to liberate the Hebrew people from slavery in Egypt, Moses protested that the people would probably ask for the name of the one who sent Moses. "What should I tell them?" Moses asked. God's response: אהיה, "I Am." If you think in code for a minute, you can see that the word translated "I am" looks a lot like יהוה, YHWH.[18] This is not a coincidence. Both words are related to the Hebrew verb היה, "to be."[19] Specifically, God tells Moses to tell the Hebrews, "I am who I am . . . YHWH, God of your ancestors, the God of Abraham, the God of Isaac, and the God of Jacob. . . . This is my name forever, my address throughout the generations."[20] Later in the same story, YHWH is identified as both "God of the Hebrews" and "Our God." In this way, the biblical writers neatly link the (new) name YHWH with the (old) names for God, including those starting with El.

This episode is sometimes called the "revelation of the divine name," which can be confusing because discerning readers will recall that YHWH shows up early and often in Genesis.[21] Without knowing that the Bible's process of development isn't transparent in its final literary form and organization, a person would rightly wonder why and how the divine name could have been used as early as Adam and Eve and by the ancestors, when it wasn't revealed until Moses.[22] Nevertheless, in Exod 6:3, God declares, "I appeared to Abraham, to Isaac, and to Jacob as El-Shaddai, but by my name YHWH I was not known to them." Some people reconcile this seeming contradiction by suggesting that God revealed more about his redemptive character and the significance of his name to Moses than to anyone before Moses, but the biblical text doesn't make this explicit. Most scholars maintain that this contradiction is simply a result of having different literary sources within the Pentateuch. In keeping with the tenor of Moses' story, the name YHWH seems to function throughout the Hebrew Bible in a way that emphasizes God's relationship with a particular people, Israel. You could say that YHWH denotes a personal nature of God— the God in an intimate and exclusive relationship with Israel.[23]

Another common biblical description of God is as YHWH Sabaoth—"LORD of hosts." The Hebrew word *sabaoth* has both military and celestial associations. The phrase "LORD of hosts" evokes images of God as a mighty general who can conscript others into his army.[24] In its starry associations, it's probably also a subtle evisceration of the Babylonian pantheon of the skies. The most powerful Babylonian deities were identified with the moon and stars, the "heavenly host." Assigning them to YHWH effectively undermined competing religions.[25]

CARE AND KEEPING OF THE DIVINE NAME

Knowing another's name is a powerful thing. Like a handle, it gives the handler some control. This seems to have been especially true in the thinking of the ancient Near East, where to know the name of a god enabled a person not only to appeal specifically and directly to that god but even perhaps to draw back the curtain a little and glimpse what made that god tick. Given such a context, God's revealing a particular name by which he could be (at least partially) understood and addressed, was to make God's self graciously available (and possibly vulnerable) to people.

One way that the Israelite God promised to be particularly present to the people was by choosing to make his name dwell among them.[26] The place that God chose to put his name came to be associated with the temple in Jerusalem,[27] so it was crucial that those very real places—building and city—be maintained as appropriately holy. God's name was inseparable from his reputation. For example, Jeremiah reports that God said, "Therefore . . . I will teach them my power and my might, and they shall know that my name is YHWH."[28] Over and over again, the prophet Ezekiel explains that God does what he does (for example, punishes and restores) so that people will "know that I am YHWH." Ezekiel was particularly fond of this phrase: it appears about sixty times in the book.

The revelation of the divine name was a gift and was not to be taken lightly. There are plenty of warnings against misusing it. One such warning is articulated in the Ten Commandments and famously translated (thanks to King James), "Thou shalt not take the name of the LORD thy God in vain."[29] Although opinions vary on what exactly this means, most agree that this commandment has to do with respecting the name of God as a representation of God's very self.

On some of the proto-biblical texts discovered at Qumran, it appears that by 200 BCE, some of the pious were reluctant even to write the four consonants of God's name, lest they offend. They used simply four dots where we would expect to see YHWH. Although there is no explicit prohibition in the Bible against ever saying God's name, by the time that the Hebrew Bible got its vowels (around 700 CE), YHWH was assigned the vowels of *adonai*, reflecting an early tradition to say "the Lord" rather than the divine name, when reading aloud.[30] That oral tradition of substituting *adonai* for YHWH carried over into the Masoretic Text, the authoritative Hebrew Bible, and is reflected in English translations where YHWH is represented (often to the puzzlement of discerning readers) with small capital letters as "the LORD."

The word "Jehovah" came out of the same tradition. It is a hybrid of the (Latin) consonants of the divine name, transliterated JHVH, plus the vowels of *adonai*, read as *e, o,* and *a*.[31] Despite its artificiality, "Jehovah" has garnered its own respect. It is the god name of choice in the American Standard Version, where every occurrence of YHWH is rendered Jehovah. It frequently appears in Christian music, and it denotes Watchtower Society members—Jehovah's Witnesses.

Sometimes the divine name appears in the Bible in a shortened form, "Yah."[32] Most often, especially in the Psalms, it appears in the phrase *hallelu yah*, meaning "praise Yah," transliterated in English versions as "hallelujah" (with the Latin *j* for *y*). Although contemporary scholars and students of the Bible vocalize the divine name as Yahweh, its pronunciation as such is a best guess, based on characteristics of Hebrew grammar and on comparison with ancient Near Eastern personal names that include forms of the name of God (like the name Daniel includes the theophoric element "El," and Christopher includes "Christ").

BAAL

There is another Hebrew word besides *adonai* that can be translated "lord." *Baal*, fairly common in the Hebrew Bible, can be translated "lord, master, owner, or husband" (at which we feminists all roll our collective eyes). Yahweh is sometimes described in the Bible as a *baal*, both literally as a lord or master to the Israelites and metaphorically as husband to his wife, Israel.[33]

However, what was a handy epithet to describe the mastery of Israel's God or God's love for and commitment to his people also appears in the Hebrew Bible as the proper name of a rival god. Baal, who appears in the Ugaritic texts as an energetic and powerful god, sometimes as the master of storms,[34] is described in the Bible as a Canaanite god whose worship the biblical writers deemed to be a covenant-breaking criminal act against the God of Israel. References to the god Baal appear sixty-seven times in the Old Testament and once in the New Testament, and always in the context of wrongful worship.

In one famous Old Testament story, Yahweh's prophet Elijah took on the prophets of Baal in a great contest of the gods to prove the superiority of Israel's God.[35] In the dramatic biblical telling, Baal lost, of course, and Yahweh's demonstration of power was followed by rain, effectively breaking a drought that had plagued the region. Biblical texts such as this contest story (or God's meeting Moses on Mount Sinai in a great thunderstorm), in light of the Ugaritic tablets and other archaeological artifacts, suggest that the biblical writers sought to show that Yahweh, not Baal, had ultimate power and mastery.

By contrast to the Ugaritic traditions, which we know from iconography discovered in Canaan linked Baal to a bull or bull calf (and the Ugaritic El is called "the Bull"), biblical texts condemn any association of Yahweh with a totem animal. The best-known such invective belongs to the biblical story of Aaron's directing the Hebrews to fashion a calf image from the gold that they wore and carried out of Egypt. Such biblical incidents in which people attribute God's liberating activity to (and then worship) calf images are told as perversions of the faith—it was Yahweh who had freed them, according to the biblical narrative (not Baal or the Canaanite El). Indeed, one of the most important and frequently repeated characteristics of Yahweh is as "the God who brought you out of the land of Egypt."

ASHERAH

In the Bible, Baal is frequently associated with Asherah, another off-limits deity—a goddess whom the wicked queen Jezebel worshipped. Like Baal, Asherah comes under attack in the Bible, especially in the books of Kings. But in her case, when I say "under attack," I mean it literally. Several texts applaud efforts to smash, burn, and otherwise destroy the "sacred poles," one translation of the Hebrew *asherah*. Citations such as these demonstrate that the term applied both to the deity herself (as a proper name) and to objects that presumably represented her—trees, for example. The *asherah* objects mentioned in the Bible were probably stylized trees that could be destroyed by burning and smashing.

The goddess Asherah, like the Canaanite El and Baal, is a prominent deity in the Ugaritic pantheon and is sometimes described as
El's wife and the mother of the gods, the "seventy sons of Asherah."[36]
Sometimes she is called in the Ugaritic stories simply "Goddess" or by
a word meaning "holy." In one case, Asherah is described as running
interference on behalf of Baal after he defeated Yamm, to convince El
to let Baal build a house. She is not unique to Ugarit but appears in
several ancient Near Eastern pantheons, including Egypt's, as well as
among other Canaanite groups.

Archaeology suggests that Yahweh may have been venerated alongside a goddess partner, Asherah, in ancient Israel. Hebrew inscriptions
dating from around 800–750 BCE, shortly after the time of Elijah,
Ahab, and Jezebel, tell of blessings by "Yahweh . . . and his Asherah."[37]
These artifacts, as well as biblical diatribes against the worship of Baal
and Asherah, suggest that deities by these names were worshipped
within ancient Israel, for a time anyway, and possibly without any
sense that such worship was heretical.[38]

THEOS AND KURIOS, FROM Lord TO LORD

With its translation, the Septuagint masks some of the diversity of Hebrew god names. *Theos* stands in for both *elohim* and *YHWH-elohim*. A
Septuagint reader, then would simply read "God" in each case and be
none the wiser. Similarly, the Greek uses *kurios*, which means "lord"
or "Lord," for the name YHWH (and sometimes for *YHWH-elohim*)
and for the Hebrew title *adonai*.[39] *El shaddai* is translated as both *theos*
and *kurios*.[40] Compare, for example, the diversity of Hebrew divine
names in Exod 6:2–3: "*Elohim* said to Moses, 'I am *Yahweh*. I appeared
to Abraham, Isaac, and Jacob as *El Shaddai*, but I did not make myself
known to them by my name *Yahweh*" with the Greek translation of
the same verses: "*Theos* said to Moses, I am *kurios*. I appeared to Abraham, Isaac, and Jacob as *theos*, but I did not make myself known to
them by my name *kurios*."

This blurring of distinctions between the Hebrew divine names
by translating them with the general words *theos* and *kurios* probably

reflects an intensified monotheism and more abstract theology. It also may have influenced the language that New Testament writers used to articulate theological ideas about Jesus and his identity in relation to (or even as) God. Indeed, if you didn't know that the Hebrew words behind the English translations "LORD" and "Lord" are different, you would miss an intriguing theological shift between the Old and New Testaments.

In the Old Testament, the name YHWH, represented in English by "LORD," refers to God. It never appears as such in the New Testament, even in quotations from the Old Testament. Rather, the title "Lord" applies to both God and Jesus, sometimes in ways that suggest an equation of the Old Testament personal God with the New Testament person Jesus.[41] The gospel of John even describes Jesus reaching back to the story of Moses' receiving the divine name from God, "I am who I am," to declare, "Before Abraham was I am," stating his identity and equality with the YHWH God of ancient Israel.[42]

The Old Testament's "name theology" came in the New Testament to be associated with Jesus. In the Old Testament, the phrase "the name of *Yahweh*" appears in eighty-three verses. Its Greek counterpart, "the name of *kurios*," appears in the New Testament in twenty verses, each of which blurs the boundary between the human Jesus and Israel's personal God.[43] For example, each of the gospels describes Jesus' Palm Sunday entry into Jerusalem as accompanied by shouts from the crowd: "Blessed is he who comes in the name of the Lord." Paul and other New Testament writers also attribute special power to "the name of the Lord." For example, Acts tells how new believers were baptized "in the name of the Lord Jesus";[44] and Paul exhorts people to "do everything in the name of the Lord Jesus, giving thanks to God the Father through him."[45]

MESSIAH

Jesus' name is a Greek transliteration of the Aramaic Yeshu(ah), from the Hebrew Yehoshua, which is normally written as Joshua, and it means something like "Yah saves." But saves from what? The New

Testament was written by people who believed that Jesus was and is uniquely able to reconcile human beings to God. Jesus' followers ultimately interpreted earlier prophecies, especially those in Isaiah about God's vicariously suffering servant "by [whose] wounds we are healed,"[46] and rituals of sacrificial atonement to conclude that Jesus bridged the gap between God and people by serving as the ultimate sacrifice, the sinless one who atones for the sin of the world. And they believed with apocalyptic hope that Jesus would or will ultimately return to earth as God's righteous judge and establish a new kingdom ("of heaven," also "of God") whereby believers would or will enjoy reward and eternal life.

This put a different spin on the idea of "Messiah" than people in Jesus' immediate community would have had. The English word "messiah" is based on the Greek transliteration *messias* of the Hebrew *meshiach*, which simply means "anointed." Originally defined in ancient Israel by the physical process of pouring oil on a priest's or king's head, anointing ("messiah-ing") was simply the concrete demonstration of God's having selected a person to serve as a religious or political leader.

The book of Leviticus tells how God established a system to consecrate priests. The crowning moment of this ritual, inaugurated by Moses, involved anointing the new priest.[47] Kings also were anointed. When God and Samuel capitulated to the people's request for a king, it was with the understanding that the human king would answer to God, the absolute and enduring king. As "God's anointed" (a "messiah"), the king was to execute God's leadership on earth, guiding the people in righteousness and ruling a nation grounded in justice and characterized by peace. He was, then, to be an ideal leader both politically and religiously.

The monarchy lasted through the early sixth century BCE, when the Babylonians decisively defeated Judah, destroyed the temple in Jerusalem, and carried Judean society's upper crust off into exile in Babylon. From then on, people hoped for a return of Israel's king, a newly anointed one, who would reestablish the nation with a global reputation governed in wisdom with justice and peace, in keeping with the dictates and characteristics of God. That is, they hoped for a messiah. The tradition that God had made an enduring covenant with King David dictated that the new king would come from the line of David (Jesse) and the tribe of Judah.[48]

Jesus' earliest followers probably expected a messiah in keeping with these traditions and thought of Jesus in those terms, but the New Testament portrays Jesus as reshaping the definition of those expectations for power and glory. When Jesus explains the necessity of his death, Peter expresses indignation and disbelief that such a thing should be. Jesus' response—"Get behind me, Satan!"—reveals how different Jesus' understanding of his role as messiah was from the traditional view held by his disciples.[49]

This particular messiah would suffer a criminal's death and return to life again, to serve as an eternal messiah. This messiah would not only lead the people to live in keeping with God's commandments but also explain and interpret the commandments in new ways, to teach a particular way of understanding what such obedience might mean. He would establish justice and peace, yes, but also hold out the hope of eternal reward and everlasting life with God as possible for all people. According especially to the gospel of John and also Paul, Jesus would push the matter of facilitating the relationship between God and God's people even further by actually *being* God, and so finally reconcile a people alienated by their human failings with a God who forgave and loved them. The significance of the messiah (specifically Jesus *as* the messiah) became greater, then, than that of a righteous and able human leader. The messiah took on the nature of divinity, being no less than God's own son.

For people schooled in the Hebrew traditions, equating a poor itinerant man from Galilee, who died as a common Roman criminal, with the biblical messiah, let alone with God, and then presuming to worship him would have been judged a grave breach of the ancient covenant with God in just the way that all the prophets warned against. For Jesus to claim to be "I am," effectively equating himself with the LORD God, would have been considered a heretical offense by any traditional Jew. Yet Jesus' followers (who were primarily Jewish, at first) believed that Jesus was indeed the fulfillment of Old Testament expectations for a messiah who would bring about a new world order, not just politically but also spiritually, in which people would be reconciled to God and in keeping with the ideals of justice and peace.[50]

CRYPTO-JESUS: OTHER NAMES AND SYMBOLS

John portrays Jesus embracing his messianic identity, and not only as defined by traditional expectations. But in the synoptic gospels, especially Mark, Jesus is portrayed as wanting to keep his identity under wraps in what scholars call the "messianic secret." When Peter defines him as the messiah, Jesus didn't correct him but commanded the disciples to keep it to themselves.[51] In Mark's gospel, Jesus shushed people over and over again, ostensibly to prevent them from blowing his cover. Some commentators explain that this was because the masses needed time to arrive at the conclusion that Jesus was a messiah of a different stripe, because Jesus' full messianic identity could be appreciated only after his death and resurrection, or because Jesus needed to do more before publicly defining himself as the messiah (since doing so would cause trouble enough to have him killed).

A movie by the comedic group Monty Python spoofs on this messianic secret. *The Life of Brian* tells the story of a man born at the same time, one stable down, and mistaken for Jesus. The adult Brian protests, "I am not the Messiah! Will you please listen? I am not the Messiah, do you understand? Honestly!" To which a girl replies, "Only the true Messiah denies his divinity." So Brian says, "What? Well, what sort of chance does that give me? All right, I am the Messiah!" And the crowd goes wild. "He is! He is the Messiah!"

Christos or Christ, the Greek translation of the Hebrew word *meshiach* or messiah, is neither Jesus' first nor his last name. It appears in the Septuagint wherever the Hebrew term "messiah" does, so it applied to anyone who was anointed. In the New Testament, it serves as a title, not a name, to describe how people understood Jesus.

According to Mark Twain, his fellow apprentice at a printing shop abbreviated JC for "Jesus Christ" in order to save space and type. He was soundly chastised by the evangelist whose pamphlet they were printing and told never to treat the savior's name so impiously again. Rather, "Put it *all* in!" So he did, and added a middle initial, for good measure: "Jesus H. Christ."[52] It's possible that this expression has its origins in an all-caps abbreviation of a Greek spelling of Jesus' name: IHC (variant, IHS). As far as we know, this abbreviation first appeared in the 600s on the special clothes of English priests; it still appears on religious vestments today. The Greek capital letter *eta* looks just like the English capital H, so many misread the letter in this way.[53] Whatever its origins, this expression lives on in curses and oaths.

Neither IHC nor IHS is etymologically related to ICHTHYS, though they all refer to Jesus. *ICHTHYS* is the all-caps spelling of the Greek word for "fish." It is also an acronym for *Iesous* (Jesus) *CHristos* (Christ) *THeou* (God's) *Huios* (Son) *Soter* (Savior). Because the Galilean Jesus and his followers spent a lot of time fishing and ate a lot of fish, it was natural for early Christians to link him with fish imagery. Some of Jesus' disciples were professional fisherman whom Jesus called with the promise that he'd make them "fishers of men."[54]

It is thought that in the early days after Jesus' death, when a Jesus follower wasn't confident that his or her new acquaintance was sympathetic to Christian beliefs, he or she would draw an arc. If the new acquaintance drew a complementary arc, forming the stylized image of a fish, then all was well—they were both Christians. (If not, well, the original drawer must have hoped that the other would only think them doodling or a bit odd and not report them as a Christian troublemaker to the Roman religious officials.)

These days, what began as a Christian resurgence of that ancient symbol, the stylized fish that you see on cars and T-shirts, has prompted variations, proliferating as fast as guppies. Among the numerous variations to appear in the resulting "fish wars" are some with stubby legs and "DARWIN" inscribed on their bodies or holding a wrench and reading "EVOLVE" in order to send a message contradicting creationists. Some fish symbols are skeletal, and some are sharks ("lawyer"-

sharks, "card"-sharks, and sharks that eat Jesus fish). "Gefilte" fish hint that the bearer is Jewish, "Lutefisk" suggests a Scandinavian driver, and "'n' chips" is just goofy.

LOGOS

While the synoptic gospels are concerned with the "messianic secret," the fourth gospel isn't shy about proclaiming the equation of Jesus with God. John begins by identifying "the Word" with both the eternal Creator and a particular human incarnation of God, thereby linking God and Jesus. This word translated "Word" is *logos* in the original Greek. In a clear riff on Genesis chapter 1, John defines the *logos* as God and "with God" from the very beginning of creation, an agent and participant in the creative act itself: "In the beginning was the *logos*, and the *logos* was with God, and the *logos* was God. He was in the beginning with God. All things came into being through him." [55] John declares that this divine Word is life itself, a life that illuminates the world with "true light, which enlightens everyone," [56] and equates it—the divine Word/life/light—with Jesus. "The Word became flesh and lived among us . . . full of grace and truth." [57]

GOD THE FATHER

Inasmuch as John identifies Jesus with God, he also distinguishes Jesus from "God the Father"—a designation that shows up throughout the New Testament, where God is described as both "the Father" generally of all believers and the father of Jesus. [58] "God the Father" creates, corrects, and redeems. He is also portrayed as capable of sending his son Jesus to teach about the Father, of saving people through Jesus' atoning death, and of bringing Jesus back to life. God the Father is characterized especially by the parental qualities of judgment, forgiveness, and love.

Jesus' own understanding of God as the gospels portray it is very much in keeping with his Jewish traditions. That is, Jesus identified God in terms of king, creator, and judge, who gave the people *torah* (in that word's broadest sense) as a means of discerning and doing God's will, who loves the world, and who chose to be especially connected to it in part through God's covenant with Israel.[59] Jesus introduced another way of imagining God, too, praying to him as *abba*, connoting the familiar and intimate relationship of a child to his or her dad. This is not as radical a break with Jewish tradition as many Christians think, however. In addition to its highly sophisticated system of rituals, priestly prayers, and sacrifice that connected a worshipper to God, Judaism included rich traditions of direct and heartfelt prayer to an immediate, compassionate, and deeply interested God. Jesus' *abba* address to God—for example, teaching his followers to pray by saying, "Our Father"—makes the relationship yet more intimate.

THE HOLY SPIRIT

The phrase literally translated "holy spirit" appears only three times in the Hebrew Bible,[60] but it appears nearly one hundred times in the New Testament. Nevertheless, New Testament ideas about the Holy Spirit (a.k.a. Holy Ghost) clearly draw from Hebrew Bible traditions of the *ruach elohim* ("the Spirit of God") or *ruach Yahweh* ("the Spirit of the LORD") that was present at creation, in-spired the ancient Judges to lead the Hebrew tribes, overtook the charismatic prophets, and revitalized the hopelessly exiled Israel. Visible only by its effects, the Spirit gives special insight and power and enables believers in all sorts of ways. Occasionally, it is represented as autonomous, even personal (who teaches and speaks, for example).[61] Consequently, although the Greek phrase *pneuma hagion* is not distinguished as a proper noun, I follow the convention of most English translations by capitalizing the words here.

Matthew and Luke credit the Holy Spirit with Mary's immaculate conception, and the Spirit descended "like a dove" on Jesus when he was baptized.[62] The gospels tell of ordinary people such as Elizabeth, Zechariah, and Simeon to whom the Holy Spirit gave special insight, and Jesus assured some of his disciples that in times of tribulation, the Holy Spirit will direct them in what to say.[63] Blasphemy against the Holy Spirit is declared to be an unforgivable offense.[64]

The gospels say little about the Holy Spirit after Jesus' baptism and before his death, but after Jesus' death it plays a significant role. John's Jesus promises that the Father will send an "advocate," or "helper" (Greek *parakletos*, sometimes represented in English translations as "Paraclete"), which he defined as the Holy Spirit; and the resurrected Jesus breathed the Holy Spirit into his disciples after saying, "As the Father has sent me, so I send you."[65]

The Holy Spirit is a constant presence in the book of Acts, where from the beginning it instructs and guides the development of the church. The most dramatic Holy Spirit moment occurs early in Acts. In an interpretation of the *ruach elohim* that the Old Testament prophet Joel foretold,[66] the author of Acts narrates a phenomenon in which there was a great wind from heaven and tongues like fire touched each of Jesus' disciples and filled them with the Holy Spirit, who enabled them to speak in other languages.[67] The baptisms that followed on that day imparted the gift of the Holy Spirit to other, new believers as well (an understanding that is still crucial to the Christian practice of baptism today). This dramatic event is remembered as the first Christian Pentecost.[68]

Paul especially develops this profile of the Holy Spirit (or simply "Spirit") and its role in Christian life as the gift of God's presence and vitality within a believer to sanctify the person, guide his or her actions and decisions, and unify members of the Christian community. The idea that God gives an enduring, vitalizing divine spirit by which he can be intimately known and who intercedes with God on behalf of believers is not limited to Acts and Paul's letters; it appears frequently throughout the rest of the New Testament.

The Christian doctrine of the Trinity—one God paradoxically comprising God the Father, Jesus the Son, and the Holy Spirit—is not spelled out explicitly as such anywhere in the New Testament. Rather, it developed out of the ways that disparate New Testament texts intimated relationships between what came to be seen by the Christian community as different aspects of and names for God. Statements such as Jesus' command to baptize "in the name of the Father, the Son, and the Holy Spirit"[69] and Paul's benediction, "The grace of the Lord Jesus

Christ, and the love of God, and the fellowship of the Holy Spirit be with you all,"[70] clearly inform this distinctive Christian theology.

IS "GOD" A BOY NAME?

Patriarchy defined the cultural context of the ancient Near East right up through the development of Christianity in the first centuries of the Common Era. Leadership and power were the prerogative of men, so when God is described in the Bible in anthropomorphic (human-like) ways, God is almost always a he-man—warrior, king, father. In the Hebrew Bible, this association of God with masculinity is strengthened by the limits of the language itself. Ancient Hebrew has no genderless pronouns (such as the English "it") and defaults to the masculine when it has to choose. As a result, God looks like a guy in the Old Testament far more often than not.

Greek does have neuter nouns and pronouns, but the language and imagery relating to God in the New Testament continued to prioritize the masculine, just as its cultural context continued to be patriarchal. The New Testament follows the Hebrew precedent by identifying *theos*-God with masculine language. The Spirit, by contrast, is tougher to pin down, not least because the biblical languages don't assign it a particular gender. The Greek *pneuma* ("spirit") is gender-neutral, mirroring the gender ambiguity of the Hebrew *ruach* ("spirit") in the Old Testament. Usually *ruach* is feminine, but sometimes it is mascu-line. In Gen 1:2, *ruach* is a feminine noun:[71] "the spirit of God [she] was hovering over the surface of the waters." The verb used here also likens God elsewhere to an eagle hovering over its nest, lending an intriguing image of God's creative activity in Genesis as perhaps like a mother tending her creation.[72]

Indeed, despite the overwhelming preference for masculine imag-ery to describe God, the Bible includes a few feminine images, too. For example, God's anguish at the apostasy of Israel is likened to that of a pained woman in labor, and God's enduring no-matter-what love for Israel is described as like that of a mother who cannot forget or forsake her children and who seeks to comfort them.[73] The creation of human beings described as "male and female in the image of God" hints at an understanding of God that includes the sexes in equal measure.[74] Finally, however, masculine language and imagery predominate in representations of God in the Hebrew Bible.

That's true in the New Testament, too, in texts informed not just by their cultural contexts but also by the Hebrew scriptures. The biblical Jesus is male, of course, and refers to God using the masculine "father" rather than "mother" or even "parent." Whether Jesus' masculinity is due to the time and place of his birth or because God determined that a man should be divinity incarnate is a question of faith. Similarly, whether Jesus' choice to refer to God as "Father" should be taken as confirmation of the masculinity of God or simply as an effect of Jesus' traditions (Jewish) and circumstances (patriarchal) is also a matter of interpretation and faith for believers today. Finally, even though Jesus challenged some patriarchal assumptions of his day, and although the early Christian church continued these innovations by including women in positions of leadership, the cultural context of the early Christian world nevertheless dictated certain constraints on both metaphysical theology and on the real-life experience of women at that time.

Definitions of God for persons of faith today are informed by the biblical images and descriptions but are finally determined by interpretation. When it comes to God's gender many people prefer to think, along with the predominant biblical imagery, of God in male terms. Others, finding such associations problematic for a number of reasons, favor language and imagery of God that prioritizes the feminine. Yet others appeal to the diversity of ways that the Bible describes God and the Bible's warnings against fashioning images of God to conclude that the best descriptions finally defy any exclusive portrait or tangible representation.

"THE GOD OF THE X TESTAMENT IS A GOD OF Y"

In grand, sweeping generalizations, many people conclude that the God of the Old Testament is an angry and vengeful God; by contrast, the God of the New Testament is loving and forgiving. As with so much about the Bible, things are seldom as simple as such pithy statements claim. Yes, many Old Testament texts tell about God's smiting people—the sinful Israelites and their pagan neighbors alike—but that is far from the whole story; there are also many stories, songs, and laws that tell of God's forgiveness, love, and acceptance of others that such simplistic generalizations overlook.[75] Yes, God in the New Testament is represented as directing divine intention and energy toward redeeming people to himself through the life, death, and resurrection of the incarnation of God in Jesus, and is described as nothing less than love itself; but that is not the whole story, either. The God of the New Testament is also demanding and judgmental.[76] In both cases, generalizing claims beg the nuances that come in part from knowing about the Bible's historical context and development.

In the Hebrew Bible, God is presented in many different ways. In the opening chapter, God is completely "out there" and "other," magnificently distinct from a universe that he brought into being effortlessly, with no human attributes other than speech. In the very next chapter, God walks around in a garden, makes people patties out of dirt, breathes, talks, worries, and regrets. In the Hebrew Bible, we have a God who picnics with friends, and who cannot be imagined like anything else; a God who holds successive generations responsible for the sins of their parents, and who declares that "every person shall be held accountable for their own actions."[77] We have a God who forbids marrying outside the community, and who facilitates the marriage of foreign women to upstanding Israelite men (the most famous being Ruth).[78] We have a God who determines to punish with violence bloody and humiliating, and who declares himself incapable of carrying out even deserved punishment, because of his great love.[79]

In the Old Testament, God breaks down and builds, demands and generously gives, punishes and forgives, rejects and embraces. Similarly, the New Testament includes images of God as both grandly other and cozily intimate; it insinuates and boldly asserts the paradoxical divinity of a very human Jesus; and it describes a Holy Spirit as an anthropomorphic advocate, mysteriously immanent in tongues of fire, distinct from humankind yet capable of "filling" a person altogether. There is constant tension in both the Old Testament and the New between God's otherness and God's likeness, between transcendence and immanence, between God's efforts to be known and God's defying human understanding. The Old Testament doesn't lend itself to a tidy, systematic theology; similarly, such definitive Christian theological positions as doctrine of Jesus' fully-human, fully-divine nature and the triune God didn't immediately follow from the New Testament but took centuries to develop. The diverse descriptions in the Hebrew Bible and the New Testament produce a many-layered profile of God, and those variations continue to stimulate dialogue and debate for both Jews and Christians about the nature and expectations of God.

CONCLUSION

I've read the last page of the Bible. It's all going to
turn out all right.

—BILLY GRAHAM

The Bible is out there in the world, subject to human interpretations
and reflected in countless disparate references serving all sorts of purposes. People talk, think about, and apply the Bible in all sorts of ways,
some of which are completely at odds with others. There is finally no
single way to discuss and understand this sacred text. Rather, the Bible's history of development, its literary and theological diversity, and
the variety of methods that people use to interpret it have generated
countless interpretations and applications. This is at least partly why
the Bible has retained its vitality and remained so significant through
the years. It has come down through the centuries not merely as a relic
dutifully dusted by a caretaking class but because it has proved to be
constantly thought-provoking, a vital and seemingly infinite source
of inspiration, debate, and human creativity for all kinds of people
everywhere.

The Bible was forged in the crucible of a hard history and represents the keen intelligence and creativity not of a single, lone individual, but of all the authors and editors who had a hand in the making,
transmission, and codifying of biblical texts. A Bible whose origins lie
in a variety of ancient times and without a single definitive translation lends itself to conversation both about it and with it. One could
even say that it *demands* such engagement. Knowing about the histori-

cal, social, and cultural context of the Bible can help us make sense of those texts and uses, even if only to wrestle with them. Finally, of course, this book tells only a fraction (of a fraction of a fraction) of the Bible's anatomy and biography. The following description of available resources directs interested readers to more information for study and contemplation.

Knowing what we do about the Bible's development and witnessing the variety of translations and interpretations out there, it's easy to understand how the history of biblical faith includes both the millennia of raucous conversations that compose the volumes and volumes of commentary and also the silence of a solitary monk, holed up in a cave, with body hair like an English sheepdog. Knowing what we do, it's also easy to understand how the Bible inhabits nonreligious spaces, too. It begs for engagement and is marvelously complex—open to the imagination of human beings from the beginning of its transmission through today.

I have sought with this book to strike a tone that invites readers who believe in the Bible as God's Holy Word and also readers who don't, because the information here doesn't require either the acceptance or suspension of such belief. For those who come to the Bible with specific religious beliefs, I encourage readers unsettled by anything in this book not to turn away from learning but to take comfort in knowing that the Bible has withstood millennia of study by believing people; to keep learning about it can strengthen and enrich one's faith. For others, too, I hope that understanding how literary characteristics and historical context affect interpretation will make it easier to appreciate the richness of biblical texts and the passion that believers bring to the Bible. The Bible "says" a lot of things. Understanding how and why people hear different things makes fruitful discussion about biblical perspectives possible.

Finally, of course, information about the Bible, such as this book seeks to provide, goes only so far. When it comes to interpreting and using biblical texts, people's individual experiences, family histories, cultural contexts, and faith traditions shape how they treat such information. As its endurance testifies, the Bible bears and even invites new iterations and reconceptions in light of our ever-changing circumstances. We can be sure that long after you and I are gone, people will continue to make new discoveries and posit new interpretations that inform ideas about the Bible. And people of all sorts—mystics and savvy businessmen, church ladies and punk musicians, hardened soldiers and romantic poets, addicts and pacifists—will draw from the rich language, evocative imagery, and spiritual depth of these texts. Over all its years (and partly because of its use over all those years), the Bible can still inspire creativity, ignite passion, comfort and disturb like nothing else.

Order of Books in the Hebrew Bible and in the Old Testament

Hebrew Bible (Masoretic Text)	Greek Septuagint Bible	Roman Catholic and Greek Orthodox Old Testament	Protestant Old Testament
Torah (Pentateuch)	*Pentateuch*	*Pentateuch*	*Pentateuch*
Genesis	Genesis	Genesis	Genesis
Exodus	Exodus	Exodus	Exodus
Leviticus	Leviticus	Leviticus	Leviticus
Numbers	Numbers	Numbers	Numbers
Deuteronomy	Deuteronomy	Deuteronomy	Deuteronomy
Nevi'im (Prophets)			
(Former Prophets)	*Historical Books*	*Historical Books*	*Historical Books*
Joshua	Joshua	Josue (Joshua)	Joshua
Judges	Judges	Judges	Judges
	Ruth	Ruth	Ruth
	1–2 Regnorum (1–2 Samuel)	1–2 Kings (1–2 Samuel)	
1–2 Samuel			1–2 Samuel
1–2 Kings	3–4 Regnorum (1–2 Kings)	3–4 Kings (1–2 Kings)	1–2 Kings
	1–2 Paralipomenon (1–2 Chronicles)	1–2 Paralipomenon (1–2 Chronicles)	
	1 Esdras	1–2 Esdras (Ezra-Nehemiah)	1–2 Chronicles
			Ezra
	2 Esdras (Ezra-Nehemiah)		Nehemiah
	Esther	Tobias (Tobit)★	Esther
	Judith	Judith★	
	Tobit	Esther (with additions)	
	1–4 Maccabees	1–2 Maccabees★	
	Poetry and Wisdom	*Poetry and Wisdom*	*Poetry and Wisdom*
	Psalms	Job	Job
	Odes	Psalms	Psalms
	Proverbs	Proverbs	Proverbs
	Ecclesiastes	Ecclesiastes	Ecclesiastes
	Song of Songs	Canticle of Canticles (Song of Songs)	Song of Solomon
	Job		
	Wisdom of Solomon	Wisdom of Solomon★	
	Sirach (Ecclesiasticus)	Ecclesiasticus★ (Wisdom of Jesus ben Sirach)	
	Psalms of Solomon		

Hebrew Bible (Masoretic Text)	Greek Septuagint Bible	Roman Catholic and Greek Orthodox Old Testament	Protestant Old Testament
(Latter Prophets)	*Prophetic Books*	*Prophetic Books*	*Prophetic Books*
Isaiah		Isaias (Isaiah)	Isaiah
Jeremiah		Jeremias (Jeremiah)	Jeremiah
		Lamentations	Lamentations
		Baruch (including the epistle of Jeremias)*	
Ezekiel		Ezechiel (Ezekiel)	Ezekiel
		Daniel (with additions; Prayer of Azariah and Song of the Three Young Men;* Susanna;* Bel and the Dragon*)	Daniel
Book of Twelve			
Hosea	Hosea	Osee (Hosea)	Hosea
Amos	Amos	Joel	Joel
Micah	Micah	Amos	Amos
Joel	Joel	Abidas (Obadiah)	Obadiah
Obadiah	Obadiah	Jonas (Jonah)	Jonah
Jonah	Jonah	Micheas (Micah)	Micah
Nahum	Nahum	Nahum	Nahum
Habakkuk	Habakkuk	Habucuc (Habakkuk)	Habakkuk
Zephaniah	Zephaniah	Sophonias (Zephaniah)	Zephanial
Haggai	Haggai	Aggeus (Haggai)	Haggai
Zechariah	Zechariah	Zacharias (Zechariah)	Zechariah
Malachi	Malachi	Malachias (Malachi)	Malachi
Kethuvim (Writings)			
Psalms	Isaiah		
Job	Jeremiah		
Proverbs	Baruch		
Ruth	Lamentations		
Song of Songs	Epistle of Jeremiah		
Ecclesiastes	Ezekiel		
Lamentations	Susanna		
Esther	Daniel		
Daniel	Bel and the Dragon		
Ezra-Nehemiah			
1–2 Chronicles			

---

*Not in Jewish or most Protestant bibles; considered deuterocanonical by Catholic scholars and relegated to the Apocrypha by Protestants.

Order of Books in the New Testament

Matthew

Mark

Luke

John

Acts

Romans

1 Corinthians

2 Corinthians

Galatians

Ephesians

Philippians

Colossians

1 Thessalonians

2 Thessalonians

1 Timothy

2 Timothy

Titus

Philemon

Hebrews

James

1 Peter

2 Peter

1 John

2 John

3 John

Jude

Revelation

Timeline of Some History
in and behind the Bible

1850 BCE	Abraham and Sarah.
1250 BCE	Moses and the Exodus from Egypt.
1200 BCE	Joshua and the tribes conquer and settle in Canaan.
1000 BCE	David becomes king over a united Israel.
922 BCE	Israel splits into a northern kingdom (Israel) and a southern kingdom (Judah).
721 BCE	Assyria conquers the northern kingdom (Israel).
621 BCE	Judean king Josiah institutes religious reforms based on the discovery of what would become the central chapters of the book of Deuteronomy.
587 BCE	Babylonians conquer the southern kingdom (Judah) and destroy the Jerusalem temple.
539 BCE	Cyrus II conquers Babylon and allows the exiled Jews to return to Jerusalem.
515 BCE	The "second temple" is completed in Jerusalem.
445 BCE	Ezra brings the Torah to Jerusalem and institutes reforms based on it.
336–323 BCE	Alexander the Great establishes an empire that includes all of the ancient Near East, bringing hellenizing influences with him.
167–164 BCE	Seleucid king Antiochus IV persecutes Jews with forced Hellenism and incites the Maccabean revolt.
142–63 BCE	Hasmonean kings (descendants of the Maccabees) rule Judah.
63 BCE	Judea becomes part of the Roman empire.
27–30 CE	Jesus' teaching and ministry, execution by Rome.
35–62 CE	Paul, a Jew who converts to Christianity, founds churches especially among gentile communities.
66–73 CE	Jews revolt against Rome.
70 CE	Roman armies raze the Jerusalem temple.
90 CE	Gathering of Jewish intellectuals and religious leaders at Jamnia to direct the reconstruction of Judaism.

A Tentative Chronology
of Hebrew Bible Writings

Approximate
Date Composition

1200–900 BCE The oldest biblical poetry, such as the Song of Deborah (Judges 5), Song of Miriam (Exod 15:21), verses from the book of Jashar (Josh 10:13), and other poems hailing Yahweh as warrior (e.g., Num 21), is orally composed.

950–850 BCE The first prose narrative of Israel's origins, the Yahwist (J) account, is composed in Judah; J's narrative is preserved in parts of the present editions of Genesis, Exodus, and Numbers. Some J passages may also survive in parts of the Deuteronomistic History (DH). The Court History (2 Sam 9–24 and 1 Kings 1–2) may also be from J's hand.

950–587 BCE Royal archives are compiled at the courts of Israel and Judah, sources for the Deuteronomistic account of the monarchy (Samuel through Kings).

800–750 BCE The Elohist (E) account of Israel's origins is composed in the northern kingdom of Israel. E passages appear in parts of the Torah and (perhaps) DH.

750 BCE The prophet Amos delivers his message orally; his disciples commit Amos's oracles to writing at an unknown later date.

746–735? BCE Hosea delivers his oral message in Israel; disciples later compile his words in written form.

740–701 BCE Isaiah of Jerusalem delivers his prophetic oracles warning of Assyria's threat to Judah; disciples later preserve Isaiah's words in parts of Isaiah 1–39.

740–700 BCE Micah delivers prophetic oracles that are later recorded and preserved in the Jerusalem temple (Jer 26:16–18).

700–621 BCE The central part of Deuteronomy (chapters 12–29) is composed.

630–609 BCE The prophetic oracles of Zephaniah are compiled.

621 BCE The prophetess Huldah begins the process of biblical canonization by affirming the authenticity of an early edition of Deuteronomy.

621–609 BCE The first edition of the Deuteronomistic History (Joshua through 2 Kings), incorporating older poetic and prose documents, is written (perhaps by the scribe Baruch in Jerusalem).

612 BCE   Nahum delivers his oracles on Nineveh's fall.

609–598 BCE   Habakkuk delivers his oracles on the Babylonian threat.

600–587 BCE   Some prophetic oracles of Jeremiah are recorded by his secretary Baruch.

587 BCE   Obadiah denounces Edom's part in Babylon's devastation of Judah and Jerusalem.

580 BCE   Ezekiel's visions in the Babylonian captivity are recorded; Baruch compiles more of Jeremiah's oracles, adding biographical material.

550–500 BCE   Collections of legal and ritual material by priestly writer(s) are inserted into JE narratives and preserved in parts of Exodus, Leviticus, and Numbers.

540s BCE   Second Isaiah delivers oracles of hope in Babylon, which are recorded later in Isaiah 40–55.

520 BCE   Postexilic prophets Haggai and Zechariah encourage rebuilding of Jerusalem temple.

500 BCE   Deuteronomistic and priestly reediting of older documents continues in postexilic Jerusalem.

500–450 BCE   Third Isaiah delivers oracles that are later incorporated into Isaiah 56–66.

500–400 BCE   The poetic dialogues in Job are composed and inserted into the framework of an old prose tale.

500–300 BCE   Additional psalms are composed and used in worship at the second temple.

490–400 BCE   The prophetic books of Malachi, Joel, and Jonah are compiled; an old folktale is rewritten, creating the book of Ruth.

450–400 BCE   Priestly editor(s) complete the revision of legal material in Exodus, Leviticus, Numbers, and Deuteronomy; Ezra returns from Babylon to Jerusalem with a revised edition of the Torah.

400 BCE   The book of Proverbs is compiled.

400–300 BCE   The process of canonization of the Torah is completed; the book of Esther is composed; disciples of a Jerusalem sage compile the book of Ecclesiastes; the books of Chronicles and Ezra-Nehemiah are written.

250 BCE   The Torah is translated into Greek, forming the first part of the Septuagint Bible.

200–100 BCE   Collections of the prophets are canonized.

165 BCE   The book of Daniel is composed.

70–130 CE   Following Jerusalem's destruction, Jewish scholars gradually develop a standardized Hebrew text.

APPENDIX 5
Major Events in New Testament History

50 CE	Paul writes 1 and 2 Thessalonians; the "Sayings" of Jesus are compiled (?).
54–62 CE	Paul writes a series of letters to various churches he has founded or visited.
54–68 CE	Nero reigns as emperor of Rome.
60–62 or 63 CE	Paul under house arrest in Rome.
62 CE	James, brother of Jesus, is martyred.
64 CE	Rome is burned, and Christians are persecuted.
66–70 CE	Gospel of Mark is written.
66–73 CE	Jewish revolt against Rome; destruction of Jerusalem and the temple★
69–79 CE	Vespasian reigns as emperor of Rome.
79–81 CE	Titus, conqueror of Jerusalem, is emperor.
80–85 CE	Gospel of Matthew is written.
80–90 CE	Gospel of Luke and Acts are written.
80–100 CE	Letter of James is written.
81–96 CE	Domitian is emperor; Christians in Asia Minor experience general hostility.
85–90 CE	Book of Hebrews is written.
90 CE (?)	Letter to the Ephesians is written; Paul's letters are collected (?).
90–91 CE	Rabbis hold council at Jamnia; rabbinic Judaism emerges from postwar reorganization.
90–100 CE	1 Clement is written; Gospel of John is composed.
95–100 CE	Various Jewish and Christian apocalypses are composed: 2 Esdras, Revelation, and 3 Baruch.
98–117 CE	Trajan reigns as emperor and persecutes some Christians.
100–110 CE	Letters of 1, 2, and 3 John are written.
100–140 CE	The Didache, Shepherd of Hermas, and Epistle of Ignatius are written; canonical New Testament books of 1 and 2 Timothy, Titus, 1 Peter, and Jude also appear.
117–138 CE	Hadrian is emperor.
132–135 CE	Jews revolt against Rome for the last time.
150 CE (?)	2 Peter is written.

★The revolt against Rome marks the end of both the Jewish state and the original apostolic church.

Abraham's Family Tree
(Genesis)

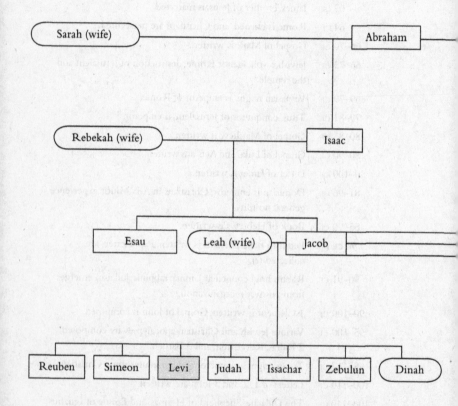

There are two different ways to count the twelve tribes of Israel:

(1) Strictly the sons of Jacob (Gen 49:28).

(2) Substituting the sons of Joseph for Levi (priests without territory) and for Joseph (Num 1:4–15).

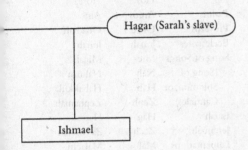

Hagar (Sarah's slave)

Ishmael

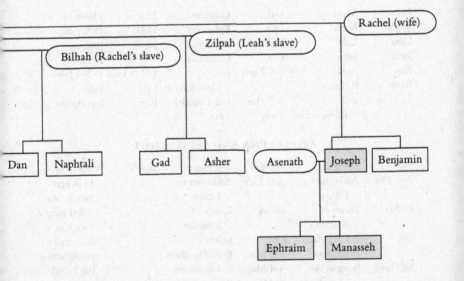

Rachel (wife)

Zilpah (Leah's slave)

Bilhah (Rachel's slave)

Dan | Naphtali

Gad | Asher

Asenath | Joseph | Benjamin

Ephraim | Manasseh

Abbreviations for Biblical Books

HEBREW BIBLE/OLD TESTAMENT

Gen	Genesis	Esth	Esther	Dan	Daniel
Exod	Exodus	Job	Job	Hos	Hosea
Lev	Leviticus	Ps	Psalms	Amos	Amos
Num	Numbers	Prov	Proverbs	Obad	Obadiah
Deut	Deuteronomy	Eccles	Ecclesiastes	Jonah	Jonah
Josh	Joshua	Song	Song of Songs	Mic	Micah
Judges	Judges		(Song of	Nah	Nahum
Ruth	Ruth		Solomon, or	Hab	Habakkuk
1–2 Sam	1–2 Samuel		Canticles)	Zeph	Zephaniah
1–2 Kings	1–2 Kings	Isa	Isaiah	Hag	Haggai
1–2 Chron	1–2 Chronicles	Jer	Jeremiah	Zech	Zechariah
Ezra	Ezra	Lam	Lamentations	Mal	Malachi
Neh	Nehemiah	Ezek	Ezekiel		

NEW TESTAMENT

Matt	Matthew	Gal	Galatians	Philem	Philemon
Mark	Mark	Eph	Ephesians	Heb	Hebrews
Luke	Luke	Phil	Philippians	Jas	James
John	John	Col	Colossians	1–2 Pet	1–2 Peter
Acts	Acts	1–2 Thess	1–2	1–2–3 John	1–2–3 John
Rom	Romans		Thessalonians	Jude	Jude
1–2 Cor	1–2	1–2 Tim	1–2 Timothy	Rev	Revelation
	Corinthians	Titus	Titus		

APOCRYPHA AND SEPTUAGINT

Bar	Baruch	1–2 Esd	1–2 Esdras	Sirach	Wisdom of
Add Dan	Additions to	Add Esth	Additions to		Jesus ben-
	Daniel		Esther		Sirach (also
Pr Azar	Prayer of	Ep Jer	Epistle of		called simply
	Azariah		Jeremiah		Sirach or
Bel	Bel and the	Jdt	Judith		Ecclesiasati-
	Dragon	1–2 Mac	1–2 Maccabees		cus, reflecting
Sg Three	Song of the	3–4 Mac	3–4 Maccabees		the Latin)
	Three Young	Pr Man	Prayer of	Tob	Tobit
	Men		Manasseh	Wis	Wisdom of
Sus	Susanna	Ps 151	Psalm 151		Solomon

RESOURCES FOR MORE INFORMATION

The first place most people go these days to learn about something, anything, is the Internet, and there are a lot of excellent resources immediately available electronically. Not all of them are helpful, though, and some are misleading, if not just plain wrong. Wikipedia entries are usually the first options to appear in response to an Internet search request. Those articles can be a good place to start, but they should never be the only or the last source used. Because Wikipedia is built on the elective contributions of anyone who wishes to write something, its information should be checked and double-checked against other reputable sources.

As far as particular websites go, the options are endless. Readers do well simply to apply the same criteria for judging their fitness as to any other resource—who produced it, why, how, and when? The two primary organizations for people studying the Bible and religion in general are, respectively, the Society of Biblical Literature and the American Academy of Religion. Their members number in the thousands and are composed mainly of people who study and teach about religion or the Bible (or both) for a living. Some members are personally religious; some are not. Both organizations have websites with a number of resources and links to aid interested readers.

Readers can be confident that the information in articles published by peer-reviewed journals and in books published by university presses is solid. The material not only is written by people highly trained (usually at the doctoral level) in the specific area addressed but also has been subjected to a process of review by others at least as highly trained and experienced. Such journals identify themselves as "peer-reviewed," if they are. (If they don't identify themselves as such, they are not.) University presses always use a system of peer review.

For most people, the trouble with the information from such journals and presses is that it often presupposes a level of familiarity with the subject that general readers don't have. In other words, such articles and books are usually written primarily for the authors' academic peers. The writers' assumptions and jargon can make these works too dense for people without academic expertise. This is not always the case, however, and many excellent university press books and journal articles are interesting and useful to general readers. I've included some of these below.

In addition to books and articles, there are a few categories of resources that may be unfamiliar to the general reader.

Concordances track the occurrence of individual words and note where they appear in the Bible. Electronic versions of bibles have made such word searching much easier, and have made print copies of concordances virtually obsolete. When conducting a word search, remember that sometimes several different English words may have only one Hebrew or Greek original behind them, and vice versa. Electronic "interlinear" bibles allow you to see biblical texts in their original languages with translations side-by-side.

If you don't know the biblical languages well enough to read Hebrew and Greek, I recommend comparing a variety of translations. Places where the translations differ usually reveal how the "original" allows for more than one reading. You can find many full-text translations on the Internet.

Lexica (plural of "lexicon"), like dictionaries, help readers define individual words. They are frequently organized in a way that reflects the grammatical constraints of the languages. For example, biblical Hebrew uses a system of three-letter root words. Many lexica arrange entries by roots rather than by the form of a particular word. In other words, to look up the Hebrew word "I am," by which God identified himself to Moses, one would search under the root of the verb "to be." Among the Hebrew and Greek lexica are:

Bauer, Walter, F. Wilbur Danker, William F. Arndt, and Frederick W. Gingrich. *Greek-English Lexicon of the New Testament and Other Early Christian Literature*, 3rd ed. (Chicago, Ill.: University of Chicago Press, 1999).

Brown, Francis, S. R. Driver, and Charles A. Briggs. *A Hebrew and English Lexicon of the Old Testament* (Oxford: Clarendon, 1907).

Holladay, William Lee. *A Concise Hebrew and Aramaic Lexicon of the Old Testament* (Leiden: E. J. Brill, 1988).

Koehler, Ludwig, Walter Baumgartner, and Johann Jakob Stamm. *The Hebrew and Aramaic Lexicon of the Old Testament*, trans. and ed. under the supervision of M. E. J. Richardson, 5 vols. (Leiden: E. J. Brill, 1994–2000).

Liddell, Henry George, and Robert Scott. *A Greek-English Lexicon*, 9th ed. (Oxford: Clarendon, 1996).

Louw, Johannes P., and Eugene A. Nida, eds. *Greek-English Lexicon of the New Testament: Based on Semantic Domains*, 2nd ed. (New York: United Bible Societies, 1989).

Muraoka, T. *A Greek-English Lexicon of the Septuagint* (Louvain: Peeters, 2002).

Dictionaries having to do with the Bible look a bit more like what we might think of as encyclopedias (just as lexica are more like what we think of as dictionaries). Entries under a single word are more detailed and topical than the brief definitions that one would find in, say, Webster's under the word "apple." For example, in the *Anchor Bible Dictionary* under the entry "Angels (Old Testament)," one can read about each of the different Hebrew terms that may describe what we think of as angels; and in its entry "Versions, English," it has pages and pages of information about different English versions of the Bible. The bibliographies following each entry or at the book's end can be helpful for locating more information on a particular topic. Some Bible dictionaries are:

Achtemeier, Paul J., ed. *HarperCollins Bible Dictionary*, rev ed. (San Francisco, Calif.: Harper-SanFrancisco, 1996).

Browning, W. R. F. *A Dictionary of the Bible* (New York: Oxford University Press, 2004).

Douglas, J. D., and Merrill C. Tenney. *Zondervan's Pictorial Bible Dictionary* (Grand Rapids, Mich.: Zondervan, 1999).

Freedman, David Noel, ed. *Anchor Bible Dictionary*, 6 vols. (New York: Doubleday, 1992–).

Freeman, David Noel, Allen C. Meyers, and Astrid B. Beck, eds. *Eerdmans Dictionary of the Bible* (Grand Rapids, Mich.: Eerdmans, 2000).

New Interpreter's Dictionary of the Bible, 5 vols. (Nashville, Tenn.: Abingdon, 2006–2009).

Commentaries, like the lexica and dictionaries noted above, come in single and multivolume versions. There is wide variety, not least because they are collections of comments about biblical texts. Some provide quite a bit of background historical information, literary analysis, and ideas for application on biblical books, even verse by verse. Others represent imaginative musings on specific biblical texts or chunks of text. A commentary may be the product of a team of highly trained scholars, or it may represent the ideas of a single individual with no biblical training who felt moved to record his or her thoughts. The following is a list of only some of the commentaries written by people who study the Bible for a living:

Brown, Raymond E., Joseph A. Fitzmeyer, and Roland Murphy, eds. *The New Jerome Biblical Commentary* (Englewood Cliffs, N.J.: Prentice-Hall, 1990).

Buttrick, George Arthur, ed. *The Interpreter's Bible*, 12 vols. (New York: Abingdon-Cokesbury, 1951–1957).

Collins, John J., ed. *Anchor Yale Bible Commentary*, 87 vols. (New Haven, Conn.: Yale University Press, 1963–).

Cross, Frank Moore, Helmut Koester, et al., eds. *Hermeneia*, 40 vols. (Minneapolis, Minn.: Augsburg Fortress, 1985–).

Keck, Leander E., et al., eds. *New Interpreter's Bible*, 12 vols. (Nashville, Tenn.: Abingdon, 1994–2002).

Mays, James L., ed. *HarperCollins Bible Commentary* (San Francisco, Calif.: HarperSanFrancisco, 2000).

Newsom, Carol A., and Sharon H. Ringe, eds. *The Women's Bible Commentary* (Louisville, Ky.: Westminster/John Knox, 1992).

NOTES

INTRODUCTION

1. Jeremy Morrison, "Bay County Animal Control to Offer Free Microchips for Pets," *News Herald*, December 27, 2007, http://www.newsherald.com/common/printer/view.php?db=newsherald&id=2115.

2. In this book, the word "Bible" is capitalized when it's used as a title (i.e., the Bible, or Hebrew Bible) but not when it's grammatically modified or appears in plural form (e.g., Jewish bible, or Christian bible, or their bibles). This is admittedly not a perfect system, and I mean no disrespect. It just looks funny to have so many capital B's on the page.

3. Tony Gosling, "Electronic ID, Microchipping, the Mark of the Beast—Some Possible Explanations," http://www.bilderberg/www.bilderberg.org/shengen.htm (accessed January 20, 2008).

4. Transliteration is different from translation. Transliteration simply renders a foreign word in characters familiar to us—e.g., גוֹיִם to *goyim*. Translation renders its meaning, in this case "nations," "(other) peoples."

CHAPTER 1: WHAT IS THE BIBLE, ANYWAY?

1. "The Bible Is America's Favorite Book Followed by 'Gone with the Wind,'" *The Harris Poll* 38, April 8, 2008, http://www.harrisinteractive.com/harris_poll/index.asp?PID=892 (accessed November 25, 2008); and "Americans Identify What They Consider 'Holy Books,'" *Barna Update*, July 7, 2008, http://www.barna.org/FlexPage.aspx?Page=BarnaUpdate&BarnaUpdateID=302 (accessed November 25, 2008).

2. Deut 21:18–21.

3. Jewish Publication Society's *Tanakh* translation.

4. This idea is represented within the Bible (Christian) itself—in one of the latest books, written long after the prophets' words of which it speaks had become sacred scripture (1 Peter 1:20–21).

5. Exod 31:18; Deut 9:9–11 (see also Exod 24:12; 32:15–16; 34:1). In that particular story, the finger of God was said to have marked the stones that Moses held. In Exod 24:4 and 34:28 and Deut 31:9, Moses does the writing.

6. For a transcript of the entire Democratic debate of September 26, 2007, see http://www.msnbc.msn.com/id/21327206/page/19/.

7. When writing about the Bible, people sometimes subdivide verses with lowercase letters. For example, the fourth verse in Genesis chapter 2 has two parts that may be identified as Gen 2:4a and Gen 2:4b. In referring to a text composed of more than one verse, it is conventional to use a dash between the references to the beginning and end. For example, Gen 1:1–2:4 refers to the passage that appears between and includes Genesis chapter 1 verse 1 and Genesis chapter 2 verse 4. In referring to two or more nonconsecutive verses, there are a couple of possibilities. If the verses are in the same chapter, the numbers are separated by a comma (e.g., Gen 1:1, 4 refers to the first and fourth verses of Genesis chapter 1). If the verses are in different chapters, a semicolon distinguishes them. For example, Gen 1:2; 3:4 refers to Genesis chapter 1, verse 2 and Genesis chapter 3, verse 4; Gen 1:1; Exod 5:6 refers to Genesis chapter 1, verse 1 and Exodus chapter 5, verse 6.

8. Also, the present chapter-verse system reflects a Christian perspective on biblical organization that differs from the older Jewish system of dividing texts into sections for use in worship and study. Jews adopted the Christian system as the standard during the Spanish Middle Ages (probably not unrelated to pressures of the Inquisition), but some minor differences remain. For example, the superscription of a psalm—telling what instruments to use or to whom the psalm is attributed—gets its own verse in Jewish bibles but is only part of the first verse in Christian bibles. The versification of the remainder of every psalm is consequently different between Jewish and Christian bibles by one. The "for unto us a child is born" verse that Handel cites is Isaiah 9:5 in the Jewish scriptures, and Isaiah 9:6 in Christian bibles.

9. *The New Oxford Annotated Bible with the Apocryphal/Deuterocanonical Books*, ed. Michael D. Coogan, 3d ed. (Oxford: Oxford University Press, 2001), 22.

CHAPTER 2: DIFFERENT BIBLES AND A HIDDEN BIBLE, TOO

1. Not yet "Bible," per se, those books nevertheless were accepted as authoritative scripture by Jews of Ptolemy II's time.

2. Furthermore, Alexandria bustled with well-educated Jews, so it is likely that the scholars were homegrown Egyptian Alexandrian Jews. See Leonard J. Greenspoon, "Between Alexandria and Antioch," in *The Oxford History of the Biblical World*, ed. Michael D. Coogan (Oxford: Oxford University Press, 1998), 320.

3. There actually were several various Greek versions and translations of the Jewish bible that circulated in the centuries straddling the year 1 CE, but most people use the term "Septuagint" to refer to any published collection of ancient Greek Jewish biblical books and leave it at that.

4. As for the h in Kh: in brief, it has to do with a grammatical convention in Hebrew that sometimes distinguishes between the beginning and ends of words—K at the beginning; kh at the end, in this case.

5. The word "testament" itself makes a theological statement, since it reflects an old use of the term as synonymous with "covenant." As binding agreements between two parties,

covenants are crucial in the Bible. In the Hebrew Bible, God makes covenants with the whole earth after the Flood, with Abraham and his family, with the Israelites through Moses, and with David. Some prophets anticipated a "new covenant," which Christians understand to be fulfilled in a special way through Jesus. The term "New Testament," then, intimates that its books tell about a new covenant between God and the world as mediated by the life, death, and resurrection of Jesus.

6. In other words, during the Christian bible's canonical process, the Old Testament, based as it was on Greek versions (translation and then some) of Hebrew books, grew to be longer than the Jewish Hebrew Bible. The result: the Western churches (Latin, then Roman) and Eastern churches (Greek, then Orthodox) include books and parts of books that do not appear in the Hebrew Bible. See note 45 in Chapter 12 for a little more information about the history of these churches.

7. For example, the movie includes a prestory, jewel, and love interest that are nowhere to be found in any biblical version of the story. See the trailer at http://www.8x.com/onenight/video_trailer.htm (accessed October 16, 2008).

8. Luther's facility with Hebrew wasn't particularly good, though, so he depended heavily on the help of others. Unfortunately, his relationship with Jews and the learned rabbis who could provide strong scholarly support was complicated by his anti-Semitism. (In a particularly hateful tract, "On the Jews and Their Lies," he warns fellow Christians of the "poisonous activities" of "these miserable, blind, and senseless people.")

9. Violence rendered richly beautiful is not unique to our time (think: Cormac McCarthy, Quentin Tarantino, *The Godfather*, Frank Miller, rock 'n' roll), and sex never goes out of style. In Caravaggio's *Beheading*, the Jewish widow and heroine, Judith, a young girl in a white blouse, leans away from the prostrate Holofernes as she grips a hunk of hair in one hand and slits his neck with the other. Blood shoots like red ribbon across the lush sheets as an old crone (presumably Judith's maid, Abra) looks on. In Artemisia Gentileschi's first painting on this theme, the women are contemporaries, their sumptuous sleeves rolled up as they wrestle the bloody Holofernes down. In a later version, deemed by its owner to be too horrifying for regular viewing, Gentileschi gives Judith both jewelry on her powerful arms and a longer, thicker sword. In Jan Massys's 1543 version, Judith sits straight, proud, and nude to the waist, looking directly at the viewer with a triumphant gaze. Holofernes's head dangles from her fist like a handbag accessory. The story of Susanna gave the artists ample opportunity to paint a nude woman. The subject usually includes several well-dressed old men ogling her lewdly. *Susanna* is also a modern opera with the apocryphal story set in mid-twentieth-century Tennessee. It is performed almost as frequently as the ever-popular *Porgy and Bess*.

10. Donald Senior and John J. Collins, eds., *Catholic Study Bible: The New American Bible, Including the Revised New Testament and Psalm, Translated from the Original Languages with Critical Use of All the Ancient Sources*, 2d ed. (New York: Oxford University Press, 2006).

11. These four parts roughly reflect the four-part arrangement of the Christian Old Testament.

12. Acts 9:1–19a.

13. For example, although tradition says that the author of the gospel of John was the apostle John, most scholars think that a disciple recorded John's teachings and that this record became the gospel attributed to John. Similarly, the letters of John should probably be

understood as the writing of people in the Johannine tradition, despite the early Christian attribution of 1 John to the apostle. It's tough to say for certain. The author of the apocalypse of John (Revelation) mentions the twelve apostles apart from himself and in the past, suggesting yet another example of writing in another's name.

CHAPTER 3: AS IT IS WRITTEN: HISTORY IN THE BIBLE

1. Gen 6:1–4.

2. Dan 3:8–30.

3. Consequently, this book does not refer to God's people in the Hebrew Bible as "Jews" until the exilic period, when Judaism probably began to take shape as a religion. Rather, they are "Hebrews" before they came to be identified with the political and geographical nation of Israel; and "Israelites" after that. (Modern citizens of the state of Israel are called "Israelis.") Some people argue that not until the rabbinic period of the first centuries (CE), when Judaism adopted the texts and traditions that especially define it still today, is the term "Jew" appropriate.

4. Hebrew Bible scholar Karel Van der Toorn goes so far as to say, "Without the Persians, there would not have been a Pentateuch." He also submits that the idea of the Torah as law is due to the Persians, too, because they called the Torah *dat*, meaning "law," rather than "instruction, advice," as the Hebrew word *torah* is best translated. See Karel Van der Toorn, *Scribal Culture and the Making of the Hebrew Bible* (Cambridge, Mass.: Harvard University Press, 2007), 251. See also Kenneth G. Hoglund, *Achaemenid Imperial Administration in Syria-Palestine and the Missions of Ezra and Nehemiah*, SBL Dissertation Series 125 (Atlanta, Ga.: Scholars, 1992), 207–240.

5. The book of Judges begins surprisingly, by assuming that those troublesome Canaanites were still in the land. This is in stark disagreement with the book of Joshua, which told how the Israelites were wildly successful in their genocide. But never mind. The books reveal different literary sources, different times, and different goals.

CHAPTER 4: CONTEXTS AND CULTURE: HISTORY BEHIND THE BIBLE

1. Josh 5:13–6:27.

2. See, for example, the archaeological reports of Kathleen M. Kenyon, *Excavations at Jericho*, 5 vols. (London: British School of Archaeology in Jerusalem, 1960–1983). Kenyon did the most groundbreaking work on Jericho. She also wrote a more general overview, *Archaeology in the Holy Land*, 4th ed. (London: E. Benn, 1979). See also Israel Finkelstein, Amihai Mazar, and Brian B. Schmidt, *The Quest for the Historical Israel: Debating Archaeology and the History of Early Israel* (Atlanta, Ga.: Society of Biblical Literature, 2007).

3. Josephus, (37–100 CE), a Jewish historian who worked for the Romans, mentions Jesus twice. He refers once to Jesus simply as the brother of James, in a passage most people accept as authentic (*Antiquities of the Jews*, 20.9.1). His other reference to Jesus provides more detail. Josephus calls Jesus "a wise man, if one should call him a man at all," for example, and says that he was "the messiah," was crucified, and on the third day appeared again to his followers.

Yet this passage, called the *Testimonium Flavianum* (*Antiquities of the Jews*, 18.3.3), is of disputed origins. Most scholars think that followers of Jesus added it to Josephus's existing work.

4. There are many excellent resources for investigating the historical context of any given character or event in far greater detail than fits in this wee chapter. A few classics plus a couple of the most recent, broad treatments include: Frank Moore Cross, *Canaanite Myth and Hebrew Epic: Essays in the History of the Religion of Israel* (Cambridge, Mass.: Harvard University Press, 1973); Amihai Mazar, *Archaeology of the Land of the Bible 10,000–586 BCE* (New York: Doubleday, 1990); Lester L. Grabbe, ed., *Can a "History of Israel" Be Written?* (Sheffield: Sheffield Academic, 1997); Michael D. Coogan, ed., *The Oxford History of the Biblical World* (Oxford: Oxford University Press, 1998); Mario Liverani, *Israel's History and the History of Israel*, transl. Chiara Peri and Philip R. Davies (London: Equinox, 2006); J. Maxwell Miller and John H. Hayes, *A History of Ancient Israel and Judah* (Louisville, Ky.: Westminster John Knox, 2006).

5. Actually, we don't have any definitive nonbiblical evidence for characters including the biblical patriarchs, Joseph, Moses, Joshua, Samson, and Solomon, or for major events such as the Flood, the Exodus, and the conquest of cities as narrated in the Bible, until Omri, a king of the northern kingdom around 880–870 BCE. Ironically, this first biblical character to gain nonbiblical attention gets only a few verses in the Bible (1 Kings 16:16–28). King Mesha of Moab's is the earliest mention of Omri, on lines 4–8 of his inscribed stele: James B. Pritchard, ed., *Ancient Near Eastern Texts Relating to the Old Testament*, 3d ed. with suppl. (Princeton, N.J.: Princeton University Press, 1969), 320, 321; William W. Hallo and K. Lawson Younger, eds. *Context of Scripture* (Leiden: Brill, 1997–2002), 2.23. The Assyrian records continued to refer to the northern kingdom of Israel as "the land of the house of Omri" long after Omri's death. For example, see Pritchard, *Ancient Near Eastern Texts Relating to the Old Testament*, 280–281, 284–285; Hallo and Younger, *Context of Scripture*, 2.113E–H. It's possible that the Mesha stele also originally referred to the "house of David," but the stone is chipped where the "D" would need to be. Although the Tel Dan stele seems to refer to the "house of David," it dates to around 800 BCE (see later in this chapter).

6. Some scholars date the Exodus earlier, assuming that the biblical story of the Exodus is related to the historical expulsion of a non-Egyptian people called the Hyksos who ruled Egypt from about 1650 to 1550 BCE. Admittedly, this is the only verifiable historical moment that shares key characteristics with that biblical narrative. But it messes up the rest of ancient Israel's chronology and doesn't fit with what is most logical for the succeeding centuries, also on the basis of the archaeological record.

7. Pritchard, *Ancient Near Eastern Texts Relating to the Old Testament*, 376–378; Hallo and Younger, *Context of Scripture*, 2.6.

8. See 1 Kings 14:25; 2 Chron 12:1–9. This pharaoh is the first one named in the biblical texts.

9. PBS broadcast a fascinating show on the topic, *The Lost Tribes of Israel*, in 2000. The companion website makes the material easily accessible: http://www.pbs.org/wgbh/nova/israel/.

10. Hezekiah is named as the sponsor of collections of sayings canonized in the book of Proverbs (25:1) and probably supported efforts by refugees from the northern kingdom to

preserve popular stories, including those about Elijah, and religious instruction such as Deuteronomy.

11. 2 Kings 18:13–19:37; Isa 36:1–37:38; 2 Chron 32:1–23. Sennacherib claims to have "locked [Hezekiah] up in Jerusalem . . . like a bird in a cage." See Pritchard, *Ancient Near Eastern Texts Relating to the Old Testament*, 287–288; Hallo and Younger, *Context of Scripture*, 2.119B.

12. 2 Kings 22:8.

13. Pritchard, *Ancient Near Eastern Texts Relating to the Old Testament*, 301–307; Hallo and Younger, *Context of Scripture*, 1.137.

14. The final fall, with the destruction of Jerusalem and its temple, is narrated in 2 Kings 24:20–25:21; and 2 Chron 36:11–20.

15. Pritchard, *Ancient Near Eastern Texts Relating to the Old Testament*, 315–316; Hallo and Younger, *Context of Scripture*, 2.124.

16. Ezra 4:1–4.

17. Neh 2:19–20; 4:1–23.

18. Sanballat, one of the leaders of the opposition against Nehemiah, is mentioned as the governor of Samaria in an Egyptian text from the same period. See A. E. Cowley, *Aramaic Papyri of the Fifth Century B.C.* (Oxford: Oxford University Press, 1923), 30:29.

19. Arguably, the entire book of Daniel concerns this matter (though it is set in Babylon, its authorship derives from a Greek context).

20. See especially Josephus, *Antiquities of the Jews*, 18.11–25; *The Wars of the Jews*, 2.119–166.

21. Matt 2:1–18.

22. Revelation comprises the visions this John had while imprisoned on the island of Patmos, probably during the reign of Domitian (81–96 CE).

CHAPTER 5: GETTING TO THE GOOD BOOK: HISTORY OF THE BIBLE

1. That is to say, not that the texts lacked authority, or at least a sense of being authoritative, until they became part of the canonical Bible, but simply that they were not composed in order to be part of a closed collection of sacred scripture. For example, there are numerous references to the texts' messages as the "word of God." The Hebrew prophets claimed to be communicating exactly that to their audiences, Paul professes to have expressed "God's word" to the Thessalonians (1 Thess 2:13), and the author of John's gospel declares that what is written there is intended to persuade people to believe in Jesus as the son of God (John 20:31). But none of these texts was composed with the goal of becoming part of a closed canon of scripture.

2. E.g., Ezra 7:6; Neh 8:1; 2 Chron 23:18; Dan 9:11; Luke 24:44; 1 Cor 9:9.

3. E.g., Exod 17:14; 24:4; Num 33:2; Deut 31:9.

4. For example, in his commentary on the Torah, Ibn Ezra noted a problem with Gen 12:6, "at that time, Canaanites were in the land," which would seem to suggest that it was written much later than Moses, after the tribes had settled and the Canaanites were no longer

in the land. In an effort not to challenge traditional readings, Ibn Ezra proposed two possibilities: that it referred to a time much earlier (before Canaanites were ever in the land); or
"there is a great mystery and the wise will be silent."

5. Gen 1:27, 31.

6. Gen 2:18, 20–23.

7. Ezra 7:1–28. See also Kenneth G. Hoglund, *Achaemenid Imperial Administration in Syria-
Palestine and the Missions of Ezra and Nehemiah*, SBL Dissertation Series 125 (Atlanta, Ga.:
Scholars, 1992), 207–240.

8. The gospel writers remember Jesus referring to his Jewish scriptures as the "law and
the prophets." (For example, see Matt 5:17; 7:12. Luke 24:44 adds the psalms.) That is how
they're referred to in Acts (13:15; 24:14).

9. For many years, scholars thought that a particular gathering of Jewish intellectuals,
called the Council of Jamnia and assembled around 90 CE, fixed the canon. Recent investigation suggests that there may never have been such a definitive moment (and may never
even have been such a council), but that the canon's closure happened somewhat more gradually. See Giuseppe Veltri, "Zur traditionsgeschichtlichen Entwicklung des Bewusstseins
von einem Kanon: Die Yavneh-Frage," *Journal for the Study of Judaism* 21 (1990): 210–226;
David E. Aune, "On the Origins of the 'Council of Javneh,' *Journal of Biblical Literature* 110
(1991): 491–493; Jack P. Lewis, "Jamnia after Forty Years," *Hebrew Union College Annual*
70–71 (1999–2000): 233–259; Jack P. Lewis, "Jamnia, Council of," n.p., *Anchor Bible Dictionary on CD-ROM*, Logos 2.1, ed. David Noel Freedman (New York: Doubleday), 1992,
1997.

10. The list comes from Athanasius, a highly respected and influential bishop of Alexandria,
Egypt, who also excoriated the use of other books as authoritative for Christianity.

11. See Chapter 9 for more details.

12. 2 Pet 3:15–16. We have little evidence to suggest that Simon Peter wrote 2 Peter.
Rather, with this attribution (and the explicit inclusion of Paul), its author simply emphasized
the church's apostolic lineage.

13. 1 Tim 5:18b (probably from the early second century CE) cites as "scripture" a saying of
Jesus' preserved in Luke's gospel (Luke 10:7, though it doesn't explicitly identify the saying
with Luke's gospel).

CHAPTER 6: WHAT'S THE BEST TRANSLATION?

1. Apart from several chapters in Daniel (Dan 2:4b–7:28), there is very little Aramaic
in the Bible, so I will follow convention by talking about Hebrew and Greek as the Bible's
original languages.

2. Neh 8:7–8. That is the most likely situation to explain the presence of persons selected
to help those gathered "to understand the torah. . . . They gave the sense, so that the people
understood the reading." It is also possible to interpret this passage to mean that the selected
persons provided commentary, not translation, of the Hebrew Torah. Given both the historical context and the biblical description, however, I find that interpretation less compelling.

3. It continued to be the lingua franca of the Near East and Middle East through the first
part of the Common Era.

4. Given their commentary-like nature, it seems that the Targums were meant to be read alongside (not replacing) the Hebrew.

5. Herbert G. Grether, "Versions, Modern Era," n.p., *Anchor Bible Dictionary on CD-ROM*, Logos 2.1, ed. David Noel Freedman (New York: Doubleday), 1992, 1997.

6. At http://www.wbtc.com (accessed June 29, 2008).

7. One example of a likely scribal error in the Masoretic Text (MT), in light of the Dead Sea Scrolls (DSS), appears in 1 Sam 10:27–11:1. Comparison suggests that the MT story of Saul and the Ammonite conflict is missing a passage. Also, the MT has an r where it probably should have d (those letters look almost identical in Hebrew). The difference is: "he kept silent" (MT = 1 Sam 10:27), and "about a month later" (DSS = 1 Sam 11:1).

8. The Samaritan Pentateuch was developed by a breakaway Jewish sect in the 300s BCE; its members appealed to the first five books as their Bible. Other useful versions for comparison include the Syriac Peshittas (translation without commentary produced by Jews in northern Syria, later adopted by Syriac Christians, who added translations of the New Testament) and the Aramaic Targums, mostly paraphrase rather than strict literal translations from Hebrew for the Persian (and post-Persian) period, Aramaic-speaking audience.

9. For a more detailed explanation of the evidence, see Emanuel Tov, "The Literary History of the Book of Jeremiah in the Light of Its Textual History," in Jeffrey H. Tigay, ed., *Empirical Models for Biblical Criticism* (Philadelphia: University of Pennsylvania Press, 1985), 211–237; Karel Van der Toorn, *Scribal Culture* (Cambridge, Mass.: Harvard University Press), 131–132, 199–203. For alternatives, see Arie van der Kooij, "Jeremiah 27:4–15: How Do MT and LXX Relate to Each Other?" *Journal of Northwest Semitic Languages* 20 (1994): 59–78.

10. For example, the *Codex Vaticanus*, so named because it's in the control of the Vatican (though it was probably written in Egypt) and dating to the fourth century CE, doesn't include that story. Entirely in Greek, the *Codex Vaticanus* vies with the *Codex Sinaiticus* for the title of oldest Bible including both Old and New Testaments that we have. Nevertheless, a good bit of the text was lost from the *Codex Sinaiticus*. Although its title refers to the monastery of Saint Catherine at Sinai, not all of its existing manuscript is there. Parts are in Germany, Russia, and the United Kingdom, too. A digital version of the *Codex Sinaiticus* is available at http://www.codexsinaiticus.org/en/.

11. Gen 1:26–27.

12. Like English, Hebrew has different words for man and male, woman and female. In Gen 1:27, the sex-specific words "male" and "female" are used. The gender-specific words "man" and "woman" are first used in Gen 2:22.

13. Gen 2:7.

14. This is the position of the biblical scholar Phyllis Trible, in *God and the Rhetoric of Human Sexuality* (Philadelphia, Pa.: Fortress, 1978).

15. In a clever twist, Adamah is the name of the commanding officer in the series *Battlestar Galactica*. His goal is to return the fleet of surviving humans to Earth.

16. The Hebrew phrase translated here as "corresponding helper" does not necessarily connote subservience. For example, God is described as "helper" to human beings. Many translations read that God took a rib from Adam's side. The Hebrew doesn't add "rib." Rather, it says simply that God "took from his side" (Gen 2:21).

17. The preface is also available in several collections and anthologies, including W. P. Ker,

ed., *Essays of John Dryden* (Oxford: Clarendon, 1900). The quotations come from this edition, p. 237.

18. Exod 34:29–30.

19. After all, the effect is described in only this one passage; and only Moses spoke with God "face to face," so we can't compare this strange resulting visage with anyone else. Nevertheless, its use in these verses is as a verb telling what happened to the "skin of Moses' face," so "horns" is probably not the best translation.

20. For my review of the development of English translations of the Bible in England through the eighteenth century, I am indebted to Benson Bobrick, *Wide as the Waters: The Story of the English Bible and the Revolution It Inspired* (New York: Simon and Schuster, 2001; Penguin, 2002).

21. From a quotation in David Daniell, ed., *Tyndale's New Testament* (New Haven, Conn.: Yale University Press, 1989), xxii.

22. This is recounted in Foxe's *Book of Martyrs*, chapter 12. One version of Foxe, edited by William Byron Forbush, is available online at http://www.ccel.org/f/foxe/martyrs/fox112 .htm (accessed June 22, 2008).

23. Indeed, this matter of Henry's wishing to marry Anne, but being refused by two popes to divorce Catherine lay at the heart of the Church of England's beginnings as a powerful Christian denomination distinct from Roman Catholicism (called till then simply "the Church").

24. Job 38:7.

25. 2 Sam 1:27.

26. Ps 23:1.

27. James laid out this "divine right of kings" in *The True Law of Free Monarchies*, 1598.

28. Cathy Lynn Grossman, *USA Today,* September 9, 2008, at http://www.usatoday.com/ news/religion/2008-09-29-bible-tour_N.htm (accessed December 6, 2008).

29. Ernest Frerichs, "Versions—English (American Versions)," n.p., *Anchor Bible Dictionary on CD-ROM,* Logos 2.1, ed. David Noel Freedman (New York: Doubleday) 1992, 1997.

30. At http://www.ebible.org/bible/web/index.htm (accessed Nov. 11, 2008).

31. At http://en.wikipedia.org/wiki/The_Free_Bible (accessed June 29, 2008).

32. At http://www.centuryone.org/obpindex.html (accessed June 29, 2008).

CHAPTER 7: WE'VE GOT ISSUES

1. Deut 23:15–16.

2. "Many Americans Uneasy with the Mix of Religion and Politics," section III, "Religion and Science," at http://pewforum.org/docs/index.php?DocID=153 (accessed January 28, 2008).

3. Creation Museum "Online Newsroom," http://www.alrcnewskitchen.com/creation museum/index.htm (accessed January 28, 2008).

4. John N. Moore, "Creationism vs. Evolution and Attention to Word Meaning," posted January 24, 2008, http://www.answersingenesis.org/articles/2008/01/24/attention-to-word -meaning (accessed January 26, 2008). Many "young earth" creationists (people who believe that the universe is only about 6,000 years old) use this language to describe the biblical sto-

ries of creation. For example, see Sean Ho, "An Eyewitness Account," July 4, 2006, http://seanho.com/church/an_eyewitness_account.html (accessed December 3, 2008); Andrew A. Snelling, "Who Is Jesus Christ? A Challenge to Christians," Institute for Creation Research, June, 2007, http://www.icr.org/articles/print/3338/ (accessed December 4, 2008).

5. Interview with Ken Ham by Christian Book Distributors (CBD), http://www.christianbook.com/Christian/Books/cms_content?page=736863&sp=1016&event=1016RNF (accessed January 27, 2008).

6. See the discussions in Chapters 3 and 5, especially, of Babylon's role in the Bible's development.

7. Proponents of "intelligent design" are not so closely wedded to a literal reading of the Bible; but they maintain that the universe is filled with phenomena so complex and sophisticated that they can only be the products of an intelligent designer, not evolution. Advocates of intelligent design are often found among "old earth" creationists—people who maintain that the world is much more than 6,000 years old, but who nevertheless reject the theory of evolution through natural selection in favor of God's immediate creative activity.

8. "Antievolution Resolutions Spreading through Northern Florida," posted January 24, 2008, http://www.ncseweb.org/ (accessed January 28, 2008).

9. The document "Ten Questions to Ask Your Biology Teacher about Evolution" is one of many examples. See the document's contents (and answers) and an article about it in "Ten Questions, and Answers, about Evolution," *New York Times*, August 23, 2008, http://www.nytimes.com/2008/08/24/us/WEB-tenquestions.html (accessed November 4, 2008); and Amy Harmon, "A Teacher on the Front Line as Faith and Science Clash," *New York Times*, August 23, 2008, http://www.nytimes.com/2008/08/24/education/24evolution.html?ref=us (accessed November 4, 2008).

10. See Warren's interview with Beliefnet's Steve Waldman, plus Warren's later clarification of his comments at http://blog.beliefnet.com/stevenwaldman/2008/12/rick-warrens-controversial-com.html, posted December 17, 2008 (accessed April 23, 2009).

11. The biblical Hebrew word here translated as "messengers" can also be translated as "angels." In the preceding episodes (Gen 18:1–33), these figures are called "men," in Hebrew, though they clearly have a special association with God. Whatever the case, in this story, the townsmen apparently perceive the visitors as men.

12. It is no coincidence that the biblical city's name came to be associated with gay sex.

13. Incidentally, some people have read the verse immediately following—in which Paul says that certain members of his audience used to be guilty of the listed behaviors but "you were washed, . . . sanctified, . . . justified, . . . in the Lord Jesus Christ and in the Spirit of our God"—as supporting efforts to "rehabilitate" gays within the faith community.

14. Paul may have come up with his own new word here, combining the Greek (Septuagint) translations of two Hebrew words meaning "man" and "bed" that appear near each other in Lev 18:22 and 20:13. See Martti Nissininen, *Homoeroticism in the Biblical World: A Historical Perspective*, trans. Kirsi Stjerna (Minneapolis, Minn.: Fortress, 1998), 114. For some recent discussions of the word, see Robin Scroggs, *The New Testament and Homosexuality: Contextual Background for Contemporary Debate* (Philadelphia, Pa.: Fortress, 1983), 107; John McNeill, *The Church and the Homosexual*, 4th ed. (Boston, Mass.: Beacon, 1993), 50; Dale

Martin, "*Arseokoitēs* and *Malakos*: Meanings and Consequences," in *Biblical Ethics and Homosexuality: Listening to Scripture*, ed. Robert Brawley (Louisville, Ky.: Westminster/John Knox, 1996), 117–136.

15. See Saul Olyan, "'And with a Male You Shall Not Lie the Lying Down of a Woman': On the Meaning and Significance of Leviticus 18:22 and 20:13," *Journal of the History of Sexuality* 5 (1994): 179–206; see 184 in particular.

16. See also Jacques Berlinerblau's balanced discussion in *The Secular Bible: Why Nonbelievers Must Take Religion Seriously* (Cambridge: Cambridge University Press, 2005), 103–104.

17. Lev 19:19.

18. Similarly, in Gen 38:9–10, a text that is used to argue that the Bible condemns masturbation, Onan is killed by God because he "spilled his seed on the ground."

19. Rom 1:28–29.

20. 1 Cor 7:1–40. In this passage, Paul concedes that marriage, and sex within it, may serve as an important deterrent to fornication (verses 2–6) but that it's not optimal (verses 32–35).

21. Rom 2:1.

22. Jeremy Walker and Associates, *For the Bible Tells Me So*, press notes, 5, http://www .forthebibletellsmeso.org/forthebible_pk.pdf (accessed February 14, 2008).

23. At http://www.sbc.net/aboutus/pssexuality.asp (accessed April 23, 2009).

24. The Hebrew terms sometimes translated in this story as "husband" and "wife" are the general words "man" and "woman." Although the narrator's explanation, "therefore a man leaves his father and mother" (Gen 2:24), is not necessarily a biblical model of marriage (e.g., Rebekah leaves her home to join Isaac's), it may reflect ideas about marriage as a monogamous union between a man and a woman.

25. Consider the famous examples of Jacob, David, and Solomon.

26. Neh 13:23–27.

27. 2 Cor 6:14.

28. For example, see Deut 25:5. On the other hand, Lev 18:16 and 20:21 forbid it.

29. The case of Sarah's slave, Hagar, is one example (Gen 16:1–2).

30. In one example of a great love leading to marriage, we read that Jacob loved Rachel so much that he served her father for fourteen years in order to rightfully marry her (Gen 29:20). Sadly, her sister Leah could never seem to win such love from Jacob, who was her husband, too (Gen 29:32). Love for one's spouse is also applauded. For example, the narrator explains that Isaac's love for Rebekah comforted him after his mother's death (Gen 24:67); the author of Ecclesiastes directs his audience to "enjoy life with the woman you love" (Eccles 9:9); and the author of Ephesians (Paul's authorship is debated) directs husbands to "love your wives just as Christ loved the church" (Eph 5:25). Titus encourages also "women to love their husbands" (Tit 2:4).

31. 1 Cor 7:8.

32. See Warren's interview of April 6, 2009, with Larry King, at http://transcripts.cnn.com/TRANSCRIPTS/0904/06/1kl.01.html and http://www.youtube.com/watch?v=bYIWSyMrhR (accessed April 23, 2009).

33. "Brian McLaren on the Homosexual Question: Finding a Pastoral Response," posted January 23, 2006, http://blog.christianitytoday.com/outofur/archives/2006/01/brian_mclaren_o.html (accessed April 23, 2009).

34. Peter Slevin, "33 Pastors Flout Tax Law with Political Sermons," *Washington Post* (September 29, 2008), A02, http://www.washingtonpost.com/wp-dyn/content/article/2008/09/28/AR2008092802365_pf.html (accessed November 4, 2008).

35. Exod 20:13; Deut 5:17.

36. Exod 21:22.

37. See also Daniel Schiff, *Abortion in Judaism* (Cambridge: Cambridge University Press, 2002), 1–26; Jacques Berlinerblau, *Thumpin' It* (Louisville, Ky.: Westminster John Knox, 2008), 158, n.48.

38. Jer 1:5.

39. Ps 139:13–15.

40. Luke 1:41–42.

41. Dan Harris and Mary Marsh, "Prosperity Gospel: Give and You Shall Receive?" January 17, 2007, http://abcnews.go.com/Nightline/Story?id=4149598&page=1 (accessed February 20, 2008).

42. At http://www.worldchangers.org/soponline/soplanding.html?site=CDM (accessed February 20, 2008).

43. At http://www.worldchangers.org/soponline/soplanding.html?site=CDM (accessed Feb. 20, 2008).

44. Interview by Laura Sheahen, posted December 2004, http://www.beliefnet.com/story/157/story_15735_1.html (accessed February 20, 2008).

45. Interview with William C. Symonds of *BusinessWeek*, May 23, 2005, http://www.businessweek.com/magazine/content/05_21/b3934014_mz001.htm (accessed February 20, 2008).

46. David Van Biema and Jeff Chu, "Does God Want You to Be Rich?" posted September 10, 2006, http://www.time.com/time/magazine/article/0,9171,1533448,00.html (accessed February 19, 2008).

47. Deut 8:18.

48. Mark 11:24.

49. John 10:10.

50. John 14:14.

51. Van Biema and Chu, "Does God Want You to Be Rich?"

52. Consider the book of Job, for example, Ps 73:3–9, and Jer 5:27–28.

53. Matt 6:19–21.

54. Matt 19:21.

55. Matt 19:24.

56. Luke 6:20.

57. Luke 6:24.

58. 1 Tim 6:10.

59. U.S. Census Bureau, "Historical Estimates of World Population," July 16, 2007, http://www.census.gov/ipc/www/worldhis.html (accessed February 21, 2008).

60. In 1967, the historian of technology Lynn White published a seminal article in *Science* in which he blames the Bible, especially Gen 1:28, for promoting anthropocentric attitudes about the earth's resources that lead inevitably to environmental degradation. See Lynn White, "The Historical Roots of Our Ecologic Crisis" 155 (3767) (March 10, 1967): 1203–1207.

61. Gen 2:15.

62. Hos 4:1–3.

63. Job 12:7; Ps 19:1.

64. Luke 19:40.

65. Jim Ball, "A Personal Greeting from the President and CEO," http://www.creation care.org/welcome.php (accessed February 24, 2008).

66. Ibid.

67. Colin Woodard, "In Greenland, an Interfaith Rally for Climate Change," *Christian Science Monitor*, September 12, 2007, http://www.csmonitor.com/2007/0912/p06s01-woeu .html (accessed February 24, 2008).

68. Adelle M. Banks, "Dobson and Others Seek Ouster of NAE Vice President," posted March 2, 2007, http://www.christianitytoday.com/ct/2007/marchweb-only/109–53.0.html ?start=1 (accessed February 22, 2008). For a copy of the letter, see http://www.citizenlink .org/pdfs/NAELetterFinal.pdf.

69. Sermon delivered February 25, 2007, http//trbc.org/new/sermons.php?url=20070225 _11AM.html (accessed February 22, 2008).

70. Ibid.

71. Tara Maxwell, *Liberty Journal*, posted February 6, 2008, http://www.liberty.edu/ libertyjournal/index.cfm?PID=16046&artid=82 (accessed February 22, 2008).

72. Because some peoples are Semitic but not necessarily Jews, many prefer the term "anti-Judaism." I use "anti-Semitism" here simply because it is still more common and more easily recognizable than "anti-Judaism," though I mean specifically to address ideas and activity that adversely target Jews.

73. Matt 27:22–25.

74. E.g., John 5:16; 6:41, 52; 7:1; 8:52.

75. Rom 3:1–2.

76. Rom 10:3.

77. Rom 9:3–4; 10:1–4.

78. Matt 16:1–12; Luke 18:9–14.

79. See not only Matt 23, but also episodes in the preceding chapter, all of which contribute to Matthew's portrayal of the Jewish authorities' role in Jesus' death.

80. Matt 5:17–20.

81. Isa 61:1.

82. Matt 26:17–20; Mark 14:12–18; Luke 2:41–42; 22:8; John 2:13.

83. For example, see Ps 22:1//Matt 27:46; Mark 15:34; Ps 22:18//Mark 15:24; Luke 23:34; Ps 31:5//Luke 23:46; Ps 69:21//John 19:28–30.

CHAPTER 8: QUOTES AND MISQUOTES

1. Gen 4:9.

2. "Earth Tells the Lessons of Cain," in *Exploring Ecological Hermeneutics*, ed. Norman Habel and Peter Trudinger (Alberta, Ga.: Society of Biblical Literature, 2008), 31–39; "Care and Keeping East of Eden: Gen 4:1–16 in Light of Gen 2–3," *Interpretation* 60(3) (July 2006): 373–384.

3. Reihan Salam, "The Facebook Commandments," September 25, 2007, http://www
.slate.com/id/2174439/ (accessed August 5, 2008).

4. "Document of the Pontifical Council for the Pastoral Care of Migrants and Itinerant
People: 'Guidelines for the Pastoral Care of the Road,'" June 19, 2007, http://212.77.1.245/
news_services/bulletin/news/20451.php?index=20451#V.%20The%20Christian%20
virtue%20of%20drivers%20and%20their%20%E2%80%9CTen%20Commandments
%E2%80%9D (accessed August 5, 2008).

5. Incidentally, feminists have long argued, tongue in cheek, that the commandments
don't apply to women. At least, it's not prohibited to covet your neighbor's husband. Indeed,
the grammar and historical context make clear that the addressees are strictly individual
males.

6. It's tempting to write that just as Eskimos have many words for snow, ancient Hebrew
has many words for killing. It does; but I am reluctant to play into the facile and ignorant
dismissal of the Old Testament as wholly violent and destructive. It is hardly that—it is much
richer and more nuanced, with plenty of creation, love, mercy, and restoration, too.

7. Lev 19:18.

8. Matt 22:37–40; Mark 12:28–34; Luke 10:25–28 (citing Lev 19:18 and Deut 6:5).

9. 1 Sam 16:7.

10. 1 Sam 16:12.

11. 2 Sam 1:19, 25, 27.

12. 2 Sam 1:23.

13. Isa 2:4; Mic 4:3.

14. Mic 4:4.

15. Joel 3:10.

16. "Lion and Lamb Love," http://www.lionandlamblove.org/ (accessed November 29,
2008).

17. Isa 11:9.

18. James Meek, "Animal Magnetism," *Guardian* (April 3, 2002), http://education.guard-
ian.co.uk/higher/biologicalscience/story/0,,678111,00.html (accessed June 17, 2008); and
"And the Lion Shall Lie Down with the Lamb," http://www.naturescornermagazine.com/
lion_lamb.html (accessed June 17, 2008).

19. Amos 5:24.

20. Ezek 25:17 reads, "I will carry out great vengeance in angry rebuke against them. They
shall know that I am the LORD, when I lay my vengeance on them."

21. "Napalm Speech Tops Movie Poll," *BBC News*, January 2, 2004, http://news.bbc
.co.uk/2/hi/entertainment/3362603.stm#quote (accessed June 1, 2008).

22. Ezek 37:1–14.

23. See especially John 10:11, 14.

24. Ps 19:1.

25. Ps 30:5.

26. Ps 84:7.

27. Ps 119:105.

28. Ps 111:10; Prov 1:7.

29. Prov 3:5.

30. It is often translated as "meaninglessness"; but this introduces a value judgment that the Hebrew word lacks.

31. Ecc 3:1–8.

32. Song 1:2.

33. Song 8:6.

34. If "Christian sex toys" sounds oxymoronic to you, its founder explains, "We pray about things before we add them to our site . . . and He's really surprised us!" "The Joy of Christian Sex Toys," *NPR.org*, March 21, 2008, http://www.npr.org/templates/story/story.php?storyId=18975616 (accessed July 15, 2008).

35. Ruth 1:16.

36. Job 19:25.

37. Job 19:23–24. I paraphrase.

38. Aramaic *tekel* = Hebrew "shekel," a unit of currency also used in modern Israel today.

39. Luke 2:8–14.

40. Many people are surprised to find that the gospel stories are quite different from one another; and neither Mark nor John has a birth story at all. There are no magi in Luke's story, and no scheming Herod, either, and there are no shepherds or manger in Matthew's story of Jesus' birth. Only Matthew describes the wise men following a star from their home in the east to find the newborn baby (in a "house," in Matthew's gospel), who must be secreted away to avoid Herod's murderous intentions. Those manger scenes with barn animals, the wise men, the shepherds, Mary, Joseph, and the new baby, with a star hanging overhead, are a composite of the different birth stories.

41. "Mr. Carnegie's Address," in *Presentation of the Carnegie Library to the People of Pittsburgh, with a Description of the Dedicatory Exercises, November 5th, 1895* (Pittsburgh, Pa.: City of Pittsburgh, [1895]), 13–14.

42. Deut 8:3; Matt 4:4; Luke 4:4.

43. Matt 5:3.

44. Luke 6:20.

45. Matt 5:6.

46. Luke 6:21.

47. Stephen Prothero, *Religious Literacy: What Every American Needs to Know—and Doesn't* (New York: HarperSanFrancisco, 2007), 182.

48. Matt 7:12; Luke 6:31.

49. Prothero, *Religious Literacy*, 182.

50. Matt 5:28.

51. Matt 5:39.

52. Matt 6:7.

53. Luke 11:2–4.

54. Matt 6:25–34; Luke 12:22–32.

55. Matt 19:26; Mark 10:27; Luke 18:27.

56. The phrase also shows up in the Hebrew Babylonian Talmud (with an elephant instead of a camel) and in the Qur'an to the same end—illustrating impossibility (*Berakoth* 55b; *Baba Mezi'a* 38b; Qur'an, "The Elevated Places").

57. Matt 5:13.

58. Barbara Bradley Hagerty, "Understanding the Gospel of Huckabee," *All Things Considered*, NPR, February 8, 2008.

59. Matt 14:13–21; Mark 6:30–44; Luke 9:10–17; John 6:1–15.

60. Matt 15:32–39; Mark 8:1–9.

61. In the context of that last gathering of Jesus with his disciples, the gospel of John features a foot-washing and the command to love and serve each other, rather than the institution of a ritual Eucharist (John 13:1–38).

62. Mark 14:22–25.

63. Matt 26:28.

64. Luke 22:19.

65. Mark 14:25.

66. Matt 26:29.

67. Luke 22:18.

68. Matt 7:6.

69. These particular Christians held Matthew's gospel, which consistently interprets Jesus in keeping with the Hebrew Bible, in highest regard. They are responsible for the *Didache*, an early Christian work that makes this argument (9.4).

70. Phil 2:6–11.

71. Isa 45:21–23.

72. Rom 14:11.

73. Rev 1:8; 21:6; 22:13.

74. John 1:10.

75. Like the biblical Hebrew of the Old Testament, the Greek of the (earliest manuscripts of the) New Testament does not distinguish between uppercase and lowercase letters. Capitalizing "Word," however, reflects the association of *logos* with God.

76. Prov 8:22–31.

77. John 8:32.

78. John 14:6.

79. John 14:11.

80. John 19:1–6.

81. For a transcript of Gingrich and Dobson's interview, see http://www.thebostonchannel.com/politics/11215421/detail.html, posted March 9, 2007 (accessed November 8, 2008).

82. John 7:53–8:11.

83. It doesn't appear in either the *Codex Sinaiticus* or the *Codex Vaticanus*.

84. John 15:9.

85. John 15:12, 17.

86. 1 John 4:7–8.

87. Such as Gen 3:19; Job 14:1–2.

88. Gen 23:1–20.

89. The kaddish prayer (not itself a biblical text), recited immediately upon burial and throughout the first year after a loved one dies, makes no mention of death. Instead, it glorifies God and prays for peace. It originated during the Middle Ages.

90. 1 Cor 15:52.

91. Rev 7:17; 21:3–4.

92. Rev 7:14, 17.

93. Isa 65:17; 66:22.

94. Rev 21:3-4.

95. From *Hamlet*, Act I, scene iii.

96. This is probably a twist on Prov 13:24: "he who spares the rod hates his son, but he who loves him is careful to discipline him."

CHAPTER 9: MEN, FAMOUS AND INFAMOUS

1. Gen 5:3-5.

2. Including Tobit, Sirach, and 4 Esdras; Luke, Romans, 1 Corinthians, 1 Timothy, and Jude.

3. Luke 3:38. Of the gospels, Luke was especially interested in making Jesus relevant to all people. Consequently, he traces Jesus' lineage back to universal, ecumenical beginnings in Adam.

4. Rom 5:12-14; 1 Cor 15:21-23, 45-49.

5. 1 Tim 2:13-14.

6. I wonder at the coincidence of cocaine distributors whose last names are Cain. Among many examples, see the following cases: Bernard Wilkerson, which lists a coconspirator named Micah Cain, http://64.233.169.104/search?q=cache:mLamLxNXeU0J:caselaw.lp .findlaw.com/data2/circs/8th/983572p.pdf+cocaine+cain&hl=en&ct=clnk&cd=1&gl =us&client=firefox-a (accessed November 14, 2008); *United States v. LaAnthony Cletae Cain* on charges of possession with intent to distribute crack cocaine, http://www.ca8.uscourts .gov/opndir/07/06/063429P.pdf (accessed November 14, 2008); Mark A. Cain, who was caught exchanging a handgun for cocaine, http://ca10.washburnlaw.edu/cases/2002/02/01 -3263.htm (accessed November 14, 2008).

7. Cain is described as someone who works the land and Abel as one who keeps animals, so two reasons people often give for God's apparent caprice are: (1) God likes meat better than vegetables, and (2) Abel specifically brought the choicest, fattiest parts while Cain simply brought what was to hand.

8. Gen 4:16.

9. Gen 8:20-9:17.

10. There is a "Noah grape" that some people cultivate for wine, though they say that the fruit doesn't travel well and has a peculiar "foxy" flavor, making it unlikely ever to unseat the popular chardonnay; see http://www.wineloverspage.com/wineguest/wgg.html#noah (accessed March 5, 2009).

11. Gen 9:24-27. It's a bit puzzling why Canaan should be explicitly cursed instead of his father, Ham, the perpetrator, except that it may have laid the groundwork for the Israelites' conquest of Canaan, or justified why non-Israelites didn't enjoy the same liberty as Israelites (Lev 25:39-46).

12. Luke 16:22-23.

13. Gen 17:9-14.

14. Gen 22:15-18.

15. Gen 18:25.

16. And even his adult actions aren't original—like Abraham, Isaac tries to pass off his wife as his sister when he is passing through enemy territory, to save his own neck.

17. Gen 28:10-22. In a curious Christian twist, this dream inspired a popular spiritual that I remember singing quite enthusiastically as a kid. In three repeating lines climbing the musical scale, we sang, "We are climbing Jacob's ladder"; but the final line of the stanza is "Soldiers of the cross," which has nothing to do with the story.

18. Gen 32:30.

19. Exod 3:1-4:17.

20. Besides the hundreds of other commandments included in the biblical Torah, Moses received a second set of laws, according to Jewish tradition, on Mount Sinai—laws that he passed down by word of mouth. This "oral Torah" began, in the early centuries of the Common Era (CE), to be written down as the Mishnah that would become the basis of the Talmud.

21. Num 14:20-35; Deut 1:26-35.

22. The reason given is not entirely clear. Numbers 20:2-12 seems to suggest that Moses didn't execute the water-from-rock procedure exactly right and failed to underscore God's holiness. In Deut 3:26, Moses apparently blames the people—God's disappointment in them made Moses guilty by association.

23. For a full transcript of the speech, see http://www.americanrhetoric.com/speeches/mlkivebeentothemountaintop.htm.

24. He's identified as the "son of Nun." Moses' own sons actually play a very small role in the biblical drama, save for a charming domestic story that takes place early in Moses' career (Exod 18:1-27). It would seem that Moses had sent his wife and two sons back to Jethro, (a.k.a. Reuel), without him. Exactly how long after the plagues and escape and all is hard to say. The narrative doesn't. After Moses escaped and led the Israelites out of Egypt, through the sea, and into the desert wilderness, Jethro met him, bringing Moses' wife and sons along. (The narrator stresses this, saying three times that Moses' wife and sons were with Jethro.) After Moses gave his father-in-law a respectful greeting, they retired. The next day, Jethro observed how Moses served to mediate and decide any and all disputes among the greater group. He took Moses aside and said, "Not good, my boy. You're going to wear yourself out like this. It's time to delegate. Appoint respectable and trustworthy people to share the burden. They can mediate the easy cases. You take the especially tough ones." (I've paraphrased.) And Moses did exactly as Jethro recommended.

25. Josh 24:1-28.

26. Judges 13:1-16:31.

27. Judges 16:30.

28. 1 Sam 2:1-10; Luke 1:46-55. "Magnificat" is the first word of the song in the Latin translation of Luke 1:46.

29. This Old Testament Saul should not be confused with the New Testament Saul, whose name became Paul.

30. There is a pun here. Saul is from the tribe of Benjamin, which means "son of the south."

31. This futuristic Saul (Tigh) discovers that he is indeed an android-like "cylon," programmed to undermine human beings.

32. 1 Sam 16:21.

33. 1 Sam 17:55–58.

34. 1 Sam 17:49.

35. March 28, 2005, http://www.nytimes.com/2005/03/28/opinion/28mon1.html (accessed November 13, 2008).

36. "Biotech's David and Goliath," AP, January 20, 2004, http://www.wired.com/politics/law/news/2004/01/61981 (accessed November 13, 2008).

37. 2 Sam 7:1–29.

38. 1 Sam 13:14.

39. 2 Sam 11:1.

40. Matt 6:29; Luke 12:27.

41. 1 Kings 3:16–28.

42. 1 Kings 4:21.

43. 1 Kings 9:1–9.

44. Gen 5:24.

45. Mal 4:5.

46. Isaiah probably had disciples who carried on prophetic work in his spirit and tradition, including the collection of oracles, his and theirs, all of which were subsequently identified with Isaiah's name.

47. Isa 6:8.

48. Jer 1:4–10.

49. Ezek 2:9–13.

50. Ezek 8:1–18.

51. Ezek 37:1–14.

52. Actually, the book is set in a time centuries earlier than it was written. It is set in the sixth century BCE but comes from a period of great tribulation in the mid-second century BCE, so what Daniel "foretells" is actually a poetic recital of events that had already happened.

53. Dan 12:1–3.

54. Rev 12:7.

55. *Henry IV, Part 2*, Act I, scene ii.

56. In Jas 5:11, the New Testament source of the phrase "the patience of Job," the Greek word meant more accurately something like "persistence," "steadfastness," or "endurance."

57. Some translations simply call him Satan with a capital S—more on this topic in Chapter 11.

58. Job 42:6.

59. Luke 2:21–52.

60. Matt 3:13–17; Mark 1:9–11; Luke 3:21–22; John 1:32–34.

61. Matt 17:1–8; Mark 9:2–8; Luke 9:28–36.

62. Matt 21:1–9; Mark 11:1–10; Luke 19:28–38; John 12:12–19.

63. They seem to disagree about the exact day, however. In the synoptic gospels, Jesus' last supper with his disciples is the Passover meal that begins the weeklong festival; in John, Jesus is crucified on "the Passover day of preparation" (John 19:14), so he is effectively identified with the lamb that is traditionally sacrificed and eaten at the meal. Some people resolve this apparent disagreement, however, by noting that John's day of preparation may refer to the day

preceding the Sabbath during (not the inaugural meal of) Passover week, thereby conforming to the crucifixion chronology of the synoptics (Matt 27:62; Mark 15:42; Luke 23:54). English translations of John 19:14 vary in suggestive ways. For example, the NIV has "the day of preparation of Passover Week" (the Greek does not include the word "week"), whereas the NRSV has "the day of preparation for the Passover."

64. John 20:31.

65. Isa 40:3; Matt 3:3; Mark 1:3; Luke 3:4–6; John 1:23. With a slight shift in punctuation, the Old Testament text is changed to meet the New Testament circumstances of John. Given the exilic context of Isaiah's prophecy and the fact that the Hebrew text lacked punctuation, the Isaiah verse should probably read, "A voice cries, 'In the wilderness prepare the way . . .'" The gospels read, "A voice cries in the wilderness, 'Prepare the way . . .'"

66. Jeff Zeleny, "Oprah Winfrey Hits Campaign Trail for Obama," *New York Times*, December 9, 2007, http://www.nytimes.com/2007/12/09/us/politics/09oprah.html?n=Top/News/U.S./U.S.%20States,%20Territories%20and%20Possessions/Iowa (accessed July 10, 2008).

67. Matt 14:3–12; Mark 6:17–29.

68. Matt 16:18.

69. Matt 16:19.

70. Matt 14:28–31.

71. Matt 26:15; 27:3–10.

72. Matt 27:3–5.

73. Mark 14:10, 43–45.

74. Luke 22:3.

75. E.g., John 6:70–71; 13:2.

76. Acts 1:15–20; Ps 69:25; Ps 109:8.

77. Matt 27:3–10. Although Matthew explains that the prophecy is found in Jeremiah, it isn't in the version of Jeremiah that became canonized. It is, however, similar to a prophecy in Zechariah 11:12–13, which seems to expand and explain Jer 18–19, that the author of Matthew's gospel may have had in mind.

78. Matt 26:22. In both Matthew's and Mark's accounts, all the disciples ask, "Is it I?" (Matt 26:22; Mark 14:19). Only Matthew portrays Judas as individually repeating the question, poignantly adding "Rabbi," to which Jesus replies, "You have said so."

79. At http://www.youtube.com/watch?v=u2MgdF6GWi0 (accessed April 26, 2009).

80. See Bart Ehrman, *The Lost Gospel of Judas Iscariot: A New Look at Betrayer and Betrayed* (Oxford: Oxford University Press, 2006); Elaine Pagels and Karen L. King, *Reading Judas: The Gospel of Judas and the Shaping of Christianity* (New York: Viking, 2007); and the National Geographic's presentation of information, with valuable links, at http://www.nationalgeographic.com/lostgospel/ (accessed November 13, 2008).

81. Luke 10:25–37.

82. See especially Amy-Jill Levine, *The Misunderstood Jew* (New York: HarperCollins, 2006).

83. Nina Bernstein, "Mrs. Clinton Says G.O.P.'s Immigration Plan Is at Odds with the Bible," *New York Times*, March 23, 2006, http://www.nytimes.com/2006/03/23nyregion/23hillary.html (accessed October 20, 2008).

84. Luke 15:11–32.

85. Timothy Keller, *The Prodigal God: Recovering the Heart of the Christian Faith* (New York: Dutton, 2008).

86. John 11:1–57.

87. John 11:35.

88. Luke 16:19–31.

89. Acts 9:4.

90. Acts 9:18.

91. 1 Cor 15:8.

92. Gal 2:11–14; cf. Acts 15:12.

93. Rom 1:16.

CHAPTER 10: LOVELY (AND NOT SO) LADIES

1. Gen 3:20.

2. Gen 3:14–19. Interestingly, nowhere does the text explicitly state that these things would be true for all subsequent snakes, women, and men (except for the enmity between the next generation of the snake and the woman). Incidentally, some later interpreters assumed that before the infraction, the snake had legs—an image that shows up in many visual renderings of the story. The Bible doesn't say, one way or the other.

3. This became especially contentious after the development of anesthesia. See Donald Caton's *What a Blessing She Had Chloroform: The Medical and Social Response to the Pain of Childbirth from 1800 to the Present* (New Haven, Conn.: Yale University Press, 1999).

4. Gen 3:1–6.

5. 1 Tim 2:11–15.

6. This Sara is sometimes also associated with the Indian goddess Kali: India is a possible site of Romani ancestry.

7. In the ancient world, conception was considered purely a female issue. Only recently, historically speaking, have people begun to appreciate that male infertility can also play a role.

8. Gen 12:10–13:1.

9. As noted above, she named the boy Isaac, "he laughs," for the absurdity of it all.

10. Gen 16:13.

11. Gal 4:22–31.

12. Gen 19:26.

13. Luke 17:32.

14. Gen 19:30–38.

15. Gen 25:21.

16. Gen 29:31.

17. Gen 34:3.

18. Gen 38:11.

19. Exod 2:4–9.

20. Exod 15:20–21.

21. Num 12:1–15.

22. Mic 6:4.

23. Josh 2:1–24; 6:22–25.

24. Matt 1:5.

25. Heb 11:31.

26. Jas 2:25.

27. Job and Psalm 89 describe this other Hebrew word, rendered "Rahab" in English, as a kind of sea monster whom God smote in the ancient, mythological past. See Job 26:12 (though the Hebrew is muddled; depending on how one reads the verse, Rahab may or may not be in it); Ps 89:9–10.

28. Gen 35:8.

29. Judges 4:1–5:31.

30. Tob 1:8.

31. Judges 16:4–31.

32. 2 Sam 11:1.

33. 2 Sam 11:2–4.

34. Her story, narrated in 1 Kings 16:31–2 Kings 9:37, overlaps with stories about the great prophets of Yahweh: Elijah and Elisha.

35. 1 Kings 16:33.

36. 1 Kings 21:23.

37. At http://en.wikipedia.org/wiki/Jezebel_(biblical) (accessed July 15, 2008).

38. E.g., see 2 Kings 9:22.

39. Gen 19:30–38.

40. Matt 1:5.

41. Amy-Jill Levine, "Ruth," in The Women's Bible Commentary, ed. Carol A. Newsom and Sharon H. Ringe (Louisville, Ky.: Westminster/John Knox, 1992), 78–84.

42. See especially Jer 44:1–30.

43. See Karel Van der Toorn, "Anat-Yahu, Some Other Deities, and the Jews of Elephantine," Numen 39(1) (1992): 80–101.

44. "Christ's Kingdom Not Based on Human Power, Pope Says," http://www.catholicculture.org/news/features/index.cfm?recnum=47863 (accessed September 10, 2008).

45. "Sarah Palin's Churches and the Third Wave: A Video Documentary," http://www.huffingtonpost.com/bruce-wilson/sarah-palins-churches-and_b_124611.html (accessed September 10, 2008). C. Peter Wagner, founder of World Prayer Center, is also a leader in this movement. Wagner published a book under his own imprint, Confronting the Queen of Heaven (Wagner Publications, 1998).

46. Rev 17:1–18.

47. Deut 29:1–30:20.

48. Josh 24:1–28.

49. Jer 31:31–34; Ezek 16:1–63; Hos 2:14–23. This Sinai covenant is distinct from the covenants that God made with the whole world: through Noah (Gen 9), with Abraham's family (Gen 12, 15, 17), and with David's dynasty (2 Sam 7) on account of the extensive conditions it imposes on the human parties.

50. Prov 3:17–18.

51. Prov 8:16, 18.

52. Prov 9:17.

53. Matt 1:1–17.

54. Isa 7:14.

55. Matt 1:23.

56. At http://www.bbc.co.uk/radio2/soldonsong/songlibrary/indepth/letitbe.shtml (accessed November 14, 2008).

57. Rom 1:3.

58. Gal 4:4.

59. Mark 3:31–35.

60. Mark 6:3.

61. Acts 1:14.

62. John 2:1–12.

63. These are all distinct from the Roman Mary whom Paul includes in a lengthy greeting (Rom 16:6).

64. Luke 10:40.

65. John 11:27.

66. John 12:1–8.

67. Luke 7:36–50.

68. Only in Luke's gospel does Mary Magdalene appear before Jesus' death. In Luke 8:2–3 she is noted as one of Jesus' female disciples, who helped provide material support for his ministry, and (following Mark's description in 16:9, part of the later addition) she is described as having been exorcised of seven demons.

69. For example, that's the context of Paul's claim in 1 Cor 15:5–8. He does not include Mary Magdalene by name among these witnesses.

70. For a good translation with discussion and commentary, see Karen L. King, *The Gospel of Mary Magdala: Jesus and the First Woman Apostate* (Santa Rosa, Calif.: Polebridge, 2003).

71. Luke 8:43–48.

72. Rom 16:1–16.

73. 1 Cor 11:3–16.

74. Ben Witherington III, "Women, New Testament," in *Anchor Bible Dictionary on CD-ROM*, Logos 2.1, ed. David Noel Freedman (New York: Doubleday), 1992, 1997.

75. 1 Cor 11:2–16.

76. Paul Ricoeur, *Freud and Philosophy: An Essay on Interpretation*, trans. Denis Savage (New Haven, Conn.: Yale University Press, 1970).

77. 1 Pet 3:1–6.

78. 1 Pet 2:18.

79. Gal 3:26–28.

80. For a fuller treatment of these issues, see Carolyn Osiek, "Reading the Bible as Women," in *The New Interpreter's Bible*, Vol 1 (Nashville, Tenn.: Abingdon, 1994), 181–187.

CHAPTER 11: FLORA, FAUNA, ETCETERA

1. At http://www.herper.com/human/script/verse10.html (accessed September 8, 2008).

2. Gen 3:1. In this story, the Hebrew word for "clever" (*arum*) plays on the word for "nakedness" (*arummim*) and later on "cursed" (*arur*).

3. For example, Proverbs favorably contrasts this quality with foolishness (Prov 12:16, 23; 13:16; 14:8).

4. Gen 2:17.

5. Gen 3:5, 22.

6. 16:1–17:5.

7. 2 Cor 11:3, 14; 1 Cor 7:5.

8. Rev 12:9; 20:2.

9. This shouldn't be confused with the serpent-staff transformation trick that Moses and Aaron performed before the pharaoh in Egypt (Exod 7:8–12).

10. Num 21:4–9. As the story goes, exasperated by the Israelites' complaining in the wilderness, God sent fiery, biting serpents. The people repented and begged Moses to get God to take away the snakes. Moses prayed, and God told him to make a *nehash nehosheth*, "bronze serpent" (in some translations, "copper"), and affix it to the top of a pole. It would work like an antidote—if people who were bitten looked on Moses' snake, they would live. John's gospel associates Moses' healing serpent with God's love and salvation through Jesus' crucifixion: "Just as Moses lifted up the serpent in the wilderness, so must the Son of Man be lifted up that whoever believes in him would not die but have eternal life" (John 3:14–15).

11. 2 Kings 18:4.

12. The most impressive find is a copper alloy snake covered in gold that was discovered at Timna. See Beno Rothenberg, *Timna: Valley of the Biblical Copper Mines* (London: Thames and Hudson, 1972), 159, plates 19, 20. See also Karen R. Joines, *Serpent Symbolism in the Old Testament: A Linguistic, Archeological, and Literary Study* (Haddonfield, N.J.: Haddonfield House, 1974); Othmar Keel and Christoph Uehlinger, *Gods, Goddesses, and Images of God in Ancient Israel*, trans. Thomas H. Trapp (Minneapolis, Minn.: Fortress, 1998), 274.

13. Mark 16:17–18. See Brian Handwerk, "Snake Handlers Hang On in Appalachian Churches," *National Geographic News*, April 7, 2003, http://news.nationalgeographic.com/news/2003/04/0407_030407_snakehandlers.html (accessed November 29, 2008).

14. Mark 16:17–18.

15. Luke 10:19.

16. Suggestions volunteered at answers.yahoo.com regarding the fruit's identity include THIS WAS A SPECIAL KIND OF FRUIT (all in caps), "the forbidden fruit in Eve's pants," "a quince," and "a fruit that wasn't carried on into our world"; see http://answers.yahoo.com/question/?qid=20080911200638AAhBMz0 (accessed September 16, 2008). Bruce Springsteen says it was a pink Cadillac.

17. Gen 2:9.

18. Gen 2:17.

19. Gen 3:22.

20. Gen 6:4.

21. Num 13:32–33.

22. Deut 2:11 equates them with the Rephaim, ancient warriors who fell to the Israelites.

23. 2 Pet 2:4 and Jude 1:6.

24. Exod 7:8–11:10.

25. In Ps 78:44–51, the order is 1, 4, 2, 8, 7, 5 (a little different), and 10 (omitting 3, 6, and 9). In Ps 105:28–36, the order is 9, 1, 2, 4, 7, 8, 10 (omitting 3, 5, and 6).

26. See Greta Hort, "The Plagues of Egypt," in two articles published by *Zeitschrift für die Alttestamentliche Wissenschaft* 69(1–4) (1957): 84–103; and 70(1–2)(1958):48–59.

27. Contrary to the movie *Magnolia*, the frogs don't rain down in Exod 8:2, but rather they swarm.

28. "Encyclopedia Metallica," http://www.encycmet.com/songs/srcreep.shtml (accessed September 11, 2008).

29. For the most part, the song was originally written for the band Exodus—how about that? "Encyclopedia Metallica," http://www.encycmet.com/songs/srcreep.shtml (accessed September 11, 2008).

30. Exod 32:1–35.

31. I Kings 12:28.

32. Translated (with the help of BabelFish) from "Hé, het lijkt de Oscars wel," http://www.cinema.nl/nff-2002/artikelen/2170291/he-het-lijkt-de-oscars-wel (accessed September 11, 2008).

33. Maev Kennedy, "Golden Calf, Bull's Heart, a New Shark: Hirst's Latest Works May Fetch £65m," July 29, 2008, http://www.guardian.co.uk/artanddesign/2008/jul/29/art (accessed September 11, 2008); and "Is Damien Hirst Still the Golden Boy?" October 9, 2008, http://www.telegraph.co.uk/arts/main.jhtml?xml=/arts/2008/09/10/bahirst110.xml (accessed September 11, 2008).

34. Matt 6:24; Luke 16:13.

35. Lev 16:7–10.

36. Actually, a lot of questions remain concerning this ritual. See Aron Pinker, "A Goat to Go to Azazel," in *Journal of Hebrew Scriptures* 7 (2007): 2–25.

37. At http://www.thefreedictionary.com/scapegoat (accessed September 12, 2008).

38. Num 19:1–10.

39. Restoration of the Jerusalem temple is crucial also, according to such believers, because 2 Thess 2:4 says that in that temple the Antichrist will declare himself to be God during the end-time.

40. Lawrence Wright, "Forcing the End," *New Yorker* 74(20) (July 20, 1998): 42–54.

41. At http://www.templeinstitute.org/archive/red_heifer_born.htm (accessed September 12, 2008).

42. This Ark should not be confused with Noah's ark. The words are different in Hebrew.

43. 1 Chron 28:2.

44. The Ark's details are enumerated in Exod 25:10–22, but the tabernacle in which the Ark was housed is described over several chapters, Exod 36:1–40:38.

45. Josh 3:1–17.

46. For example, see the story of how the Israelites took the city of Jericho (Josh 6:1–27).

47. 1 Sam 5:1–6:18.

48. 2 Sam 6:1–17.

49. 2 Kings 25:13–17; Jer 52:17–23. An ancient Jewish tradition maintains that Jeremiah spirited the Ark away to Egypt after the Babylonians took over. Eusebius, a Christian of the

fourth century, reports the same thing in his introduction to the gospels: *Praeparatio Evangelica*, Book 9.39. For other ancient Jewish theories, see C. L. Seow, "Ark of the Covenant," *Anchor Bible Dictionary on CD-ROM*, Logos 2.1, ed. David Noel Freedman (New York: Doubleday), 1992, 1997.

50. Paul Raffaelle, "Keepers of the Lost Ark?" *Smithsonian Magazine*, December 2007, http://www.smithsonianmag.com/people-places/ark-covenant-200712.html?c=y&page=1 (accessed September 20, 2008).

51. David Van Biema, "A Lead on the Ark of the Covenant," *Time*, February 21, 2008, http://www.time.com/time/health/article/0,8599,1715337,00.html (accessed September 20, 2008). See also Tudor Parfitt, *The Lost Ark of the Covenant: Solving the 2,500 Year Mystery of the Fabled Biblical Ark* (New York: HarperOne, 2008).

52. Frank Joseph and Laura Beaudoin, *Opening the Ark of the Covenant: The Secret Power of the Ancients, the Knights Templar Connection, and the Search for the Holy Grail* (Franklin Lakes, N.J.: New Page, 2007); Graham Phillips, *The Templars and the Ark of the Covenant* (Rochester, Vt: Inner Traditions/Bear & Co., n.d.).

53. For example, Michael Rood believes that it was taken away by means of an ancient elevator into a hiding spot under the temple before the Babylonians could get their hands on it. See http://www.michaelroodministries.com/mm5/merchant.mvc?Screen=CTGY&Store _Code=ARA&Category_Code=Video (accessed September 20, 2008).

54. Rev 11:18.

55. 2:248.

56. That's not all. In biblical Hebrew, מִי (pronounced "me") is "who"; הוּא (pronounced "who") is "he"; הִיא (pronounced "he") is "she"; and דָּג (pronounced "dog") is "fish." In other words, it sounds like: me is who, who is he, he is she, and dog is fish.

57. Job 40:15–24 describes Behemoth; Job 41:1–34 (the whole chapter) is devoted to Leviathan (in *Tanakh* the relevant text is numbered differently: Job 40:25–41:26).

58. "Young earth" creationists are so called because they believe the earth to be about 6,000 years old, with calculations based on Genesis.

59. Cynthia Wolfe Boynton, "ESPN, Now a Behemoth Still at Home in Tiny Bristol," July 13, 2008, http://www.nytimes.com/2008/07/13/nyregion/nyregionspecial2/13espnct.html (accessed November 28, 2008); E. Scott Reckard and Michael A. Hiltzik, "How BofA Became Industry Behemoth," September 16, 2008, http://articles.latimes.com/2008/sep/16/business/fi-bofa16 (accessed November 28, 2008).

60. Job 41:25 (41:17 in the Hebrew Bible) The Hebrew *elohim* ("gods") in this verse is sometimes translated "the mighty" (e.g., in KJV, NET, ASV, and NIV) to avoid the suggestion that God would talk about other gods.

61. Ps 74:14; Ps 104:26; Isa 27:1.

62. *Keilalphabetischen Texte aus Ugarit*, Vol. 1, ed. M. Dietrich, O. Loretz, and J. Sanmartín, AOAT 24 (Neukirchen-Vluyn: Neukircher-Verlag, 1976), 1.5.I.1. See also M. Dietrich, O. Loretz, and J. Sanmartín, eds., *The Cuneiform Alphabetic Texts from Ugarit, Ras Ibn Hani, and Other Places*, (*Die Keilalphabetischen Texte aus Ugarit*, 2d enlarged ed.) (Münster: Ugarit-Verlag, 1995), 1.3.III.40–42, for a story in which the goddess Anat, not Baal, is the (unnamed) creature's undoing.

63. 2 Esdras 6:49–52. This book, a composite of 4, 5, and 6 Ezra, is part of some Orthodox bibles.

64. For a brief but engaging description, see Clifford A. Pickover, *Wonders of Numbers* (Oxford: Oxford University Press, 2000), 196. See also Eric W. Weisstein, "Leviathan Number," from *MathWorld*—A Wolfram Web Resource, http://mathworld.wolfram.com/Leviathan Number.html (accessed September 12, 2008).

65. "Prayer Vigil Targets the Devil's Day," June 5, 2006, http://news.bbc.co.uk/2/hi/europe/5049516.stm (accessed September 14, 2008).

66. One particularly gruesome practice was to light crucified Christians on fire to serve as living torches along his parade path. See the first-century *Annals* of Tacitus (Book XV).

67. Duane F. Watson, "Six Hundred and Sixty-Six," *Anchor Bible Dictionary on CD-ROM*, Logos 2.1, ed. David Noel Freedman (New York: Doubleday), 1992, 1997.

68. "Social Security Number (SSN) and the Mark of the Beast (666)," updated November 4, 2007, http://www.greaterthings.com/Conspiracy/SSN_SocialSecurityNumber_666/ (accessed September 14, 2008).

69. Terry Watkins, "What about Barcodes and 666?" Dial-the-Truth-Ministries, 1995, http://www.av1611.org/666/barcode.html (accessed September 14, 2008).

70. E.g., 1 Sam 4:17; Phil 2:25 (human); Gen 31:11; Acts 8:26 (supernatural). Only with the Latin Vulgate are human and divine messengers distinguished by different terms—*nuntius* and *angelus*, respectively.

71. E.g., Prov 13:17; Matt 25:41, 2 Cor 12:7.

72. E.g., see Gen 16:11; 2 Kings 1:3; Exod 23:20; Ps 78:49, respectively.

73. Although it refers to a group of only males, it can also refer to a group including females, too. For example, the phrase literally translated "sons of Israel" refers to the Israelites (men and women, boys and girls, alike). Groups of only females are described in a different way.

74. E.g., Ezek 9:2.

75. E.g., Zech 1:7–17.

76. Dan 9:21; 10:13, 21.

77. Nearly all descriptions of the cherubim describe their association with God's throne—the wings of cherubim are imagined and represented as extending over the Ark of the Covenant (e.g., Exod 25:18–22). Ezekiel also depicts them with four faces and wings attending the mobile glory of God (Ezek 10:1–22). Isaiah describes visions of six-winged seraphim whose thunderous voices rang out above God's throne to declare, "Holy, holy, holy is Yahweh Sabaoth! The whole earth is full of his glory" (Isa 6:2–4).

78. Num 21:6.

79. Acts 12:21–23.

80. Matt 13:39–42.

81. 1 Sam 16:14, 15, 16, 23; 18:10; 19:9.

82. Besides those references to Saul's tormenting spirit, see Judges 9:23. Similarly, 1 Kings 22:22–23 and 2 Chron 18:22 tell how God put a "lying spirit" into certain prophets' mouths.

83. Deut 32:17; Ps 106:37.

84. For example, Ps 91:6 poetically describes pestilence as like a predatory criminal "stalking" in the darkness.

85. Isa 34:14.

86. It appears seven times in the Greek translation of Hebrew Bible texts, including the reference to idol worship (Deut 32:17) and the Lilith beast (Isa 34:14).

87. Matt 8:28-34; Mark 5:1-20; Luke 8:26-39. In Mark and Luke, the man's name is Legion, reflecting the many demons that plague him.

88. 1 Sam 29:4.

89. 2 Sam 19:22 (2 Sam 19:23 in the Hebrew Bible).

90. E.g., 1 Kings 5:4 (1 Kings 5:18 in Hebrew Bible).

91. Num 22:1-41.

92. Num 22:30.

93. Num 22:32-33.

94. Zech 3:1.

95. See also Victor P. Hamilton, "Satan," *Anchor Bible Dictionary* on *CD-ROM*, Logos 2.1, ed. David Noel Freedman (New York: Doubleday), 1992, 1997; T. J. Wray and Gregory Mobley, *The Birth of Satan: Tracing the Devil's Biblical Roots* (New York: Palgrave, 2005).

96. Respectively: John 12:31 and Matt 9:34; Matt 13:38; John 8:44.

97. Mark 1:13; Luke 4:2.

98. Rev 12:9.

99. Isa 14:12.

100. Isa 14:4-23.

101. Lucifer was also used as a name for the planet Venus, as Cicero explains in *De Natura Deorum* (Book 2); and Virgil uses "Lucifer" interchangeably with "day star" in *Georgics* (Book 3). Both date to around 50 BCE.

102. 2 Kings 1:2-3.

103. Peter Green, "The World of William Golding," *Review of English Literature* 1(2) (April 1960): 65-66; Bernard F. Dick, *William Golding* (New York: Twayne, 1967), 27-28. Harold Bloom cites both of these sources in *William Golding's* Lord of the Flies (New York: Chelsea House, 1996).

104. See Luke 11:18; Matt 12:26-27.

105. Rev 1:20.

106. Gen 49:8-12.

107. Rev 5:5.

108. Rev 5:6-14.

109. Num 24:17.

110. Matt 2:2. Here, Matthew is probably looking back to a prophecy in the Torah (Num 24:17), which he understands to be fulfilled in Jesus.

111. For example, see the website Bethlemstar.net, devoted to explaining the historicity and religious implications of the star.

112. Margie Wylie, "Science Offers New Theories on Star of Bethlehem," *Religion News Service*, 2004, http://www.beliefnet.com/Faiths/Christianity/2004/12/Science-Offers -New-Theories-On-Star-Of-Bethlehem.aspx (accessed February 25, 2009).

113. Isa 60:1, 5, 6, 11.

114. A recent study suggests that it has measurable antidepressive qualities. See http://www .fasebj.org/Press_Room/07_101865_Press_Release.shtml (accessed September 17, 2008);

and http://www.fasebj.org/cgi/content/abstract/fj.07-101865v1 (accessed September 17, 2008). Some people eat frankincense for indigestion, and a recent study shows that it may relieve the symptoms of arthritis. See "Frankincense Provides Relief for Osteoarthritis," BioMed Central, news release, July 29, 2008, http://www.washingtonpost.com/wpdyn/content/article/2008/07/30/AR2008073001481.html (accessed September 17, 2008).

115. Even you can buy some: http://www.catholicsupply.com/CHURCHS/incense.html or http://www.cenacle.co.uk/products.asp?partno=C0203 (accessed September 18, 2008).

116. Woldeselassie Ogbazghi, Toon Rijkers, Marius Wessel, and Frans Bongers, "Distribution of the Frankincense Tree *Boswellia papyrifera* in Eritrea: The role of Environment and Land Use," *Journal of Biogeography* 33(3) (March 2006): 524–535. Despite their tenacity, trees that have wept resinous tears are weakened and less able to reproduce. See Toon Rijkers, Woldeselassie Ogbazghi, Marius Wessel, and Frans Bongers, "The Effect of Tapping for Frankincense on Sexual Reproduction in *Boswellia papyrifera*," *Journal of Applied Ecology*, 43(6) (December 2006): 1188–1195.

117. For example, see Exod 30:34; Lev 2:2, 15, 16, 5:11; 6:15; 24:7.

118. W. W. Müller, "Frankincense," *Anchor Bible Dictionary on CD-ROM*, Logos 2.1, ed. David Noel Freedman (New York: Doubleday), 1992, 1997.

119. Mark 15:23.

120. Erkki Koskenniemi, Kirsi Nisula, and Jorma Toppari, "Wine Mixed with Myrrh (Mark 15.23) and Crurifragium (John 19.31–32): Two Details of the Passion Narratives," *Journal for the Study of the New Testament* 27(4) (June 2005): 379–391.

121. Ps 22:18.

122. Ps 69:21.

123. John 19:39. Myrrh's only other New Testament appearance is in Revelation, in a long list of valuable merchandise (Rev 18:13).

124. Exod 30:23; Ps 45:8.

125. Matt 27:29; Mark 15:18.

126. At http://www.nysun.com/opinion/congos-crown-of-thorns/67306/, November 30, 2007 (accessed September 18, 2008).

127. The story of the relic in Notre Dame is the best-known and begins in Jerusalem in the early fifth century. At http://www.notredamedeparis.fr/Veneration-of-the-Crown-of-Thorns (accessed September 18, 2008); http://www.stonyhurst.ac.uk/article_1235.shtml (accessed September 19, 2008); http://www.basilicasantacroce.com/basilica_reliquie.aspx (accessed September 19, 2008).

128. See "Holy Grail" in the Catholic Encyclopedia, http://oce.catholic.com/index.php?title=Holy_Grail%2C_The (accessed September 19, 2008).

129. Michael Baigent, Richard Leigh, and Henry Lincoln, *Holy Blood, Holy Grail* (New York: Dell, 1982); Dan Brown, *The Da Vinci Code* (New York: Random House, 2003).

130. At http://en.wikipedia.org/wiki/Christian_cross (accessed November 28, 2008).

131. For a discussion of the archaeological evidence of a crucifixion, see J. H. Charlesworth, "Jesus and Jehohanan: An Archaeological Note on Crucifixion," *Expository Times* 84 (1973): 147–150.

132. Both Mormons and Jehovah's Witnesses eschew the cross altogether, citing its absence among early Christians (who used a stylized fish to symbolize their belief in Jesus), the temp-

tation to worship the cross itself (Jehovah's Witnesses especially are concerned about this hint of idolatry), and the abhorrent nature of a torturous execution by crucifixion.

133. The Rapture Ready Index, "like a Dow Jones Industrial Average of end time activity . . . [or] prophetic speedometer," "factor[s] together a number of related end time components into a cohesive indicator, and . . . standardize[s] those components to eliminate the wide variance that currently exists with prophecy reporting." See http://www.raptureready.com/rap2.html (accessed September 21, 2008).

CHAPTER 12: SITES TO BE SEEN

1. Gen 2:10–14.

2. Sirach 24:25.

3. Gen 2:15.

4. With the exception of a few references that matter-of-factly mention Eden as a place like any other (2 Kings 19:12; Isa 37:12) and as a person's name (2 Chron 29:12, 31:15; Ezek 27:23), Eden is remembered occasionally elsewhere in the Bible as a primordial, ideal place (e.g., see Isa 51:3; Ezek 36:35).

5. These "cherubim," a transliteration of the Hebrew word, may be modeled on the fantastic, imposing winged guardians of Babylonian and Assyrian gates.

6. Gen 8:4.

7. William Snelling, "Amazing 'Ark' Exposé," *Creation* 14(4)(September 1992):26–38, http://www.answersingenesis.org/creation/v14/i4/report.asp.

8. William Tynan and Leon Jaroff, "Phony Arkaeology," *Time*, July 5, 1993, http://www.time.com/time/magazine/article/0,9171,978812,00.html.

9. Stefan Lovgren, "Noah's Ark Quest Dead in Water—Was It a Stunt?" *National Geographic News*, September 20, 2004, http://news.nationalgeographic.com/news/2004/09/0920_040920_noahs_ark.html.

10. Kate Ravilious, "Noah's Ark Discovered in Iran?" *National Geographic News*, July 5, 2006, http://news.nationalgeographic.com/news/2006/07/060705-noahs-ark.html.

11. Gen 11:1. This would seem to be in sharp contradiction to the preceding chapter, which tells that people had spread out and spoke different languages. Despite this arrangement, the narrative in chapter 11 allows readers to assume that it gives specific background information for the broad overview of generations and nations described in chapter 10.

12. Gen 11:7.

13. Paul's Christian missionary work extended the geographical scope of biblical literature to include places in modern Turkey, Greece, and Italy.

14. Gen 11:31.

15. Fred Jeter, "Teams Compete So Military Dad Can See Son Play," *Richmond Times-Dispatch*, July 4, 2008, http://www.inrich.com/cva/ric/sports.apx.-content-articles-RTD-2008-07-04-0013.html (accessed November 23, 2008).

16. Gen 12:1.

17. Gen 12:10.

18. Ptolemy I was one of Alexander's military officers who gained control of the Egyptian region after Alexander's death.

19. For example, see Lev 22:33; Ps 81:10; Amos 2:10.

20. For example, see 2 Kings 17:4.

21. Matt 2:13–21.

22. According to the documentary hypothesis, the Yahwist and Priestly writers used the name Sinai; the Elohist and Deuteronomist used Horeb.

23. Exod 19:16–25; 20:18–21.

24. Although Jesus didn't visit Sinai, as far as we know, there is a famous painting at the monastery of Saint Catherine—the Jesus Pantokrator icon. It is similar enough to the image on the Shroud of Turin for some people to doubt the authenticity of the shroud, imagining rather that the two shared a sixth-century model. The monastery is most famous for housing a great deal of the *Codex Sinaiticus*, one of the earliest Greek biblical manuscripts (dating to the fourth century CE). See more about the book, and digital samples, at http://www .codexsinaiticus.net/en/ (accessed November 23, 2008).

25. For examples, see the conversations of the filmmaker Simcha Jacobovici with an archaeologist and professor of Hebrew Bible at the University of California-Berkeley, Ronald Hendel, and with the editor of *Biblical Archaeology Review*, Hershel Shanks, http://web .archive.org/web/20070502122212/http://www.bib-arch.org/bswbOOexodusbeware.html and http://web.archive.org/web/20070528054314/www.bib-arch.org/bswbOOexodus.html, respectively (accessed November 25, 2008).

26. The Hebrew noun *midbar* refers to an undomesticated area and is used to describe the area between Egypt and Canaan. Given what we know about some of the wild places in the Bible, namely, that most are arid, it also bears the translation "desert."

27. 1 Kings 19:11–13.

28. See Lev 20:24; Deut 31:20; Jer 11:5.

29. It seems that the biblical writers were intentional about forging this collective identity. Many scholars think that at least some of the people who identified themselves as Israel were actually native Canaanites. Through declarations of identity and belief such as we see at the end of Deuteronomy and of Joshua, they accepted the Exodus experience and the Sinai covenant for themselves in the same way that many of us today celebrate Thanksgiving as "our story," despite the fact that our particular ancestors did not come to the United States on the *Mayflower*.

30. Nine seafaring groups of pirate raiders and occasional mercenaries, including the Philistines, are mentioned in Egyptian sources from the reigns of Merneptah and Rameses III (between 1210 and 1150 BCE). Some of them also appear in sources from Anatolia and Egypt decades earlier. The term "Sea Peoples" to describe these groups is a modern one.

31. Josephus, *Antiquities of the Jews*, 9.277–91; P. Shen et al., "Reconstruction of Patrilineages and Matrilineages of Samaritans and Other Israeli Populations from Y-Chromosome and Mitochondrial DNA Sequence Variation," *Human Mutation* 24 (2004): 248–260. The Samaritans today, most of whom live in one of two sites in modern Israel, understand themselves to be descended from ancient Israelite tribes.

32. John 4:1–30.

33. John 7:53–8:11.

34. 1 Kings 8:25; cf. 2 Sam 7:12–16. In other words, the covenant went from being unconditional to being conditional.

35. Ps 50:2.

36. Ps 137:1.

37. Isa 14:32.

38. Isa 8:18.

39. Isa 2:3–4.

40. Heb 12:22.

41. Gen 14:18.

42. 2 Chron 3:1.

43. That the Babylonian Talmud has had far greater influence on Judaism than the Jerusalem-Palestinian Talmud attests to an intellectually and spiritually rich Babylonian Jewish community lasting well into the first centuries of the Common Era.

44. In Revelation, Babylon serves as a code word for Rome, the great world power at the time of Revelation's writing.

45. Constantinople (modern Istanbul), not Rome, was the capital city of the Roman empire during Constantine's time. Whereas Alexandria, Antioch, and Jerusalem diminished in strength after the birth of Islam, Constantinople and Rome continued to be major centers of Christian power. They diverged over the centuries, however, in their ideas about how to conduct worship and business, until they split formally in 1054 into the Roman Catholic and Eastern Orthodox churches.

46. Josh 3:7–4:24.

47. Luke 5:1; 1 Mac 11:67. John occasionally (three times) calls it the sea of Tiberias. Matthew and Mark refer to a Galilean region as Gennesaret (Matt 14:34; Mark 6:53).

48. Isa 8:23; Isa 9:1, respectively.

49. Mic 5:2 (5:1 in the Hebrew Bible).

50. John 7:42.

51. John 1:46.

52. Matt 2:23.

53. Isa 11:1.

54. Christian tradition commonly uses this word, from the Latin *passus*, having to do with suffering, to refer specifically to that period of Jesus' arrest, trial, and crucifixion.

55. 2 Sam 15:30.

56. Zech 14:4.

57. Matthew apparently read the poetic parallelism of Zech 9:9 literally—Jesus called for and rode both a donkey and her colt (Matt 21:1–7). The other synoptic gospels take into account the prophecy's literary form to read a single animal (Mark 11:1–10; Luke 19:28–38).

58. Associated Press, "Armenian, Greek Worshippers Come to Blows at Jesus' Tomb," http://www.haaretz.com/hasen/spages/976409.html (accessed September 4, 2008).

59. Associated Press, "Monks Clash at Jerusalem Site," *Richmond Times-Dispatch*, November 10, 2008, A7.

60. Rev 16:16.

61. Judges 5:19.

62. 2 Kings 23:29.

63. Job 7:9.

64. Isa 38:18.

65. 1 Sam 2:6.

66. Ps 103:4.

67. Jonah 2:6.

68. Rev 9:11.

69. In a creative twist, Jehovah's Witnesses appeal to a couple of other texts in Revelation (9:1; 20:1) to conclude that this Abaddon is actually Jesus, from heaven, who destroys Satan in hell.

70. It also appears in several of the deuterocanonical books, including Tobit, the Greek version of Esther, Wisdom of Solomon, Sirach, Baruch, Prayer of Azariah, 2 Maccabees, and 4 Esdras.

71. Rev 20:13; 6:8; 20:14, respectively.

72. 2 Kings 23:10; 2 Chron 28:3; 33:6.

73. Matt 23:33.

74. Matt 5:22, 29, 30; 10:28; 18:9; 23:15, 33; Mark 9:43, 45, 47; Luke 12:5; Jas 3:6; 2 Pet 2:4.

75. Matt 5:29, 30; Mark 9:47; Jas 3:6.

76. Matt 5:22; 18:9; Mark 9:43; Jas 3:6.

77. 2 Pet 2:4. In Greek mythology, Tartaros is the name of the dark and gloomy site (and the god of that place), deep underground (in some sources it's below Hades), wherein the Titans were imprisoned after a cosmic battle with the high god, Zeus (see Hesiod's *Theogony*, lines 720–735).

78. Matt 8:12; 13:42, 50; Matt 22:13; 24:51; 25:30; 27:45.

79. Jude 1:6–7.

80. God dwells in the heavens but is not limited to them, according to the Old Testament. After all "The LORD made heaven and earth" and could "come down" at will; "heaven, even the highest heaven can not contain him" (e.g., Exod 31:17; Ps 18:9; 2 Chron 2:6, respectively).

81. Dan 12:1–2.

82. Luke 24:50–51.

83. 1 Thess 4:16–17.

84. Matt 5:10–12; John 14:2–3.

85. Rev 7:9–17.

86. For example, compare Matt 4:17 with Mark 1:15.

87. Matt 7:21.

88. Matt 13:33.

89. Matt 13:31–32.

90. Isa 66:18–23.

91. Rev 3:12; 21:1–5. Hebrews describes a heavenly Jerusalem to which people ascend (Heb 12:22).

92. Rev 21:21.

93. Matt 16:19.

94. Gal 4:21–5:1.

95. John 3:27.

CHAPTER 13: GOD NAMES, BEINGS, AND DOINGS

1. Gen 1:1.

2. Exod 20:3; Deut 5:7.

3. Job 1:6; 2:1.

4. Ps 95:3.

5. In the gospel of John, Jesus appeals to this psalm as justification for calling himself God's son, and seems to interpret the "gods" of the psalm to refer to humans who received God's word (John 10:33–36). Some interpreters have taken the "gods" of this psalm to refer to humans all the way through—to unjust rulers, in particular.

6. Gen 1:26.

7. Gen 3:22.

8. Isa 6:8.

9. E.g., Ps 96:4–5; 135:5–7, 15–18. In a striking example of how the Hebrew Bible reflects both monotheism and henotheism among the ancient Israelites, David declared within the very same speech, both that "There is no God but you [Yahweh]" and that God drove out the other peoples "and their gods" from Canaan (2 Sam 7:18–24).

10. E.g., Isa 37:19; Jer 2:27; Ezek 20:32; Hab 2:19.

11. E.g., Isa 40:18 ("God"); Ezek 28:2 ("a god").

12. For a summary, see David Biale, "The God with Breasts: El Shaddai in the Bible," *History of Religions* 21(3) (1982): 240–256.

13. Gen 17:1–2; 28:3; 35:11.

14. Excavations at Ras Shamra, site of the ancient city-state of Ugarit, began with the discovery in 1928 of a burial tomb yielding artifacts of interest. Excavations continued through the 1970s (with a break for World War II), revealing what archaeologists judged to be houses, temples, and palaces. Several religious tablets were discovered near the temple; a number of others come from residential areas near palace complexes; and many were housed in the palace itself, in rooms devoted to the royal archives.

15. See the story of El's feast in M. Dietrich, O. Loretz, and J. Sanmartín, eds., *The Cuneiform Alphabetic Texts from Ugarit, Ras Ibn Hani, and Other Places, Die Keilalphabetischen Texte aus Ugarit*, 2d enlarged ed. (Münster: Ugarit-Verlag, 1995), 1.114.

16. There is one possible Ugaritic reference in what may be a shortened form of the divine name YHWH, where the word yw apparently refers to a son of El. See *Die Keilalphabetischen Texte aus Ugarit* 1.1 col. IV line 14; and Simon B. Parker, ed., *Ugaritic Narrative Poetry*, SBL Writings from the Ancient World 9 (Atlanta, Ga.: Society of Biblical Literature, 1997), 89. That the biblical nation's name and people are called Isra-el, not Isra-ya, has led some scholars to conclude that El, not Yahweh, was the earliest name for ancient Israel's particular God. See Mark S. Smith, *The Origins of Biblical Monotheism* (New York: Oxford University Press, 2001), 142–145.

17. Exod 3:13–18; cf. Exod 6:2–13.

18. What's more, people familiar with biblical Hebrew can attest that the first and third letters (reading from right to left) in both cases are notorious shape-changers: in some grammatical circumstances, a yod may become a vav, or vice versa.

19. So the bumper-sticker quoting R. Buckminster Fuller, "God Is Verb," has real biblical basis.

20. Exod 3:15.

21. To avoid confusion, readers should distinguish between the sources proposed by the documentary hypothesis and the divine names themselves. That is, although most scholars think that the divine name Elohim predates the name YHWH, the J source (which favors the divine name YHWH) is thought to be earlier than the E source (which favors the divine name Elohim).

22. The narrator of Gen 4:26 explains that as early as Adam and Eve's grandchildren "people began to call upon the name YHWH." Abraham also "called on YHWH by name" (Gen 12:8), and so did Isaac (Gen 26:25).

23. The phrase "YHWH God of Israel" appears almost 100 times in the Hebrew Bible; and "YHWH your God" appears about 400 times.

24. E.g., 1 Sam 17:45, Ps 24:10.

25. E.g., Judges 5; Isa 40:26.

26. E.g., Deut 12:11.

27. 1 Kings 5:5.

28. Jer 16:21.

29. Exod 20:7; Deut 5:11.

30. When a particular Hebrew passage already included *adonai* (as in *adonai YHWH*), the vowels from *elohim* were used. The tradition of substituting *adonai* for the divine name is also reflected in the Septuagint and may have begun as early as the second temple period beginning around 500 BCE. Many Jews today, concerned about degrading the divine name, use *ha Shem* (or translate, "the Name"), when they come across YHWH. Some apply their caution to the written word "God" in English, choosing to represent it as "G-d."

31. Either the e is a transliteration of the first Hebrew vowel of *adonai*, or it reflects *elohim*. Most people attribute this usage to a Christian translator working in the early 1500s; but it appeared already in 1270, in Raymond Martin's "Pugio Fidei"; see the *Jewish Encyclopedia*, Vol. 7 (New York: Funk and Wagnalls, 1901-1906), 88.

32. E.g., Exod 15:2; Ps 115:18; 118:5; Isa 12:2.

33. Hos 2:16 plays on this use of *baal* as both "husband" and "master," distinguishing God's future relationship to Israel as like a marriage not of mastery but of intimate partnership: "in that day . . . you will call me 'my *ish*' [literally "my man," an idiom for husband] and no longer 'my *baal*' [literally "my master," also idiomatic for "my husband"].

34. In a lengthy Ugaritic narrative, Baal defeated the chaotic personification of sea named Yamm and a personification of death named Mot (*yam* and *mot* are also the Hebrew words for "sea" and "death," respectively), to gain tenuous control as king of the universe. This "Baal cycle" or "epic of Baal" is narrated on a number of tablets and includes Baal's struggles with a third contender, Ashtar, associated with the stars and heavenly bodies, possibly the planet Venus in particular. See James B. Pritchard, ed., *Ancient Near Eastern Texts Relating to the Old Testament*, 3rd ed. with suppl. (Princeton, N.J.: Princeton University Press, 1969), 129–142; William W. Hallo and K. Lawson Younger, eds., *Context of Scripture* (Leiden: Brill, 1997–2002), 1.86.

35. 1 Kings 18:1–46.

36. See Dietrich, Loretz, and Sanmartín, *The Cuneiform Alphabetic Texts from Ugarit, Ras Ibn Hani, and Other Places*, 1.4.VI.46; John Day, "Asherah," *Anchor Bible Dictionary on CD-ROM*, Logos 2.1, ed. David Noel Freedman (New York: Doubleday), 1992, 1997.

37. One such inscription, which identifies Yahweh with Samaria, the capital of the northern kingdom of Israel, was discovered at a caravan crossroads in the Sinai south of Judah, called Kuntillet 'Ajrûd. See Z. Meshel, "Kuntillet 'Ajrûd: A Religious Centre in Northern Sinai," *Expedition* 20 (1978): 50–54; P. Beck, "The Drawings from Horvat Teiman (Kuntillet Ajrûd)," *Tel Avid* 9 (1982): 3–86; W. G. Dever, "Asherah, Consort of Yahweh?" *Bulletin of the American Schools of Oriental Research* 255 (1984): 21–37; http://www.fas.harvard.edu/~semitic/wl/digsites/SLevant/Kun tilletAjrud2006/ (accessed July 25, 2008). Another is from Khirbet el-Qom, an area near Hebron in the hill country of Judah. See W. G. Dever, "Iron Age Epigraphic Material from the Area of Khirbet el-Kôm," *Hebrew Union College Annual* (40–41) (1970): 139–204; L. T. Geraty, "The Historical, Linguistic, and Biblical Significance of the Khirbet el-Kôm Ostraca," in *The Word of the Lord Shall Go Forth*, ed. C. L. Meyers and M. O'Connor (Winona Lake, Ind.: Eisenbrauns, 1983); Ziony Zevit, "The Khirbet el-Qôm Inscription Mentioning a Goddess," *BASOR* 255 (1984): 39–47.

38. See also Judith M. Hadley, *The Cult of Asherah in Ancient Israel and Judah: Evidence for a Hebrew Goddess*, Oriental Publications 57 (Cambridge: Cambridge University Press, 2000); Mark S. Smith, *The Origins of Biblical Monotheism* (New York: Oxford University Press, 2001).

39. The word *kurios* also applies generally to human lords (e.g., Matt 18:32).

40. The Septuagint also renders El Shaddai in Ezek 10:5 as *theo[s] shaddai*. In the case of Shaddai alone (without El), the Greek sometimes translates it as *pantokrator*, a term that means "all-powerful" (reflected in the English translation "Almighty").

41. The issue is portrayed as cause for consternation and puzzlement among the Hebrew scholars of Jesus' community who cannot figure out how the anticipated Christ could be both the son of David, as they claim, and someone that David would call "my lord" (i.e., someone with priority in terms of both chronology and power, though David's son). Jesus stumps them, quoting from Ps 110:1 in its Greek translation. Rather than "The LORD (Hebrew YHWH) said to my lord (Hebrew *adonai*)," Jesus uses, "The Lord (Greek *kurios*) said to my Lord (Greek *kurios*)" (Matt 22:41–46).

42. John 8:58; Exod 3:14.

43. The phrase "the name of *Elohim*" appears only two times in the Hebrew Bible: Ps 69:31; Dan 2:20 (in Aramaic). Likewise, its Greek counterpart, "the name of *theo[s]*," appears only a few times in the New Testament (Rom 2:24; 1 Tim 6:1; Rev 16:9).

44. Acts 8:16; 19:5.

45. Col 3:17.

46. Isa 53:5.

47. See especially Lev 8:1–13.

48. E.g., 2 Sam 7:16.

49. Matt 16:23; Mark 8:33.

50. Exactly how Jesus as Messiah should be understood is not consistently represented in the

New Testament, and the divinity of Jesus continued to be debated for centuries—even after 325 CE, when it became a foundational principle of Christian doctrine as articulated by the Council of Nicaea.

51. Matt 16:20; Mark 8:29–30; Luke 9:20–21.

52. Roger Smith, "The H of Jesus H. Christ," *American Speech* 69(3) (Autumn 1994): 332.

53. Ibid., 331–335.

54. Matt 4:19; Mark 1:17.

55. John 1:1–3a. This sounds a great deal like the Hebrew concept of *hokmah*, "wisdom," which infuses the world and the created order. To examine the world and to learn from it is to gain in wisdom and be closer to God, according especially to the Old Testament "wisdom literature."

56. John 1:9.

57. John 1:14.

58. John also identifies Jesus with God the Father, claiming, for example, "The Father and I are one" (John 10:30).

59. Jouette M. Bassler, "God (in the NT)," *Anchor Bible Dictionary on CD-ROM*, Logos 2.1, ed. David Noel Freedman (New York: Doubleday), 1992, 1997.

60. Ps 51:11; Isa 63:10, 11 (*ruach qodesh*).

61. 2 Sam 23:2; Luke 12:12; John 14:26; Acts 13:2. Both the Hebrew word *ruach* and the Greek word *pneuma* are used for "wind" and "breath" as well as "spirit." The Hebrew noun appears in both masculine and feminine forms; the Greek is gender-neutral.

62. Mark 1:10; Luke 3:22; John 1:32. In Matt 3:16, it is the *pneuma theo[s]*, translated "Spirit of God."

63. Luke 1:41, 67; 2:25; Mark 13:11.

64. Matt 12:32; Mark 3:28–29; Luke 12:10. Exactly how this should be understood is a matter of some dispute, but the gospels present it as so serious as to be the only truly unforgivable sin.

65. John 14:16–17; John 20:22. This is probably meant to recall the story of God's breathing life into the first human being (Gen 2:7).

66. Acts 2:16–21; Joel 2:28–32.

67. Acts 2:1–4.

68. It took place on an existing Jewish holiday. Pentecost is the Greek name for a Jewish festival ("Feast of Weeks") observed fifty days (seven weeks) after and including Passover. Originally an agricultural festival, it came to be associated with God's giving the Torah to Israel. The Christian Pentecost, which celebrates the gift of the Holy Spirit, occurs on the fiftieth day after and including Easter.

69. Matt 28:19.

70. 2 Cor 13:13.

71. The Greek translation uses *pneuma*, a neuter noun.

72. Deut 32:11. The eagle in this text is masculine, however.

73. Isa 42:14; 49:15; 66:13.

74. Gen 1:27.

75. E.g., Jer 31:31–34; Num 14:18; Isa 66:18, respectively.

76. E.g., Jesus taught that those who failed to look out for the unfortunate, poor, and out-

cast would be judged as failing to care about God, cursed, and consigned to eternal fire (Matt 25:31–46); and Revelation describes a divine horseman who "in righteousness judges and makes war," whose mouth lets fly a smiting sword, who rules with an iron rod, and "treads the winepress of the fury of the wrath of Almighty God" (Rev 19:11–15).

77. E.g., Gen 18:1–16; Isa 46:5; Exod 20:5; Ezek 18:1–4.

78. Deut 7:3; Ezra 10:2.

79. This ambivalence dominates the books of the Latter Prophets. For an example within the same book, compare Hos 5:8–14 with 11:8–9.

INDEX